JUDGES
&
JUSTICE
&
LAWYERS
&
LAW

BOOKS BY FRANCIS M. NEVINS

MYSTERY FICTION

Publish and Perish (1975)
Corrupt and Ensnare (1978)
The 120 Hour Clock (1986)
The Ninety Million Dollar Mouse (1987)
Into the Same River Twice (1997)
Beneficiaries' Requiem (2000)
Night of Silken Snow and Other Stories (2001)
Leap Day and Other Stories (2003)
Night Forms (2010)

NONFICTION ON THE MYSTERY GENRE

Judges & Justice & Lawyers & Law (2014)
Ellery Queen: The Art of Detection (2013)
Royal Bloodline: Ellery Queen, Author and Detective (1974)
The Sound of Detection: Ellery Queen=s Adventures in Radio (1983)
Cornell Woolrich: First You Dream, Then You Die (1988)
The Sound of Detection (revised and expanded edition) (2002)
Cornucopia of Crime (2010)

ON MOVIES

The Films of Hopalong Cassidy (1988)
Bar-20: The Life of Clarence E. Mulford, Creator of Hopalong Cassidy (1993)
The Films of the Cisco Kid (1998)
Joseph H. Lewis: Overview, Interview and Filmography (1998)
Paul Landres: A Director' Stories (2000)
Hopalong Cassidy: On the Page, On the Screen (2008)
The Cisco Kid: American Hero, Hispanic Roots (2008)

ANTHOLOGIES & COLLECTIONS (EDITED OR CO-EDITED)

The Mystery Writer's Art (1970)
Nightwebs by Cornell Woolrich (1971)
The Good Old Stuff by John D. MacDonald (1982)
Exeunt Murderers by Anthony Boucher (1983)
Buffet for Unwelcome Guests by Christianna Brand (1983)
More Good Old Stuff by John D. MacDonald (1984)
Carnival of Crime by Fredric Brown (1985)
Hitchcock in Prime Time (1985)
The Best of Ellery Queen (1985)
Leopold's Way by Edward D. Hoch (1985)
Darkness at Dawn by Cornell Woolrich (1985)
The Adventures of Henry Turnbuckle by Jack Ritchie (1987)
Better Mousetraps by John Lutz (1988)
Mr. President—Private Eye (1988)
Death on Television by Henry Slesar (1989)
Little Boxes of Bewilderment by Jack Ritchie (1989)
The Night My Friend by Edward D. Hoch (1991)
The Anthony Boucher Chronicles 2001-02
Night & Fear by Cornell Woolrich (2004)
Tonight, Somewhere in New York by Cornell Woolrich (2005)
The Keeler Keyhole Collection by Harry Stephen Keeler (2006)
Love and Night by Cornell Woolrich (2007)

JUDGES
&
JUSTICE
&
LAWYERS
&
LAW

*Exploring the Legal Dimensions
Of Fiction and Film*

Francis M. Nevins

PERFECT CRIME BOOKS

Crime@PerfectCrimeBooks.com

Perfect Crime Books™ is a registered Trademark.

Printed in the United States of America.

ACKNOWLEDGMENTS

Chapter 1 first appeared in *Legal Education for the 21ˢᵗ Century*, ed. Donald B. King (Fred B. Rothman & Co., 1999). An expanded version (in English) was published in *Recht-Gesellschaft-Kommunikation: Festschrift für Klaus F. Rohl,* ed. Stefan Machura & Stefan Ulbrich (Nomos Verlags-Gesellschaft, 2003). Chapter 2 first appeared in *18 Legal Studies Forum 177* (1994), Chapter 3 in *19 Legal Studies Forum 57* (1995), and Chapter 4 in *24 Legal Studies Forum 43* (2000). Chapter 5 comes from material first published in *Legal Reelism: Movies As Legal Texts,* ed. John Denvir (University of Illinois Press, 1998); *28 Vermont Law Review 915* (2004); and *Law and Popular Culture,* ed. Michael Freeman (Oxford University Press, 2005). Chapter 6 comes from material first published in *Legal Reelism: Movies As Legal Texts,* ed. John Denvir (University of Illinois Press, 1996). Chapter 7 first appeared as Chapter 15 of *Prime Time Law: Fictional Television As Legal Narrative,* ed. Robert M. Jarvis & Paul R. Joseph (Carolina Academic Press, 1998). Chapter 8 first appeared in *24 Legal Studies Forum 611* (2000), and Chapter 10 in *48 UCLA Law Review 1557* (2001). Chapter 9 first appeared in *30 University of San Francisco Law Review 1097* (1996). An expanded version appeared in *Screening Justice,* ed. Rennard Strickland et al. (William P. Hein & Co., 2006).

Library of Congress Cataloging-in-Publication Data

Nevins, Francis M.

Judges & Justice & Lawyers & Law

ISBN: 978-1-935797-69-2

First Edition: December 2014

For Dean Mike Wolff
and all my colleagues
on the Saint Louis University law faculty,
present and past, living and dead,
who supported me
as I created and refined the seminar
that generated the essays in this book

JUDGES
&
JUSTICE
&
LAWYERS
&
LAW

CONTENTS

Photographs follow Page 262

OPENING STATEMENT

May it please the court. . . . Oops! Wrong kind of opening statement.

Some time before I joined the St. Louis University law faculty, my future colleagues enacted a requirement that, before he or she graduated, each student must take a course or seminar "of a humanistic nature." Most students satisfied this requirement by taking either Legal History or Legal Philosophy, also known as Jurisprudence. Since our student body had grown exponentially since I joined the faculty, I suggested that more options should be available to satisfy our requirement and proposed a seminar on "Law, Lawyers and Justice in Popular Fiction and Film." Details on how my seminar was constructed will be found in Chapter 1 of this book. During the 20-odd years I offered that seminar more or less on an annual basis, I began writing and publishing lengthy essays on some of the material it covered. Most of the chapters in this book are new and (I hope) improved versions of those essays.

What was a pioneering venture when I created my seminar has spread to many another law school, and the scholarly literature on the subject has grown with its general acceptance, as witness books like *The Lawyer and Popular Culture*, ed. David L. Gunn (Rothman & Co., 1993), Paul Bergman and Michael Asimow's *Reel Justice: The Courtroom Goes to the Movies* (Andrews & McMeel, 1996), *Law and Popular Culture*, ed. Michael Freeman (Oxford University Press, 2005), *Law and Popular Culture*, ed. David Ray Papke et al. (LexisNexis, 2007, 2d ed. 2012), and, most recently, *Law and Popular Culture*, ed. Michael Asimow & Shannon Mader (Peter Lang, 2013). Law journals have likewise welcomed contributions to the subject. Of the ten chapters in this book, four first appeared in West Virginia University's Legal Studies Forum, one apiece in the University of San Francisco and UCLA's law reviews, and one in the law journal published by the University of Vermont. Of course, you don't have to be a law professor, or even a lawyer, to be interested in what I like to call jurisfiction and juriscinema, and my hope is that this collection will help to spread interest in these subjects beyond the confines of the legal profession.

Of all the people who helped make the book a reality, I owe the deepest debt to my secretary, Sharon Baird, who helped me out of many a corner into which with my computer ineptitude I had painted myself. Thanks again, Shari!

FRANCIS M. NEVINS
St. Louis, Missouri May 11, 2014

CHAPTER 1

Using Fiction and Film as Law School Tools

There are any number of ways in which fiction and film can be used as teaching tools in law school, and in one way or another all law professors do it, but perhaps I've worked out more ways of making use of these tools than most of my colleagues. As I talk us through a few of the ways in which fiction and film can perform functions in legal education, the obvious starting point is the one we all share.

In every course we teach, the casebook is an anthology and every case or problem in it is a story. When we and our students tease out the meanings and implications of these stories, we are doing something quite similar to what professors of literature do with the novels and stories and plays they discuss with their students. Every essay examination question we write is a species of story. Every hypothetical we propound in class is a skit, another species of story. Whether we are conscious of it or not, we are using these forms of fiction as classroom tools every working day of our lives. Indeed part of what made law teaching enjoyable, at least to me, is precisely that it could be done through stories, both those I or another professor made up and those that really happened. And if we use stories well, classroom hours become enjoyable to our students too.

Devising little skits or dramas can add life and zest even to courses that have the reputation of being dull and dreary. The course in Estates and Administration, which before retiring I offered once and frequently twice a year, is not required for graduation at St. Louis University but is well known to be necessary for the bar examination so almost everyone takes it. Many students have told me that they went into that course expecting to be bored silly but were pleasantly surprised by how interesting it turned out. One reason why, I believe, is because the subject matter permitted me to use various forms of fiction with great freedom. If Shakespeare was right when he said that cowards die many times before their deaths, then I was the ignoblest coward of them all, having died thousands of times in class as I played the role of testator in the little dramas I devised. I've married my students, had children with them, divorced them, married them to each other, killed them off. Usually I cast the students in the front rows as the other main actors in these little dramas. Thanks to this form of fiction, much of the law of wills, trusts and estates became more vivid and involving not only for my students but for me as well.

The same tools can be used with equal effect in all sorts of other courses, for example Copyright Law. In the mid-1960s when I was a law student at NYU, I had so little sense of the shape of my own future that not only did I fail to take the course on copyright, I never even met the professor who taught it, Walter Derenberg, one of the superstars of the field. By the time I came to St. Louis University and became a law professor myself, I had begun to sell some fiction of my own and needed to learn some copyright law in self-defense. Since there was no course on copyright in the curriculum here, I created one. For well over thirty years I was the only person ever to have taught that subject here. The size of the class tended to range between 35 and 50 each year, an amazing feat considering how little copyright law is practiced in St. Louis. Maybe these figures were a function of the unusual approach I employed.

In the course on copyright law I made use of the same forms of fiction that served the course in wills, trusts and estates, but I also had to use fiction in other and more fundamental ways, simply because so much of the subject matter of copyright law deals with creative work. Not only did I have the pleasure all copyright professors share—that of talking about masters like Hemingway,[1] Saroyan,[2] Salinger,[3] Hitchcock,[4] Bartok,[5] Shostakovich[6]—but, since I happen to have written a bit of fiction myself, I was able to indulge in the unique pleasure of using my own output in my little skits and dramas. What a hoot to toss out a hypothetical about Steven Spielberg wanting to buy the movie rights in one of my novels!

Discussing the radically different regimes under the present Copyright Act of 1976 and the previous 1909 act that continues in large measure to govern all work that predates 1978, I didn't need to invent a hypothetical novel or borrow one from Hemingway or Faulkner and draw a timeline of its copyright life on the chalkboard. As luck would have it, my own first novel, *Publish and Perish*, came out in 1975, when the 1909 Act was the only copyright regime we had. I could hold up a copy of that book and we could explore such questions as the duration of copyright protection it enjoyed under the 1909 Act, the changes in duration after the enactment of the 1976 statute, the need to renew the copyright in that book in its 28th year of copyright life, the 1992 statutory amendment that eliminated the need for formal renewal, and many more. If the spirit moved me I'd display the back of the dust jacket with its photograph of the handsome young author and make some aptly rueful remark about the aging process. Then I could hold up a copy of my second novel, *Corrupt and Ensnare*, which as chance would have it came out in 1978, soon after the effective date of the present statute, and our discussion of the differences in the legal regime governing this title as opposed to my first novel took on—I hope!—a special vividness. When the subject shifted to collective works I could bring in an old issue of *Ellery Queen's Mystery Magazine* with a story of mine in it and, with luck, impart the same vividness to the analysis of what rights in that story are owned by the magazine publisher and what rights by me. When anthologies came under consideration, I could hold up a copy of one of the twenty-odd I've edited and expound with great specificity on what rights I as editor own and what rights remain the property of the author or authors of the stories I brought together. At the point where the Supreme Court's landmark decision in the *Feist* case[7] came up, I could display some compilations of raw data I prepared for various books, such as the comprehensive checklist which concludes my biographical-critical book *Cornell Woolrich: First You Dream, Then You Die*—a checklist which arranges all of Woolrich's more than 200 magazine stories alphabetically by the titles of the magazines in which he appeared and, within each magazine listing, chronologically in order of publication—and ask my students whether after *Feist* that checklist enjoys any copyright protection. Is it any wonder that I enjoyed teaching this course more than any other?

I also devised a unique way of using fiction and film in a copyright course which may be worth a few minutes' discussion. One of the biggest challenges in this course is teaching the concept of substantial similarity. How should students be exposed to the analytic problems and techniques involved where the court has to decide whether the defendant's work is so similar to the plaintiff's work as to constitute copyright infringement? The traditional approach is simply to assign various judicial opinions that contain long-winded comparative plot summaries of the contending works—works which of course the students haven't read.[8] I never considered that a helpful way to teach substantial similarity. But what were the alternatives? It would be unwieldy to the point of absurdity for a professor to make students read a complete novel, and then run in class a full-length movie which arguably infringes the novel, and expect the students to take detailed notes over a two-hour period while keeping in their minds everything that transpired in the novel.

But suppose there were a story, only ten or twelve pages long, and a movie about fifteen minutes long which was both similar to and different from the story in enough respects so that reasonable minds would differ as to whether they were substantially similar?

About twenty years ago I stumbled upon just the right combo. The story was "The Services of an Expert" by Harry Stephen Keeler (1890-1967), one of the truly inspired nuts of American literature.[9] The movie was "Smooth Fingers" (1949), one of the first films ever made exclusively for TV. Keeler apparently never heard of this little picture but many years ago I came upon a 16mm print of it and, in a rare thunderclap of insight, recognized at once that chance had put in my hands a matched pair that solved my problem perfectly. Everyone would read the ten-page story beforehand and take detailed notes and the 15-minute film would be run in class the following week, leaving ample time for a long discussion of whether they were substantially similar. At the end of the exercise I would poll the class, asking how many would have found for Keeler if they were on the jury and how many for the makers of "Smooth Fingers." That the result of the show of hands was different each year demonstrated to me that my approach was working. Several other law schools are now using the same story and film in the same way I do.

In two of the seminars I offered on a regular basis, fiction and film literally constituted the subject matter. One of these was a seminar on Law and Literature of the sort that many law schools offer. The first thing I would tell students who expressed interest in this seminar is that it wasn't a substitute for a college literature course, that it was appropriate only for students who already had some reasonable familiarity with at least a respectable number of the works we were going to study. I went out of my way to make this point because many of the great works of literature that deal with legal themes are not concerned with those themes in any central sense. In my seminar we would isolate the legal themes in those works and concentrate on them predominantly even if, as in Dostoevsky's *The Brothers Karamazov*, the law element was less than central.[10]

Because I happen to have spent some time studying Greek drama when I was young, my seminar began with Aeschylus and the Oresteia trilogy—*Agamemnon*, *The Libation Bearers* and *The Furies*—which collectively constitutes the most powerful pro-law fiction ever written.[11]

Then we would move to Sophocles and the *Antigone,* and then to the two great legal plays of Shakespeare, *The Merchant of Venice* and *Measure for Measure.* The novels of Dickens are too long to cover fully in my seminar but we spent some time on the law-related chapters of *The Pickwick Papers* and *Bleak House.* Then we would read *The Brothers Karamazov,* and Melville's *Billy Budd,* and Kafka's *The Trial* and "In the Penal Colony," and Richard Wright's *Native Son,* and Camus' *The Stranger.* I usually stopped there, roughly fifty years from when I was offering the seminar. The works I chose are traditional and not in the least innovative but others who offered the same seminar tended to be more daring in their choices.[12] Law and Literature satisfied not only our seminar requirement but also our rule that each student must complete a course or seminar of a humanistic nature. I can't claim that it contributed directly to making my students more competent lawyers but I continue to hope that it helped make their lawyering more human.

During the late 1970s I also created out of whole cloth a new seminar in which fiction and film penetrated the law school curriculum. Its nickname was Law and Film, its full title was Law, Lawyers and Justice in Popular Fiction and Film, and its subject matter, as the complete name indicates, was the treatment of the themes of law, lawyers and justice in the popular fiction and movies of the twentieth century. We actually began very late in the nineteenth century, with Justice Holmes' seminal essay "The Path of the Law"[13] and "The Corpus Delicti," a story by Melville Davisson Post (1869-1930) that came out almost simultaneously with the publication of Holmes' essay. These two works are another matched pair, dealing with the lawyer as servant of what Holmes called "the bad man." Post's story, now a century old but still reprinted regularly,[14] is about a lawyer named Randolph Mason whose client has a problem. He's about to marry a beautiful New York socialite but his blackmailing former mistress is threatening to go public and stop the wedding. Mason's advice: "This growth must be cut out at the roots." Not to mince words, he advises his client how he can kill this woman and, if he happens to be caught, admit the murder in open court and still walk away free as a bird. The client does happen to be caught but Mason's defense forces the judge to direct a verdict of not guilty. End of story. Is it any wonder that even today Post remains a key figure in law-related fiction? He was our first important author of tales about law and lawyers in the 20th century, and in my seminar we read several more besides this early classic and, if I may throw in a plug for the next chapter of this book, trace his evolution "from Darwinian to Biblical lawyering."[15]

Around 1920 Post was displaced as our premier lawyer author by Arthur Train (1875-1945), creator of the immortal Mr. Tutt, whose eighty-odd adventures in jurisprudence ran regularly in the *Saturday Evening Post* from 1919 until Train's death. Most of the later tales in the Mr. Tutt series are formulaic and not worth reviving but about twenty of the earlier ones remain extremely interesting today,[16] and we would read five in my seminar.

In the early 1930s, around the time Train's stories became routine, his role as America's lawyer storyteller was taken over by Erle Stanley Gardner (1889-1970), the creator of Perry Mason. From the perspective of my seminar the meatiest Perry Mason novels were the earliest, published between 1933 and 1936, when Mason functioned not as we remember him from Raymond Burr's portrayal in the much later TV series, as a ponderous bureaucrat mindful of the law's niceties, but rather as a tiger in the social Darwinian jungle.[17] Among the other works we would read are William Faulkner's "Smoke" and "Tomorrow,"[18] Louis Auchincloss' "Power in Trust" and "The Tender Offer," two grandly cynical stories by Lawrence Block, and a pair of novellas by lawyer-science fiction writer Charles L. Harness.[19]

We also, of course, watched law-related movies. Most of what we saw in class came from one of the three golden ages of American films dealing with the themes of law, lawyers and justice. From the first of these golden ages, the 1930s, the most important film to my way of thinking is *Counsellor at Law* (1933), directed by William Wyler, from a script by attorney Elmer Rice based on his hit 1931 stage play of the same name, and starring John Barrymore as a manic-depressive workaholic lawyer driven to near suicide by several personal and professional crises erupting at the same time. This film takes place entirely in a lavish Art Deco suite of law offices in a New York skyscraper, with not a moment of courtroom action, so that we don't have to endure the nonsensical trial sequences which make so many law films of the Thirties—and later decades too—laughable to viewers who are attorneys.

The second golden age of movies relevant to my seminar roughly coincides with the peak years of the Warren Court and gave birth to such classics as *12 Angry Men, Anatomy of a Murder, To Kill a Mockingbird* and *Inherit the Wind*,[20] not to mention TV series like *Perry Mason* and *The Defenders*. Two of the features with which I represented this period—Hitchcock's *The Wrong Man* (1957) and the first version of *Cape Fear* (1962)—go against the idealistic grain of their time. Then to do justice to the Warren Court ethos I would run a genuine unsung classic of this period, *Man in the Middle* (1963), starring Robert Mitchum, the *Cape Fear* sociopath, as a career military officer with some legal training who's faced with the choice of destroying his career to save, not an innocent black man as in *To Kill a Mockingbird*, but a white racist maniac (brilliantly portrayed by Keenan Wynn) who clearly is not worth the sacrifice.[21]

My seminar coincided with much of the third golden age of movies dealing with law, lawyers and justice, the age that gave us *Dirty Harry* (1971), *. . . And Justice for All* (1979), *Breaker Morant* (1979), *The Star Chamber* (1983) and *Criminal Law* (1989), to name just a handful of relatively recent films whose hallmark is an acid contempt for law, lawyers and the legal system. I would represent this period with one of the last films directed by Tony Richardson, a little-known gem called *The Penalty Phase* (1986), starring Peter Strauss as a liberal trial judge who's about to enter a tough re-election battle and facing the nightmare of having to nullify the conviction of a sociopath who tortured and murdered dozens of teen-age girls because the arresting officers violated his constitutional rights.[22] This film, structured as a duel between the ethos of films like *To Kill a Mockingbird* and that of our own post-Warren Court anti-Warren Court era, was the perfect vehicle for drawing together the themes I dealt with in this seminar. Whenever I wanted the seminar to end on a lighter note I would close with the wildly funny and cynical comedy *Trial and Error* (1997), in which an unsuccessful actor (Michael Richards) makes a shambles of the system when he takes over for an inebriated lawyer buddy (Jeff Daniels) and, with forensic skills absorbed from watching Gerry Spence on the tube, defends a con artist (Rip Torn) whose mail-order house sells ordinary Lincoln-head pennies at $17.50 each as bronze busts of Abe.

What I hope to have suggested here is that fiction and film are law school tools: in traditional courses like Estates, in more exotic courses like Copyright, in traditional humanistic offerings like Law and Literature, and in eccentric inventions of my own like the seminar on Law and Film. When used properly they can enrich both law students and the law school curriculum. And they can make life more interesting for some of us who are law professors.

NOTES

1. *Estate of Hemingway v. Random House, Inc.,* 23 N.Y. 2d 341, 244 N.E.2d 250 (1968).

2. *Saroyan v. William Saroyan Foundation,* 675 F. Supp. 843 (S.D.N.Y. 1987).

3. *Salinger v. Random House, Inc.,* 811 F.2d 90 (2d Cir. 1987).

4. *Stewart v. Abend,* 495 U.S. 207 (1990).

5. *Bartok v. Boosey & Hawkes, Inc.,* 523 F.2d 941 (2d Cir. 1975).

6. *Shostakovich v. Twentieth Century-Fox Film Corp.,* 196 Misc. 67, 80 N.Y.S.2d 575 (Sup. Ct. 1948).

7. *Feist Publications, Inc. v. Rural Telephone Service Co., Inc.*, 499 U.S. 340 (1991).

8. See, e.g., *Sheldon v. Metro-Goldwyn Pictures Corp.*, 81 F.2d 49 (2d Cir. 1936).

9. In recent years Keeler has become the subject of a number of first-rate websites. For one of the most elaborate and well-informed, see http://xavier.xu.edu/~polt/keeler.html.

10. In *The Failure of the Word: The Protagonist as Lawyer in Modern Fiction* (1984), Richard H. Weisberg argues that *The Brothers Karamazov is* centrally about legal themes. For the opposing view, which on this issue is much closer to mine, see Richard Posner, *Law and Literature* (2d ed. 1998). I organized much of my Law and Literature seminar by pitting Posner's book and Weisberg's two volumes—*The Failure of the Word* and *Poethics and Other Strategies of Law and Literature* (1992)—against each other.

11. The most helpful books I found in teaching Aeschylus and Sophocles are H.D.F. Kitto, *Form and Meaning in Drama* (1956) and Walter Kaufmann, *Tragedy and Philosophy* (1968). Neither Posner nor Weisberg discuss all the works covered in my seminar but most are discussed by one or the other if not both.

12. My colleague Henry Ordower, who is an authority on medieval Norse literature, includes material not only from that tradition but from various third world sources in his Law and Literature syllabus, to the exclusion of a number of Western literary classics.

13. 10 *Harvard Law Review* 457 (1897).

14. Its first appearance was in Post's collection *The Strange Schemes of Randolph Mason* (1896) and its most recent in Elizabeth Villiers Gemmette's anthology *Law in Literature: Legal Themes in Short Stories* (1992).

15. See Chapter 2 of this book.

16. See Chapter 3 of this book.

17. See Chapter 4 of this book.

18. Faulkner had no legal training but was fascinated by law, and his treatment of legal themes is the exclusive subject of Jay Watson, *Forensic Fictions: The Lawyer Figure in Faulkner* (1993).

19. For a generous collection of short fiction by this author, including the two novellas used in my seminar, see Charles L. Harness, *An Ornament to His Profession* (1998).

20. Thomas J. Harris discusses these and other Warren Court film classics in his book *Courtroom's Finest Hour in American Cinema* (1987).

21. For a discussion of this film and the Howard Fast novel on which it was based, see Chapter 9 of this book.

22. For a full account of this film, see Chapter 10 of this book. See also Gale Patrick Hickman, "The Writing and Filming of *The Penalty Phase*," 48 *UCLA Law Review* 1583 (2001).

CHAPTER 2

From Darwinian to Biblical Lawyering:
Melville Davisson Post

Whatever else we may be, each of us is the child of the social circumstances of our world; and so is each work that we create. One of the circumstances that can decisively shape a nation's literature and certainly has shaped the literature of the United States is its legal thought, the categories in which its laws are framed, the habits of mind and action in its legal community, the roles lawyers play and the ways nonlawyers judge them. A great deal of scholarly research and sometimes of speculative ingenuity has been devoted to exploring the links between events in 19th-century American legal history and such major works of American fiction as Cooper's *The Pioneers*, Hawthorne's *The House of the Seven Gables* and Melville's *Billy Budd*.[1] It seems clear to me that American legal development is also intimately linked with American fiction of the 20th century—and not just with what academic literary critics have canonized as great literature but with popular fiction too. In this chapter I shall concentrate on one especially interesting popular fiction writer and explore what his work tried to tell us about law, lawyers, lawyering and justice.

Our starting point is almost exactly 100 years ago, when Darwin's image of the natural world as a vast, violent and never-ending struggle for survival had been translated by social Darwinians like Herbert Spencer into a portrait of the human world; when American industrialists and railroad builders and stock-market speculators made huge fortunes and millions of immigrants poured into the United States to escape lives of unspeakable degradation in Europe and found only slightly less degradation, made bearable perhaps by the faith that now they were living in the land of opportunity.

The American legal community's foremost social Darwinian of the time, indeed the foremost legal thinker in all of our history, was Oliver Wendell Holmes, Jr. (1841-1935), who in the late 1890s wrote the most important jurisprudential essay of his career.[2] Holmes' aim in "The Path of the Law" was to isolate law's identifying characteristics and to distinguish law from morality. "If you want to know the law and nothing else, you must look at it as a bad man, who cares only for the material consequences which such knowledge will enable him to predict, not as a good one, who finds his reasons for conduct, whether inside the law or outside of it, in the vaguer sanctions of conscience."[3] The material consequence which concerns "the bad man" is the incidence of public force.

> "You can see very plainly that a bad man has as much reason as a good one for wishing to avoid an encounter with the public force, and therefore you can see the practical importance of the distinction between morality and law. A man who cares nothing for an ethical rule which is believed and practiced by his neighbors is likely nevertheless to care a good deal to avoid being made to pay money, and will want to keep out of jail if he can."[4]

Holmes doesn't address what is the duty of the lawyer whose client happens to be a "bad man," but the answer seems to follow as night follows day. Given the amoral client Holmes posits, the attorney's obligation is to stifle any moral qualms he may have and exert all his efforts to keep the client just this side of the often arbitrary technical line that separates legal from illegal conduct. In both theory and practice this remains the prevailing view among American lawyers and legal ethicists today. It is also the view expounded in the early stories of American popular culture's first important lawyer author, Melville Davisson Post.

What first attracted Post to this philosophy is not clear since his only biographer to date was a librarian lacking both legal training and curiosity about Post's jurisprudential development.[5] But if we read the memoirs of authors who were more or less Post's contemporaries, we sense that social Darwinism was simply in the air everyone breathed who lived and thought in the robber-baron era at the end of the nineteenth century. Take for instance Theodore Dreiser (1871-1945), who during the 1890s was scratching out a bare-bones existence as a newspaper reporter, first in Chicago, then in St. Louis, Pittsburgh and other centers of industry. Thirty years later, not yet the author of *An American Tragedy* but already recognized as a major American novelist, he wrote about that time in his memoir *Newspaper Days*. Dreiser was a man torn down the middle between his Marxist egalitarian identification with the oppressed and his social Darwinian conviction that both the rich and the poor deserve to be what they are. That split is captured in his reflections on the Darwinian decade that had begun thirty years before.

"Indeed, the spirit of America at that time, as I see it now, was remarkable. It was just entering then upon the most lurid phase of that vast, splendid, most lawless and most savage period in which the great financiers, now nearly all dead, were plotting and conniving the enslavement of the people and belaboring each other for power. . . . Money, money, money. It was the greatest lure of all. You could see it in the faces of the people, in their step and manner. Power, power, power—everyone was seeking power in the land of the free and the home of the brave. They were wildly desirous to place themselves above their fellows—to push them down into a kind of abject, cringing wage slavery, and this in the face of their constant yelping about equality, fraternity and the like. There was almost an angry dissatisfaction with inefficiency of any degree, or slowness, or age, or anything indeed which did not tend directly to the accumulation of riches. The American of that day wanted you to eat, sleep and dream money and power."[6]

The more fiction one has read by Americans shaped in the 1890s—including the work of authors as far apart as Clarence E. Mulford (1883-1956),[7] Arthur Train (1875-1945)[8] and Erle Stanley Gardner (1889-1970)[9]—the more one becomes convinced that Dreiser's take on the decade was right. Any fuller account of Melville Davisson Post's youthful attraction to social Darwinism must await a fuller biography if there ever is one.

***

Post was born in Harrison County, West Virginia on April 19, 1869, eight years after West Virginia became a separate state. His father, Ira Carper Post (1842-1923), was a local aristocrat and well-to-do cattleman. His mother, Florence May Davisson (1843-1914), was the great-granddaughter of Daniel Davisson (1749-1819), who was one of the founding fathers of the area, having settled in 1773 on prime land in what was to become Clarksburg, West Virginia. Melville was the second of their five children and the first of their two sons. He grew up in an atmosphere of rural gentility and fervent Methodist Episcopal religion. After eight years at the local elementary school on Raccoon Run, he was allowed two years without formal education. In the fall of 1885 he was enrolled in Buckhannon Academy, transferred to the University of West Virginia two years later, graduated in 1891 and, after a single year of legal studies, was awarded a Bachelor of Laws degree in 1892. Later that year he was admitted to West Virginia's bar.

During Melville's childhood and adolescence his father had begun dabbling in West Virginia Democratic Party politics and wound up being elected to the state legislature. The year young Post received his law degree he attended the state Democratic convention at Parkersburg, made a speech on behalf of one of the candidates for governor, and was chosen as a presidential elector-at-large and later as secretary of the Electoral College. Whatever his early political ambitions may have been, he subordinated them to the private practice of law. He formed a partnership with attorney John A. Howard, set up an office in Wheeling and, over the next eight years, established a reputation as an expert at collecting bad debts. He also represented corporations and accused criminals.

His first literary ambitions date back to the years at Buckhannon Academy, and some examples of his juvenilia are preserved among the family papers at West Virginia University. It was probably around 1894 or '95 that he began experimenting with fiction. By the spring of 1896 he seems to have completed the seven stories that made up his first book, and the collection was published by G. P. Putnam's Sons later that year as *The Strange Schemes of Randolph Mason*.

Jurisprudence apart, the character of Randolph Mason follows in the tradition of the tormented protagonists of Poe. He hails from Virginia and is described in the tale that introduces him, "The Corpus Delicti," as "the mysterious man of New York . . . as grand, gloomy, and peculiar as Napoleon ever was. . . . He wanders through [his club] usually late at night, apparently without noticing anything or anybody. . . . [H]e reminds me of a great world-weary cynic, transplanted from some ancient mysterious empire." (23-25)

Mason is not only a lawyer but the quintessential lawyer for his time, a born-again social Darwinian who conceives of law in completely amoral terms and uses his knowledge of its technicalities to help criminals get away with their crimes. According to "The Corpus Delicti" his specialty is criminal defense work and he's become

"famous for his powerful and ingenious defenses. He

found holes in the law through which his clients escaped, holes that by the profession at large were not suspected to exist, and that frequently astonished the judges. His ability caught the attention of the great corporations. . . . He pointed out methods by which they could evade obnoxious statutes, by which they could comply with the apparent letter of the law and yet violate its spirit, and advised them well in the most important of all things, just how far they could bend the law without breaking it." (24-25)

All the early Mason stories abound with endorsements of the philosophy to which Holmes in "The Path of the Law" was about to give classical expression. From "Two Plungers of Manhattan":

Client: "[W]e are ready to follow your instructions to the letter in any matter that is not criminal."
Mason: "The transaction will be safely beyond the criminal statutes, although it is close to the border line of the law."
Client: "'Beyond' is as good as a mile; let us hear your plan." (87-88)

In "Woodford's Partner" Mason lectures his client:

"Sir, the law of self-preservation is the great law governing the actions of men. All other considerations are of a secondary nature. The selfish interest is the great motive power. . . . Men do not bear a hurt if the hurt can be placed upon another. It is a bitter law, but it is, nevertheless, a law as fixed as gravity." (117-118)

The same social Darwinism is espoused by other characters in these stories. "The Error of William Van Broom" ends with a

17

prosecutor telling the merchant who was the target of a Mason scheme:

> "All wrongful and injurious acts are not punished by the law. Wrongs to become crimes must measure up to certain definite and technical standards. These standards are laid down rigidly by the law and cannot be contracted or expanded. They are fixed and immutable. The act done must fit closely into the prescribed measure, else it is no crime. If it falls short, never so little, in any one vital element, the law must, and will, disregard it as criminal, no matter how injurious, or wrongful, or unjust it may be. The law is a rigid and exact science." (175)

Dismissing charges against one of Mason's clients, the judge in "The Sheriff of Gullmore" says:

> "The law cannot be figured out. It is certain and exact. It describes perfectly what wrongs are punishable as crimes, and exactly what elements must enter into each wrong in order to make it a crime. All right of discretion is taken from the trial court; the judge must abide by the law, and the law decides matters of this nature in no uncertain terms." (250)

And in "The Animus Furandi" we learn that Mason's secretary Courtlandt Parks shares his employer's philosophy.

> "The world is a fighting station. The one intention of the entire business world is robbery. The man on the street has no sense of pity; he grows rich because he conceives some shrewd scheme by which he is enabled to seize and enjoy the labor of others. His only object is

to avoid the law; he commits the same wrong and causes the same resulting injury as the pirate. The word 'crime,' Hogarth, was invented by the strong with which to frighten the weak; it means nothing. Now listen, since the thing is a cutthroat game, why not have our share of the spoil?" (263)

After these disquisitions one expects Post's early tales to portray a dog-eat-dog world without any moral aspects. This is indeed what we find in some of the stories, but in others Post inconsistently smuggles in moral elements, usually by stressing the selfless motivation of the "bad man" client or the wickedness of Mason's target. These strategies spoil the tales in which Post adopts them but strongly suggest that he's not terribly comfortable with the social Darwinism his spokesmen profess.

In "The Corpus Delicti," first, best known and strongest of the early Mason stories, the client is Richard Warren, alias Samuel Walcott, whose vast property and forthcoming marriage to beautiful young socialite Miriam St. Clair are threatened when his spurned Mexican mistress threatens to expose him as an impostor and a murderer. Mason's solution to the problem is simplicity itself. "This growth must be cut out at the roots." (44) In other words, the man has to kill the woman, but in such a way that it doesn't count as murder under the law. The scheme involves his visiting her house disguised as a Mexican, stabbing her to death with "a great Mexican knife," (51) cutting up her body in her steel bathtub, and then using sulfuric acid to dissolve the body literally into nothing. As luck would have it, he is picked up by the police in his Mexican disguise right after finishing his grisly work and is put on trial for murder. His defense counsel of course is Randolph Mason, who at the close of the prosecution's case moves for a directed verdict of not guilty. Under the doctrine of *Ruloff v. People*,[10] where there is no eyewitness to the crime but only circumstantial evidence that a murder was committed, then purely circumstantial evidence that the defendant was the murderer is legally insufficient for a conviction and, as Mason says, "this Court must compel the jury to acquit him." (68) "Your Honor," responds the District Attorney, "this doctrine is monstrous. . . . If this is the law, then the law for the highest crime is a dead letter. The great commonwealth winks at murder and invites every man to kill his enemy, provided he kill him in secret and hide him. . . ." (68-69) The court, however, has no choice in the matter. "I have no right of discretion," the judge instructs the jury. "The law does not permit a conviction in this case, although every one of us may be morally certain of the prisoner's guilt. I am, therefore, gentlemen of the jury, compelled to direct you to find the prisoner not guilty." (71) From which the jury, the spectators and of course the readers see that "when the skillful villain sought to evade it . . . how weak a thing [the law] was." (74)

The remaining six stories in *The Strange Schemes of Randolph Mason* are variations on the theme of the Darwinian lawyer but in a minor key inasmuch as Mason's advice enables his clients to get away with crimes less serious than murder. In "Two Plungers of Manhattan" Mason works out a scheme to help a pair of brothers obtain the quick $5,000 they need to corner the market in some commodity or other. By moralistic coincidence he picks as the target for his scheme the corrupt retired shoe tycoon whose machinations had ruined his clients' father years before. The scheme calls for one of the brothers to make a $25,000 down payment on the tycoon's mansion and then to turn it into a livery stable, forcing the tycoon to pay a $7000 premium to buy back the property. The $2000 that the brothers don't need for their speculation becomes Mason's fee.

In "Woodford's Partner" young Carper Harris, confidential clerk for a large Baltimore wholesaler, is robbed of $20,000 of the firm's money while on a train journey to New York. Knowing that his bosses will at least fire him and probably charge him with theft too, he appeals for help to his cattle-dealer brother William, who goes to Mason for a scheme to recoup the lost money. Mason has William travel to West Virginia and talk beef speculator Thomas Woodford into forming a cattle partnership. As soon as each man has deposited

$5,000 in a partnership account at a local bank, William cleans out the account and hops the first train for New York. Woodford then makes legal moves to have William extradited to West Virginia to stand trial. "You have violated no law," Mason assures his client; "you have simply taken advantage of its weak places to your own gain and to the hurt of certain stupid fools." (146) The state of New York proves Mason a good legal prophet by refusing the request for William's extradition. Thus, as Post sums up, "[t]he blow which Fate had sought to deliver with such malicious cunning against [Carper Harris] had been turned aside, and had fallen with all its crushing weight upon the shoulders of another man. . . ." (150)

The client in "The Error of William Van Broom" is professional gambler Camden Gerard, who's been using his winnings to support his younger sister but has lost everything he owns in a long streak of bad luck. Mason sends him to Wheeling, West Virginia to visit Van Broom, the local jeweler. Gerard presents a forged letter of introduction from a New York diamond importing house, hints that he wants to offer Van Broom a piece of a lucrative international oil deal and agrees to buy a diamond necklace from Van Broom for $3500. But when the two men go to the bank, ostensibly so that Gerard can withdraw the money from his account, he simply ducks out with the necklace and catches a train for New York. As the local prosecutor later informs Van Broom, there is no basis on which to demand Gerard's extradition. Presenting the forged letter of introduction was not *per se* a crime. "He bought the jewels and you trusted him. He is no more a law-breaker than you are. He is only a sharper dealer." (173) Van Broom's disgusted response may well be shared by most readers. "[W]hat is the good of the law anyhow?" (176)

The most amoral of all the tales in the collection is "The Men of the Jimmy." On a cold and snowy night, Mason is enticed to a country house on the Hudson, seized by a gang of thieves, and forced to devise a plan whereby they can legally raise the money they need to bribe some guards so that their imprisoned companions can escape. Mason as usual is not at a loss for a plan. The child of wealthy Cornelius Rockham had been kidnapped—not by these thieves—several days earlier.

21

Following Mason's instructions, the most presentable of his new clients, a man named Barker, visits Rockham and says that at 11:00 that night he will tell where the child is and take Rockham to the place, but only if Rockham pays him $5,000 in advance. Rockham agrees, and has some police officers wait for eleven o'clock with him. At the appointed hour nothing happens except that Barker slips the $5,000 to one of his confederates in a tobacco pouch. When Barker is tried for obtaining money under false pretenses, Mason demands a directed verdict of not guilty, arguing that making a false statement about a future event doesn't fall within the definition of the crime. The district attorney simply cannot believe "that the law is so defective and its arm so short that it cannot pluck forth the offender and punish him when by every instinct of morality he is a criminal. If this be true, what a limitless field is open to the knave, and what a snug harbor for him is the great commonwealth of New York!" "[S]ir," the judge replies, "this is not a matter of sentiment; it is not a matter of morality; it is not even a matter of right. It is purely and simply a matter of law, and there is no law." (204) What happened to the kidnapped child Post never bothers to tell us.

Almost equally amoral is "The Sheriff of Gullmore" which comes next in the book. Colonel Moseby Allen is about to conclude his term as sheriff of his West Virginia county and make an accounting of funds to his successor. His problem is that he's lost $30,000 in county revenue speculating on Wall Street. Mason's secretary, Courtlandt Parks, brings the sheriff's plight to Mason's attention: unless Allen can find $30,000 in a hurry, his innocent father and brother will have to forfeit the bond they put up when Allen took office. Mason comes up with a scheme so that the loss falls instead on the head of Jacob Wade, the newly elected sheriff, and on whoever *his* bondsmen happen to be. Allen is indicted but the West Virginia judge is compelled to rule, as Mason had known, that what Allen did was neither embezzlement nor larceny nor any other crime. The result, concludes His Honor, "is not reason or justice, but it is the law." (255)

"The Animus Furandi" opens with a conversation between Mason's secretary Courtlandt Parks and private investigator Braxton Hogarth in which we learn that Mason had become a sort of Poe character after having lost his fortune in France thanks to some governmental "treachery," and that since his return to New York Parks has been secretly soliciting criminal business for Mason so as to help his boss recover both intellectually and financially. As part of a scheme to feather his own nest, Parks introduces Hogarth to Mason as a man with a problem akin to that of several previous clients: he needs to raise a quick $20,000 to save his son from being charged with embezzling that amount from a New Jersey bank. The scheme Mason hatches takes us back once more to West Virginia where Walson, the manager of a coal company, is transporting a $20,000 payroll to the mine in a box under his buckboard seat. Hogarth handcuffs the manager, identifies himself as a detective, claims that Walson is a fugitive desperado and marches him back to town, leaving the buckboard with its cashbox out on the open road. By the time the "mistake" is straightened out and Walson goes back to retrieve the $20,000, the buckboard has been burned and the money stolen. Later in New York, Hogarth and Parks visit an illegal gambling den, lose the booty at faro and take it back from the dealer at gunpoint. They get caught on the spot but, as the district attorney informs the chief of police, for various technical reasons what they did was not robbery. The chief's last remark sums up much of the story. "[W]on't there be hell to pay when the crooks learn the law?" (286-287). The final scene shows a "grim, emaciated and rigidly ugly" Mason sailing back with Parks to France.

Into some of these earliest Randolph Mason stories Post had permitted the intrusion of moral aspects at odds with his Darwinian premises and hinting at a jurisprudential struggle within him. The five new tales issued by Putnam in 1897 as *The Man of Last Resort* begin with Mason back in New York and once again counseling the "bad man" (and woman) how to commit crimes while staying within the law but culminate in the apparent death of both Post's protagonist and his Darwinian vision.

In a preface Post reveals that he'd taken quite a blast of critical heat for publishing *The Strange Schemes* and, from the critics' perspective, showing potential criminals the loopholes in the law through which they might wriggle. His defense, the obvious one under the circumstances, was that the Randolph Mason stories were intended as object lessons in how the legal system should be improved. To those who argued that he could better serve this purpose by privately pointing out legal flaws "to a few political leaders" he replied that no law is legitimate unless rooted in "the will of the people" so that he had no choice but to address his lessons to the electorate at large. Almost twenty years later, this view of juridical legitimacy was to form the basis for one of his most powerful law stories.

The first, longest and weakest of the five tales collected in *The Man of Last Resort* is "The Governor's Machine." The setting is a nameless southwestern state, most likely New Mexico, part of the "mighty new land" which "stood open with its doors wide. Any combatant who pleased could enter. . . . If he were fittest, he could win." (30-31) Alfred Randal, the handsome New Englander who's become governor, has been using his office to accumulate a personal fortune that will make him worthy of the woman he loves. Unfortunately the alcoholic crony known as Billy the Plunger whom Randal appointed secretary of state has lost $50,000 in state funds to an obese gambler. Randal is determined to save his buddy from prison and disgrace by making good the loss out of his own profits from public service even if it means he can never propose to his wealthy sweetheart. Billy saves Randal from his own nobility by coming to New York and obtaining from Randolph Mason a scheme to recoup the money some other way. The plan turns out to be ridiculously simple. Billy gets the fat gambler Crawley to lend him $50,000 for speculation in oil futures and signs a note giving Crawley 12% interest on a 30-day loan plus one-eighth of Billy's profits. Randal signs the note as surety. Crawley's money is used to replace the embezzled state funds and, thirty days later, the signers refuse to repay the $50,000. Crawley's suit against them is quickly dismissed by the court on the ground that a futures contract is a species of gambling contract and therefore unenforceable.[11] Post takes almost 100 pages of awkward prose and inept construction to reach this lame climax, and Mason never comes on stage for a moment.

Much tighter and more purely Darwinian is "Mrs. Van Bartan." Mason's client, the former Columbia Summers, is a West Virginia belle whose family had fallen on hard times until her marriage to a man she doesn't love, Gerald Van Bartan, the weak and useless only son of a deceased iron tycoon whose widow, herself near death, is so fiercely opposed to the union that she's prepared to cut Gerald out of her will and leave all the family property to her church. Mason draws out of his client the one fact she's tried to keep from him—that the man she really loves, Robert Dalton, happens to be her mother-in-law's attorney—and tells her that she must do whatever it takes to entice Dalton into sabotaging the will he draws for the old lady. This is precisely how things work out. Gerald's mother dies, and it quickly becomes apparent that the will Dalton drafted for her isn't worth the paper it's written on since it leaves her estate "to St. Luke's Episcopal Church." A church *per se* is not a legal entity capable of holding title to property, which means that the will is void and Gerald takes by intestate succession. His career ruined by newspaper coverage of the affair, Dalton sails off to become a law professor in Japan. (I am not making this up.) Columbia Van Bartan tearfully visits Mason again to revile him in the ripest of terms. "Yes, thanks to your devilish ingenuity, I obtained [what I wanted], but at what a cost! I have the money, but it is daubed over with the blood of a man's heart. . . . I charge you, do you hear me, I charge you with the ruin of this man's life." "Madam," replies Mason, ". . . I am not concerned with the nonsense of emotion." (133-134). He walks out of the room and the story ends. Why he didn't give her the obvious advice—arrange a little accident for her husband and take off with the Van Bartan fortune to become a Japanese law faculty wife —does not appear. We may have here a sort of negative infusion of morality, or perhaps Post thought the story was already sufficiently drenched in social Darwinism.

Next comes "Once in Jeopardy," almost ninety pages of leaden exposition, structural ineptitude and painfully obvious legal gimmickry. Robert Gilmore is unique among Mason clients in that he consults the lawyer *after* committing his crime, whose genesis he explains in a long dull monologue. He and his partner Brown Hirst had schemed for Hirst to marry an unsuspecting woman, take out $200,000 in life insurance with her as beneficiary, fake his own suicide and slip off to Europe, after which Gilmore would court and marry his widow, take control of the insurance proceeds and eventually desert her and join Hirst overseas. But when the time came to go out with Hirst and fake a suicide, Gilmore, who had actually fallen in love with Mrs. Hirst, had thrown his partner over a bridge into the raging Tug River hundreds of feet below. Refusing to believe that her husband killed himself, Mrs. Hirst has hired a private detective to prove it was murder. Gilmore is convinced he'll be caught and begs Mason to save his life. Mason's advice: Gilmore must be framed for the murder and put on trial in West Virginia where the faked evidence against him will explode and he'll be acquitted so that he can never be tried again on the same charge. The balance of this long-winded story details the working out of the plan but befuddles the reader because the only *false* evidence presented at Gilmore's trial is his own confession, which turns out to be inadmissible. In terms of plot mechanics this is the sloppiest of all the Randolph Mason exploits.

The shortest, most vividly written and interesting story in the collection is "The Grazier." The scene once again is West Virginia and the title character is Rufus Alshire, a giant of a man who runs cattle on his spread and "loved the open sky, and the blue hills, and the monster oak trees, and hated in his heart with a stubborn bitter spirit of rebellion the least shadow of restraint." (232) This majestic man of the hills, who quite clearly foreshadows Post's immortal Uncle Abner, has a legal problem. His land is mortgaged to the hilt and his promissory notes have been bought up by a rapacious oil company whose bosses have learned that there's a huge pool of black gold beneath his property. Alshire ventures all the way to New York to seek the advice of his young friend Jerry Van Meter. While crossing a traffic-choked Manhattan street, Alshire and Jerry save a man from being run over by a horse-drawn mail wagon. As chance or providence would have it, the man is Mason's secretary Courtlandt Parks, and suddenly the lawyer has another client. But this client is unlike any in Mason's experience: he refuses to save his property by committing a crime. Mason is outraged by such scruples. "Commit a crime! No man who has followed my advice has ever committed a crime. Crime is a technical word. It is the law's name for certain acts which it is pleased to define and punish with a penalty. None but fools, dolts, and children commit crimes." (252) Alshire is unmoved by this legalism and insists that he won't commit any moral wrong even if technically it's legal. Mason explodes in fury.

> "Moral wrong! A name used to frighten fools. There is no such thing. The law lays down the only standard by which the acts of the citizen are to be governed. What the law permits is right, else it would prohibit it. What the law prohibits is wrong, because it punishes it. This is the only lawful measure, the only measure bearing the stamp and sanction of the State. All others are spurious, counterfeit, and void. The word moral is a pure metaphysical symbol possessing no more intrinsic virtue than the radical sign." (252-253)

Luckily Alshire has no moral qualms about Mason's ultimate plan for him, which involves his leasing oil rights to close friends like Jerry who don't live in West Virginia so as to stall the foreclosure on his property for years and give him time to drill for the oil himself. The final lines of dialogue between the two men are pregnant with Post's future as a writer of stories about the legal system.

Alshire (astonished): "Is all this possible?"

Mason: "To the law all things are possible—even justice." (257)

The description of Mason in the final paragraph, his form thin and gaunt with swollen purple veins showing on his forehead, suggests that the attorney is unwell.

The collection closes with another short and relatively tight story, "The Rule Against Carper." Social Darwinian entrepreneur Russell Carper has spent years looting a bankrupt company for which he'd been appointed receiver, but finally after endless delaying maneuvers the court is about to enter a decree ordering him to account and he can't because he's been ruined in the stock market. In a long introspective sequence we learn that the woman he loved had broken her engagement when she found out about his legal but vile business practices and that he had tried but failed to convince her that social Darwinism was ordained by God and not to be questioned by mere man. Desperate, Carper goes out that night to seek the help of Randolph Mason, his last hope, only to find that the medical problems hinted at in "The Grazier" have grown much worse: the lawyer is "raving like a drunken sailor" and at the point of death from "acute mania." At this juncture Carper accepts the fact that his ruination is well deserved. "For seven years he had flown the black flag of piracy. . . . Every man who had passed up a prisoner on to the deck of his galleon, had walked the plank. It was now his turn. It was justice." (284) He goes home and, we are to understand, kills himself. Mason never appears and, we are to understand, is also dead, or as good as dead anyway. And so he was for the next ten years. When at last he was resurrected, the newly incarnated Mason had nothing in common with the old version except his legal expertise and his name.

***

During the ten years that followed *The Man of Last Resort* Post wrote next to nothing, devoting himself almost exclusively to politics, law and, later, to his family. In 1898 he was elected chairman of West Virginia's Democratic Congressional Committee. Three years later he cut his professional ties with John A. Howard and formed a new partnership with John McGraw, an older and politically better connected attorney. The firm of McGraw & Post, based in Grafton, specialized in representing coal mines and railroads. In 1903 the thriving establishment lawyer married Ann Schoolfield in Philadelphia. Their only child, born on February 5, 1905, was named Ira Carper Post II, after Post's father. The child died of typhoid fever at the age of eighteen months. Devastated by this and other tragedies whose exact nature remains obscure, Post soon afterwards ended his partnership with McGraw and in fact cut all his ties to both law and politics. From this point until his death he was identified by the public and himself simply as a writer.

In 1906, after being wooed for several years, Post signed a contract with the popular *Pearson's Magazine* to resurrect Randolph Mason and write a new series of stories about him. The timing, and a reference in the *Pearson's* promotional announcement (". . . we believe that they will prove to be the most interesting stories of the mystery class that have been produced since the original cases of Sherlock Holmes"), make it clear that the magazine was hoping to duplicate Conan Doyle's resurrection of the sage of Baker Street in 1903, after the world had come to believe that Holmes had plunged with Professor Moriarty into the Reichenbach Falls. In order to make the new Randolph Mason tales marginally more Holmes-like, Mason's secretary Courtlandt Parks was transformed into a first-person narrator in the manner of Dr. Watson.

That was a minor change in the format of the series compared to the total and totally unexplained character transformation that Mason himself underwent at the behest of the *Pearson's* editors. "[I]t seemed to us," they explained in their promotional announcement, "that for magazine purposes, a new series of stories would be much stronger, and more universally satisfactory to our readers, if Randolph Mason could be made the champion of right instead of the tutor of criminals." Post, the editors claim, "accepted our view of the matter and worked out his cases accordingly." How much he was paid for agreeing does not appear, but the last two stories in *The Man of Last Resort* make it plain that Post needed no bribe to renounce social Darwinism. In any event, the promo in *Pearson's* was followed by a statement signed by Courtlandt Parks himself, in which he explains his employer's activities as tutor to criminals as the result of an "attack of acute mania"—which in fact is what *ended* that phase of Mason's career—and then informs us that since his recovery the attorney's *raison d'etre* is "to find within the law a means by which to even up and correct every manner of injustice. He would consider no case which did not contain this element, a wrong for which the law in its regular course offers no redress." But he protests (perhaps too much) that Mason has not developed morals or a conscience but rather has chosen to specialize in redressing the balance of justice because it's hard to do. "Take a situation so hopeless as to be called fated or inevitable, add, in the correction of it, a necessity to return the injury directly and in an exact measure to the author of it, and one has a difficulty not easily possible of solution to human intelligence." The claim that Mason in these stories is operating purely as a technician is justified in the sense that Post usually doesn't stack the deck by making the clients simplistically sympathetic, as Arthur Train would often do by having his character Mr. Tutt represent a nice young man or woman in love. But where the earlier Randolph Mason tales had offered a Darwinian view of law and lawyering with occasional inconsistent overtones of morality, the *Pearson's* stories tend to portray the lawyer protagonist in the service of secular common decency and the legal system itself as having the resources to bring about the decent result despite the invocation of specific rules of law by the antagonist, who more often than not is an avatar of the Holmes "bad man."

Pearson's ran a new Randolph Mason story in each of its monthly issues from February 1907 through May 1908—a total of thirteen tales, three of them divided into two installments each—and later in 1908 all thirteen were published in book form by Edward J. Clode as *The Corrector of Destinies*. Most of the tales are cut to a single pattern, with a client victimized by a scoundrel coming for redress to Mason, who invariably finds a judicial decision he can use to make the client whole. The stories frequently involve financial skullduggery among railroad, coal and oil tycoons in Virginia or western Pennsylvania, and more often than not the linchpin of Mason's counterstrategy is a case decided by the West Virginia Supreme Court. For a sense of how the reconstituted Mason operates we need not explore each of the thirteen stories at length. Two of them, one rather weak and the other the best in the collection, will suffice.

Mason's client in "Madame Versay" (*Pearson's*, March 1907) is an aristocratic Old South matriarch, and the problem she presents is that a hapless young man in the family has been seduced and befuddled into stealing the ancestral jewels and turning them over to the avaricious New York "variety actress" of the title. The woman can't be prosecuted because that would require prosecution of the young man too and the besmirchment of the family's honor, but she's willing to sell the jewels back to the matriarch for $10,000 cash. Mason arranges for the payoff to be made in Richmond, Virginia, capital of the old Confederacy, and in Confederate money. When the furious Madame Versay threatens to have him prosecuted for passing counterfeit currency, Mason is ready with a citation to *United States v. Barrett*,[12] holding that because Confederate money doesn't and never was intended to simulate U.S. money, it can't be considered counterfeit.[13]

In "The Life Tenant" (*Pearson's*, October 1907) the client is a tubercular young man named Hopkins, who will die if he doesn't move almost at once to the Marquesas Islands. Mason determines that a tropical lifestyle will cost Hopkins $1200 up front and the same amount every year thereafter and uses his legal wiles to secure the money. At a judicial sale of tax-delinquent land in West Virginia, Hopkins had purchased a tract that he happened to know was rich in coal. The only mine actually on the land was a backyard pit operated by the old farmer who had lost the property for unpaid taxes. Later Hopkins discovered that he'd bought not fee simple title to the tract but a mere life estate, valid only for what was left of the decrepit old farmer's life. Under the general rule of law, a life tenant may not conduct mining operations on his property but is limited to making his living by farming the land's surface. To make matters worse, a voracious soft coal trust knows of the wealth beneath the land and is gleefully waiting for the old farmer to die so it can begin full-scale excavations. Mason forces the trust to buy out his client's interest by citing *Koen v. Bartlett*,[14] in which the West Virginia Supreme Court had ruled that where a mine is already in operation on a piece of property, no matter how small the mine may be, even a backyard pit like the old farmer's, a life tenant may legally "gut the land of every ounce of value." (164)

Certain weaknesses recur in many of these stories. Too often Post couches either the problem or Mason's solution, or both, in long arid stretches of narrative unrelieved by a syllable of dialogue or characterization. Mason usually is offstage when his schemes come to climax. Most of the subordinate players in these little dramas are simplistically drawn. And, reading the thirteen tales close together, one is overwhelmed by their generic similarity and prone to forget what makes each story different.

But there is also much to enter on the credit page of the ledger. The writing in these tales is much leaner than in the earlier Randolph Mason collections. Mason himself remains an effectively Poesque figure, an obsessive recluse living in an old mansion "on the west side of Broadway below Wall Street" (7) that he has turned into "one huge library of law books" (9), his domestic needs attended to by an Italian peasant couple who live in the basement and his administrative needs by Parks. Post vividly draws Mason "in a heavy black oak chair before the fire . . . his face thrown partly into shadow by the flaming logs on the hearth. The masterful iron face, the lean, hard jaw with its projecting chin, the fearless, bony nose appearing in the fantastic light flattened a little at the end, like that of a beast of prey, and the craggy forehead—all colored, browned, reddened by the fire." (52-53; from "The Burgoyne-Hayes Dinner.") "[H]is chin up, his jaws looked like the close-fitting bars of a trap, his eyes wide open, but the eyeballs dull, his body erect, rigid almost, in its gray tweeds, and the long, nervous fingers gripped behind his back." (115; from "The Interrupted Exile.") He doesn't orate anywhere near often enough but when we do hear him speak, his words ring with the sort of austere majesty and authority that most readers of Post will associate with his later and much better known character Uncle Abner.

From the first story in the new series, "My Friend at Bridge" (*Pearson's*, February 1907):

> Winfield Gerry: "The scheme of things seems to require a hell. Matters must be adjusted somewhere."
> Mason: "This one will be adjusted here." (14)
> Gerry: ". . . The Fifty-eighth National Bank will never shoulder such a loss. These debts aggregate three hundred thousand dollars."
> Mason: "The Fifty-eighth National Bank will not lose a dollar."
> Gerry: "Then I do not know how under heaven Egan Bedford can be got to cash the checks!"
> Mason: "It is sufficient that I know." (17)

From "The Interrupted Exile" (*Pearson's*, July and August 1907):

> Mason: "Nothing is ended until it arrives at its adjustment."
> Parks: "Then this is a case for the Court of Final Equity, if it ever sits."
> Mason: "It is a case for me." (124)

From "The Last Check" (*Pearson's*, September 1907), where Mason is being retained by the dying president of an insurance company:

> Curtis: "And, now, if only I could return the money to the insurance company; if only I could even matters with

that cold, cruel, cunning political intriguer, I should die happy."

Mason: "Then you will die like the saints. The Assurance Company of North America will not lose a dollar, and matters will be squared once for all with this politician."

Curtis: "Human pity has always promised the impossible to the dying; but it is no kindness."

Mason: "Sir, I promise nothing; I merely point out the inevitable."

Curtis: "The inevitable! Why, only the hand of God could perform the thing you speak of."

Mason: "Pardon me; your own hand has already done it." (145)

If we think ahead to the numinous ambience of the Uncle Abner stories Post was to write later, we might imagine that Randolph Mason too is being portrayed as a sort of time-traveling Old Testament prophet. Post takes special pains to keep that temptation away from us and to make us see Mason as a totally secular righter of wrongs. In "The Last Check," for example, one of the characters says to Mason: "I consider this thing to be a providence of God." "On the contrary," Mason replies, "it is a mere principle of law." (147) And in "The Virgin of the Mountains" (*Pearson's*, December 1907 and January 1908), the longest and weakest story of the thirteen, the Italian marquis whom Mason in a momentary reversion to his old self had gotten off for a sadistic but in his view justified murder says: "Mr. Mason, I wish to thank you for my life." "Sir," Mason tells him, "I had no interest in your life. The adjustment of your problem was the only thing of interest to me." (227) Every so often the author remembers that his character is still supposed to be an amoral technician.

In "The Intriguer" (*Pearson's*, April and May 1908), with which the collection ends, Post not only creates the single genuinely interesting female character in the series but links her with his recurring Social Darwinian theme. When Margaret Garnett speaks of the joy of the battle to survive, Post bathes her in a kind of mystic glow much as the directors of 1950s religioso movies did when a holy man preached the word of God. "Straining muscle against straining muscle, wits fiercely hand to hand, with the cross for the conquered. That's the fine thing, Courtlandt, that's life! only let the fight be fair." (276-277) Margaret's father, railroad mogul John A. Garnett, is about to be ruined by the schemes of U.S. Marshal Thomas B. Wood, who's demanding control of Garnett's line as a *quid pro quo* for turning in his badge. Despite Margaret's pleas to let the Darwinian chips fall where they may, Mason steps in and advises Garnett to agree to the deal. What the lawyer knows and no one else in the tale seems aware of is that any contract giving a public official some benefit in return for his resignation from office is invalid. But at the end of the story, after Wood has been defeated, Margaret trumps Mason's ace by announcing that she's going to marry the ex-marshal, so that in due course he'll control her father's properties anyway. This is far from a world-class story but it hints that the battle of jurisprudential values in Post's heart was still raging as he put his first lawyer character to rest.

***

The year 1908 was triply significant in Post's creative life. It saw the publication of the third and last Randolph Mason collection; of the twenty-fifth and last Mason story, the never reprinted and never collected "The Marriage Contract" (*Pearson's*, June 1908), in which Mason functions less as a lawyer and more as a sort of universal uncle to young lovers in distress; and of the first of more than two dozen tales he was to sell to America's premier popular fiction magazine. That tale, "The Trivial Incident" (*Saturday Evening Post*, December 19, 1908), deals with a civil suit by an aggrieved black teenager against a small-town banker, and in terms of racial enlightenment the story is decades ahead of its time. At least two other non-series Post tales of roughly the same vintage—"The Locked Bag" (*Saturday Evening Post*, February 4, 1911) and "The Fairy Godmother" (*Saturday Evening Post*, April 15, 1911)—are also of legal interest. These three and eight other non-series stories from various magazines were published in book form, with revisions and a framing structure to give them the superficial appearance of a novel, as *The Nameless Thing* (Appleton, 1912). By then Post had already created another series character, his finest and most enduring contribution: the immortal Uncle Abner.

In most of the eighteen Abner stories Post published in the second decade of the last century, he sought to transcend human law altogether and to focus on the divine law standing above man's puny structures of (in)justice. The tales are set in the remote western area of Virginia around the middle of the 1800s, before the Civil War split off that region into a separate state, and their radiant center is Abner, a huge, bearded, grimly austere and supremely righteous countryman who smites wrongdoers and mends destinies as if he were a Biblical prophet magically transplanted to the New World. Through his storylines, characterizations, narrative and dialogue, Post filled these tales with a power and majesty echoing the language of the King James Bible, capturing the essence of evangelical Protestantism and integrating it into detective fiction with the same supreme skill that G.K. Chesterton at the same time was lavishing upon his Father Brown stories in the service of rationalist Catholicism.

The character of Uncle Abner was probably based on Ira Carper Post, to whom Post dedicated *Uncle Abner: Master of Mysteries* when that collection of the first eighteen stories in the series was published by Appleton in 1918: "To MY FATHER whose unfailing faith in an ultimate justice behind the moving of events has been to the writer a wonder and an inspiration."

What makes the dedication especially fitting is that most of these tales are permeated by the theme that chance does not exist, that "[t]here was a purpose in every moving of events" which is described interchangeably as providence or "the justice of God." Post does not pretend that divine justice is synonymous either with human justice or with the law as it stands but in several of the stories he stresses that taking the law into one's own hands to achieve justice of either the human or divine variety is a vain and foolish endeavor; that these things should be left to the inscrutable providence that governs all.

In the first few paragraphs of the first tale in which he appears, "The Angel of the Lord" (*Saturday Evening Post*, June 3, 1911, as "The Broken Stirrup-Leather"), Abner is described by the narrator, his young nephew Martin, as "one of those austere, deeply religious men who were the product of the Reformation. He always carried a Bible in his pocket and he read it where he pleased. . . . Abner belonged to the church militant, and his God was a war lord." (41-42) In a later tale, "The Riddle" (*Metropolitan Magazine*, September 1912), Martin says of his uncle: "He was one of those austere, deeply religious men who might have followed Cromwell, with a big iron frame, a grizzled beard and features forged out by a smith. His god was the god of the Tishbite [i.e. the Old Testament prophet Elijah], who numbered his followers by the companies who drew the sword." (212) And in "The Straw Man" (*Red Book*, April 1915) Abner is described as

> "a big, broad-shouldered, deep-chested Saxon, with all those marked characteristics of a race living out of doors and hardened by wind and sun. His powerful frame carried no ounce of surplus weight. It was the frame of the empire builder on the frontier of the empire. The face reminded one of Cromwell, the craggy features in repose seemed molded over iron, but the fine gray eyes had a calm serenity, like remote spaces in the summer sky. The man's clothes were plain and somber. And he gave one the impression of things big and vast." (227)

He is a landowner and cattle raiser and, though not trained as a lawyer, he seems to have a vast fund of legal knowledge on which he draws as the occasion demands. But the atmosphere of these stories is numinous, not legalistic, and the aura surrounding Abner is not lawyerlike but thunderously prophetic. If we focus on the legal dimension of the tales about him we risk losing sight of what was most crucial for his creator, but focus on that dimension we must.

"The Angel of the Lord," the first tale in the series, is one of several in which Post aims to show the absence of chance and the presence of divine purpose everywhere. The only point of legal significance is that Dix, the evildoer who overtakes young Martin at a lonely Virginia inn and plans to kill him during the night and steal the cattle sale money he's carrying for his kinfolk, refers to his antagonist as "Lawyer Abner with his brief" and "Lawyer Abner, with your neat little conclusions." (57)

In the second Abner story, "The Wrong Hand" (*Saturday Evening Post*, July 15, 1911), Post pits Abner against Gaul, a diabolical hunchback who has cursed and rejected God because he was born deformed, and legal language abounds in the Socratic colloquy between the two. "We do not have our possessions in fee in this world, Gaul, but upon lease and for a certain term of service. And when we make default in that service the lease abates and a new man can take the title." (31) Abner personally drafts a deed covering Gaul's land and forces the hunchback to convey the property to his dead brother Enoch's son by proving that Gaul obtained the land by fratricide. The theme of the right division of land among a dead man's successors will recur in several later Abner stories.

"The House of the Dead Man" (*Saturday Evening Post*, September 30, 1911) reprises the situation of the Randolph Mason story "The Sheriff of Gullmore" and features yet another sheriff who has stolen tax revenues his bondsmen are obliged to make good. The tale is permeated by divine providence but lacks any specific legal aspect.

The earliest Abner story of overpowering legal interest is "The Tenth Commandment" (*Saturday Evening Post*, March 2, 1912). Post's figure of evil in this story is at once a Holmesian "bad man," demanding his rights under the law with no regard for morality, and a classic Shylock, suing to dispossess a neighbor because of a technical defect in the other's deed until Abner, following in the footsteps of Shakespeare's Portia, trumps the "bad man" with another and stronger rule of law. The dialogue between these antagonists deserves to be quoted at length.

Abner: "You got this wedge of land on which your house is built by a lawsuit, did you not?"

Dillworth: "I did; but if men do not exercise ordinary care they must suffer for that negligence."

Abner: "Well, the little farmer who lived here on this wedge suffered enough for his. When you dispossessed him he hanged himself in his stable with a halter."

Dillworth: "Abner, I have heard enough about that. I did not take the man's life. I took what the law gave me. . . ."

Abner: "It is the law, but is it justice, Dillworth?"

Dillworth: "Abner, how shall we know what justice is unless the law defines it?"

Abner: "I think every man knows what it is."

Dillworth: "And shall every man set up a standard of his own, and disregard the standard that the law sets up? That would be the end of justice."

Abner: "It would be the beginning of justice, if every man followed the standard that God gives him. . . ."

Dillworth: ". . . You would saddle every man with the thing you call a conscience, and let that ride him. Well, I would unsaddle him from that. What is right? What is wrong? These are vexed questions. I would leave them to the law. Look what a burden is on every man if he must decide the justice of every act as it comes up. Now the law would lift that burden from his shoulders, and I would let the law bear it."

Abner: "But under the law, the weak and the ignorant suffer for their weakness and for their ignorance, and the shrewd and the cunning profit by their shrewdness and by their cunning. How would you help that?" . . .

Dillworth: "But why should it be done? Does Nature

do it? Look with what indifference she kills off the weakling. Is there any pity in her or any of your little concerns? I tell you these things are not to be found anywhere in Nature—they are man-made."

Abner: "Or God-made."

Dillworth: "Call it what you like, it will be equally fantastic, and the law would be fantastic to follow after it. As for myself, Abner, I would avoid these troublesome refinements. Since the law will undertake to say what is right and what is wrong I shall leave her to say it and let myself go free. What she requires me to give I shall give, and what she permits me to take I shall take, and there shall be an end of it." (160-164)

Post surprisingly gives Dillworth the last word in the Socratic dialogue but Abner of course prevails in the practical sense, tricking the proto-Darwinian into signing over his lawsuit to Abner himself by promising to hand back seven-eighths of what he recovers. As soon as the ink is dry on the paper he announces that he's dropping the suit and gleefully points out that he's kept his promise to the letter since seven-eighths of nothing is nothing. This is one of the most perfect 20th-century adaptations of the core of *The Merchant of Venice* and one of the finest of all the tales of Uncle Abner.

"The Riddle" (*Metropolitan Magazine*, September 1912) opens with Abner riding into the county seat to appear before a grand jury, but there is no particular legal interest in this tale of a murdered miser and the meaning of the taunting clue to the location of his hidden gold that he left behind him: "Why don't you look in the cow?"

"The Devil's Tools" (*Metropolitan Magazine*, March 1913) introduces into the series a new regular character, the pompous and grandiloquent Squire Randolph. When some valuable emeralds are pried out of his daughter Betty's heirloom necklace shortly before her wedding day, Randolph suspects Mammy Liza, the proud old slave who's been in his family for generations, and conducts a quasi-hearing into the theft. Abner intervenes and, while spied upon by young Martin, discovers the truth and makes sure no one else will.

The next two tales have no connection in terms of narrative but thematically they form a matched or rather a mismatched pair. "An Act of God" (*Metropolitan Magazine*, December 1913) brings Abner and Martin to a county fair, not for fun but on grim business, to expose a villainous deaf mute named Blackford. Before they can do anything the scoundrel is "accidentally" stabbed to death during a gypsy knife-thrower's performance. Squire Randolph pompously opines that the death should be categorized as, in the legal sense, an act of God, but Abner knows better and confronts the gypsy that night. Even though he can prove Blackford's death was murder, he has said nothing, he explains, because he "feared that the justice of the law might contravene the justice of God. . . ." (75) The gypsy agrees completely with Abner's view of the situation. "Monsieur, I have done an act of justice, not as men do it, but as the providence of God does it." (80)

If that story seems an open invitation to take the law into one's own hands, it's counterbalanced by "A Twilight Adventure" (*Metropolitan Magazine*, April 1914), which is likely to remind today's readers of the classic anti-vigilante Western novel and movie *The Ox-Bow Incident*. On the trail, Abner and Martin come upon some cattlemen who have transformed themselves into a lynch mob and are about to hang two strangers they believe guilty of rustling and murder. Abner listens to the flimsy circumstantial evidence against the pair, twists it around so that it seems to prove the guilt of the mob's chief instigator, then clears that man and gives the vigilantes an object lesson in the need for due process of law.

The most famous, most often reprinted and by all odds the quintessential Abner story is "The Doomdorf Mystery" (*Saturday Evening Post*, July 18, 1914), in which Abner accompanies Squire Randolph, the local justice of the peace, in investigating the death of a demonic farmer by a fowling piece hanging on a wall in a totally sealed room. The tale is beautifully written and superbly constructed, with a powerful climax built around Post's recurring theme of the justice of God. But it lacks any special legal dimension, and so do "The Hidden Law" (*Metropolitan Magazine*, August 1914) and "The Treasure Hunter" (*Saturday Evening Post*, August 14, 1915), which come next in the series.

"The Straw Man" (*Red Book*, April 1915) takes place on a court day and its plot depends on the law of succession, with Abner exposing an attorney who, with a remainder interest in certain land subject to two life estates, has murdered the one life tenant and framed the other. Thematically, however, there is minimal legal dimension to the tale.

"The Edge of the Shadow" (*Red Book*, May 1915) takes place shortly before the Civil War and portrays Abner as the classic man in the middle, between a maniacal abolitionist on the one side and, on the other, a diabolical slaveholder who anachronistically spouts Nietzschean atheism. Abner argues that the country's only chance to avert a hellish conflict is to enforce rigidly both the rights of due process and the concept of equality before the law. If there is little here to interest legally oriented readers, "The Mystery of Chance" (*Red Book*, July 1915) and "The Concealed Path" (magazine publication unknown) offer even less as Abner twice again teaches the lesson that what seems to be chance is really the working of providence.

The legal element returns with a vengeance in "The Age of Miracles," which was a non-series story when it appeared in magazine form (*Pictorial Review*, February 1916) but was revised for book publication with Abner and Squire Randolph replacing the original protagonists. The reason why Post originally kept this tale out of the Abner cycle is not far to seek: thematically it's the same story as "The Tenth Commandment" only without the Socratic colloquy. The rapacious brothers Adam and Benton Wolf have taken land from its rightful owner through a technical defect in his deed, leaving their victim dead and his daughter Julia homeless. "It was a proceeding at law," Randolph comments. "It was the law that did the thing, and we can not hold the law in disrespect." Abner replies: "But the man who uses the law to accomplish a wrong, we can so hold. He is an outlaw, as the highwayman and the pirate are." (137) Now Adam has apparently shot himself in the face with his own fowling-piece and lies in his coffin ready for the earth. With Randolph in tow, Abner visits Benton Wolf and asks him to undo this wrong and convey the land to Julia.

> "The property is not yours. You got it by a legal trick, the judge who heard you was bound by the technicalities of language. But you are old, Wolf, and the next Judge will go behind the record. He will be hard to face. He has expressed Himself on these affairs. 'If the widow and the orphan cry to me, I will surely hear their cry.' Sinister words, Wolf, for one who comes with a case like yours into the Court of Final Equity." (150)

Without becoming philosophical like his forerunner Dillworth in "The Tenth Commandment," Benton insists on his rights under the law and refuses to sign—until Abner proves that Adam Wolf's death was not an accident but fratricide.

The only courtroom story in the Abner series, "Naboth's Vineyard" (*Illustrated Sunday Magazine*, June 4, 1916), is also Post's classic exposition of the meaning of the sovereignty of the people. Abner and young Martin are attending the trial of a young farmhand for the murder of Elihu Marsh. The young woman who kept house for the dead man stands up in court and confesses to the crime herself but Judge Simon Kilrail refuses to direct a verdict for the defendant. After an enigmatic late-night conversation between the judge and Abner, the trial resumes next morning. Abner stands up in court and unaccountably demands that Kilrail step down from the bench. The judge holds Abner in contempt. "You threaten me," Abner intones, "but God Almighty threatens you." Then, turning to the courtroom spectators, he proclaims: "The authority of the law is in the hands of the electors of this county. Will they stand up?" Then "[s]lowly, in silence, and without passion, as though they were in a church of God, men began to get up in the courtroom." Squire Randolph, then Martin's father, then various tradesmen, then a Catholic priest and two Protestant circuit riders, and finally old Nathaniel Davisson, a real-world great-granduncle of Post, "a just man, and honorable and unafraid." As Martin sums up the scene: "I saw that law and order and all the structure that civilization had builded up, rested on the sense of justice that certain men carried in their breasts. . . ." (334-336) When Post says "men" he means it literally—no women included, nor Jews nor black men either, which is precisely how things stood in the Virginia of the 1850s—but the scene makes it clear that Post is trying to be as inclusive as the facts of history permit. The sheriff refuses Kilrail's order to arrest Abner for contempt. "I would obey the representative of the law," he says, "if I were not in the presence of the law itself!" (337) At this point Abner accuses Judge Kilrail of the murder of Elihu Marsh, and Nathaniel Davisson forces the judge to remain in the courtroom and listen while Abner sets forth the incriminating evidence. Kilrail then withdraws into his chambers and shoots himself. As recently as 1987 Post's surprise denouement, albeit without the overlay of political philosophy, was borrowed by Hollywood for the courtroom thriller *Suspect*.

"The Adopted Daughter" (*Red Book*, June 1916) pits Abner against yet another prototype of the Holmes "bad man" demanding his legal rights, the disputed property this time being a young octoroon woman whom Sheppard Flornoy had bought but never formally adopted nor legally emancipated. Upon Sheppard's sudden death, his dissolute brother Vespatian claims the woman. "[Sheppard's] adopted daughter—sentimentally, perhaps! Perhaps! But legally a piece of property, I think, descending to his heirs. . . ." (305) As in "The Age of Miracles" Abner defeats the evildoer's legal claim by proving that he murdered his brother.

Uncle Abner: Master of Mysteries, published in 1918, stayed in print for at least twenty years and was praised to the rooftops by American critics for generations.[15] But the jurisprudential aspects of the Abner stories have largely gone unnoticed, and most of the interest in these tales has been limited to students of the crime-detective genre. As I hope I've demonstrated, they deserve no less attention from those whose concern is the development of American fiction on the subjects of law, lawyering and justice.

Between 1910 and 1925 Post published dozens of short stories about other series characters and additional dozens of nonfiction pieces, many on legal topics, in the *Saturday Evening Post*, *Hearst's Magazine*, *Pictorial Review*, *Collier's*, *McCall's*, *Red Book* and elsewhere. Most of the nonfiction is still buried in microfilm copies of the *Saturday Evening Post* but most of the short stories were collected, sometimes with revisions to shoehorn them into series format, in volumes like *The Mystery at the Blue Villa* (1919), *The Sleuth of St. James's Square* (1920), *Monsieur Jonquelle, Prefect of Police of Paris* (1923) and *Walker of the Secret Service* (1924), all issued by D. Appleton & Co., the publisher of the Abner collection. Little of this work has weathered the years well and none of it deals with legal themes.

***

Post's life after *Uncle Abner* was a slow descent into stillness. Near the end of 1919, thirteen years after the death of his infant son, pneumonia killed his wife. That same year Arthur Train began publishing his Mr. Tutt stories in the *Post*, and the creator of Randolph Mason and Uncle Abner quickly lost his pre-eminence as America's foremost teller of tales about the law. Post's beloved father, the inspiration for Abner, died in September 1923 at the age of 81. Melville hunkered down in his palatial West Virginia home, The Chalet, about twelve miles from Clarksburg, and hugged solitude like a security blanket. Visitors were welcome only when his flag was hoisted to the top of its pole. He drank more than was good for him. He hunted small game, played polo, occasionally invited neighbors for horseback sports and a picnic lunch. One of those neighbors, a young woman named Agnes Smith Parrish, set down her impressions of him almost half a century later.

"As a person, Melville was, to put it bluntly, a
darling. Quirky, not like other people; thin, but moving
slowly and deliberately; given to long observant
silences, often broken by memorable comments or
amusing anecdotes. After dinner . . . he moved from
chair to chair, and once explained that it was a sign of
approaching old age always to sit in the same chair. I
didn't realize it then, but whatever his age he must have
been, while I knew him, a very lonely man."[16]

In 1924 he roused himself long enough to conduct a vigorous
campaign for John W. Davis, a fellow attorney who was that year's
Democratic candidate for the presidency. Davis lost to Calvin
Coolidge by a huge margin but remained permanently grateful for
Post's support and showed his gratitude thirty years later when he
was asked to select a law-related short story for an anthology and
chose "The Corpus Delicti." Post, he wrote in his brief introduction,
was "an old friend of my West Virginia days—a friend who
sometimes borrowed my law books to do research for his
magnificent lawyer stories."[17] But by the middle 1920s Post's literary
output of all types had slowed to a trickle, and just after Christmas
1926 he drafted his will, naming his two nieces as principal life
beneficiaries of his estate.

In the following two years he revived Uncle Abner in four final
stories published in *Country Gentleman*: "The Devil's Track" (July
1927), "The God of the Hills" (September 1927), "The Dark Night"
(November 1927) and the double-length "The Mystery at Hillhouse"
(May and June 1928). The first and third of these have no legal
dimension at all, while the thematic material in the second and
fourth comes straight out of much earlier Abner stories. In "The God
of the Hills" Abner visits Judge Bensen on cattle-buying business
only to find that the jurist has been clubbed to death the night before
and that Squire Randolph is conducting an investigation. Bensen
had been about to hand down his decision in the matter of Caleb

Greyhouse who, shortly before his unexpected death, had added a holographic codicil to his will, disinheriting his daughter for falling in love with a family enemy and devising his property to his conniving brother Barnes Greyhouse. Abner searches the judge's library, finds an old Virginia case (with no citation provided) ruling that a holographic codicil is invalid if appended to a non-holographic will, and pins Bensen's murder on the evil brother. In the first installment of "The Mystery at Hillhouse" Post recycles the anti-lynching storyline of "A Twilight Adventure" all but verbatim as Abner stymies a vigilante mob in pursuit of a stranger suspected of old Webster Patterson's murder by showing that the circumstantial evidence makes the mob leader look more guilty than the suspect. In the second installment Squire Randolph holds a quasi-formal inquest into Patterson's death and suspicion is spread equally among four men until Abner offers a solution reminiscent of "The Doomdorf Mystery." With this overblown and feeble rehash the Abner cycle limps to its end.

***

By then Post had already launched his final series of stories, a group of fourteen published in *American Magazine* and, with one exception, collected in book form as *The Silent Witness* (Farrar & Rinehart, 1930). The protagonist of these tales is Colonel Braxton, who like Abner dwells in western Virginia in the years just before the Civil War but, unlike Abner, is a lawyer.

> "He was a big man, with a face expressionless as a mask, except when he wished to contort it with a stamp of vigor. His black hair was brushed sleek, an immaculate white handkerchief, tucked into his collar, covered the white bosom of his shirt to protect it from the ash of the cigar that was always present, even in the courtroom." (118-119)

Braxton's oratorical style and philosophy are very close to Abner's but, perhaps precisely because his law practice roots him more firmly in the workaday world, he seems less impressive a figure. In at least two of the fourteen stories he presents himself as literally on divine missions, assigned to a case, so to speak, by the highest Court of all. As in the Abner series, the main theme is metaphysical—that chance is an illusion and God's justice and providence the omnipresent reality—and the criminological secondary theme is the characterization of circumstantial evidence as a silent witness that always tells the truth and can never be made to lie. Our concern of course is with the stories' legal dimension.

In "The Forgotten Witness" (*American Magazine*, September 1926; collected in *The Silent Witness* as "The Cross-Examination") Braxton defends a petty criminal against the charge that he locked the county sheriff in the closet of his house and stole the tax money the sheriff had collected. The appearance of the closet door, which Braxton arranges to be brought into court, demolishes the sheriff's testimony and frees the framed client.

"The Survivor" (*American Magazine*, October 1926) introduces into the series Dabney Mason, clerk of the circuit court, a foppish but honorable and courageous functionary who serves as a sort of Squire Randolph figure in some of the Braxton stories. More important, this tale shows how far Post had moved from his youthful social Darwinism. Old Peregrin Monroe had written a will leaving his vast estate to whichever of his two nephews outlives the other, a disposition that all but forces them into fighting a pistol duel to determine who is fittest to survive and prosper. ". . . It would lead to my estate descending to the better man . . . . It will be as these newfangled scientists affirm—a survival of the fittest! . . . " (74) Under Monroe's will, if the nephews should die at the same time, his estate "shall go to found a negro colony in Massachusetts." (73) The duel indeed leaves both men dead and Braxton, representing a beautiful distant relative of the younger nephew, tries to overcome the legal presumption of simultaneous death and prevent the money from being used on a "fool errand into Massachusetts. . . ." (77)

"The Invisible Client" (*American Magazine*, December 1926) opens with the statement that Braxton "used to say that he practiced in two jurisdictions: the courts of Virginia, and God's court." (48) In this case he sees himself before the latter. Wealthy Junius Hagan was shot to death in his home the night before he was to sign a will that would turn his mansion into an orphanage, and his wicked nephew David Grier takes the property by intestate succession. Braxton unaccountably feels "a direction to himself . . . to go forward . . . , on faith, as under sealed orders." (56-57) He drafts a deed conveying the mansion to the orphanage and reserving to Grier a life estate, forces Grier to sign it by proving he killed his uncle, and settles back to await the justice of God, which causes Grier to die in a train wreck within the month.

"The Heir at Law" (*American Magazine*, February 1927) is another intestacy story, but without a murder or a *deus ex machina*. Braxton's adversary this time is Caleb Lurty, who is about to take the estate of his dead brother Marshall by intestate succession, to the exclusion of Marshall's illegitimate daughter. The discussion of injustice in the law of succession sounds almost feminist today.

> Braxton: "Upon what theory of justice, Mr. Lurty, could such a law be founded? In what manner is our paternal ancestor of greater value to us, that a child's estate should go to the father, while the mother who brought him into the world takes nothing?"
>
> Lurty: "Upon the theory, sir, that the man made the fortune."
>
> Braxton: "Upon the theory, rather, that the man made the laws!" (144)

Braxton saves the day by discovering a will in favor of the daughter that Marshall had signed before his death and Caleb had found and hidden.

"The Leading Case" (*American Magazine*, June 1927) is one of only two Braxton stories that is told by a functioning first-person narrator, a youth similar to Martin in the Abner cycle. The case which brings the nameless boy, his father and everyone for miles around into court has to do with a legal element we have seen in Post stories several times before, a defect in a deed to property bought at a tax sale. When the property turns out to be rich in coal, a certain Ebenezer Ponsford shows up with a warranty deed to the land, apparently signed by Patrick Henry, governor of Virginia, back in 1786, and sues to eject the apparent owner, whose lawyer of course is Colonel Braxton. As in the Abner story "Naboth's Vineyard," Post describes "the people as the source of justice, as they were the source of authority in a republic." (264) But even though popular sentiment is unanimously against Ponsford, Post surprisingly gives equal time to the view that the law's the law regardless of justice. "If good men from worthy motives broke the law down in one instance, evil men in another instance, from unworthy motives, would also break it down. And so there would be no principles established, and no clear-laid rules by which men could be guided in the conduct of their affairs." (265) Braxton cuts the Gordian knot of law vs. fairness by proving Ponsford's deed a forgery.

In "Colonel Braxton Chooses a Client" (*American Magazine*, April 1928; collected in *The Silent Witness* as "The Guardian"), Braxton is asked to represent Ridgewood Carter, brother and legatee of the late Martha Carter, whose will left everything to Ridgewood except some priceless old plate which she bequeathed to her impoverished niece Sarah Carrington. The plate has been stolen from the Carter house, apparently by thieves coming in from the Ohio River, and Ridgewood wants Braxton to draft a deed under which he'll give Sarah title to the house and she'll give him title to the plate. Braxton, having concluded that Ridgewood himself stole the plate, insists on adding a technical clause to the deed that will ruin his own client's scheme. How can he possibly justify this breach of lawyerly ethics? Because his true client in the matter, he insists, was not Ridgewood but "The Guardian of the Fatherless" (115), God himself!

"Colonel Braxton Hears the Silent Voices" (*American Magazine*, September 1928; collected in *The Silent Witness* as "The Mute Voices") is another pure evidence story. Fairfield Harris, who is in love with Julia Monroe, is charged with having shot to death the wealthy and despicable Duncan Cruger on the evening of the day Cruger had forced Julia into marriage. Braxton as defense counsel turns a trail of blood drops into a Not Guilty verdict.

One of the most fascinating of all the Braxton stories is "The Vanished Man" (*American Magazine*, February 1929). Without a client, Braxton becomes involved in the mysterious disappearance of old Captain Berkley, the life tenant of certain valuable land bordering the Ohio River, and with the captain's companion, a proud and compassionate black man known as Horton, who is determined to maintain the property as Berkley's steward during the seven years before there will be a legal presumption of death. Complicating the situation is Pittsburgh lawyer Evert Brewster, who has been retained to oust the black man if possible. "The man was within the technical ethics of his profession," Post remarks. "But human affairs were on a larger plane. There was always a moral right under every legal right if the latter ought to stand. And as the moral right was, so would the legal right be also. There could be no justice in the absence of a moral right." (212) When Braxton discovers what happened to Captain Berkley and why Horton won't depart from the land, he agrees to keep his knowledge to himself. "For I have learned one thing—one thing in a long experience of life—I have learned to keep silent and to stand aside when the inscrutable Providence of God is moving to the adjustment of some troubled matter in the affairs of men!" (233)

"The Mark on the Window" (*American Magazine*, April 1929) is yet another evidence story. At the end of his long career, Judge Benton Woods is shot to death with a deer rifle while standing on the courthouse balcony and trying to calm down some gun-toting settlers who are protesting the inundation of their homes and fields by waves from riverboats. Braxton, appointed as a special judge to take Woods' place and find his murderer, uses a primitive form of ballistics to do it.

In "The Dead Man's Shoes" (*American Magazine*, June 1929) Braxton and the court clerk Dabney Mason go out to visit vicious Benedict Brant, who has succeeded to a huge estate after the death of his older brother Maynard in an apparent boating accident. Benedict plans and has the clear legal right to turn his house by the Ohio into "a place of revel for the river boats—that foothold for the devil that this law-abiding community of Virginia was so determined to bar out." (34) First Braxton tries to persuade Brant not to exercise his rights under the law, lest he have "the eternal forces of God to reckon with." Brant replies: "I don't care a curse for the eternal forces of God. . . . My brother is dead; I take the property by inheritance, and I shall do as I please with it. . . ." (39) As both Braxton and Abner had done in earlier stories, the good lawyer once again prevails by proving that the "bad man" came into his property rights by murdering his brother.

"The Mystery at the Mill" (*American Magazine*, August 1929) is the only Braxton story that wasn't collected in *The Silent Witness*. According to Post's biographer, Braxton "solves a cruel murder and then observes what seems to be the avenging agency of God settling the misdeed. . . ."[18] There is no indication of any legal dimension to the tale.

"The Guilty Man" (*American Magazine*, September 1929) is yet another evidence story, this time with Braxton in the unaccustomed role of prosecutor before the grand jury whose members are considering whether to indict the fugitive Richard Pickney for the murder of his uncle. Braxton uses a bloody handprint on a window blind to pin the crime on the dead man's other nephew.

"The Witness in the Metal Box" (*American Magazine*, November 1929; collected in *The Silent Witness* as "The Metal Box") is the second and last Braxton story with a genuine first-person narrator, a young boy whose grandfather brings him to court. The grandfather, we learn, is the son of none other than Daniel Davisson, Post's own great-great-grandfather, which means that the young narrator must be either Post's great-grandfather or at least a great-granduncle. What brings the old man and the boy to court is a will contest. Braxton represents the daughter of the late Alexander Harrington, who apparently left a holographic will disinheriting the woman and devising his vast estate to his brother Blackmer Harrington. Blackmer plans to use the estate "to seize some islands in the West Indies and add them to the Republic. . . . Once seized, the American Government would annex the territory, and by that much the Republic would be advanced on its manifest destiny." (14-15) Even though Judge Lewis knows that a decision in Blackmer's favor will drag the United States into another imperialist war, he seems to have no choice but to hold the will valid — until Braxton opens the circular metal box of the title and uses its contents to prove the will a forgery.

The last story in the cycle, indeed the last tale Post ever wrote and the only one he didn't live to see in print, is "The White Patch" (*American Magazine*, September 1930). Braxton visits the ruthless politician Bushrod Johnson, who has won a ruinous $20,000 libel suit against a newspaper publisher named Culpepper, and asks him not to levy on his judgment, so that the land Culpepper had received under the will of his late wife and devised in his own will to her daughter by a previous marriage will go to the young woman as intended. Johnson refuses to take less than his full legal entitlement and rejects Braxton's appeal to religion as garbage. Braxton then reveals that he's just discovered Culpepper's dead body and that Johnson will never collect a penny on his judgment since under Virginia law "personal actions pending in the courts — like slander, like libel — abate at the death of the parties. They are wiped out by death, as though they had never existed." (310) It's hard to accept that this rule would nullify a judgment handed down before the party's death and Braxton gives us no citation. Is it possible that Post's creative life ended with a patent mistake of law?

***

Post's stories near the end of the decade were not only thematically repetitious but few and far between. A mere three (including the two-part last appearance of Uncle Abner and a pair of Braxtons) came out in 1928, another six (all of them Braxtons) in 1929, and just one, the final Braxton, in 1930. On June 23 of that year, twelve days after a serious fall from his favorite polo pony, Melville Davisson Post died in the Clarksburg hospital at age 61. He was laid to rest in the Elkview Masonic Cemetery between his wife and his infant son. A large marble slab across his grave is incised with a statement of his credo.

> The universe toils in some tremendous purpose. Be not disheartened because the understanding of that purpose is denied you. . . . Reflect, that over aeons, over light years, over ages inconceivably extended, the energies of God, patient and unwearied, have been shaping the design of every earth creature out of the germ of life, and what could you have seen—at any point of that interminable way—in your brief flash of human consciousness, but the rise and fall of tides, the progressions of the seasons, and no change. Go forward with a high face. The mysterious energies of God labor to some divine perfection.[19]

Clearly what is evoked on Post's tombstone is not the God of Abraham, Isaac and Jacob, of Elijah and Abner but rather an impersonal creative force of the sort that William James called "a stream of ideal tendency embedded in the eternal structure of the world."[20] How Post's final credo squares with the Biblical perspective that permeated his tales of Uncle Abner and Colonel Braxton remains a mystery. Had he kept his deepest convictions to himself and built his fictional world around religious beliefs more acceptable to the *Saturday Evening Post*? In his last years could he have gone beyond Christianity and into a philosophic faith, and might this explain why he wrote so little near the end? Whoever tries to connect Post's fiction with his ultimate testament must also account for why his tombstone contains not a word about the forces that had dominated his stories from the beginning: law and justice. I leave these tasks to his next biographer if any.

Post has been dead more than eighty years now but his influence has never died and, in the sense that amoral lawyer characters dominate the landscape of contemporary fiction and film, that influence is stronger than ever today. His first book, *The Strange Schemes of Randolph Mason*, was reprinted in hardcover in 1972. The first and most radical of his early Randolph Mason stories, "The Corpus Delicti," has been included over the decades in a number of anthologies.[21] S.S. Van Dine, the first American detective novelist to reach the bestseller lists, clearly alluded to the climax of Post's story during aesthete-amateur detective Philo Vance's discourse on law, reason and common sense: "[A] court often acquits a prisoner, realizing full well that he is guilty. Many a judge has said, in effect, to a culprit: 'I know, and the jury knows, that you committed the crime, but in view of the legally admissible evidence, I declare you innocent. Go and sin again.'"[22] What made "The Corpus Delicti" so powerful—the lawyer's ability and willingness to advise a client how to commit a cold-blooded murder, admit the deed in open court and walk away free—was developed by Erle Stanley Gardner, with clear acknowledgment of his source, into the centerpiece of *The Bigger They Come* (1939), first of the long series of novels he wrote under the byline of A.A. Fair about disbarred attorney turned private eye Donald Lam. More recently the crime novelist Lawrence Block has published several stories dealing with New York lawyer Martin Ehrengraf, whose philosophy and style of practice make Randolph Mason look like a saint. In "The Ehrengraf Method" (*Ellery Queen's Mystery Magazine*, February 1978) he arranges for the release of a wealthy young man who is a serial killer of women by the simple ploy of committing a murder himself with the same technique while his client is in jail, and in "The Ehrengraf Presumption" (*Ellery Queen's Mystery Magazine*, May 1978) he gets Client A off on a murder charge by framing B for the crime, then takes on B as a client and gets him off in turn by framing C. Block has no legal training and his protagonist serves clients not by taking advantage of glitches in the system but by breaking the law in whatever way will work. The chasm that divides Ehrengraf from Randolph Mason is as good a measure as any of how far the profession is presently held in contempt.

Fortunately Mason is not Post's only character that has survived. The 1918 collection *Uncle Abner, Master of Mysteries* remained in print for at least two decades and was reissued in paperback as recently as 1975, while two years later the entire cycle of 22 Abner stories, rearranged in the order of their apparent composition, was published by a university press with a host of scholarly apparatus but no special emphasis on their aspect as stories about law.[23] Indeed the Abner series has been carried on in our own time, though again without appreciable legal dimension, by John F. Suter in a cycle of fourteen new tales published in *Ellery Queen's Mystery Magazine* between 1980 and 1986. No less a figure than William Faulkner made use of certain elements of the Abner and the Colonel Braxton stories in short works like "Smoke" (1932),[24] "Tomorrow" (1940) and "An Error in Chemistry" (1946)—all collected in *Knight's Gambit* (1949)—and in his 1948 novel *Intruder in the Dust*.[25] These Yoknapatawpha County chronicles center on lawyer Gavin Stevens, who despite his mild manner and cosmopolitan tolerance bears a certain cousinly resemblance to the attorney characters in the later stories of Post. Much of the fiction with Gavin as protagonist is presented from the viewpoint of his teen-age nephew Chick Mallison, whether or not the boy is physically present, just as the Uncle Abner tales are usually seen from the perspective, whether or not *he* is physically present, of Abner's young nephew Martin. Faulkner's convoluted prose of course is light years removed from the austere simplicity that Post learned from the King James Bible and adapted to his own purposes, but some of the central concerns in Post's stories, ranging from the proper descent of land to the nature of justice, figure just as prominently in Faulkner's. What matters most, however, for those of us who come to Melville Davisson Post with a background and interest in law is not his impact on other writers but the duel of jurisprudence that was fought in his fiction and apparently in his mind and heart. The conflict begins in the early Randolph Mason stories (1896-97), where the legal philosophy is rigidly social Darwinian but with occasional moral infusions at odds with the dog-eat-dogma. By the time of *The Man of Last Resort*'s final tales, Darwinism has been challenged and then rejected on moral grounds. In the later Randolph Mason stories (1906-07) the lawyer still claims to be an amoral technician but usually operates as a sort of Portia figure, using legal technicalities to defeat victimizers armed with different technicalities, although Mason's moral basis unlike Portia's is resolutely secular and rooted in common human decency. The Uncle Abner series (1911-18) transforms social Darwinism into the quintessence of evil but the righteous protagonist is no longer a lawyer and, despite the *Merchant of Venice* overtones in a few early tales like "The Tenth Commandment," the tendency is to eschew the legal order entirely as of no account from the protagonist's stern religious perspective. In the Colonel Braxton stories (1926-30) social Darwinism is still the philosophy of godless Shylocks and the viewpoint character has become a blend of good lawyer and thundering prophet: an uncomfortable blend in tales like "The Guardian" where it's suggested that an attorney should betray his client if he hears the voice of God telling him to do it. In thirty-five years of creative life Post traveled the long road from one end of the religious-jurisprudential spectrum to its opposite, with all too infrequent stops in the sensible secular middle ground. But the conflicting currents of legal thought that animate some of his best stories are what makes them of continuing interest to students of law in literature today.

NOTES

1. See Brook Thomas, *Cross Examination of Law and Literature: Cooper, Hawthorne, Stowe, and Melville* (Cambridge University Press, 1987).
2. Oliver Wendell Holmes, Jr., "The Path of the Law," 10 Harvard Law Review 457 (1897). Holmes first presented this essay on January 8, 1897

as a speech at the dedication of a new building at Boston University School of Law.

3. *Id.* at 459.

4. *Id.* at 459.

5. See Charles A. Norton, *Melville Davisson Post: Man of Many Mysteries* (Bowling Green University Popular Press,1973). All biographical information about Post in the present chapter is taken from this work.

6. Theodore Dreiser, *Newspaper Days*, ed. T.D. Nostwich (University of Pennsylvania Press, 1991), at 490-491. This work was first published in 1920.

7. See Francis M. Nevins, *Bar-20: The Life of Clarence E. Mulford, Creator of Hopalong Cassidy* (McFarland & Co., 1993).

8. In Chapter 3 of this book I discuss the development of Train's jurisprudence in the long-running Mr. Tutt series from early social Darwinism through several other stances, none of them rooted in religion as was the later work of Post.

9. It may seem incredible that someone born in 1889 could have been profoundly influenced by the social Darwinism of the 1890s, but Gardner's biographer has documented that while in fourth grade the future creator of Perry Mason wrote a school composition on the Greek myth of Atalanta, stressing the theme that whoever does not win the race dies. See Dorothy B. Hughes, *Erle Stanley Gardner: The Case of the Real Perry Mason* (Morrow, 1978), at 35-36.

10. 18 N.Y. 179 (1858).

11. See *Irwin v. Williar*, 110 U.S. 499 (1884).

12. 111 Fed. 369 (D.N.D. 1901).

13. More precisely, the court held that one who passes *counterfeit* Confederate money, clearly labeled as such, couldn't be prosecuted for counterfeiting. One wonders what idiots would be in the market for such worthless paper 35 years after the end of the Civil War.

14. 41 W. Va. 559, 23 S.E. 664 (1895).

15. "All of these stories are masterly examples of the justifiable surprise ending, yet have the logic and dramatic power which we have come to associate with Athenian tragedy." Edward J. O'Brien, *The Best Short Stories of 1918* (Small Maynard, 1919), at 360. "In conception, execution, device and general literary quality these stories of early Virginia, written by a man who thoroughly knows his *metier* and is also an expert in law and criminology, are among the very best we possess." Willard Huntington Wright, Introduction, *The Great Detective Stories* (Scribner, 1927), at 23-24. "No reader can call himself connoisseur who does not know *Uncle Abner* forward and backward." Howard Haycraft, *Murder for Pleasure: The Life and Times of the Detective Story* (Appleton-Century, 1941), at 97. The Abner collection is "second only to Poe's *Tales* among all the books of detective short stories written by American authors." Ellery Queen (Frederic Dannay), *Queen's Quorum* (Little Brown, 1951), at 68. Outside the United States, however, the critical estimation differs. According to one eminent commentator, "the attraction the [Abner] stories have for Americans simply does not exist for others. To English readers, Abner is likely to seem a distant and implausible figure." Julian Symons, *Mortal Consequences: A History from the Detective Story to the Crime Novel* (Harper & Row, 1972), at 85.

16. Charles A. Norton, *supra* note 6, at 50.

17. John W. Davis, Introduction to "The Corpus Delicti," in *Fiction Goes to Court*, ed. Albert P. Blaustein (Henry Holt, 1954), at 2.

18. Charles A. Norton, *supra* note 6, at 228.

19. *Id.* at 62.

20. William James, *The Varieties of Religious Experience* (Harvard University Press, 1985), at 401. This work was first published in 1902.

21. Anthologies that include this story range from Albert P. Blaustein's *Fiction Goes to Court*, *supra* note 18, to Elizabeth Villiers Gemmette's *Law in Literature: Legal Themes in Short Stories* (Praeger, 1992), which also includes Post's "The Animus Furandi."

22. S.S. Van Dine, *The "Canary" Murder Case* (Scribner, 1927), at 11. Van Dine was the pseudonym of art critic Willard Huntington Wright (1887-1939). See John Loughery, *Alias S.S. Van Dine: The Man Who Created Philo Vance* (Scribner, 1992).

23. Melville Davisson Post, *The Complete Uncle Abner* (University of California/San Diego Extension, 1977).

24. No Faulkner specialist seems to have noticed that the plot of "Smoke" is a collage of elements from the Colonel Braxton stories "The Mark on the Window," "The Guilty Man" and "The Witness in the Metal Box" and the late Uncle Abner stories "The Devil's Track," "The God of the Hills" and "The Mystery at Hillhouse." A full account of how Faulkner wove together pieces of these six tales into his own fabric has yet to be written.

25. Post's influence on Faulkner is usually overlooked by Faulkner scholars. For one notable exception, see Michael Grimwood, *Heart in Conflict: Faulkner's Struggles with Vocation* (University of Georgia Press, 1987), at 195-200.

CHAPTER 3

Mr. Tutt's Jurisprudential Journey: Arthur Train

Younger readers of law-related fiction tend to identify the genre with relatively recent novels like Scott Turow's *Presumed Innocent* and Tom Wolfe's *The Bonfire of the Vanities*, both published in 1987, or, if they have slightly longer memories, with works like John Jay Osborn Jr.'s *The Paper Chase* (1971). Middle-aged readers are more likely to think back to the golden years of the Warren Court and figures like Perry Mason and Atticus Finch. But long before any of those books and barristers sprang from their creators' imaginations, *the* lawyer of American fiction was Arthur Train's Mr. Tutt.

Ephraim Tutt took center stage in more than eighty short stories, most of them published in the *Saturday Evening Post* between 1919 and 1945, then assembled into hardcover collections issued by Charles Scribner's Sons and irregularly reshuffled into large "Best of Mr. Tutt" volumes. After Train's death his once hugely popular character faded into oblivion. Having re-examined all the Mr. Tutt stories for this chapter, I am satisfied that oblivion is precisely what many of them deserve. Train's best tales, however, still hold their rewards, stemming not from the quality of his prose, which suffers all too often from lawyerly leadenfootedness, nor from the complexity of his characters, who all too often are stereotypes or worse, but rather from the links connecting them with Train's law practice and life and, most important of all, from their treatment of some of the fundamental themes of jurisprudence.

***

Arthur Cheney Train's book of reminiscences and reflections on his life fills five hundred pages, many of them published in a five-part *Saturday Evening Post* serialization (17 September-15 October 1938) before the hardcover edition was released. But those in search of what made him tick as a person will find reading *My Day in Court* (Scribner, 1939) an exercise in frustration. If a prize were offered for writing the biographically least helpful book about oneself, Train would easily make the short list.[1] He tells plenty of war stories from his years as prosecutor, private attorney and full-time author and shows in rich detail how his fiction often grew out of his legal files. But of his life outside working hours he says hardly a word,[2] and almost every one of the 100 subheadings under the index entry for "Train, Arthur" relates either to writing or law, so that even the most basic facts about him must be hunted for in other sources.[3] And since no one in the almost 70 years since his death has found him interesting enough to warrant a genuine biography, the connections that this essay will draw between his best known fiction and his life are limited willy-nilly to his professional careers.

As his zeal for privacy may have hinted, Train was a New England Brahmin, "the native of a region traditionally inclined towards predestination. . . ." (6) He was born on September 6, 1875 into a family well endowed with money and prestige and spent his youth in "the almost rural environment of the sunny side of Marlboro Street, on Boston's Back Bay." (161) His father, Charles Russell Train (1817-1885), is described in *My Day in Court* as a "rather stocky" man (481), as "a friend of Lincoln and Charles Sumner, a veteran of the Civil War, and afterwards Attorney General of Massachusetts," (370) an office the senior Train held between 1872 and 1879.[4] (Several sources wrongly give the dates as between 1873 and 1890.) As a child Arthur was taken by his father "to the homes of Emerson, Holmes, Lowell and Longfellow, and on

Sunday afternoons to the old Union Club where I met the 'war governors' John D. Robinson and John D. Long, Generals Grant and Sheridan and many veterans of lesser distinction and valor, such as Benjamin F. Butler." (370) This is all we ever learn about Charles Russell Train. Arthur's mother, born Sarah M. Cheney (1836-), is never mentioned once.

"I cannot remember when I did not have an overmastering impulse to write. It was a passion even in my childhood." (5) Train attended Boston's Prince School, then Boston Latin School, then St. Paul's School in Concord, New Hampshire, then, inevitably, Harvard. While a student at prep school and college he "deluged the weeklies and monthlies with contributions." (5) He studied at Harvard from 1892 to 1896, "a time when any American boy could get there as broad and enlightened an education in composition and literature as at either Oxford or Cambridge." (5) His major of course was English, and at the urging of professors like George Lyman Kittredge and Charles Townsend Copeland he "devoured . . . the works of Meredith, Hardy, Howells, Stevenson, Mary E. Wilkins, Sarah Orne Jewett, and during my junior and senior years of Conrad and the newly discovered Rudyard Kipling. . . ." (5) He received his A.B. from Harvard in 1896 but didn't then set out to make his name as a writer because "among the circle of Bostonians to which my family belonged, the writing of fiction was looked upon as, at best, a frivolous and even as a rather scandalous vocation. A young man who insisted upon becoming an artist, author, musician or sculptor was apt to find himself a disinherited outcast. . . . The New Englander of my boyhood days had a right to life and liberty of a sort, but not to the frank pursuit of happiness."(6) Besides, the creative life was presumed to mean a life without money, and "[p]overty and respectability did not walk hand in hand in Puritan New England, where a comfortable bank account has always been regarded as a sign of God's grace." (6) Like any prudent son of a former Massachusetts attorney general, Train chose to enroll in Harvard Law School.

In *My Day in Court* he draws a veil around his three years as a law student, describing himself as "an honor man" (131) but mentioning not a single course, professor, incident or insight from that period. If one judged by its impact on his future career as a fiction writer, the event most crucial to Train's development during law school was the publication of Justice Holmes' seminal essay "The Path of the Law."[5] In April 1897, late in his second semester, he married Ethel Kissam (1875-1923), who bore him three daughters and a son, but none of these five rate space in his reminiscences either.[6] He received his LL.B. in 1899, became a member of the Massachusetts Bar later that year, and spent "a few months in a conventional Boston law office" (6) before relocating to New York City, where he worked briefly and without pay for the Legal Aid Society and then found a job with the firm of Robinson, Biddle & Ward at 160 Broadway. But he quickly became "bored, impatient and unhappy" (6) with private practice and used family connections to get himself appointed an Assistant District Attorney for New York County, starting January 11, 1901. That at first the position was an unpaid slot suggests that Train at this time was being subsidized by his mother or a bequest in his father's will.

His office was on the fourth floor of the Criminal Courts Building, at the corner of White and Centre Streets, connected by the "Bridge of Sighs" over Franklin Street with the Tombs Prison. Train describes the place as "a hideous monstrosity of red brick with stone trimmings, . . . its buckling walls having been made repeatedly the object of official condemnation as a menace to human life—criminal and otherwise." (11) The building, covering a full city block, was "one of the gloomiest structures in the world. Tier on tier it rises above a huge central rotunda, rimmed by dim mezzanines and corridors upon which the courtrooms open, and crowned by a . . . glass roof encrusted with soot through which filters a soiled and viscous light. The air is rancid with garlic, stale cigar smoke, sweat and the odor of prisoners' lunch. The corridors swarm with Negroes, Italians, blue-bloused Chinese, black-bearded rabbis, policemen, shyster lawyers and their runners, politicians big and little." (11)

Here Train came into daily contact "with murderers, thieves, burglars, gangsters and confidence men, defaulters, English 'ticket-of-leave men,' unfrocked priests, ex-convicts, 'lamisters,' army deserters, outcast and erring sons and daughters, pimps, prostitutes, exiles, impostors." (12) He tried thousands of cases and prosecuted "some hundreds of murderers, several of whom went to the chair. Yet the astonishing thing was that I discovered few who seemed thoroughly bad or even worse than a multitude who had escaped entanglement in the criminal law." (12-13) Even the career criminals in their non-working hours "were apt to be homebodies, like more reputable citizens, fond of their children and friends, responsive to sympathy or kindness and keenly appreciative of fair treatment." (13) The sea of faces was so vast that "at the end of seven years . . . I could not, when I met a man on the street, tell in most cases whether I had gone to college with him, prosecuted cases before him as a juror or sent him to jail." (370)

Train the aspiring author would have had to be deaf, blind and without a sense of smell not to recognize the potential of this environment, and it was during his years with the District Attorney's office that he began to sell both fiction and nonfiction to some of the country's highest-paying magazines. His first published story appeared in the summer of 1904 and his first *Saturday Evening Post* tale a year later.

Within a few years of his appointment as a prosecutor Train burned out. "The trial of cases had become almost automatic. I could make an objection in my sleep and a summation appropriate to any variety of offense while only half awake. I had acquired all the criminal law necessary—which really was very little indeed." (253) What kept him from leaving the job was both "its drama and the fact that it offered so much literary material. Moreover, the regularity of my official working hours, which were from 10 a.m. to 1 p.m. and from 2 to 4, followed by a short period of consultation or preparation for the next day, assured me an amount of time for writing impossible in civil practice." (253) Finally, in the summer of 1908, he resigned. "It took a considerable amount of resolution to give up a salary of $7500 for working five hours a day, with a six weeks' summer vacation; a comfortable office with no overhead, where . . . one was kowtowed to and flattered; where there was always something exciting going on, and where one could count on a dozen or so jolly fellows to have lunch with and swap stories every day. Yes, it was a distinct wrench to tear oneself away from that disgusting, grimy old building and an even greater one to break the habits formed over so long a period." (253)

Train launched his private practice by renting a one-room office at 32 Nassau Street but the venture was not a success and he became so depressed that for a while he was unable to write. "Occasionally I would be assigned to defend some penniless murderer (usually with another lawyer to whom the presiding judge wished to show a favor and with whom I had to split the $500 fee) and would be astonished to find how easy it was, after my experience as an assistant district attorney, to throw nuts into the prosecution's machinery." (254) But the noncriminal cases he hoped for rarely came his way. "My ignorance of civil law and procedure was abysmal, and I never much improved it. I can see now that through unfitting myself for the general practice of my profession, by specializing for seven years in the prosecution of crime, I hastened the inevitable denouement of abandoning law for letters. . . . One of the chief reasons that I became a writer was because I never in fact became a lawyer. If I was retained, as sometimes happened, to try a civil case it was always prepared and briefed for me by another attorney beforehand, I acting only as counsel. In this way I managed from time to time to make a fair showing. But, after trying without intermission a continuous stream of exciting cases for seven years, I could not bear to sit kicking my heels waiting for clients to turn up." (257) Instead of taking down his shingle and becoming a full-time writer as common sense would have seemed to dictate, he took the opposite route and opened a new office at 30 Broad Street in partnership with George H. Olney, a nephew of the man who had served as Grover Cleveland's Secretary of State.

"The first year of Train & Olney was neither legally nor

financially exciting." (261) Late in the summer of 1910 Train accepted an appointment as a deputy special attorney general to take over the district attorney's office in corrupt Queens County and "prosecute all the political crimes I could ferret out. . . . " (262) In the spring of 1911 he set sail for Europe to study continental legal systems and wound up in Italy as a *de facto* journalist reporting on the trial of various members of what we now call the Mafia. Later that year he got into a dispute with a magazine editor over whether he or the magazine owned various rights in one of his serial stories, a dispute that forced him to learn some copyright law and eventually to become one of the founders of the Authors League of America, drafting author-friendly allocation-of-rights contracts which the League would then pressure periodicals to adopt. In the fall of 1913 Train returned to the District Attorney's office but both he and his then boss, Charles Albert Perkins, "closed our desks in the old Criminal Courts Building on December 31, 1915" (335) and opened up a new partnership. "We took a suite of offices at 61 Broadway, overlooking the East River, and furnished them handsomely in new mahogany and even with a potted palm. There we sat and waited for business," (336) with Perkins reading advance sheets while Train wrote stories and novels, including the earliest tales of his most famous character, Mr. Tutt.

What came the firm's way was "a mixture of queer unrelated cases, many of them with a criminal flavor, drawn to us by our reputation as former prosecutors—divorces, separations, annulments, actions for alienation of affections, the defense of blackmail cases (in which we were unusually successful), will contests, accident and libel suits, embezzlements, and an occasional murder case." Perkins did all the witness interviews, legal research and brief drafting, with the courtroom work left to Train, who discovered "that private law practice and the observation of the daily life of the city going on around me offered as much dramatic material for fiction as had the criminal courts." (336) In the summer of 1918, more than a year after the United States had entered World War I, Train volunteered for service, was commissioned a major in the Judge Advocate General's office and found himself performing idiotic duties under the official label of Military Intelligence, working out of what he called a "rookery" on F Street in Washington, D.C. Soon after resuming civilian life and law practice he began to write and the *Saturday Evening Post* to publish the Mr. Tutt stories, which not only made him a household name but conferred on him the role of America's lawyer author, the emissary between our legal system and its subjects.

Late in 1921 he abandoned the practice for keeps, "with some forebodings but no qualms. For over twenty years . . . I had lived upon the crimes and weaknesses, economic disasters, and sexual entanglements of my fellow men. . . . I have neither remorse nor regrets that I no longer earn my living out of the misfortunes or difficulties of others." (368) As a full-time writer he continued to turn out several tales of Mr. Tutt every year in addition to other works of fiction and journalism. For his day's output he would "seek congenial surroundings, usually an alcove in the library of my club [the Harvard Club of course], where I am unlikely to be interrupted and where I have no other distractions—except the snoring of those about to die of old age hard by." (491) After an hour of revising his previous day's product he would "go ahead at high pressure for a couple of hours until, having written some fifteen hundred or two thousand words, I gradually taper off. After some form of light exercise followed by lunch, I am at it again for another two or three hours, varied by research work or the correcting of proof. . . . On a good day I will work six or seven hours, and on a poor one from two to three." (492) He was unable to compose on a typewriter because "I make too many corrections and interlineations" and refused to dictate his material "because, if I do, I become as stilted, verbose and redundant as a solicitor writing to a client." (492) His writing was done "in longhand at a table with a soft draughting pencil on a hard-surfaced yellow pad. . . . " (492) Train finds space in *My Day in Court* to reproduce a sample page of manuscript, to tell us the precise brand of pencil he favored and how he'd vary his posture if his back or neck ached, but fails to let us know that his first wife died less than two years into his new regime, on May 15, 1923; or that two and a half years later, on January 6, 1926, he married again; or that his second wife, Helen Coster Gerard (1889-1982), was the mother of his second son.[7] From *My Day in Court* alone one might easily conclude that except for his writing Arthur had no life at all.

The writing continued to support Train's family in affluence through the booming Twenties and the Depression-scarred Thirties, when they enjoyed both a fine home at 113 East 73rd Street in Manhattan and a summer place called Sol's Cliffs in Bar Harbor, Maine. On the evidence of his stories it would seem that he spent most of his leisure time pursuing fish. Early in 1941 the 65-year-old Train was elected president of the National Institute of Arts and Letters. Two years later, on the publication of *Yankee Lawyer: The Autobiography of Ephraim Tutt* (Scribner, 1943), Train found himself the center of a legal and literary donnybrook when countless readers who had somehow missed the 80-odd Mr. Tutt adventures in the *Post*, and the twelve hardcover collections (including two huge omnibus volumes) that Scribner had published regularly since 1920, leaped to the conclusion that Ephraim Tutt was just as real a person as Arthur Train or they themselves. All sorts of people wrote to Train claiming they were related to his creation or demanding that Mr. Tutt handle a case for them.[8] A Philadelphia attorney named Lewis R. Linet discovered that *Yankee Lawyer* was fiction and sued in New York Supreme Court to have the book's publication enjoined on grounds of breach of implied warranty and consumer fraud. Representing Train was the eminent attorney John W. Davis, who argued that no implied warranty attaches to any literary work and, more narrowly, that any reasonable purchaser of the book should have known it told the life story of an imagined character, like Daniel Defoe's alleged autobiography of Robinson Crusoe.[9] The absence of the names Linet and Train from the Table of Cases volumes of West's Fifth Decennial Digest (1936-46) suggests that the controversy never generated a published judicial opinion. Probably the complaint was dismissed.

Train's health failed soon after the dust of this imbroglio blew away, and during most of 1945 he commuted from home to hospital for a series of operations. On December 22, just a week after the National Institute of Arts and Letters re-elected him as its president, he died of cancer.

***

If we believe Train's autobiography, Mr. Tutt began life in his mind as an abstraction, a symbol of the lawyering philosophy Train had evolved during his seven years in the District Attorney's office. The Manhattan of the 20th century's first decade was teeming with near-penniless immigrants still steeped in their native cultures— Italian, Syrian, Chinese and a dozen more—often unable to read or speak English and without a clue as to the nature of their legal obligations in their adopted homeland. Most of the people Train prosecuted were from one or another of these ethnic groups. The charge against them was usually murder or a similar serious crime against a fellow ethnic and the defense counsel was incompetent or a shyster. Train came to believe it was part of his role to redress the balance. On one occasion "where the prisoner's attorney had been so inept and antagonizing in his manner as to seriously prejudice his client's interests and I had leaned over backwards to even things up with the jury, the defendant on his conviction, being asked if he had anything to say before justice was pronounced, replied: 'I want to thank Mr. Train for his interest in me. He has done more to help me than my own lawyer.'" (110)

In time, Train tells us, there dawned on him a realization that had eluded him during all his philosophy classes at Harvard, namely that neither the legal system nor life itself offered justice. "Just as the laws of Nature were harsh and implacable, whose results must needs be set aright, if at all, in an apocryphal Hereafter, so the Laws of Man rarely, or never, did exact justice in any individual case. We merely did the best we could by applying legal rules-of-thumb based on the doctrine of averages, which we hoped in the long run—a very long run indeed—did make for justice." (113) The saving grace of a system Train saw as intolerable was that "within the technical limits set by the statutes jurors, sometimes aided by prosecutors on the one hand and [defense] attorneys on the other, did the best they could to even things up." (114) He believed it was the right and indeed the responsibility of jurors to "apply whenever possible the rules of ethics rather than of strict law or at least to allow considerable play to ethical considerations." (114) It was his experience "that juries, so far from doing what they were supposed to do, really treated crimes as sins, and temporarily acted as vicarious representatives of the Almighty in deciding what ought to be done about the transgressors" and it was his conclusion that "on the whole, although it wasn't the Law, this was a good thing. . . . " (114) Far from seeing himself as a guardian on the ramparts, saving civilization from the lawless, he was convinced "that even the worst [criminal defendants] had something admirable about them and should be judged, not according to legislative standards, but by their own, for which usually they were not responsible. . . . " and "that kindness, loyalty and courage were better tests of a man's rectitude than his respect for the letter of the statutes." (114) These views moved Train in the direction of "judging, and often acting, by technically extra-legal considerations, according to what might be called the laws of God rather than those of Man. . . ." (115)

They also moved him to the first stage in the creation of his most famous character. "Gradually," he says, "there materialized in my mind a sort of protagonist of real Justice. . . . Whenever I got up to try a case, no matter who was defending it in the flesh, this imaginary champion simultaneously arose and stood beside the defendant, his hand on the latter's shoulder. . . . Out of this ectoplasm" grew "the character of Ephraim Tutt, a sort of `father-in-law' of the ignorant, helpless and underprivileged—a voluntary defender of those unjustly accused of crime." (115)

This "early conception of a visionary adversary, defending the morally innocent but legally guilty, who by utilizing the technicalities of the law secured real justice for the prisoners at the bar," (481) developed no further until shortly after Train's discharge from the Army. Late one evening in March 1919, having just seen a performance of *Potash and Perlmutter*, Montague Glass' hit comedy play about two Jews in the garment trade,[10] it occurred to Train that "had the two characters been lawyers . . . they could have been made, to me at least, equally or even more amusing." (481) At that instant "Ephraim Tutt first stirred in my creative consciousness. In fact he burst forth full panoplied in hat, cane and stogy. . . ." (481) The image came to him from the memory of a white-painted clamshell ashtray in his parents' house in Boston. On the inside of the shell a tall thin figure in stovepipe hat and frock coat was portrayed bending over to take a light from a short fat figure, the two men joined at their cigar tips. The pudgy figure reminded Train of his father and the slender one of a family friend but the names that suddenly sprang into his mind were Tutt and Mr. Tutt. The slender man, who developed into Ephraim Tutt, the one and only Mr. Tutt of the subsequent story cycle, Train envisaged "sitting in a swivel chair in his old-fashioned law office, his feet encased in 'Congress' shoes, crossed upon the desk in front of him. . . ." while the short tubby fellow, simply Tutt or on occasion Samuel Tutt but never Mr. Tutt, stood in the imaginary office with "his hands clasped beneath his coattails. . . ." (482)

The next day Train went down to Atlantic City for an appointment with the legendary *Saturday Evening Post* editor George Horace Lorimer. That night after dinner at the Trocadero Hotel with Lorimer and two other regular contributors to the *Post*, Train said something to the editor about the embryonic characters taking form inside him. Next morning as the two were being wheeled along the boardwalk in Atlantic City's version of the rickshaw, Lorimer remarked: "You know, there might be a series in that suggestion of yours." (483) Then he recounted an anecdote from a St. Louis newspaper which he thought Train could adapt into the first tale in such a cycle. The result was "The Human Element," first of more than eighty Mr. Tutt stories that the *Post* would publish over the next quarter century.[11]

Almost twenty years after that beginning and half a dozen before his death, Train devoted a chapter of *My Day in Court* to the origins of his by then world-renowned character. Ephraim Tutt's physical appearance, he said, was borrowed from "an elderly Southern lawyer who, about twenty years ago,[12] haunted one of the New York clubs. With his high-shouldered, ramshackle figure, his clean-shaven, wrinkled face, his long white hair, this courteous old Virginian was the counterfeit presentment of my hero—*counterfeit* I am glad to record, since he was later expelled from the club for stealing writing-paper." (484) In terms of characterization, Train went on, "I suppose that Mr. Tutt is a combination of most of the qualities which I would like to have, coupled with a few that are common to all of us. One critic has disposed of him by saying that his popularity is due to the fact that he is a hodge-podge of Puck, Robin Hood, Abraham Lincoln and Uncle Sam. I am willing to let it go at that." (484) Train said nothing in *My Day in Court* about where the name Tutt itself came from but dealt with the question in a later essay, "The Best Tutt Story of All," which comprises the first chapter of his last story collection, *Mr. Tutt Finds a Way* (Scribner, 1945). "I had known only one Tutt in my youth, an attractive girl from St. Louis, and, needing a short, snappy name for my old hero . . . unblushingly filched hers." (14)

My Day in Court claims that the plot of each Mr. Tutt story was "based on a formula, precisely as is a stage play. At the beginning the characters are introduced and a legal problem posed (Act I). The 'suspense,' or 'menace,' element is thereupon developed to a point at which it is seemingly impossible for justice to triumph (Act II). Then the old lawyer pulls a legal rabbit out of his stovepipe hat and saves the situation (Act III). Justice, in the shape of Mr. Tutt, triumphs over merely technical Law. . . ." (486) This is a fair account of what the stories had evolved into by the late Thirties, but if it accurately described the entire series we would have little excuse for revisiting Mr. Tutt almost 70 years after his creator's death. However, by going back to the beginning and examining the stories in roughly chronological order, we discover that at least for the first several years they are neither as formulaic nor as reassuring as Train near the end of his life would have us believe.

In 1919, when he created Mr. Tutt and his cohorts, Train identified law, lawyering and the legal system with the brutality of the Criminal Courts Building, and one primary value of the early stories in the cycle is that they catch the textures of that world so vividly. The dark oppressive courtrooms, the smells in the ancient corridors, the bureaucratic infighting, the prosecutors with their code of convict-the-bastard-whatever-it-takes, the abuses of power by political hacks in judges' robes, all are evoked with an acid cynicism suggestive of Mark Twain but unfortunately in a somewhat heavyhanded, longwinded and lawyerly style showing little trace of Twain's black humor.[13] The Darwinian jungle atmosphere of the Criminal Courts Building is matched by that of New York's streets, and many early tales in the series include scenes in ethnic enclaves packed with immigrants clawing for survival, corrupt nightstick-wielding Irish cops, and petty criminals preying on other members of their own group.

In Train's world, however, there is one safe haven where the rule of dog-eat-dog does not apply, namely the offices of Tutt & Tutt, Attorneys and Counselors at Law, located in lower Manhattan at 61 Broadway, where over the course of the early stories we are introduced to the men and women who make up Mr. Tutt's professional family. Most frequently encountered is Samuel Tutt, the short and paunchy junior partner, who is no relation to Ephraim but, as we learn in "The Human Element," wanted to work with him because "I feel that with you I should be associated with a good name." (*Tutt and Mr. Tutt*, 4.) Next in importance stands Minerva Wiggin, a single woman in her forties who has an LL.B. but, rather than maintaining her own practice, functions as the firm's chief clerk and at times as Mr. Tutt's conscience.[14] Of equal value in another way is Bonright "Bonnie" Doon, Train's version of a streetwise tough guy with heart of gold, who serves as in-house investigator and as the firm's "runner," haunting the courthouse and the Tombs on the lookout for clients he can steer to his employers. The remainder of the office force consists of Willie Toothaker, an orphan boy unofficially adopted by Mr. Tutt and kept around to perform odd chores;[15] Ezra Scraggs, an alcohol-soaked old scrivener who performs his Bartleby tasks in a wire cage in the outer office;[16] and Miss Sondheim, the sexy but seldom seen stenographer. The atmosphere within this privileged space is harmonious, tolerant, mutually supportive, with work coming to a halt every afternoon at five when Miss Wiggin brews tea, Mr. Tutt enjoys a stogy and a bottle of malt extract, and we are treated to a lively discussion of legal history or philosophy that somehow or other bears on the case at hand. For thousands of *Saturday Evening Post* devotees the offices of Tutt & Tutt were as real as their own workplaces, and Ephraim's ancient house on West 23rd Street, with its book-musty den and sea-coal fire and horsehair rocker and inexhaustible supply of juristic reflection and (presumably) pre-Prohibition alcohol, was as vivid in countless readers' imaginations as the quarters of the two London bachelors who resided at 221B Baker Street. Those who revisit Mr. Tutt's world today may wish he'd spent less time playing high poohbah to the fraternity known as the Sacred Camels of King Menelik, but the dromedarian antics must have struck *Post* subscribers of our grandparents' time as funny.

In Train's early stories of Mr. Tutt the case confronting Ephraim is usually criminal and the client is a poor man—occasionally Caucasian, more often an ethnic—charged with murder or some other serious offense. But there are vast differences among the tales of this general type. In some, as so often in the real world then and now, the defendant is guilty and without moral justification, so that Mr. Tutt functions much like the first incarnation of Melville Davisson Post's Randolph Mason, an amoral hired gun finding legal loopholes.[17] What sets these stories apart from the rest of the series is that they portray everyone and everything within their ken—the legal system and its lackeys, the defendant and his milieu, even Ephraim Tutt himself and his colleagues—with the sort of genial, detached contempt that Train's contemporary H.L. Mencken was lavishing at the same time on *boobus*

Americanus and his institutions. The more cynical about the system a reader may be today, the more he or she will tend to admire the Mr. Tutt stories of this sort. It's unfortunate that the cynicism of these tales shades over at times into a politically incorrect depiction of certain ethnic groups that casts doubt on the stories' revivability in our so sensitive era.

What unifies the other early Mr. Tutt stories of this general type is that Train mutates from a Menckenesque stance to one reminiscent of Lincoln Steffens or Upton Sinclair,[18] portraying the system as an obscene monster thirsting for the blood of the oppressed and Mr. Tutt and associates as the righteous remnant, battling law to achieve justice. Within this framework of social protest and class war we need to distinguish (although Train doesn't) between stories where the defendant is an innocent victim of mistake or malice on the part of witnesses or the system or both and stories where he is legally guilty but acted with moral justification. Then within the latter grouping we must distinguish further (although our subjective values are bound to affect the process) between those where the moral justification Train offers seems plausible and those where it falls flat.

Anyone who expects a neat organic development of the series from one of these types of story to another is simply not in the world Train made. The order in which the *Post* ran the tales, which presumably reflects the order of their composition, shows stories of all these varieties cheek by jowl with one another, with stories of the same general type that straddle or defy my distinctions, and with stories not of this general type at all. Yet throughout these early tales, regardless of the role he plays—defender of the underdog, gun for hire, flimflam artist, mender of romantic destinies, amateur detective or a blend of two or more of these parts—Mr. Tutt's philosophy, rhetoric and tactics remain consistent. The result is that the stories at one end of the spectrum paint the entire legal system and its functionaries as vicious, hypocritical and absurd, while the stories at the other end reassure us, much like the later and more conventional Mr. Tutt tales to be covered in due course, that the good lawyer can use the resources of the the law itself to bring about justice.

***

Train devoted most of Chapters XVI and XVII of *My Day in Court* to his prosecutions of Italian defendants. He claimed that during his time in the District Attorney's office foreign-born Italians constituted up to 45 per cent of those convicted of homicide (164) and described "the incredible ignorance and superstition existing among the Neapolitans, Calabrians and Sicilians who lived, often ten to twelve in a room, in the tenements of Elizabeth and Mulberry Streets in Manhattan, or Union Street in Brooklyn." (164) In later years as a defense lawyer he represented "an Italian laborer [who] had shot and killed two police officers . . . in pursuit of him" (254) and, arguing that his client had merely used reasonable force against the excessive force of his uniformed victims, persuaded the prosecution to accept a plea to manslaughter in the second degree. (255) It comes as no surprise to learn that the client in the first Mr. Tutt story is Italian. "The Human Element" (#1; 7 June 1919, as "The Trial of Angelo Seraphino"; *Tutt and Mr. Tutt*) not only introduces Ephraim and his menage but provides the paradigm of the early tales in the series where the immigrant defendant is legally guilty, morally justified (in Train's view anyway), and persecuted by a vindictive judge, a corrupt prosecutor and the system in general as cruelly as was Jean Valjean in *Les Miserables*. Train, who cared neither to write nor read detective fiction,[19] leaves no doubt as to the facts in the case. Angelo Serafino, who "makes an honest living by blacking shoes near the entrance to the Brooklyn Bridge" (8), walked one day into the barbershop of Tomasso Crocedoro and "put a bullet through his head." (9) Angelo's wife Rosalina had been engaged to Tomasso, who had jilted her and then after her marriage "seized every opportunity which presented itself to twit Angelo about the matter." (8) As Angelo himself bursts out in court at the close of his trial: "I killa that man! He maka small of my wife! He no good! He bad egg! I killa him once—I killa him again!" (38) Train might easily have given Angelo

77

stronger motivation, say by having him claim that Tomasso raped or attempted to rape his wife, but seems to feel that what he's provided is enough. Assigned as defense counsel by the sadistic Judge Babson, who "hates Italians" (9), and with the ruthless sleazeball "Bloodhound" O'Brien appearing for the prosecution, Mr. Tutt knows that he's been set up for a fall by a "precious pair of crooks, who for their own petty and selfish ends played fast and loose with liberty, life and death." (17-18) That he wins a Not Guilty verdict in the teeth of the facts and judicial hostility is due to no legal skill on Mr. Tutt's part but purely to the whim of chance. Unable to sleep the night before the case went to the jury, he had stepped into St. Patrick's Cathedral very early that morning and fallen asleep in a pew where he happened to have been seen by the jury's foreman. "At first we couldn't see that there was much to be said for your side of the case, Mr. Tutt; but when Oi stepped into the cathedral on me way down to court this morning and spied you prayin' there for guidance I knew you wouldn't be defendin' him unless he was innocent, and so we decided to give him the benefit of the doubt." (42) This last scene replicates the anecdote from the St. Louis paper that George Horace Lorimer had suggested to Train as the germ of his first Mr. Tutt story.[20] The rest comes from Train's intimate knowledge of criminal prosecutions in early 20th-century New York, and of course from his vivid imagination.

"The Hepplewhite Tramp" (#4; 16 August 1919, as "In Re: Sweet Land of Liberty"; *Tutt and Mr. Tutt*) pits Train's radical social consciousness against his pervasive cynicism and his protagonist against an obscenely rich Manhattanite, drawn not from life as Train with his background might easily have done but rather as a cartoonish caricature, the first of many such in the series. Bibby, butler to the elegant Mr. John De Puyster Hepplewhite, is showing his master's equally elegant houseguest Mrs. De Lancey Witherspoon to the bedroom assigned to her in Hepplewhite's Fifth Avenue mansion when they're shocked out of their wits to find lying between the pink silk sheets a scruffy and foul-smelling tramp.

Michael Casey, who claims that he found the front door of the mansion slightly ajar and was just "snooping round looking for something to eat" (247), is promptly arrested and charged with breaking and entering, burglary and other offenses set forth in the legalese gobbledygook of indictment clerk Caput Magnus.[21] Next we see the two Tutts engage in the first of the long jurisprudential dialogues that enliven several early tales in the series. "The fellow who steals a razor or a few dollars," Ephraim maintains, "is regarded as a mean thief, but if he loots a trust company or takes a million he is a financier. The criminal law . . . is administered for the purpose of protecting the strong from the weak, the successful from the unsuccessful, the rich from the poor. . . ." (244) This is when Bonnie Doon, just back from the Tombs, offers them the tramp case, which Mr. Tutt seizes upon as the perfect illustration of his point. "If John De Puyster Hepplewhite fell asleep in somebody's vestibule the policeman on post would send him home in a cab; but if a hungry tramp does the same thing he runs him in. If John De Puyster Hepplewhite should be arrested . . . they would let him out on bail; while the tramp is imprisoned for weeks awaiting trial, though under the law he is presumed to be innocent. Is he presumed to be innocent? Not much! . . . Just because this poor man—hungry, thirsty and weary—happened to select a bed belonging to John De Puyster Hepplewhite to lie on he is thrown into prison, indicted by a grand jury, and tried for felony! Ye gods! `Sweet land of liberty!'" (250) Mr. Tutt subpoenas Hepplewhite as a defense witness, brings a $100,000 civil suit against him for false imprisonment, all but reduces the poor plutocrat to jelly on the stand and delivers a fire-breathing summation, but in one of the few genuine surprise twists in a Train story, the tramp is convicted anyway. "Your argument was fine—grand—" confides Juror Number Six, "but nobody could ever make us believe that your client went into that house for any purpose except to steal whatever he could lay his hands on. . . ." (271) Casey then admits to the court that the jury was right: he's a professional burglar who, on hearing the butler and Mrs. Witherspoon coming into the bedroom, "dove for the slats and played I was asleep." (271)

In this duel between the Mencken and Upton Sinclair components of the series, Mencken wins hands down.

Even more cynical is "The Dog Andrew" (#7; 15 November 1919; *Tutt and Mr. Tutt*), which was based on an assault case Train prosecuted early in his career. "I think," he tells us in *My Day in Court*, "that I am one of the few attorneys who has actually ever brought to trial a defendant charged with using his dog 'as a dangerous weapon.'" (57-58) The fictional version opens with an account of the stupid feud between the Appleboys and the Tunnygates, two couples with adjacent summer cottages on the shores of Long Island Sound. Train carefully arranges the story so that we can't tell these absurd fat men apart, nor their equally fat and stupid wives either. (I had to teach myself to form a mental picture of Oliver Hardy when I saw one name in the text and of W.C. Fields when I saw the other.) The feud begins with a boundary dispute. Herman Tunnygate, hectored by his obese bride, starts taking a shortcut to the beach by forcing his way through the hedge that separates his and the Appleboys' property. Bashemath Appleboy borrows the vicious Andrew from her aunt upstate, her husband Enoch posts "BEWARE OF THE DOG" and "NO TRESPASSING" signs, and when next Herman breaches the hedge, chunks of his trousers and rear end wind up between Andrew's jaws. Tunnygate retaliates by having Appleboy arrested for assault with a dangerous weapon. Mr. Tutt is offering a hilarious discourse on the history of criminal proceedings against animals when in walks Bonnie Doon and hands them Appleboy as a client. Ephraim considers the case beneath his dignity and refuses to try it himself but masterminds the lesser Tutt's defense, which is based on lack of scienter (even though Train has already shown us that Enoch's and Bashemath's scienter is as big as their bellies) and on the old saw that every dog is entitled to one bite. All the parties lie through their teeth at the trial and, as chance would have it, the judge comes from the same upstate town as Bashemath's aunt and knows from firsthand knowledge that Andrew is a vicious beast. When he directs a verdict of not guilty, it's clear that Train means us to see the legal system as a grotesque farce. Flash forward 35 years: When then vice-president Richard M. Nixon was asked to select a favorite lawyer story story for an anthology, "The Dog Andrew" is what he chose, calling Train "my favorite author" and this tale "[o]ne of his best. . . ."[22] To my knowledge none of Nixon's legion of biographers has mentioned the point.

The dog bite trial is a paragon of decorum next to "Mock Hen and Mock Turtle" (#8; 29 November 1919, as "Ways That Are Dark"; *Tutt and Mr. Tutt*), which in large part comes from two murder cases Train tried—one for the prosecution, the other for the defense—and discussed in his memoirs.[23] The story opens with a brief introduction to New York's Chinatown. "No one better than the Chink himself realizes the commercial value of the taboo, the bizarre and the unclean. . . .[T]he Chinaman always gives his public exactly what it wants." (43) The Asian enclave is in the middle of an 80-year-old war between the Hip Leong and On Gee tongs, "a feud imposing a sacred obligation rooted in blood, honor and religion upon every member, who rather than fail to carry it out would have knotted a yellow silken cord under his left ear and swung himself gently off a table into eternal sleep." (47) Mock Hen, who has a white wife and professes to be a "Christian Chinaman . . .purely for business reasons" (54), is one of four Hip Leongs assigned to kill rival tong member Quong Lee. Unluckier than his comrades, Mock is recognized fleeing from the murder scene by a cop and other witnesses. Despite his attempt to create a detective-story perfect alibi for himself at the Hudson House social settlement he frequents when passing as a Christian, he's arrested and charged with murder. At a mind-boggling fee, the Hip Leong legal committee retains Mr. Tutt for the defense. Ephraim, we are told, "had hardly seen a dozen Chinamen in his life—outside of a laundry." (60-61) But he recognizes "what the law did not, namely that a system devised for the trial and punishment of Occidentals is totally inadequate to cope with the Oriental. . . ." (60) The courtroom scenes that prove his point are at once reminiscent of *Alice in Wonderland* and prophetic of *Catch-22*: well over forty days of trial time, an army of perjured Chinese witnesses for both prosecution and defense, an interpreter provided by each tong and an umpire interpreter to resolve the endless wrangles between his colleagues, the beheading of a white rooster in the courthouse basement to solemnize the Asians' testimony.[24] Only when the white woman from Hudson House takes the stand and innocently confirms Mock's false alibi is "Bloodhound" O'Brien forced to ask the court for a directed verdict of acquittal. Following a gargantuan banquet in Mr. Tutt's honor—as if he had anything to do with this farce except to sit there—Mock Hen is gunned down by On Get assassins on a Chinatown street. As the cop on the beat whispers to Mr. Tutt: "[W]hy in hell couldn't they have done it three months ago?" (88) With its blend of pervasive disgust, Theater-of-the-Absurd courtroom hijinks, a jurisprudential thesis too radical even for Critical Race buffs and language that nowadays would get Train prosecuted under every Hate Speech code in the country, this story is by all odds law fiction's counterpart to *The Birth of a Nation*.

Judging from his remarks in *My Day in Court* (111, 160), Train apparently developed special antipathies to New York's Chinese and Syrian populations as a result of courtroom encounters; and the treatment he gave the former group in "Mock Hen and Mock Turtle" he metes out to the latter in "The Kid and the Camel" (#14; 3 April 1920; *By Advice of Counsel*). The beast of the title plays no part in the story except as a clumsy device to involve Mr. Tutt in a murder stemming from the ongoing religious war between two Maronite sects transplanted to lower Manhattan. Coney Island concessionaire Kasheed Hassoun, charged with the murder of Sardi Babu, is prosecuted by William Montague Pepperill, a naive young Boston Brahmin who seems to be Train's sardonic self-portrait, and defended of course by Mr. Tutt. Ephraim again argues that the American legal system is incompetent to treat unassimilated alien populations justly and predicts to his tyro adversary exactly how the trial will proceed. "The defense will produce many witnesses— probably as many as the prosecution. Both sides will tell their stories in a language unintelligible to the jury, who must try to ascertain the true inwardness of the situation through an interpreter. They will realize that they are not getting the real truth—I mean the Syrian truth. As decent-minded men they won't dare to send a fellow to the chair, whose defense they cannot hear and whose motives they do not either know or understand. They will feel, as I do and perhaps you do, that the only persons to do justice among Syrians are Syrians." (69) Pepperill refuses Ephraim's offer to plead to Man One (as we all learned to call it from watching *Law & Order*) and a furious Mr. Tutt vows to make a fool of him in court. The trial with its dozens of perjurers on both sides is highlighted by the hilarious cross-examination of star prosecution witness Habu Kahoots. The jury deadlocks twice and only then, apparently having never bothered to ask his client what really happened, does Mr. Tutt stumble on the truth.

Ephraim's client in "By Advice of Counsel" (#15; 17 April 1920, as "The Passing of Caput Magnus"; *By Advice of Counsel*) is a flabby dweeb named Theophilus Higgleby, who is charged with bigamy and cheerfully admits the fact: while already married to one Tomascene Startup in Chicago, he took to wife one Alvina Woodcock in New York. "May I ask why?" inquires Samuel Tutt politely. "Why not?" Higgleby replies. "I'm a traveling man." (145) Caput Magnus, who as usual drafted the indictment, is this time forced by his superiors to try the case himself. Ephraim demolishes the prosecution's law-jargon wonk by what Train's reminiscences describe as an ancient defense,[25] establishing that Higgleby is not a bigamist but a trigamist. Since the indictment alleges the defendant was lawfully married to X at the time he married Y, proof of an even earlier marriage to W compels the court to direct an acquittal. "Your client seems to have loved not wisely but too well," remarks the judge to Mr. Tutt good-naturedly (180).

If Ephraim in that tale seemed a clone of Melville Davisson Post's first version of Randolph Mason, he resumes muckraking crusader garb in "The Shyster" (#16; 7 August 1920; *By Advice of Counsel*). As an Assistant District Attorney, Train encountered a number of criminal defense lawyers whose practice was to bilk clients out of huge fees by delaying their trials again and again and keeping them locked up in the Tombs indefinitely. Most of his plot comes from one such case.[26] A Jewish teenager with the not very Jewish name of Tony Mathusek is wrongly accused of hurling a brick through the window of Froelich's butcher shop. Delany, the cop who arrested him, is a brutal and corrupt thug in league with Raphael B. Hogan, the fat and elegant king shyster of the city. Once engaged as defense counsel, Hogan schemes with his runner Joey Simpkins to seek one postponement after another until the attorney fees eat up every cent of Tony's mother's savings. Mr. Tutt wanders into the case almost by accident and, with the aid of a sympathetic judge, ousts Hogan as defense counsel. After exposing Delany on the witness stand as a perjurer, Ephraim sets the stage for the shyster's ultimate disbarment.

In "Beyond a Reasonable Doubt" (#17; 11 September 1920; *By Advice of Counsel*) he again represents a legally guilty but morally justified ethnic, this time on the misdemeanor charge of practicing veterinary medicine without a license. Danny Lowry, an Irish immigrant in his seventies, can't read or write and lacks all the legal qualifications for a D.V.M. but has loved animals all his days and lives only to care for them and his teen-age granddaughter Katie. With automobiles having made the horse all but obsolete, New York's licensed vets are frantic to root out unauthorized competition and hire a detective to entrap Danny into taking five dollars for the care of a sick horse, upon doing which the old man is dragged off to a police station. Katie enlists Mr. Tutt for the defense but legally Ephraim has none and must bet on the moral sense of juries and the obscene absurdity of the situation. His fury explodes when the *agent provocateur* freely admits on the stand that he'd told Danny he was a physician. "It's your business to pretend you're a doctor when you're not, and you walk the streets a free man; and you want to send my client to Sing Sing for the same offense!" (292) Mr. Tutt eavesdrops on the jury's deliberations much as Train himself admits he was wont to do as a prosecutor,[27] so that we get to overhear the twelve good men and true effectively nullifying the law. "Who shall ever again have the temerity to suggest that the jury system is not the greatest of our institutions?" (311)

"The Bloodhound" (#26; 10 June 1922; *Tut, Tut! Mr. Tutt*) pits Ephraim against an adversary familiar to us from "The Human Element": William Francis "Bloodhound" O'Brien, "who viewed it as his duty to his God, his country, and himself to convict, by any means at his command, every hapless defendant brought to the bar of justice." (8) From *My Day in Court* we learn that the character was based on an Assistant D.A. of Train's acquaintance who "justified to some extent the stock portrayal of villainous prosecutors so familiar to theatregoers. . . ." (101) But the trick O'Brien uses here came from "one of the most famous prosecutors this country has ever known, a lawyer of high repute, [who] once boasted in my hearing of having secured a conviction in a weak case by sending for a copy of Byrnes' *Professional Criminals of America*, holding it so the jury could read the title, and pretending to be reading from its contents—asking the defendant such questions as 'Didn't you . . . blow up the bank at Red Bank, on March 6, 1898?'— there being no such statements in the book. Can I be blamed for never having any respect for the man thereafter?" (104) In Train's fictional version of the incident, Paddy Mooney, on the street again after fourteen months in Sing Sing on a trumped-up charge, blunders into a botched robbery. Both he and Mulligan, the real criminal, are arrested by the corrupt cop Delany, who plants a gun on Paddy before bringing him in to the station house for a beating. O'Brien offers Mulligan a sweetheart deal in return for his testimony against the innocent Paddy. Mr. Tutt is assigned to the defense and demolishes the perjury until all charges against Paddy are dropped except that of carrying the concealed weapon Delany planted on him. This is when the desperate O'Brien resorts to the ploy Train described in *My Day in Court*. Ephraim then makes his adversary take the stand and be sworn and, to quote Train's memoirs again, asks "whether, when he took the book in his hands and appeared to read from its pages, he had in fact been reading something that was printed there. . . . If he . . . insisted that he had been reading from the book—Mr. Tutt would offer it in evidence, and have him sent up for perjury. If he . . . admitted that he had been making the whole thing up—he would be ruined." (104nl) The Bloodhound chooses disgrace over prison and admits the truth. "Now, gentlemen," says Ephraim to the jury, "you may convict my client if you wish." To which the foreman replies: "The hell we will! The fellow we want to convict is O'Brien!" (38)

Most of Mr. Tutt's cases over the next several years were on the civil side and the most juristically interesting of them will be discussed in later sections. It's not until "Yaller Dog" (#43; 9 February 1929; *The Adventures of Ephraim Tutt*) that he is again pitted against O'Brien, and even though this case too seems hopeless, at least the judge has a humane streak. Ephraim's client, teen-age Gussie Menken, had known that the brutal beat cop Grady was out to beat him up and, seeing Grady coming down the street late one evening, had ducked into Jacob Grossman's unlocked store and living quarters while Grossman was out mailing a letter. The boy had hidden behind a counter, knocked over some cans of tomatoes and was caught, beaten, and charged by Grady with a huge assortment of offenses including breaking and entering, burglary, grand larceny and assault. The trial scene is preceded by several anecdotes from Train's own experience, later retold as fact in *My Day in Court*, such as the case of the black defendant by the name of Moses Cohen (62) and the man charged with attempting to steal a ship's anchor (23). During a withering cross-examination Ephraim proves that Grady has been reciting a set speech given him to memorize by O'Brien. But what precipitates the jury's acquittal of Gussie is Mr. Tutt's arranging for a mangy yellow dog to be let loose in the courtroom at just the psychological moment so that the compassionate ones among the twelve good men and true will see the analogy between the dog and Ephraim's hapless young client.

"Mr. Tutt Plays It Both Ways" (#49; 13 May 1933; *Tutt for Tutt*) is a masterpiece of legal cynicism, centering on a ploy so audacious that we'd write Ephraim off as a disgusting shyster if Train hadn't assured us early on that the client for whom the gimmick is pulled was innocent. Prohibition is still in force when young gas station attendant Tony Torsielli falls in love with Rosy, the 18-year-old daughter of "Macaroni Mike" Angelo. Like other local restaurateurs, Mike is making regular payoffs to federal revenue agent Shay in return for permission to sell the illegal liquor he buys from bootlegger Joe Cavorti. When Tony learns too much about this situation, Cavorti and Shay plot to lure the young man to Fort Morris, site of a long abandoned federal military post, and kill him. The plot gets botched and Cavorti winds up killing Shay, with Tony caught on the spot and charged in federal court with the agent's murder. Ephraim is assigned as defense counsel but Samuel bets him $500 he can't win this one: clearly the dumbest wager in the Train canon. First Mr. Tutt argues before the federal judge that the United States can't try Tony because jurisdiction over Fort Morris automatically reverted to the state of New York when the post was abandoned. Then when his client is indicted and tried by the state, Ephraim contends that New York has no jurisdiction because Fort Morris remains federal property and its military function is merely dormant!

Train again called on his by now ancient experience in the District Attorney's office in a few other late stories like "Mr. Tutt, Take the Stand!" (#56; 13 July 1935) and "Life in the Old Dog Yet" (#59; 2 May 1936), both collected in *Mr. Tutt Takes the Stand*, and yet again in "Jefferson Was Right" (#67; 25 September 1937, as "Mr. Tutt and Mr. Jefferson"; *Old Man Tutt*), one of the strongest tales from the last decade of the series, with Ephraim defending another proletarian innocent against the sadistic Judge Babson and the vicious prosecutor whose nickname and surname have unaccountably changed to "Bulldog" O'Brion. Newspaper delivery truck driver Vance Halloran, a saintly sort who sponsors outings for the slum newsboys on his route, is charged with the murder of Michael Kelly, a fellow driver with whom he'd quarreled. Halloran claims that he happened to be walking in the same block with Kelly when the shot that killed his enemy was fired from an alley—the same alley where a cop had found both Halloran and the murder gun a few minutes later. Assigned to this all but hopeless case and forced to go to trial without adequate preparation time against a conviction-crazy prosecutor determined not to let the jury hear the only fact in Halloran's favor—that at the time of the murder he was on his way home to celebrate his first wedding anniversary—Ephraim stands on principle, engages in fierce oral duels with both O'Brion and the judge, compares the proceeding to a Nazi court and comes close to being jailed for contempt, all with the hope that the jury will become outraged, follow Jefferson's dictum that "rebellion to tyrants is obedience to God" (27), and acquit Halloran in protest. Less than five years before his death, in "His Honor, The Judge" (#77; 29 March 1941; *Mr. Tutt Comes Home*), Train revived the original format of the series one last time, and proved that it still held much of its early power.

***

Throughout the twenty-six years of the Mr. Tutt series Train would every so often cast his hero in nonforensic roles: as a righteous trickster outfoxing a scoundrel the law can't touch,[28] as a benevolent uncle who brings or keeps a nice young man and woman together,[29] as a fisherman,[30] once in a blue moon as an amateur detective.[31] Ephraim's exploits of these sorts run the gamut from satisfactory to abysmal but have little or no legal component and therefore get short shrift here. The remaining stories whose juristic themes deserve detailed discussion stem from Train's years as a general practitioner when, having left the District Attorney's Office, he was pleased to discover that law's civil side offered as much raw material for fiction as the criminal. Over time he became increasingly dependent on civil subjects, in particular the law of wills and estates, and his stories in this vein present in retrospect a clear line of evolution that culminates in what all too soon became the Mr. Tutt formula.

What these tales uniformly stand against is a jurisprudential view to which one of the greatest American judges gave classical expression five years before Train launched his best known series.

88

"To enforce one's rights when they are violated is never a legal wrong, and may often be a moral duty. . . . . [T]he law, which creates a right, can certainly not concede that an insistence upon its enforcement is evidence of a wrong. A great jurist, Rudolf von Ihering, in his 'Struggle for Law,' . . . maintains the thesis that the individual owes the duty to himself and to society never to permit a legal right to be wantonly infringed. . . . [This thesis] has, at least, its germ of truth."[32]

For the rest of the Mr. Tutt cycle and of Train's life, this in a nutshell is the philosophy of the enemy; an enemy variously conceived but ultimately taking the form of modern avatars of Shylock.[33]

The theme is first sounded in the magnificent "Hocus-Pocus" (#10; 3 January 1920; *Tut, Tut! Mr. Tutt*), which centers on the interaction between wills law and evidence law and opens with an apt quotation from Train's friend Dean John H. Wigmore, seemingly deriding much of the latter subject as a "system which decides controversies by mumbling magic formulas before a fetich."[34] Shortly before her death, wealthy widow Caroline Grover had had Mr. Tutt draw her will, cutting off her despicable brothers and leaving virtually everything to her young ward Lucy Aymar. The will, drafted pursuant to the client's detailed memorandum of instructions, had been duly executed, witnessed by three women friends of Mrs. Grover (although she shared the will's contents with only one of them), and returned to the offices of Tutt & Tutt for safekeeping. But after Mrs. Grover's death no one in the office can find the will and, upon learning that it was somehow mislaid, her brothers sue for a declaratory judgment that they take the estate by intestate succession. Under Section 1865 of New York's then Code of Civil Procedure the establishment of a lost will required, among other things, that its provisions be "clearly and distinctly proved by at least two credible witnesses, a current copy or draft being equivalent to one witness."[35] The friend to whom Mrs. Grover read her will counts of course as one witness but the memorandum of instructions, which substantively meets the criteria for a "current copy or draft," is apparently inadmissible under Section 829 of the Code as a communication between lawyer and client.[36] A dialogue between Mr. Tutt and Lucy Aymar introduces a theme Train will revisit in several stories to come: rules of law vs. codes of honor.

> Lucy: "But no honest person would invoke any such law to defeat the perfectly obvious intention of one of his relatives!"
>
> Ephraim (playing devil's advocate): ". . . Have we really any right to complain because our adversaries insist that the game be played to a finish according to the legal code?"
>
> Lucy: ". . . [W]hatever the law may be, it seems to me that no honest person should invoke it to accomplish what he personally thinks to be a wrong or a suppression of the truth."
>
> Ephraim: "Quite so. But you are talking now about honor, not about law—an entirely different thing."
> (131-132)

The trial scene that ensues is one of Train's finest, with the rigorous Justice Pettingill interpreting the statutes inflexibly and ruling against each of Mr. Tutt's ingenious arguments for the memorandum's admissibility. After court adjourns, Train offers a Socratic colloquy in Mr. Tutt's office.

> Ephraim: ". . . Here we have a crowd of reputable witnesses who know exactly what was in Mrs. Grover's will . . . and yet for one reason or another the judge excludes practically every bit of evidence in the case. It's not only absurd, it's preposterous! It isn't equitable—it's criminal! . . . It almost makes me want to turn Bolshevik!"

Miss Wiggin: "You're quite Bolshevik enough already! You know perfectly well that though the law may work hardship in individual cases it is the crystallized wisdom of human experience. . . . [O]ur first duty is to obey the law whatever it is—no matter what the result may be. If we lawyers do not respect the law, who will?. . . . Even if the enforcement of a law is to result in what seems to be a wrong, to connive at an infraction or evasion of it is a greater one—the greatest that a lawyer can commit, for it attacks the very foundation of society."

Ephraim: "Quite right—as usual!"

Samuel: ". . . There's no use in being over-conscientious. You've got to have common sense about everything. . . . I won't stand seeing people robbed—even by the law that Miss Wiggin seems to think so perfect."

Ephraim: "How are you going to help yourself?" (143-145)

Samuel's suggestion is that Section 829 would no longer be a problem if Willie Toothaker should sneak into the Grover house and plant the memorandum of instructions in the dead woman's desk. This is precisely how justice and testamentary intent are made to triumph at the story's climax. As Train comments in an aside to the reader: "It is the business of the recording angel and not mine—of which I am very glad—to determine just how outrageous Mr. Tutt's conduct was and what should be done with him in the hereafter." (148) In Ephraim's very next published exploit, "Contempt of Court" (#11; 31 January 1920; *By Advice of Counsel*), which was apparently written before "Hocus-Pocus" but appeared in the *Post* three weeks later, a wealthy and socially conscious woman chooses to be jailed rather than reveal a legally unprotected confession from a justified murderer. Clearly Train did not think men alone are capable of honor.

The comic villain in "You're Another!" (#18; 2 October 1920; *By Advice of Counsel*) is Edna Pumpelly, a fat ludicrous *nouveau riche* from

Athens, Ohio, aboil with frustration at her failure to command the respect of New York's social elite. Snubbed by her genuinely patrician next-door neighbor Mrs. Rutherford Wells, Edna conscripts her husband J. Pierpont Pumpelly's attorneys into devising a scheme for revenge. After an altercation on the street with the Wells chauffeur, she waddles into City Magistrate's Court and swears out a summons against Mrs. Wells "for violation of Section Two, Article Two of the Traffic Regulations providing that a vehicle waiting at the curb shall promptly give way to a vehicle arriving to take up or set down passengers. . . ." (239) Mrs. Wells' friend John De Puyster Hepplewhite, familiar to Train's readers from "The Hepplewhite Tramp," advises her to consult Mr. Tutt. At this point we are treated to another Socratic colloquy among Ephraim, Samuel and Miss Wiggin, probably the longest Train ever wrote.

> Ephraim: "[U]nfortunately—or perhaps fortunately from our professional point of view—our lawmakers from time to time get rather hysterical and pass such a multiplicity of statutes that nobody knows whether he is committing crime or not."
>
> Samuel: "In this enlightened state it's a crime to advertise as a divorce lawyer; to attach a corpse for payment of debt; to board a train while it is in motion; to plant oysters without permission; or without authority wear the badge of the Patrons of Husbandry."
>
> Miss Wiggin: "Really, one would have to be a student to avoid becoming a criminal." (247)

As might be expected after this interlude, the rest of the story shows pompous Mrs. Pumpelly pummeled by a barrage of Magistrate's Court summonses for one picayune legal infraction after another: "for violation of Section One, Article Two, of the Police Traffic Regulations in that . . . you permitted a vehicle owned or controlled by you to stop with its left side to the curb on a street other than a one-way traffic street; and also for violation of Section Seventeen, Article Two of Chapter Twenty-four of the Code of Ordinances of the City of New York in that . . . you caused or permitted the same [vehicle] to proceed at a rate of speed greater than four miles an hour in turning corner of intersection highways, to wit, Park Avenue and Seventy-third Street. . . ." (254) "[F]or allowing your drop awnings to extend more than six feet from the house line. . . . [F]or failing to affix to the fanlight or door the street number of your house. . . ." (264-265) And on and on *ad infinitum* and *ad nauseam* until Mrs. Pumpelly hollers Uncle and dismisses her complaint against her neighbor.

Perhaps Train's finest story on the law-vs.-honor theme is "That Sort of Woman" (#20; 5 March 1921; *By Advice of Counsel*). Priggish Harvard-educated playboy Payson Clifford Jr., executor and residuary legatee under his late father's will, finds a letter accompanying the will and asking him to pay $25,000 from the estate "to my very dear friend Sadie Burch, of Hoboken, N.J." (191) The assumption is that the woman was Payson Senior's mistress. Samuel Tutt, from whom the young man seeks advice, acts precisely like the lawyer in service to the "bad man" Holmes posited as the key to understanding legality in "The Path of the Law."[37] Since the letter is not a part of the will it isn't legally binding, so that Payson Junior is perfectly within his rights to ignore it and keep the $25,000 for himself.

> Samuel: ". . . As executor you're absolutely obliged to carry out the terms of the will and disregard everything else. You must preserve the estate intact and turn it over unimpaired to the residuary legatee."
> Payson: "But I am the residuary legatee!"
> Samuel: "As executor you've got to pay it over in full to yourself. . . ." (203)

When Ephraim hears of this he invites young Payson to his home on West 23rd Street, gets him joyously drunk on old burgundy and cognac, and prevails on him to spurn his legal rights, follow the gentleman's code of honor and give the woman the money. Thanks to a standard *Saturday Evening Post* plot twist that the story would have been stronger without, Payson gets to keep the cash and his honor too.

If ever Mr. Tutt plays the shyster *par excellence* it's in "Nine Points of the Law" (#30; 26 July 1924, as "Status Quo: Or, Nine Points of the Law"; *Page Mr. Tutt*). His clients in this distasteful episode are the impoverished widow and children of Rupert Talliaferro II, who for the past five years have been living with their pet goat as squatters in a shanty on the side of a 60-foot-tall hill on 236th Street in upper Manhattan. The realty company that owns the lot, and can show clear title stretching back more than a century to the children's great-grandfather, has engaged Marcus Marcus' construction firm to bulldoze the property and put up a skyscraper. Enter Mr. Tutt, with the claim that the Byzantine verbiage of the grant to the great-grandfather gave him only a life estate, with the result that the entire chain of title after him is a nullity and that the Talliaferro children own not just the lot in issue but roughly half a billion dollars' worth of adjacent realty to boot. Ephraim's tactics are of the sort that have given lawyers the high reputation they enjoy today. He genially insults the Jewish sheriff charged with removing the family. "You have to know Latin to be a lawyer. To be a sheriff you have to know only Yiddish." (35) He camps out on the hilltop with his clients and the goat, refusing to come down until Marcus pays a fortune to settle his claim. When the other side goes to court for an eviction order, Mr. Tutt, knowing that Marcus will lose a fortune thanks to a penalty clause in his contract unless the skyscraper is up by a certain day, uses devious tactics to obtain one delay after another. When his friend and fellow Sacred Camel Judge Affenthaler happens to be assigned the case, Ephraim in a private meeting pointedly reminds His Honor: "King Menelik expects every Sacred Camel to do his duty." (57) When Affenthaler balks at handing the Talliaferros all of New York City north of 110th Street and rules against Mr. Tutt's spurious claim on a Friday afternoon, Ephraim makes a quick trip to

Albany and arranges with the governor, a friend and also a Camel, to elevate Affenthaler at once to the Appellate Division but to hold off notifying the judge for a few days so the promotion can be announced to him as a surprise birthday gift. Thus when Affenthaler signs the order of ouster on Monday morning, neither he nor anyone except Mr. Tutt knows that he no longer has jurisdiction. The result is yet another long delay, and the furious Marcus is finally forced to fork over $100,000 to settle the suit.

Among the longest, finest and funniest of the entire series is "When Tutt Meets Tutt" (#40; 10 September 1927; *When Tutt Meets Tutt*). Train based this tale on his experience representing the contestants in the litigation over the will of Amos F. Eno,[38] which according to *My Day in Court* "occupied us for years. . . ." (337) and "was largely responsible for my giving up the law. I felt that life was too short for that sort of thing." (338) Samuel Tutt accepts the case Train's firm had taken on in the real world, seeking to overturn on grounds of testamentary incapacity the will of cat-loving Commodore Enoch Lithgow, an apparent suicide who left only $100,000 to each of his ten nieces and nephews and the rest of his $4,000,000 estate to various cultural institutions and a home for homeless cats. If Samuel wins, the firm will receive a 50% contingency fee totaling two million dollars. Unfortunately some of these cultural institutions have already retained Ephraim at a far more modest figure to defend the will.

> Ephraim: "We can't be on opposite sides of the case at the same time. It's unethical."
> Samuel: "Ethics hell! What's ethics between friends? . . . There ain't any such thing, east of a million dollars."
> Ephraim: "Well, illegal then!"
> Samuel: "That's different!—Are you dead sure it's illegal?" (232-233)

Holmes' "bad man" couldn't have said it better. To avert the conflict of interest, Samuel resigns from Tutt & Tutt and opens his own firm.

"[Y]ou can't expect me to let a million dollars go by without reaching for it!" (235). The trial is a masterpiece worthy of Lewis Carroll: platoons of medical "experts" with professional opinions dictated by their fees, a 96-page hypothetical question that takes 2½ hours to read into the record, savage disputes over whether the Commodore was in the habit of bleating like a goat or telling creditors that "the rabbit" would pay them, a butler whose Cockney haccent ypnotizes both Samuel hand Is Onor hinto talking the same dialect, an anti-cat summation that must rank with the world's daffiest courtroom rhetoric, and a surprise ending when Commodore Lithgow himself erupts into the proceedings, disinherits all the relatives who were trying to break his will, and is held in contempt of court for not being dead. Anyone who can read this magnificent deconstruction of the system and still wants to be a lawyer belongs in the cuckoo's nest Jack Nicholson flew over.

Equally wondrous in its raw cynicism is "Mr. Tutt, Father-in-Law" (#48; 25 March 1933; *Tutt for Tutt*). While visiting another firm on business, Mr. Tutt discovers that impecunious law clerk Garrett Pell has just been fired for the crime of falling in love with Phyllis Kelly, daughter of the firm's most arrogant partner. Ephraim gives the young man a job with Tutt & Tutt and has him take a case Kelly had turned down, representing the relatives of Ezra Buckmeister in a suit to invalidate the late mogul's will, which left his entire estate to the Metropolitan Research Foundation. "The law, my son, is never clear. If it were, we lawyers couldn't make a living. . . . [A]n attorney should never be too sure that a will cannot be broken somehow. . . . It's sound legal doctrine that where there's a will there's a way—to break it. . . . [M]ental incompetency . . . undue influence, fraud, duress, mistake, void gift, lapsed legacy, fallen arches, cold in the head, *contra bonos mores, e pluribus unum, sic semper tyrannis,* wind on the tummy—any old thing. . . . " (41-42) Once the objections to probate are filed, Ephraim stalls the case for almost eight months, until the long anticipated death of one of his own clients, multimillionaire Joseph McGregor, whose will left $5,000,000 to the same Metropolitan Research Foundation. He has McGregor's will probated in nothing flat, then moves to bring the Buckmeister case before the surrogate's court, where Pell proves that, due to the recent McGregor bequest, the Foundation will exceed the $20,000,000 in assets permitted to a charitable corporation under §15 of New York's General Corporation Law if it's given the Buckmeister bequest. Therefore, Pell argues, Buckmeister's $1,000,000 must be distributed to his relatives as in intestacy. With the $50,000 that constitutes his half share of Tutt & Tutt's 10% contingency fee Pell is able to marry Phyllis Kelly.

***

A person who demands his rights under the law where one with a sense of honor would waive them is not far removed from a person who uses his legal rights to hurt or ruin others. The latter character type is commonplace in the work of Train and many another modern author of law-related fiction and indeed constitutes the 20th-century version of the demonic figure in English literature's first and richest masterpiece on legal themes, *The Merchant of Venice*.

The core of Shakespeare's play, at least as most readers perceive it,[39] is simultaneously juristic and religious. Shylock, being a Jew, is *eo ipso* a bloodsucking monster whose weapon of choice and polestar is the law. The other major characters, being Christians, are paragons of simple human decency. When Shylock demands the pound of Antonio's flesh to which the law entitles him, Portia invites him to choose decency over legality and waive his right. Being a Jew, Shylock indignantly refuses. Portia in effect replies: If law is what you want, then by God law is what you shall have! As if by magic she then produces another rule of law that trumps Shylock's legal right and leaves him devastated.

It took the slaughter of six million to dump the play's religious component into the garbage heap of history, but all it took for fiction writers concerned with legal themes to decouple and build upon Shakespeare's juristic nucleus was a usable secular substitute for the evil Jew. Such a replacement came to hand with the advent of social Darwinism in the late nineteenth century and, more precisely, with Holmes' superb evocation of "the bad man" in "The Path of the Law." By the time Train began working with these story elements, other lawyer authors like Melville Davisson Post had been at it for twenty years or more,[40] and even some nonlawyer writers who were Train's contemporaries made effective use of the pattern now and then.[41] But it was Train who reduced the practice to what he himself called a formula[42] and devised more variations on the theme than any of his colleagues.[43]

The effect of this story framework operates independently of any particular author's subjective intent. Taken as integral texts with a unified vision, both *The Merchant of Venice* and Shakespeare's other great juristic play *Measure for Measure* seem to propose that we reject and transcend everything connected with law, that we live without rules, by love and forgiveness alone. Taken in isolation, however, the "courtroom" scene in *The Merchant of Venice* offers a different perspective, purely secular and radically at odds with the religious thrust of the play as a whole: that a legal system can and will generate justice out of its own resources, at least when the "good lawyer" employs them. Whether Shakespeare himself believed this is both undiscoverable and irrelevant. Likewise, when the same framework is used by 20th-century authors like Post or Train, no matter how cynically they may have viewed their legal environment, the effect of their stories is to leave readers with a warm fuzzy feeling about the system.

The *Merchant of Venice* framework is not impossibly rigid but offers a number of variations. What the Shylock figure invokes may be either a broad principle of law or an arcane technicality, and what the Portia figure invokes in reply may be either as well. Train used all four of these basic variants in different tales. What is at once most difficult for the author and most satisfying to the reader is a story where the Portia figure prevails by a legal rule of the same precise type as her adversary's or by turning his rule back on itself. Train pulled off this feat only on rare occasions.

The pitfalls inherent in using this framework are both easy to discern and hard to avoid. If Shylock must invoke Rule A and Portia must counter with Rule B, those rules dictate the plot. Where the rule comes from a statute, the author must cram into the storyline every predicate to the statute's applicability; where it stems from a judicial decision, he must devise a plot on all fours with the facts of the case. Either way he has precious little room to be creative. And even if he's skillful enough to leap over this pitfall in individual stories, recycling the framework too often will sooner or later reduce his tales to ritualistic exercises in repetition that leave readers yawning. This is what happened to Train as, during the Thirties and early Forties, he drew from the Shakespearean well over and over again.

Train himself succinctly captured part of what tends to go wrong in these formulaic later stories when he remarked in *My Day in Court*: "The further one gets from personal experience the paler does the blood become." (444) But he compounded this problem by setting all too many of his variations on the Shakespearean theme in the mythical upstate New York hamlet of Pottsville, where every time Mr. Tutt stops off on a fishing vacation he finds some widow or orphan or inoffensive Sacred Camel being cheated under color of law, usually by the villainous local attorney, Squire Hezekiah Mason, or by one of Mason's "bad man" clients. Ephraim invariably trumps his adversary's legal weapon with another and more humane rule of law, but Squire Mason always returns to oppress another helpless innocent and before long, no matter how often Train compares him to Shylock, the modern reader is bound to conjure up images of Wile E. Coyote. These Pottsville outings are rarely of great juristic interest, but those who would like to sample one may find "The Doodle Bug" (#41; 1 October 1927; *When Tutt Meets Tutt*) more palatable than most. Train's finest adaptations of the juristic core of *The Merchant of Venice* have nothing to do with Pottsville but rank with his most interesting stories and deserve our attention here.

His first effort in this tradition and one of his grandest is "In Witness Whereof" (#22; 7 May 1921; *Tut, Tut! Mr. Tutt*). Years before the story begins, Ephraim had drawn millionaire widower Cabel Baldwin's will leaving everything to his daughter Lydia. Now Mr. Tutt receives a visit from fat slimy Alfreda, who had surreptitiously married the old man after serving briefly as his nurse. The new Mrs. Baldwin offers a huge fee if Ephraim will prepare a codicil to her husband's will, leaving generous bequests to several high-powered charities, other large gifts to members of Alfreda's family and the vast bulk of his estate to the lady herself. Mr. Tutt realizes that he's being asked to connive at undue influence but, after making Alfreda state that not she but her husband is the client, he agrees to draft the codicil. At this point Train interposes several pages of legalese attempting to justify Ephraim's decision along servant-of-the-bad-man lines. The scene in Baldwin's bedroom with Alfreda all but physically forcing the enfeebled old man to sign the document is a masterpiece, but the last laugh goes to Mr. Tutt. He manipulates Alfreda into signing the codicil as a witness so that, after Baldwin dies and the will and codicil are offered for probate, it quickly becomes clear that the later document is fatally defective because Alfreda is both witness and legatee. Her only recourse is to renounce the huge bequest in the codicil and rely on the other gifts to her relatives. No sooner has she done so than Ephraim pulls out an argument that invalidates those bequests too, and so on and on in a splendid duel between the Portia and Shylock philosophies of law.

"The Liberty of the Jail" (#25; 15 April 1922; *Tut, Tut! Mr. Tutt*) shows the Shylock and Portia aspects of the formula integrated into a glorious unity, although in the real-world case he adapted for the plot Train seems to have played the Shylock part.[44] Wallace Barrington, a young widower with an aged mother and four small children, is run down and maimed for life by T. Otis Crabb, who was drunk and driving his wealthy wife Lucretia's car on a party with some girlfriends. Mr. Tutt pays the Barrington family's bills while bringing suit. "It isn't exactly ethical for us to pay 'em, but what's a little ethics when an old woman and four children are starving?" (89) He wins a $50,000 verdict against both the Crabbs but then his troubles begin: T. Otis owns no separate property and Lucretia flatly refuses to pay the judgment.[45] Ephraim threatens to have T. Otis imprisoned for debt if the money isn't paid.[46] The Crabbs' lawyer, Aaron T. Lefkovitsky, devises a cunning countermove based on quirks in New York law. As long as Lucretia gives bond in the amount of the judgment and her husband's boozing-and-wenching buddy Algie Fosdick acts as surety, T. Otis is entitled to the "liberties of the jail," which means he is legally in prison but actually enjoys complete freedom of movement throughout New York County. Indeed he can even go beyond the "jail" and spend long weekends living it up in Atlantic City provided that Algie goes with him and that they both return on Monday before Fosdick can legally be served with process in an action on the bond. It's not what he knows but whom he knows that enables Mr. Tutt to trump this ploy. Thanks to having the general superintendent of Penn Station as a poker pal, Ephraim arranges for the Monday train on which T. Otis and Algie are returning to New York to be halted for three minutes in the tunnel under the Hudson at a point where the front end of the train with Algie in it is in New York and the rear cars, to which T. Otis has been lured by the hint of a new sexual conquest, are in New Jersey. This gimmick permits Algie to be lawfully served with process in the action to forfeit Lucretia's bond.

"Mr. Tutt Is No Gentleman" (#50; 8 July 1933; *Tutt for Tutt*) fuses the law-honor and Shylock-Portia oppositions into a magnificent tale with a glorious flimflam to boot. In the earlier "Mr. Tutt's Revenge" (#42; 1 September 1928; *The Adventures of Ephraim Tutt*), which lacks juristic interest, Ephraim had been invited into the Wanic Club, whose members own a palatial lodge and the exclusive fishing rights on a salmon-rich stretch of the Santapedia River in the fictitious Canadian province of St. Lawrence. As the present story opens, he and his colleagues are basking in this angler's paradise when they are invaded by Judge Philo Utterbach Quelch, a distant relative of the late Bishop Charteris, who figured in "Mr. Tutt's Revenge," and the successor to the bishop's share in the Wanic Club. For the past two years Quelch has landed a bigger salmon than any other Club member, and if he has the same luck this year he'll be entitled to the Golden Salmon, a trophy created by Bishop Charteris for whichever Wanic member kills the largest fish in the so-called Home Pool for three seasons in a row. Quelch is an odious toad who has no code of honor and, like Holmes' "bad man," lives solely by the rules of law—and is determined to use his legal knowledge to win the Golden Salmon. On the night of his arrival he engages in a superb juristic dialogue with Ephraim and another club member.

Ephraim: "Do you contend that if two men are fishing a stream and one hooks a salmon, the other has a legal right to gaff and take it, on the ground that he was the one to reduce it to actual possession?"

Quelch: "I most certainly do! . . . The fish belongs to the one who gets him."

Warburton: ". . . What would you think of a man who gaffed another man's fish?"

Quelch: "As a judge, my task, should such a case come before me, would be solely to interpret and apply the law according to my best lights."

Ephraim: ". . . So that if another fisherman hooked the same fish foul, it would belong to whichever could manage to land him?"

Quelch: "That is not only my position but it is the law!"

Warburton: "Don't you think that among sportsmen such a performance would justly be regarded as contemptible?"

Quelch: "It is time that sportsmen, so-called, realized that they are governed by the rules of law like everybody else."

Ephraim: "So you'd take another man's fish if you hooked him foul?"

Quelch: ". . . I only say that under the law I would have the right to do so, if I chose."

Ephraim: "But do you think any man calling himself a gentleman would do a thing like that?"

Quelch: ". . . Will you kindly inform me in what respect a person calling himself a gentleman differs

from any one else? . . . Honor is honor, and law is law. . . .
The only basic test of the rightfulness or wrongfulness of
an action is whether that action is legal or illegal." (173-
175)

The issues raised in this dialogue become concrete as the story
proceeds, with Quelch exploiting his knowledge of old common-law
rules regarding wild animals (or *ferae naturae* as he likes to call them) to
take all sorts of unfair advantages and maximize his chance of winning
the Golden Salmon. At the climax, when Mr. Tutt has apparently
hooked a leviathan of a fish that will cost Quelch the trophy, the
Honorable Philo hooks the fish foul and, in the last hours before the
contest closes, exhausts himself desperately trying to reduce the fish to
possession or, as anglers would say, to land him, only to discover that
he's been flimflammed by Mr. Tutt and wrestling with a waterlogged
pair of his own overalls. Ephraim and his colleagues cap the exposure
of Quelch's character by turning law back on its abuser as Portia did on
Shylock and expelling him from the Wanic Club for conduct
unbecoming a gentleman.

Unlike any other Train story, "Take the Witness" (#57; 28 September
1935; *Mr. Tutt Takes the Stand*) is set entirely in court and all but a few
pages deal with Mr. Tutt's savage cross-examination of the tale's
Shylock figure, predatory hussy Laura Lavelle, whose business is to
maneuver rich young men into written offers of marriage and then sue
them for breach of promise when they come to their senses.[47] After
ripping the woman to pieces on the witness stand, Ephraim follows
Portian precedent by invoking an obscure doctrine of contract law on
the effect of mailing an acceptance of an offer but retrieving the letter
before it's delivered. Most of Train's later stories in the *Merchant of
Venice* vein are routine but this one is a gem.

***

When Arthur Train died, the world of Mr. Tutt died with him.
Although the five years before and the fifteen years after his death saw
the first great flowering of the softcover reprint, only one of Train's

story collections was ever published in paperback.[48] Although the same twenty years witnessed the rise and fall of dramatic radio and the rapid expansion of television from an infant to a behemoth insatiably gobbling up story material, only one attempt was ever made to bring Mr. Tutt to either medium.[49] When Scribner tried to revive interest in the character with another omnibus volume, *Mr. Tutt at His Best* (1961), the book failed to find an audience.

A number of years ago Professor Philip Stevick wrote that "[n]one of [Train's] fiction, including the Tutt stories, is likely to endure."[50] Commentators who share Train's legal background tend to think more highly of the series as a whole.[51] Even his fondest lawyer admirers, however, must concede that his tendency to longwinded exposition and character stereotypes and his reliance in all too many of the later Mr. Tutt stories on formulaic plot gimmicks make much of his output indigestible today. What I hope to have demonstrated in this chapter is that about two dozen exploits of Train's once renowned protagonist remain as rewarding as ever. To my mind there are five factors which, either singly or in various combinations, demarcate what is living in the canon from what is comatose or dead: (1) the vividness with which a story conveys the flavor of criminal practice in immigrant-thronged New York early in the last century; (2) the intensity with which a story portrays the criminal justice system as a machine for grinding the wretched of the city, innocent and guilty alike; (3) the cynicism with which a story treats the legal system and all its functionaries as an absurd and grotesque farce; (4) the skill with which a story pits adherence to the aristocrat's code of honor against insistence on one's rights under the law; and (5) the success with which a story reworks the core of *The Merchant of Venice*, substituting Mr. Tutt for Portia and the Holmesian "bad man" for Shylock in a forensic duel whose outcome suggests that the ministrations of a good lawyer can coax the system to produce justice. The Mr. Tutt stories that still earn high marks under these criteria seem to me well worth resurrecting for a new generation.

NOTES

1. In fairness I must point out that Train describes his book merely as "reminiscences" and "in no sense an autobiography." (3)

2. "There has been nothing of significance to others in my private life and I have excluded all reference to it as far as possible." (3)

3. Typical of Train's treatment in reference works is Prof. Philip Stevick's entry in *Dictionary of Literary Biography, Volume 86: American Short-Story Writers, 1910-1945, First Series,* ed. Bobby Ellen Kimbel (Gale Research Co., 1989), at 298-305. It's unfortunate that Stevick consistently gives the first name of Train's best known character as "Ephriam" rather than the correct "Ephraim" but it's symptomatic of how completely the Mr. Tutt stories have been forgotten. For the most insightful recent commentary on Train, see Jon L. Breen, *Novel Verdicts: A Guide to Courtroom Fiction* (Scarecrow Press, 1984), at 162-169. Although the author is not a lawyer, this book is by far the finest treatment of its subject to date. However, since Breen limits himself to discussing only works of fiction with significant courtroom scenes, his commentary on Train omits the Mr. Tutt stories that are full of juristic interest but don't involve a trial.

4. For a thumbnail sketch of Train's father's life, see William T. Davis, *History of the Judiciary of Massachusetts* (Boston Book Co., 1900), at 289. By a previous marriage Charles Russell Train was the father of Charles Jackson Train (1845-1906), a career naval officer who rose to the rank of Rear Admiral and died of uremia while stationed in China as Commander in Chief of the U.S. Asiatic Fleet. See New York *Times,* 4 August 1906, at 1 (Charles Jackson Train obituary). The admiral's son, also named Charles Russell Train (1879-1967), rose to the same naval rank before his retirement. See New York *Times,* 10 December 1967, at 87 (Charles Russell Train obituary). Arthur Train refers briefly to both men in *My Day in Court,* 348.

5. Oliver Wendell Holmes, Jr., "The Path of the Law," 10 Harvard Law Review 457 (1897). Holmes first presented this essay as a speech at the dedication of a new building at Boston University School of Law. We have no reason to believe Train attended the ceremony but it's quite reasonable to suppose that he read the published essay when it appeared in his own school's law journal.

6. The Kissams were distant relatives of the Vanderbilts. Ethel Kissam Train had something of a literary career of her own while married to Arthur, publishing magazine stories and at least two books, *Son* (Scribner, 1911) and *Bringing Out Barbara* (Scribner, 1917). A huge collection of Ethel's short fiction, *Son and Other Stories of Childhood and Age*, was published by Scribners in the year of her death. When she died—on May 15, 1923, of bronchial pneumonia—one of her daughters was still single, one was married and living in New York City and the third was married and living in Paris. As of Arthur's death in December 1945, the single daughter was married, the Paris-based daughter had divorced and married again, and the New York-based daughter was still married to her original husband. Ethel's only son, Arthur Kissam Train (1902-1981), was a student at Oxford when his mother died and a Lieutenant Commander in the Navy at his father's death. He became a translator, a frequent contributor to *Reader's Digest* and other periodicals, and the author of at least two books, *The Story of Everyday Things* (Harper, 1941) and *Spoken Like a Frenchman* (Doubleday, 1966). See New York *Times*, 17 May 1923, at 19 (Ethel Kissam Train obituary); 23 December 1945, at 18 (Arthur Train obituary); 21 July 1981, Section B, at 10 (Arthur Kissam Train obituary).

7. Helen was divorced from her first husband, Sumner Gerard (1874-1966), a lawyer and real estate developer with conservative political ties. Gerard entered Harvard Law School in the fall of 1897, a year behind Train, but left the following spring to enlist in Theodore Roosevelt's Rough Riders and fight in the Spanish-American War. See New York *Times*, 12 March 1966, at 27 (Sumner Gerard obituary). Helen had three sons by Gerard. The only child of her second marriage was John Train

(1928-), an investment counselor and prolific author of nonfiction. See 2 *Who's Who in America* 3375 (47th ed. 1993).

8. See Train's account, "The Best Tutt Story of All," in *Mr. Tutt Finds a Way* (Scribner, 1945), pp. 1-7. This essay was first published as "Should I Apologize?" in the *Saturday Evening Post*, 26 February 1944.

9. Train himself suggested this defense in remarks printed in the New York *Times*, 16 May 1944, at 23. His account of the litigation, "Mr. Tutt Pleads Not Guilty," is included in *Mr. Tutt Finds a Way* (Scribner, 1945), pp. 228-241. (This essay was first published in the *Saturday Review of Literature*, 2 December 1944).

10. One reference source describes the play as a "[l]ong-run Jewish dialect farce about a couple of feuding business partners (Barney Bernard and Alexander Carr) who hire a Russian refugee bookkeeper." Edwin Bronner, *The Encyclopedia of the American Theatre 1900-1975* (A.S. Barnes, 1980), at 379. According to Bronner, the play opened at the George M. Cohan Theatre on August 16, 1913 and ran for 441 performances. *Ibid.* Clearly either Train's recollection of the date he attended the show was years off the mark or else what he went to see was a revival.

11. The *Post* offered a total of 86 Mr. Tutt tales, all but two of which found their way into one or more of the collections published by Scribner. Also found in those collections are seven Mr. Tutt stories not published in the *Post*; two quasi-fictional pieces ("Tootle" and "Mr. Tutt's Queerest Case," both in *Old Man Tutt*) that hardly count as stories at all; and two magazine articles ("The Best Tutt Story of All" and "Mr. Tutt Pleads Not Guilty," both in *Mr. Tutt Finds a Way*) in which Train discusses his protagonist.

12. Since *My Day in Court* appeared in the *Post* in 1938 and as a book a year later, one might easily suppose that by "twenty years ago" Train meant around 1918-19. However, this passage of his reminiscences is taken verbatim from his Preface to the first omnibus volume of Mr. Tutt stories, *The Adventures of Ephraim Tutt* (Scribner, 1930), at ix. The Virginian lawyer must therefore date back to around 1910.

13. "No lawyer can spend ten years drawing papers and retain his freedom of expression," Train declares in *The Autobiography of Ephraim Tutt*. . . . "[T]he factual attitude becomes part of his make-up. His style ceases to be free. He becomes literal, pedantic, over-precise, unable to see the woods for the trees. . . . The longer they stay at it [i.e. the practice of law] the less they become qualified to give rein to fancy. Lawyers, as a rule, do not become poets, playwrights or novelists—at any rate not of the first rank. They rarely produce great literature." (375-376) Whether Train means to include himself in his stricture remains unclear. "I was never in earnest about the law," he says. "I was always a sort of legal play-boy. Even so, my professional training has decidedly stood in my way." (375)

14. She gets to dominate the twenty-ninth tale in the series, which was published under three different titles: in the *Post* (3 May 1924) as "Miss Wiggin's Love Affair," in *Page Mr. Tutt* (Scribner, 1926) as "The Maiden and the Tar," and in *The Adventures of Ephraim Tutt* (Scribner, 1930) as "Captain Ahab."

15. Willie more or less takes center stage in the twelfth Mr. Tutt story, "Toggery Bill" (14 February 1920; *Tutt and Mr. Tutt*), which describes how Ephraim first met the youth and used a legal quibble to save him from a burglary charge.

16. Ezra has his moment in the sun in the twenty-eighth tale, "The Cloak of St. Martin" (3 March 1923; *Tut, Tut! Mr. Tutt*).

17. See Chapter 2 of this book.

18. Train praises the muckraking journalism of Steffens and his colleagues at *McClure's Magazine* in *My Day in Court* (37, 41, 208-209), and his bibliography shows that three of his own early pieces were published in the same crusading periodical.

19. "I have rarely written what are technically known as detective stories and take small interest in them." *My Day in Court*, 161.

20. Research in the St. Louis *Post-Dispatch* files for late 1918 and early 1919 has failed to unearth the item Train described.

21. There really was a Caput Magnus or at least a man who claimed that was his name. Train prosecuted him for practicing medicine without a license. *My Day in Court*, 60-61.

22. Albert P. Blaustein, ed., *Fiction Goes to Court* (Henry Holt, 1954), at 32.

23. Train recounts the case he defended at pp. 255-257 of *My Day in Court* and the one he prosecuted at 34-36. The defendant in the latter case was "a notorious Chinaman" called Mock Duck, and when it was over Train's fellow Assistant District Attorneys nicknamed him Mock. *Id.* at 132.

24. Small wonder that the *Post* ran this story as "Ways That Are Dark." The title comes from a once popular and now infamous 60-line poem by Bret Harte, "Plain Language from Truthful James" (1870), whose closing verse runs:

> Which is why I remark,
>
> And my language is plain,
>
> That for ways that are dark,
>
> And for tricks that are vain,
>
> The heathen Chinee is peculiar, —
>
> Which the same I am free to maintain.

Bret Harte, *Stories and Poems*, ed. William Macdonald (Oxford University Press, 1947), at 575-576. It has been argued that the butt of this poem and of Harte's short stories about Asians in the old West is not the "heathen Chinee" but white racism. "Vigorously opposed to racial injustice in general and to its application to the Chinese in particular, Harte struck out at such injustice on numerous occasions." Wilton Eckley, "Bret Harte," in *American Writers: A Collection of Literary Biographies, Supplement II, Part I: W.H. Auden to O. Henry*, ed. A. Walton Litz (Scribner, 1981), at 350-351.

25. *My Day in Court*, 61.

26. *Id.* at 48-49.

27. "If the reader feels some surprise at my familiarity with what went on under the supposed sanctity of the jury room, I should frankly explain that I made it a practice to listen at the open transom from the top of a small and most convenient step-ladder." *Id.* at 35.

28. Two typical examples of this type are "Wile Versus Guile" (#2; 3 July 1919) and "Lallapaloosa Limited" (#6; 13 September 1919), both collected in *Tutt and Mr. Tutt*.

29. The tales with Ephraim in this capacity include "In re Misella" (#9; 6 December 1919), which is so completely irreconcilable with every other story in the series that it has never been reprinted or collected in any form, and "The Viking's Daughter" (#37; 5 February 1927), collected in *When Tutt Meets Tutt*.

30. The sport figures prominently in several Mr. Tutt stories where law takes a back seat to vivid descriptions of angling in the wilderness. The most extreme instance of this sort of tale is "Tutt for Tutt" (#45; 21 March 1931), collected in *Tutt for Tutt*, which has no legal dimension at all but merely recounts a salmon fishing duel along Canada's Nipsicodiac River between Ephraim and an unsportsmanlike British plutocrat.

31. "The Hand Is Quicker Than the Eye" (#5; 30 August 1919, as "Matter of McFee"), collected in *Tutt and Mr. Tutt*, is the earliest story in the series that qualifies for the fair-play detective genre. Other tales in which Mr. Tutt operates simultaneously as lawyer and sleuth are "The Acid Test" (#33; 12 June 1926), collected in *Page Mr. Tutt*, and "The King's Whiskers" (#74; 30 December 1939), collected in *Mr. Tutt Comes Home*. Train's finest detective story and the last truly worthwhile tale in the series is "With His Boots On" (#81; 12 September 1942), collected in *Mr. Tutt Finds a Way*.

32. Cardozo, J., in *Morningstar v. Lafayette Hotel Co.*, 211 N.Y. 465, 468, 105 N.E. 656, 657 (1914).

33. One is not surprised to learn that von Ihering in *The Struggle for Law* also discusses *The Merchant of Venice*, and concludes that Shylock was

the victim of a miscarriage of justice. For an account of the dispute about Shylock among 19th-century German jurists, see George Keeton, *Shakespeare's Legal and Political Background* (Barnes & Noble, 1968), at 148-150.

34. 3 Wigmore, *Evidence* §1938nl (1st ed. 1904). This was still the current edition when Train wrote his story. The object of Wigmore's scorn was a series of judicial decisions on the admissibility of nonexpert opinion evidence as to a person's sanity.

35. The present and more liberal version of this statute is New York Surrogate's Court Procedure Act §1407 (McKinney 1983).

36. This section carved out an exception where the decedent's attorney also witnessed the will, which is why Train made sure the witnesses to Mrs. Grover's will didn't include Mr. Tutt. New York's present version of the statute would have aborted this story from the start. See New York Civil Practice Law & Rules §4503(b) (McKinney 1977).

37. "If you want to know the law and nothing else, you must look at it as a bad man, who cares only for the material consequences which such knowledge will enable him to predict, not as a good one, who finds his reasons for conduct, whether inside the law or outside of it, in the vaguer sanctions of conscience." Oliver Wendell Holmes, Jr., "The Path of the Law," 10 *Harvard Law Review* 457, 459 (1897).

38. In the endless litigation over Eno's will, the firm of Perkins & Train appeared in at least three of the proceedings that led to reported opinions. See *In re Eno's Will*, 196 App. Div. 131, 187 N.Y.S. 756 (1st Dep't 1921); *In re Eno's Will*, 118 Misc. 186, 192 N.Y.S. 840 (Surr. Ct. 1922); *In re Eno's Estate*, 118 Misc. 431, 193 N.Y.S. 759 (Surr. Ct.), *aff'd mem.*, 202 App. Div. 739, 194 N.Y.S. 931 (1st Dep't 1922).

39. For an exceptionally counter-intuitive reading of the play, see Richard Weisberg, *Poethics and Other Strategies of Law and Literature* (Columbia University Press, 1992). Weisberg argues that "unlike any (male) Christian character, [Shylock's] speech is usually direct, literal, precise." (97) ". . . [T]he moneylender stands in open court for the

sanctity of verbal expressions of commitment." (98) "The attack upon Shylock in court thus constitutes also an attack upon verbal obligation. . . . And Portia's victory there . . . demarcates the ascendancy of the casual breach of promise, the lighthearted breaking of the sacred oath." (98) Shylock speaks "as a committed Jew and thus as a believer in direct dealing and in oath keeping." (99) ". . . [He insists] on the bond, on law, on justice. . . ." (99) Weisberg interprets the often overlooked fifth act of the play as the vindication of Shylock's ethic in that "the keeping of promises [is] equated with the preservation of both direct ethical commitment and precise textual responsibility." (96) Act V signifies "the subtle ascendancy of ethics over comedy, of law over equity, of oaths over breaches, of commitment over mediation." (101) "Shylock may be gone, but his unmediated approach to commitment lingers on." (102) "Finally shorn of the male mediations of . . . courtroom disguise, Portia speaks in her own voice and makes her beliefs known. . . . Jewish commitment finally prevails over Christian mediation. . . . Law conquers equity, and the covenant regains its ascendancy." (103) "Shylock is gone but not forgotten. And we are left to ponder whether his values are not somehow better, more direct, more forceful." (104)

40. See Chapter 2 of this book.

41. Several years before his classic crime novels like *The Maltese Falcon* (1930) and *The Glass Key* (1931) had made him famous, Dashiell Hammett employed the framework in an uncharacteristic but satisfying little story, published in magazine form as "The New Racket" (*Black Mask*, 15 February 1924) and in the now rare collection *The Adventures of Sam Spade and Other Stories* (Bestseller, 1944) as "The Judge Laughed Last." Unfortunately the tale was not included in either of the "major" collections of Hammett's short fiction published after his death.

42. *My Day in Court*, 486.

43. Train claimed in *My Day in Court* that "almost every Tutt story . . . is based, in part at least, on personal experience." (337) But he also admitted that for years he had "offered a standing honorarium to any one calling my attention to a decision, principle or 'quirk' of the law"

that he could use in a story. "I have advertised in *The New York Law Journal* and my offer is today posted on the bulletins of a majority of the law schools throughout the United States. I have received thousands of letters in reply, but in twenty years only eight persons have suggested an available point." (487) Most of Train's variations on *The Merchant of Venice* were apparently the fruit of his own legal research, with the element of "personal experience" generally minor in nature. In the stories where Mr. Tutt ventures far from his usual haunts—to the Montana-Canada border in "The King's Whiskers" (#74; 30 December 1939), or to New Mexico's Cocas Pueblo reservation in "And Lesser Breeds Without the Law" (unpublished in magazine form but probably written around 1940)—it's safe to assume that the vividly described local color stems from a vacation trip. Both the above tales were collected in *Mr. Tutt Comes Home*.

44. "'The Liberty of the Jail' tells how Perkins and I actually found a means whereby one of our clients, who had been sent to jail, was able to spend his weekends at Atlantic City." *My Day in Court*, 488.

45. Why didn't he simply levy on Mrs. Crabb's separate property? Well, if he had it would have aborted an excellent story.

46. This was still legally possible at the time and even later, as Ferdinand J. Wolf demonstrates in his notes (pp. 569-572) following the reprint of the story in the omnibus volume *Mr. Tutt's Case Book* (Scribner, 1936). Mrs. Crabb however could not have been jailed because what was then section 1488 of New York's Code of Civil Procedure (later Section 829 of the Civil Practice Act) severely restricted the use of this remedy against a woman.

47. During Train's years in private practice he represented the victims in several cases of this sort which he describes in *My Day in Court* (338-342). Like their he-said-she-said counterparts today, such suits were little more than legally sanctioned varieties of blackmail. In one of the earliest Mr. Tutt stories, "Samuel and Delilah" (#3; 2 August 1919, as "Tutt vs. the 'Spring Fret'"; *Tutt and Mr. Tutt*), Samuel Tutt begins by

representing a woman with the same racket and winds up being taken by her for several thousand dollars.

48. *Tutt and Mr. Tutt* was issued by Bantam Books in 1946 but sales were apparently so poor that neither Bantam nor any other firm offered paperback editions of the other collections. Thirty-five years after its publication, the Bantam volume became the subject of a review essay that is all too brief and suffers from a misleadingly comprehensive title but certainly conveys appreciation for the role Mr. Tutt played as, so to speak, the Atticus Finch of his time. See Karl T. Piculin, "Tutt and Mr. Tutt: The Arthur Train Stories Revisited," 5 *ALSA Forum* 79 (1980).

49. *The Amazing Mr. Tutt*, a summer replacement series heard briefly on the CBS radio network beginning in July 1948, starred Will Wright as Ephraim, with John Beal as Bonnie Doon. For short accounts of the series, see John Dunning, *Tune In Yesterday: The Ultimate Encyclopedia of Old-Time Radio 1925-1976* (Prentice-Hall, 1976), at 26-27, and John Dunning, *On the Air: The Encyclopedia of Old-Time Radio* (Oxford University Press, 1998), at 24. The single attempt to translate Mr. Tutt to television was a 30-minute pilot film, "Strange Counsel," directed by Jerry Thorpe from a teleplay by Ellis Marcus and Harold Swanton. Whether the script was an original or an adaptation of a Train story is unclear. Walter Brennan portrayed Mr. Tutt as a foxy country grandpa, based not in Manhattan but in a Pottsvillesque small town in upstate New York. Vera Miles guest-starred as a young woman who comes to Ephraim with the claim that someone has tampered with her late grandfather's will. See Vincent Terrace, *Encyclopedia of Television, Volume I: Series, Pilots and Specials, 1937-1973* (Baseline/Zoetrope, 1986), at 308. The pilot never sold but was broadcast September 10, 1958 on *Colgate Theater*, a short-lived NBC summer replacement series.

50. Philip Stevick, "Arthur Train," *supra* note 3, at 305.

51. The fullest lawyerly treatment of the Mr. Tutt stories in recent times is found in Chapter 10 of Thomas L. Shaffer, *American Legal Ethics: Text, Readings, And Discussion* (Matthew Bender, 1985). Shaffer reprints two of the tales discussed in the present chapter—"The Hepplewhite

Tramp" and "In Witness Whereof"—and thoughtfully probes their ethical dimension. Despite the mind-boggling titular misnomer, see also Philip H. DeTurk, "Tutt: An Annotated Bibliography of Arthur Train's Tutt Short Stories," Tarlton Legal Bibliography Series #39 (University of Texas Law Library, 1993).

CHAPTER 4

Samurai at Law: Erle Stanley Gardner

Erle Stanley Gardner has been dead more than forty years but what he accomplished in his eight decades on the planet still survives. Beginning in the middle 1920s he wrote hundreds of tales—many the length of short novels—for the pulp magazines whose lurid covers filled the nation's newsstands in the time between world wars. In his first full-length novel, *The Case of the Velvet Claws* (1933), he created Perry Mason, fiction's most celebrated attorney, the courtroom dynamo who was to become the protagonist of 82 books (1933-71), a movie series (1934-37), a long-running radio series (1943-55), a legendary television series (1957-66), and a cycle of two-hour TV movies (1986-93) that are still regularly seen on cable and satellite today. As if that weren't enough for one lifetime, Gardner also created several other book-length series including one (1937-49) about a prosecuting attorney and another (1939-70) about a disbarred lawyer turned private detective and his irascible female partner. Small wonder that he liked to refer to himself as "the fiction factory."

Gardner was born on July 17, 1889 in the small town of Malden, Massachusetts to a mother whose ancestors came over on the Mayflower and a civil-engineer father descended from a long line of sea captains. This boy whose earliest years coincided with the golden age of social Darwinism was a born combatant, with a boundless zest for competition and an unstoppable drive to succeed. In 1899, while in fourth grade, he wrote a school essay on the Greek myth of Atalanta, the theme of which is that whoever doesn't win the race dies. Later that year his family moved west, settling in 1902 in a prosperous California mining town. Wander though he did throughout his life, Gardner called the Golden State his home from that day forward.

He spent his early teens traveling with his father through remote stretches of California, Oregon and the Klondike, developing a zest for outdoor living that was to become a hallmark of his fiction. In school he was a maverick and a troublemaker, earning pocket money by boxing in unlicensed matches, and his interest in the law seems to have grown out of hunting for loopholes in the California statutes that made prizefighting illegal. After completing high school in 1909 he was admitted to Valparaiso University in Indiana but was soon expelled for slugging a professor. He went back to California, apprenticed himself to one established attorney after another and, in 1911, passed the state bar. Over the next twenty years he discovered that litigation was a form of combat at which he could excel, and he earned a reputation as one of the state's most flamboyant trial lawyers. Many of his clients came from the Chinese community of Oxnard and the first book-length study of Gardner, now almost 70 years old, reconstructs a number of the forensic scams he perpetrated on their behalf. During one of the city's periodic anti-lottery crusades, Gardner was representing twenty Chinese accused of selling lottery tickets. While all the defendants were out on bail and just before the first batch was to be brought in for trial, Gardner made some secret arrangements with the leader of the local Asian community. The next day a plainclothesman "picked up a Chinese who was booked as Ah Lee. . . . At the station the Chinese prisoner gave a friendly greeting to a deputy sheriff." When the deputy learned that the prisoner had been booked as Ah Lee, he told the detective: "That's not Ah Lee." Detective: "That certainly is Ah Lee. . . . I bought a ticket from him a week ago, and I just arrested him at Ah Lee's laundry." Deputy:

"I've known Ah Lee for ten years. He does my Sunday shirts. This is Wong Duck, the butcher." Detective: "But I tell you he was running the laundry. . . . He was bossing the others around. What would a butcher be doing running a laundry?" Deputy: "Who knows why a Chinaman does anything?" Next the detective identified another defendant from whom he had purchased a lottery ticket as Ho Ling, the grocer. Deputy: "He's Ong Hai Foo, the druggist . . . the biggest dealer in dried-lizard medicine in Southern California." Detective: "But I tell you he was running Ho Ling's grocery when we arrested him. . . . He was waiting on customers. Why would a druggist be selling vegetables?" The answer of course is that Gardner had had dozens of Asian merchants exchange identities so that each would be booked under another's name. After it became clear that the key prosecution witness had wrongly identified several defendants, all twenty cases were quietly dismissed.[1] This is simply one specimen from the bag of courtroom tricks and fireworks which, when he began writing novels, Gardner handed over to his alter ego Perry Mason.

Since the practice of law could not contain his energies, Gardner launched a number of sales businesses as a sideline. But he was a born wanderer, to whom the four walls of a law office or courtroom were like the walls of a prison cell, and the only way he could think of to make decent money and still enjoy a free-ranging lifestyle was to establish himself as a professional writer. But he quickly discovered that writing fiction wasn't the same as writing briefs. "It was like trying to sign my name with my left hand," he said many years later. "I knew what I wanted to do but for the life of me I couldn't do it." (DBH 73) He collected a drawerful of rejection slips but his Can Do spirit never flagged and as soon as one magazine had bounced a story he'd mail it out to another. In the spring of 1921, as he put it, "Glory be, I clicked!" (DBH 74) His first sales were a pair of humorous skits for which the pulp magazine *Breezy Stories* paid him ten or fifteen dollars apiece.

For the next two years he sold hardly a word. "I wrote the worst stories that ever hit New York," he said near the end of his life. "I have the word of an editor for that, and he hadn't seen my worst stories because the worst ones I wrote under a pen name." (DBH 77) Finally thanks to sheer persistence he sold one of those pseudonymous tales ("The Shrieking Skeleton," as by Charles M. Green, *Black Mask*, December 1923), and from then on he appeared with mind-boggling frequency in the so-called pulps that made up most Americans' entertainment in the days before radio and TV. *Black Mask, Top-Notch, Argosy, West, Clues, Air Adventure, Detective Fiction Weekly, Three Star, Prize Detective, Detective Action Stories, Gangland Stories, Western Trails, Gang World, Dime Detective*—the entire list of magazines in which he published would fill most of a page.

How did he keep up this pace without coming apart? "For a period of several years," he said, "I pounded out stories on the typewriter at the rate of a novelette every third day, and at the same time practiced law, much of it trying cases in front of juries, which I can testify is a very exhausting occupation." (DBH 83) After a full day at the office or in court and an evening at home dictating legal memoranda and correspondence, Gardner would sit down at the typewriter around 10:00 P.M. and start work on a story. "I would work until one, one-thirty, or two o'clock in the morning when I would be so dog-tired that whenever I would stop to rest I would fall asleep in the chair and have nightmares, dreaming for the most part about the characters in the story, waking up a few seconds later all confused as to what had been in the story and what had been in my dream. At that time I would go to bed. I would sleep about three hours a night, waking up around five or five-thirty in the morning. Then I would take a shower, shave, pull up my typewriter and write until it came time to go to the office. It's a wonder that I didn't kill myself with overwork. If I finished one story at twelve-thirty at night, I couldn't go to bed without starting another." (DBH 83) Night after night he would pound away at those typewriter keys until his fingers bled. Eventually he switched to a primitive dictating machine and set himself a fiction quota of 100,000 words a month.

The genre pulps in which Gardner appeared were flimsily bound and stapled and printed on dirt-cheap paper which the years have turned dirt-brown, but copies today are hard to come by and often command astronomical prices. Even if you had the time and fortune to assemble a complete library of the pulps that featured Gardner stories, whenever you opened the pages of an issue to enjoy his contribution you'd run the risk that the magazine might fall apart in your hands. And frankly, many of those early tales don't hold up all that well seventy-five to ninety years later. They were uniformly written in a fiendish hurry and some of them wind up with plot complications not only unexplained but beyond explicability. Yet even the weaker stories are often filled with the kind of raw vivid inventiveness and taut immediacy that have long since vanished from fiction, and the outstanding ones are as readable today as they were when Hoover and FDR sat in the White House.

As his friend Freeman Lewis wrote shortly after Gardner's death: "He was a born story-teller. In over forty years as a publisher, I never met a writer so generously endowed with that quality. In an evening's conversation (perhaps monologue would be a better word) he would produce more ideas and plots for books than most writers come by in a lifetime." (DBH 309) Writing as much and at such white-hot speed as he did, it's small wonder that he often lost track of various elements in his plots. In his defense he argued that "[e]very mystery story ever written has some loose threads" (DBH 163) and claimed that the breakneck pace of his novels and stories made it all but impossible for readers to catch the plot flubs. "After all, on a trotting horse who is going to see the difference? The main thing is to keep the horse trotting and the pace fast and furious." (DBH 302)

The number of series characters Gardner created for the pulps defies belief. In the Western genre alone he wrote ten stories for *Black Mask* (1924-32) about Bob Larkin, an adventurous juggler who uses a billiard cue instead of a gun; eight tales for the same magazine (1925-35) featuring Black Barr, a gunfighter who considers himself an instrument of God's justice; three stories apiece about The Old Walrus (1926-27) and Buck Riley (1927-28) and two apiece about Fish Mouth McGinnis (1926-31) and Sheriff Billy Bales (1928). The 21 Whispering Sands tales he wrote for *Argosy* (1930-34) are perhaps his finest work in this genre, with their rich descriptions reflecting his lifelong love of the desert.[2] He also wrote a surprising number of science-fiction novels without any series characters.[3]

The majority of his pulp stories, however, were contemporary crime thrillers, most of them with protagonists somewhat reminiscent of the "good badman" characters of the sort that were portrayed again and again by silent Western film star William S. Hart. Among the longest running and best known of his series characters in this vein are Ed Jenkins, the Phantom Crook (72 stories for *Black Mask*, 1925-43)[4] ; Speed Dash, the Human Fly (20 stories for *Top-Notch*, 1925-30); Lester Leith (66 stories, 1929-43), an aristocratic thief and amateur sleuth whose butler is really an undercover cop assigned to nail him; Sidney Zoom (17 stories for *Detective Fiction Weekly*, 1930-34), an aloof and godlike sleuth who, like his creator, "aided misfortune, but detested weakness" and whose only friend is a police dog; Dan Seller, the Patent Leather Kid (14 stories, 1930-34); Senor Arnaz de Lobo (23 stories, 1930-34), a sort of Zorro figure without the cape and mask; and Paul Pry (27 stories, 1930-39), another gentleman thief and amateur detective, sidekicked by a one-armed hulk with the improbable name of Mugs Magoo. Then there's a small army of the shorter-lived series characters including Major Copely Brane (8 stories for *Argosy*, 1931-34), Rex Kane (3 tales for *Detective Action Stories*, 1931-32), Steve Raney (7 stories for *Clues*, 1932-33), El Paisano (5 stories for *Argosy*, 1933-35), Stan Wider, The Man in the Silver Mask (3 tales for *Detective Fiction Weekly*, 1935), Barney Killigen (4 stories for *Clues*, 1938-39), Ed Migrane, The Headache (3 tales for *Detective Fiction Weekly*, 1939-40), and several more to boot. Random samplings in these series suggest that legal elements appear in them sometimes but not to an overwhelming extent. What almost all Gardner protagonists have in common is that they're scam artists.

Take, for example, Paul Pry, the impossibly debonair young

adventurer who debuted in the October 1930 issue of *Gang World* and, after appearing in all but four of the magazine's 25 issues, continued his career in the pages of *Dime Detective*.[5] Pry makes his living hijacking stolen goods from the underworld and then collecting huge rewards from the rightful owners. In each of his early exploits he concocts an elaborate scam to frustrate the latest crime coup of gangster mastermind Big Front Gilvray; and if you can ignore Gardner's graceless and verbose style and just enjoy the clever plotting, these episodes can be almost as much fun as a brace of Roadrunner cartoons, with "A Double Deal in Diamonds" (*Gang World*, February 1931) having special appeal thanks to vivid action scenes on board an interurban tramcar.

After awhile the duels with Gilvray vanish and each later story in the series is a self-standing unit. In "Dressed to Kill" (*Dime Detective*, 1 September 1933), Pry and his sidekick Mugs Magoo are having supper at a nightclub when Mugs, who has a photographic memory for faces and an encyclopedic knowledge of the underworld, pieces together information he happens to have about several fellow diners and tells Pry they're about to witness the surreptitious delivery of a letter from a certain imprisoned gem thief to his lawyer. Sniffing stolen jewels in the air, Pry deftly snatches the letter before it can be delivered and takes it back to his table, only to find sitting there a lovely lady who allows him to seduce her in record time, then tells him she's being blackmailed and asks him to accompany her to a masquerade ball and steal back for her some compromising letters. It's hardly a surprise when we learn that the indiscreet letters and the stolen jewels are connected, but it's still fun to watch Pry walk into the lion's mouth, tweak the noses of the ungodly and emerge with all the boodle in sight.

"The Finishing Touch" (*Dime Detective*, August 1938) also opens with Paul and Mugs enjoying dinner at a night spot. Two jewel-cases containing identical gems happen providentially to be in Pry's pocket. Mugs spots a certain lovely lady in the club and tells Paul she's an ex-convict whose underworld bosses are forcing her to work the badger game on amorous males. The scheme Pry devises on the spot is never explained to his partner or us but calls for him to allow the woman to work the badger game on him and steal one of the twin jewels while at the same time Mugs flashes the other stone around the nightclub's bar. When the scheme goes haywire, Pry instantly concocts another, this time trying to convince the thieves that he has a geiger counter that can locate stolen jewels.

In the twenty-seventh and last tale in the series, "It's the McCoy" (*Dime Detective*, January 1939), Paul and Mugs are relaxing at a baseball game when Magoo intercepts code signals between a jewel thief and a master fence. Pry instantly cracks the code, audaciously breaks into the signaled conversation and waits for the crooks' reaction, which is not long in coming. A young woman steps in front of his car as he's leaving the ballfield parking lot. Her "doctor" tells Pry that she has an incurable disease that will kill her in a few weeks and asks him to take her out every night and make her last hours happy. (How many defendants in auto negligence suits must wish they had hit so forgiving a victim!) Paul then sends Mugs to the city's best hotel disguised as a visiting rajah, complete with a fake ruby in his turban and some out-of-work black showgirls as his harem. The argument between Magoo and a bad-tempered belly dancer is one of the funniest scenes Gardner ever wrote. When Pry tells his dying girlfriend that he's a professional thief with designs on the rajah's ruby, she breaks out in gales of enthusiasm for the scheme, saying "I don't think it's exactly a crime to rob the very rich" and "After all, the world owes you a living." Once again Pry's master plan is never explained but it works perfectly and our heroes come out of the climactic bloody battle unscathed and the richer by two suitcases full of jewelry while the poor dying maiden gets stuck with the red glass from Mugs' turban.

At around the same time he created Paul Pry, Gardner also launched an even longer-running series about the light-fingered larcenist Lester Leith, whose forte is solving crimes by analysis of newspaper reports and then hijacking the loot before he exposes the criminal to the stupid police.[6] Lead-witted Sergeant Ackley has planted an agent in Leith's palatial penthouse but Lester has long been aware that his valet is a spy and delights in twisting poor Scuttle into a pretzel each time the game is afoot: sending him out on humiliating wild goose chases, ridiculing his every word, almost but never quite letting the servant know that his cover is blown, manipulating events so that Scuttle and Ackley slam into each other full tilt while he nimbly slips between them with the boodle. Most of Leith's 66 adventures are hastily assembled and prone to loose plot threads but unfailingly rich in verve and zip and bounce and sheer readability. One of the finest in the series is "The Candy Kid" (*Detective Fiction Weekly*, 14 March 1931), a walloping bamboozler of a tale in which Leith leads the forces of law and order around by their noses as everyone searches for the rajah's rubies which an unlucky stickup artist had snatched and then apparently hidden somewhere in a candy factory moments before being swiss-cheesed by police bullets. Before he's finished Lester finds uses for fifty dollars worth of chocolate, an electric soldering iron, a string of firecrackers, a police siren, a blowtorch, and a mad scheme to save heat by pretending November is July.

The tales at the end of the cycle are just as wild and crazy as the early entries in the series. In "Something Like a Pelican" (*Flynn's Detective Fiction Magazine*, January 1943), Leith happens to be on the sidewalk below when a mysterious woman throws a silver fox cape out of a furrier's window to the accompaniment of screams for the police. Puzzled, he returns to the neighborhood that night just in time to witness the abduction of a secretary in the precision instrument company across the street from the furrier's. It soon develops that the blueprints for a new invention were stolen from the company's vault during the fur-tossing diversion and the caper turns into a race for the plans between Leith and the police and a fight between Leith and the company over the innocent secretary's claim for damages. The plot would have been killed in its tracks by a thorough police search at the get-go but this is a fun story, paced like a rocket, spiced with laconic wit and boasting the added dividends of satire on amateur authors and expert-sounding shotgun lore. In "The Black Feather" (*Flynn's Detective Fiction Magazine*, July 1943), the police spy Scuttle is replaced as Leith's valet by Singra Bhat, who pretends to be a Burmese detective but is actually a Japanese spy planning to steal a secret treaty from a sick diplomat in a hotel and pin the blame on Lester. Meanwhile Leith becomes interested in a jewel theft and sets out to hijack the loot with the help of a siren-equipped baby carriage, some smoke bombs, and a wacky scheme to produce 16mm movies for home viewing. With this 66th and last caper the series ended.

***

Of more immediate interest to us here are those of Gardner's magazine stories that deal directly with law, lawyers, lawyering and justice. His first series of direct relevance to these subjects lasted for six separate but thematically connected stories, written (or more likely dictated) and published in *Black Mask* during the period when he was making the transition from pulp magazines to hardcover novels.[7] Protagonist of these tales is Ken Corning, a young man fresh out of law school who, for no particular reason except that it's a Darwinian challenge, sets up practice in a metropolis which for sheer corruption rivals (and no doubt was strongly influenced by) the poisonvilles in Dashiell Hammett's *Red Harvest* (1929) and *The Glass Key* (1931). Hardly is the paint dry on Corning's office door when he begins to run afoul of the politicians in control of the York City government. In each tale he represents a far from admirable person who's being framed on a criminal charge by some of the local powers that be and in each tale he clears his client not by any lawyerly skills but by getting out into the streets and concocting an imaginative scam that flushes out the truth. Assisting him in these schemes is his secretary Helen Vail, who is the prototype of Della Street as Gardner first drew her: a tough-talking but good-hearted dame who gladly takes risks from which the most loyal secretary in the real world would run screaming. Corning's ultimate adversary, political boss Carl Dwight, comes onstage only in the first tale and has vanished down the memory hole long before the last.

In "Honest Money" (November 1932) the client is speakeasy proprietor Esther Parks, who's been locked up on a phony charge of attempting to bribe Sergeant Perkins of the local Prohibition squad. A few hours after he's retained Corning to handle the case, Mrs. Parks' obese husband is shot down on the street. Corning goes into action and soon discovers that she's being railroaded because she had inadvertently discovered too much about corruption in the city water department. The tale ends with a gunbattle and the release of Corning's client but, in a touch of truly Hammett-like cynicism, nothing happens to the murderers.

In "The Top Comes Off" (December 1932) Corning gets involved in what seems a private matter as a mysterious woman hires him to represent George Colton, who's in jail charged with the murder of his wife's lover, politically connected realtor Harry Ladue. Corning quickly realizes that the woman is Mrs. Colton, and that she's on the brink of suicide. This time the murderer turns out to be Sergeant Perkins, the corrupt cop from the first Corning story, who, being relatively low on the political food chain, winds up having to pay for his crime.

The client in "Close Call" (January 1933) is Amos Dangerfield, a politically ambitious businessman who has gone into hiding at Corning's suggestion after being accused of the hit-and-run murder of hostile newspaper publisher Walter Copley. Once again it's a political frameup, which Corning explodes by setting a trap that proves the man who claims to have witnessed the killing is actually the assassin for hire who did it. Neither he nor his higher-ups is arrested for the crime.

"Making the Breaks" (June 1933) opens with Helen Vail coming to Corning in the middle of the night after having money planted on her that is tied to a murder case her boss is defending. Clearly the powers that be are out to discourage Corning from representing ex-convict and small-time burglar Fred Parkett, who's been charged with a street killing on evidence he claimed the arresting officer planted on him. With the help of an undercover Federal agent,

Corning establishes that the real killers were the men who claimed they witnessed the murder and the police detective.

"Devil's Fire" (July 1933) begins in medias res with Corning at the scene of another street murder, this one apparently the result of a violent argument between underworld bosses Frank Glover, who wound up dead, and George Pyle, who's charged with the murder. A sniveling small-time crook by the name of Henry Lampson buttonholes Corning on the street, claims he saw the murder and offers to testify in Pyle's favor if he's paid off. When Corning refuses to give a bribe, Lampson goes to the police and makes a deal to frame the lawyer for suborning perjured testimony. Eventually Corning sets up a scam involving a rigged target-shooting competition to lure the real killer out of the woodwork.

"Blackmail with Lead" (August 1933) brings the series to an end of sorts. Corning is retained by small-time criminal Sam Driver, who's accused of killing his partner Harry Green, and soon finds that the case is linked to the murder of wealthy George Bixel in a lonely mountain cabin several months before. When a rapacious slattern who knows some of the truth is bought off and sent packing, Corning gets Helen Vail to impersonate the woman and rigs a charade that exposes the facts.

***

In 1931, when most of the country was in the pit of the Depression, Gardner made over $20,000 from pulp writing, in addition to his income as a lawyer, but his success almost killed him. He decided that the only way to free himself for the nomadic life he wanted to live was to phase himself out as a lawyer, cut back his torrent of wordage for the pulps and start writing, or rather dictating, novels for hardcover publication. The result was Perry Mason, who debuted in *The Case of the Velvet Claws* (1933) and eventually made his creator one of the wealthiest and most widely read authors in the history of the world.

What accounts for the mind-boggling success of the Mason novels? Gardner himself never claimed they were written with any grace. His characterizations and descriptions tend to be perfunctory and are often reduced to a handful of lines that he recycled in book after book. Indeed virtually every word not within quotation marks could be left out of any Perry Mason exploit and little would be lost. For what vivifies these novels is the sheer readability, the breakneck pacing, the involuted plotting, the fireworks displays of courtroom tactics based in large part on Gardner's own law practice in Oxnard, and the dialogue, that inimitable Gardner dialogue whose every line, whether spoken in or out of court, is a jab in a complex form of oral combat.

The first nine Mason books, published between 1933 and 1936, are set in the dog-eat-dog milieu of the free enterprise system in the depths of its worst depression, and Gardner, born scrapper that he was, revels in it. The Mason of these novels is a tiger in the social Darwinian jungle, totally self-reliant, asking no favors, despising the weaklings who want society to care for them, willing to take any risk for a client no matter how unfairly the client plays the game with him. On the first page of *The Case of the Velvet Claws* we are told of Mason: "He gave the impression of being a thinker and a fighter, a man who could work with infinite patience to jockey an adversary into just the right position, and then finish him with one terrific punch." (1) A few pages later there is this telling exchange between Mason and the beautiful treacherous woman who has consulted him. Mason: ". . . Nobody ever called on me to organize a corporation, and I've never yet probated an estate. I haven't drawn up over a dozen contracts in my life, and I wouldn't know how to go about foreclosing a mortgage. People that come to me don't come to me because they like the looks of my eyes, or the way my office is furnished, or because they've known me at a club. They come to me because they need me. They come to me because they want to hire me for what I can do." Woman: "Just what is it that you do, Mr. Mason?" Mason: "I fight!" (5)

Variations on this scene recur throughout Gardner's early novels, in which Mason again and again says of himself: "I am a paid gladiator." If Gardner had wanted to show off his erudition he might have had Mason call himself the servant of the bad man

Holmes had evoked in "The Path of the Law"[8]; if he had wanted to connect back with his Western stories he might have had Mason describe himself as a hired gun; if his affinity had been for Japanese rather than Chinese culture he would probably have called his character a samurai. In the last analysis all these formulations have the same meaning. And Della Street in her first incarnation is cut from the same cloth: in the words of Gardner's publisher Thayer Hobson, "a gal who would poison her mother, eat unslaked lime, and twist a baby's wrist for the man she cared for." (DBH 130)

Any doubts that these characters clearly reflect their creator are dispelled by a glance at Gardner's voluminous correspondence. At the outset of his career as a novelist he wrote his publisher: "I want to make my hero a fighter, not by having him be ruthless with women and underlings, but by having him wade into the opposition and battle his way through to victory. . . . More than that, I want to establish a style of swift motion. I want to have characters who start from scratch and sprint the whole darned way to a goal line. . . ." (DBH 102) The letter he wrote his publisher at the end of 1934 is full of similar imagery: "Let's plant our feet firmly on the ground, double our right fists, measure the distance with a nice left lead, and sock all competitors right between the eyes. Yours for a belligerently successful 1935." (DBH 124)

In *The Case of the Velvet Claws* Mason outlines his creed to private detective Paul Drake. "I'm a lawyer. I take people who are in trouble, and I try to get them out of trouble. I'm not presenting the people's side of the case, I'm only presenting the defendant's side. The District Attorney represents the people, and he makes the strongest kind of a case he can. It's my duty to make the strongest kind of a case I can on the other side, and then it's up to the jury to decide. That's the way we get justice. If the District Attorney would be fair, then I could be fair. But the District Attorney uses everything he can in order to get a conviction. I use everything I can in order to get an acquittal. It's like two teams playing football. One of them tries to go in one direction just as hard as it can, and the other tries to go in the other direction just as hard as it can. . . . My clients aren't blameless. Many of them are crooks.

Probably a lot of them are guilty. That's not for me to determine. That's for the jury to determine." (259-260)

Perry Mason as Gardner first created him does indeed use everything he can, and usually his tools are the little people whose financial desperation in the pit of the Depression forces them to accept almost any risk in return for a little money. In *The Case of the Velvet Claws* Mason pays twenty dollars to a hotel switchboard operator to tell him what number a certain person called and then with twenty-five bucks bribes a policeman who lost his shirt at poker the previous night to get confidential information from the phone company as to who has that number. Later in the same novel he loosens the tongue of a hostile witness by pretending to frame him for a murder, and at the climax he manipulates estate funds to prevent a murderer who is not his client from obtaining money for his defense. In *The Case of the Counterfeit Eye* (1935) Mason is searching for a woman to impersonate a prosecution witness. Mason: "Go to an employment agency and find a young woman [of a certain description] who is hungry. . . . Be damn sure she's hungry." Della Street: "How hungry?" Mason: "Hungry enough so she won't argue with cash." Della: "Will she go to jail?" Mason: "She may, but she won't stay there, and she'll be paid for it if she does. . . ." (180) Della brings back a young woman and Mason's talk with her goes in part as follows. Mason: "Been out of a job long?" Woman: "Yes." Mason: "Ready to do anything that's offered?" Woman: "That depends on what it is." Mason says nothing. Woman: "I don't give a damn what it is." Mason: "That's better." (200)

Indeed Mason in his original incarnation will even twist evidence to get a guilty client acquitted, and does so in *The Case of the Howling Dog* (1934). "I've told you before, and I'm telling you again, that I'm not a judge and I'm not a jury. I'm a lawyer. The district attorney does everything he can to build up a strong case against the defendant. It's up to the lawyer for the defendant to do everything he can to break down the case for the district attorney. . . . [A defense lawyer is] a partisan, a representative hired by the defendant, with the sanction of the state, whose solemn duty it is to present the case of the defendant in its strongest light. That's my creed and that's what I try to do." (290-291) At the end of this powerful novel, after Mason has twisted the evidence so that the client he knew to be guilty has been acquitted by a jury and can never be tried again, an ambivalent Della Street says to him: "You are a cross between a saint and a devil." "All men are," he replies. (294)

If the original Mason seems an amoral and unattractive character, from Gardner's perspective this was already a sanitized version of what he wanted to present. Chapter X of *The Case of the Counterfeit Eye* (1935) contains a fascinating dialogue between Mason and the newly elected district attorney Hamilton Burger. "You've got a reputation for being tricky," Burger says, "and I find that you *are* tricky, but I think they're legitimate tricks . . . I think an attorney has a right to work any legitimate trick in order to bring out the truth. . . . I notice that your tricks aren't for the purpose of confusing a witness, but for the purpose of blasting preconceived notions out of his head, so that he can tell the truth. . . . District attorneys have a habit of wanting to get convictions. That's natural. The police work up a case and dump it in the lap of the district attorney. It's up to him to get a conviction. In fact, the reputation of a district attorney is predicated on the percentage of convictions he gets on the number of cases tried. . . . When I took this job . . . I wanted to be conscientious. I have a horror of prosecuting an innocent person. . . . Your courtroom technique is clever, but it's all of it founded on having first reached a correct solution of the case. When you resort to unorthodox tricks as a part of your courtroom technique I'm opposed to them, but when you use those tricks to bring about a correct solution of a mystery I'm for them. My hands are tied. I can't resort to unorthodox, spectacular tactics. Sometimes I wish I could. . . ." Mason replies: ". . . I don't ask a man if he's guilty or innocent. When I start to represent him, I take his money and handle his case. Guilty or innocent, he's entitled to his day in court, *but* if I should find one of my clients was really guilty of murder and wasn't legally or morally justified, I'd make that client plead guilty and trust to the mercy of the Court. . . . If a person is morally justified in killing, I'll save that person from the legal penalty if it's possible to do so." (171-174) The last sentence clearly refers to what Mason did for the guilty client in *The Case of the Howling Dog*. However, in a letter to his publishers from the same period Gardner said that he had toned down his conception of Mason "in order to make it appear that he wouldn't defend a man and try to get him off if he thought that person was guilty of cold-blooded murder without any moral justification." But he bitterly resented having to water down his Darwinian notion of law practice and would have preferred his books to reflect the real-world fact "that the burning question which confronts a man accused of crime who enters the office of any reputable criminal attorney is not the question of his guilt or innocence but the question of whether he has the necessary retainer available in the form of spot cash." (DBH 123)

Love him or hate him, he told the truth as he knew it.

For Perry Mason as Gardner first created him, the core value is loyalty to his client, despite the client's despicable character and acts, regardless of how unfairly the client deals with him. In *The Case of the Velvet Claws* Mason is retained by a seductive blonde who initially conceals her identity from him but turns out to be Eva Belter, a predatory and promiscuous woman whose wealthy husband owns a scandal magazine. When George Belter is shot to death, Eva tries to force Mason to keep her out of trouble by telling lies that make Mason himself seem to be the murderer. At what seems to be the climax of the novel, Mason—emulating the climactic scene between Sam Spade and Brigid O'Shaughnessy in Dashiell Hammett's classic *The Maltese Falcon* (1930)—accuses Eva of the murder and, when she confesses her guilt, turns her and the evidence to convict her over to the police. This apparent betrayal of a client causes Mason's secretary to lose faith in him, as Gardner explained to his publisher, "until the very last, when she suddenly realizes he was working for his client all the time instead of against her, and . . . they get back to a basis of Della Street worshipping Mason's fighting loyalty." (DBH 106)

Describing exactly how Gardner pulled off this feat would ruin a fascinating novel for those who haven't read it, but his strategy is a a brilliant creative variation on the often slavishly imitated *Maltese Falcon* denouement.

If Mason the samurai stands for Gardner's ideal of good lawyering, what is his notion of a bad lawyer? In *The Case of the Caretaker's Cat* (1935) Mason is consulted by a crippled servant at the mansion of the late Peter Laxter, whose grandsons and testamentary legatees are trying to make the man get rid of his beloved cat. Mason sends a letter claiming without any firm legal basis that the provision in Laxter's will requiring the caretaker's continued employment impliedly allows him to keep the cat, and that any action against the animal would breach that condition and lead to the forfeiture of their bequests. The grandsons consult Nathaniel Shuster, whom Mason holds in absolute contempt. "He poses as a big trial lawyer, but he's a bigger crook than the people he defends. Any damn fool can win a case if he has the jury bribed." (21) "If there's anything in reincarnation, he must have been a Chinese laundryman in a prior existence. Every time he snickers, he sprays his audience, like a Chinese laundryman sprinkling clothes." (22) "He's a disgrace to the profession, and he gets us all into disrepute." (33) "Shuster will try to egg his clients into a fight, and I'll either have to back up or play into his hands. If I back up, he makes his clients believe he's browbeaten me into submission, and charges them a good fee. If I don't back up, he tells them their whole inheritance is involved and soaks them a percentage. That's what I get for running that bluff about a forfeiture of the inheritance." (23) Sure enough Mason's adversary is the shyster his name unsubtly suggests. "It's going to be a hard fight; it's going to be a bitter fight. I've warned my clients of that. You're a resourceful man. You're a sly man. If you don't mind the expression, I'll say you're a cunning man. Lots of us would take that as a compliment; I take that as a compliment myself. Lots of times my clients say, 'Shuster is cunning.' Do I get sore? I don't! I say that's a compliment. . . . I warned my clients that Winifred [Peter Laxter's disinherited granddaughter] was going to try to break the will. I knew she'd try it by every means in her power, but she couldn't claim the grandfather was of unsound mind, and there's no question of undue influence. So . . . she picked on Ashton and his cat." Shuster refuses to settle the dispute unless "Winifred signs an agreement that she won't contest the will. . . ." Mason: "I don't know anything about Winifred. I've never met her and haven't talked with her. I can't ask *her* to sign anything." Shuster, rubbing his hands gleefully: "We couldn't settle on any other basis. It's a matter of principle with us. . . ." Mason, finally losing his temper: "You know damn well I'm not representing Winifred. You knew that that letter of mine meant exactly what it said, but you knew you couldn't kid your clients into paying big fees over a cat, so you dragged in this will-contest business. . . . You've frightened your clients into believing they've got to get Winifred's signature on a release. That's laying the foundation for a nice fat fee for you." Shuster screams: "That's slander!" Mason, to the grandsons: ". . . I'm not your guardian. I'm not going to break my neck trying to save your money. If you two want to give that cat a home, say so now; that's all there'll be to it. If you don't, I'll make Shuster earn his fees by dragging you into the damndest fight you've ever been in. . . ." (25-29) The moral is clear: a good lawyer will do almost anything for a client but will not generate a dispute for the lawyer's own profit.

How did the original Mason mutate into the radically different character whom younger audiences are familiar with from TV? As we've seen, the process began as early as 1935 with the initial dialogue between Mason and Hamilton Burger in *The Case of the Counterfeit Eye*. It accelerated around 1937 when the *Saturday Evening Post*, which had previously published many a story by Melville Davisson Post and Arthur Train, began offering huge sums of money for the right to serialize Perry Mason novels before their appearance in hardcover. But Gardner in return had to tone down the series even more, in order to satisfy the magazine's requirements. He did so in a way that was nothing short of brilliant. I will guarantee you in advance, he said in effect to his readers, that

Mason's clients will always be innocent, so that you can enjoy the way I have him skate on the thin edge of the law and pull all sorts of sneaky courtroom tricks without being bothered by any moral qualms about the cause he is serving. We might call this Gardner's personal contract with America, a contract which he kept from the late 1930s until his death.

At first Gardner was ambivalent about what he must have regarded as a Faustian bargain. In December 1936, just after completing the first Mason novel that the *Post* accepted for serialization, he described the book to his publisher as a case "with lame canaries and moving vans and silenced rifles and firebugs and trick garages and substituted amnesia victims and what the hell have we. . . . No real life lawyer would ever have been mixed up in a mess like that." (DBH 131) But only a few years later, in *The Case of the Perjured Parrot* (1939), Gardner denounced precisely the kind of lawyer he had told his publishers he had originally wanted to portray as a hero. Mason, reading his mail, says to Della Street: "Oh, Lord, here's another one. A man, who's swindled a bunch of people into buying worthless stock, wants me to prove that he was within the letter of the law." (6) The echo of Melville Davisson Post's early Randolph Mason tales[9] resounds loud and clear for those with ears. "You know, Della," Mason continues, "I wish people would learn to differentiate between the reputable lawyer who represents persons accused of crime, and the criminal lawyer who becomes a silent partner in the profits of crime. . . . I never take a case unless I'm convinced my client was incapable of committing the crime charged. . . ." (6)

In the Mason novels published between the late 1930s and the late 1950s, not only are the clients always innocent but the ruthlessness is muted, "love interest" plays a stronger role, and Mason becomes increasingly more stodgy, to the point that by the end of this middle period he refuses even to drive above the speed limit. But the oral combat remains as breathlessly exciting as ever, the pace as frantic and the plots as twisty, the best of them centering on various sharp-witted and greedy people battling over control of capital. Mason of course is still Gardner's alter ego but in several novels of these years he creates a second surrogate in the person of a philosophic old entrepreneur who delights in living on his own in the wilderness, as Gardner did himself.

One of the most interesting of these stand-ins is Fremont C. Sabin, whose obituary is summarized in the first chapter of *The Case of the Perjured Parrot* (1939).

> "Just touching sixty, he represented a strange figure of man; one who had wrung from life all that it offered in the way of material success; a man who literally had more money than he knew what to do with. . . . [F]or the most part he did not believe in philanthropy, thinking that the ultimate purpose of life was to develop character; that the more a person came to depend on outside assistance, the more his character was weakened.
>
> ". . . Sabin had believed that life was a struggle and had purposely been made a struggle; that competition developed character; that victory was of value only as it marked the goal of achievement. . . .
>
> "[He] had placed something over a million dollars in trust funds for charitable uses, but he had stipulated that the money was to go only to those who had been incapacitated in life's battles: the crippled, the aged, the infirm. To those who could still struggle on, Sabin offered nothing. The privilege of struggling for achievement was the privilege of living, and to take away that right to struggle was equivalent to taking away life itself." (9-10)

Gardner's admiration for this man is so obvious that it comes as no great surprise when later in the book he turns out not to be dead at all.

Most of the Perry Mason novels Gardner wrote during the roughly twenty years that constitute his middle period are still highly readable today and a few offer rewards out of the ordinary. *The Case of the Rolling Bones* (1939) features two courtroom scenes, a wild complex plot, subtly planted clues to the truth and a pair of first-rate Mason scams, one on the street when a cop tries to give him a speeding ticket and another in court when he uses his office switchboard operator to play mind games with a hostile witness. A full-blown jury trial complete with closing arguments is the centerpiece of *The Case of the Careless Kitten* (1942), in which Della Street is charged with helping to hide a key prosecution witness. *The Case of the Crooked Candle* (1944) is considered in some quarters the finest pure detective novel in the Gardner canon, with its exceptionally long trial sequence, diagram, timetable, and detailed technical testimony about tides. In *The Case of the Half-Wakened Wife* (1945) the sky falls in on Mason more thunderously than in almost any other novel: not only is he fired by his client in mid-trial but he gets sued for defamation of character by someone he wrongly accused of the murder his client is being tried for. *The Case of the Fiery Fingers* (1951) features two jury trials with separate defendants and one of Mason's longest and most sustained cross-examinations of a hostile witness. There are many other gems in the canon awaiting rediscovery by readers with the good sense to overlook the formulaic elements that even in the best of Mason's cases are repeated endlessly.[10]

***

At around the same time he was reinventing Perry Mason for the benefit of the *Saturday Evening Post*, Gardner created another fictional world which in many respects was closer to his heart. The setting is Madison City, county seat of a farm district in rural California a couple of hours' drive from Los Angeles. The protagonists are Doug Selby, an idealistic young man who has just been elected District Attorney, and Rex Brandon, a crusty middle-aged former rancher turned sheriff who is clearly something of a stand-in for Gardner himself. There is also a large supporting cast of recurring small-town characters who, according to Gardner's friend Dean John H. Wigmore, "give the [series] a solid permanence in good literature."[11]

For our purposes the most important of these is criminal lawyer R.B. Carr, who "looked more like a successful actor than a practicing attorney. . . ." (8) and (although by this time Gardner hated Hollywood) seems tailor made to be played by John Carradine or some other preternaturally slim purveyor of movie menace. The fascination of the nine-volume D.A. series (1937-48) is that here Gardner reversed the polarities of the Perry Masons: the prosecutor and sheriff are the heroes and the defense lawyer a shyster of the first water, whose highest priority is (in Gardner's own words of a few years before) whether his client "has the necessary retainer in the form of spot cash. . . ." and whose cunning tricks on behalf of the guilty are confounded again and again like those of Squire Mason in Arthur Train's Mr. Tutt stories.[12] But there's a fundamental difference between Gardner's series and Train's. In the Mr. Tutt tales the duel is typically legalistic, with Squire Mason wielding some arcane rule of law in order to assist his evil client and Ephraim countering with an even more arcane rule of law. Carr in the D.A. series typically serves his odorous clients by hocusing evidence and Selby defeats him by detective work that ferrets out the truth.

Carr first appears in the third and perhaps finest Selby book, *The D.A. Draws a Circle* (1939), when he buys a house in Madison City, claiming he wants a retreat from the hurly-burly of Los Angeles criminal practice. Hardly has he moved in when a nude corpse is found in the barranca between Carr's house and that of lovely Rita Artrim, who was so outraged at the prospect of a shyster neighbor that she'd consulted Selby about legal means of forcing him out. Lying side by side in the body are two bullets from different guns. Whichever bullet entered the man first killed him instantly, and Selby soon suspects that Carr has covered for the murderer by himself shooting into the corpse just so as to be able to create a reasonable doubt if his client is brought to trial. At the climax it's revealed that Carr's plot was even more devious than suspected, but this is typical of the tactics Selby confronts in subsequent books. By the time the series ends, with *The D.A. Takes a Chance* (1948), Carr has been forced to marry a woman who knows too much about one of these schemes and is rooting about for a way of divorcing her without freeing her to testify against him.

***

In the same year that saw the sanitized Perry Mason debut in the *Saturday Evening Post* and the first Doug Selby novel appear in hardcover, Gardner took us back into the social Darwinian jungle when he launched yet another lawyer series for *Black Mask,* the pulp in which he had his roots. In the firm of Jonathan & Boniface there works a young man named Peter Wennick who plays six roles to the hilt: apprentice lawyer, ardent lover, wheeler-dealer, flim-flam man, snappy sleuth, and lively first-person narrator. To call the relations between him and the senior partners unorthodox is like calling King Kong a cute little monk. On the surface Pete is a law student with a sideline of chasing the secretaries, and only the surface is visible to Cedric L. Boniface, the plump, smug, precedent-spouting academician who has "bluish-white eyes, looking like two peeled hard-boiled eggs"[13] and gives the firm its image of conservative respectability. In reality Pete doesn't have the slightest interest in law. "Who wants to talk intelligently with lawyers? They don't even talk intelligently among themselves." [14] He works directly and solely for E.B. Jonathan, an amoral old Machiavellian with eyes "as smoothly moist as a snake's tongue" and a voice "as smooth as butter on hotcakes"[15], and his true function is to go outside the law to crack cases for the firm without cracking the firm's image.

Pete makes his first appearance in "Among Thieves" (September 1937) when the firm is retained to defend a young man named James Raymore who is charged with the cold-blooded murder of his lover's husband. Hardly has he set foot in the small city of Loma Vista where the crime took place than Pete learns he's in a hub of political corruption that has been cloned, as it were, from York City in Gardner's Ken Corning series, and suspects that Raymore was the victim of an official frame-up. Posing as a real-estate sharpshooter ready to pay whatever bribes it takes to get a certain piece of property rezoned, Pete is put in touch with the slimeballs who run the city and begins playing them against each other in the tradition of the Continental Op in Hammett's *Red Harvest* (1929). He uses a worthless check to open an account in the local bank under a phony name but then discovers that the name he's chosen for himself happens to be that of a wealthy investor, which means he's inadvertently committed the crime of forgery. Before this long and lightning-paced tale is over he gets trapped in the middle of a gun duel between political gangsters, extracts a confession from a wounded conspirator by pretending to be a doctor ("The anterior sclerosis shows symptoms of a traumatic regurgitation in the cardiac reflexes")[16] and falsely telling the man he's dying, endures a flogging with rubber hoses in the back room of police headquarters, and sues the city's political boss for assault and false arrest.

In "Leg Man" (February 1938) the firm is retained by Mrs. Olive Pemberton to keep a certain red-headed golddigger from starting a lawsuit against her husband Harvey. Posing as Olive's long-lost brother, Pete visits the Pemberton residence, wangles an invitation to stay on for a few days, and that evening begins spying on Harvey's brokerage business from the adjoining office suite which helpful Olive has conveniently rented and bugged. Then Pete conjures up a noble scam to recover Harvey's passionate love letters from the redhead—a plan that calls for him to impersonate in rapid succession a masked burglar, a cop and a second cop—but the con game is interrupted when Harvey is found murdered and helpful Olive tries to frame Pete for the crime. An inspired combination of speed, luck, bluff, fast talk and nimble brainwork pulls Pete out of the fire in this wonderful mini-novel.

In "Take It Or Leave It" (March 1939) the firm becomes entangled in another web of politics and murder reminiscent of Gardner's earlier *Black Mask* tales about Ken Corning. With Mayor Layton Spred and the municipal council of the city of Marlin facing a recall election after the exposure of massive corruption, the editor of the leading anti-administration newspaper is found shot to death on Spred's doorstep. The mayor claims he acted in self-defense, shooting at what he thought was a prowler, but when the ballistic evidence makes him out a liar, he and his lovely daughter Millicent retain J&B for the defense. Pete visits Marlin posing as a slot-machine racketeer, edges into the smoke-filled back rooms where the city's crooked politics is conducted, charms all the females and hocuses all the evidence in sight, and figures out the real murderer while Cedric L. Boniface sits in the law library researching precedents. Pete's solution is of arguable fairness but the story is briskly paced and with a beautifully simple and ironic key gimmick.

One of the many strengths of the short-lived Wennick series is its sardonic treatment of sacred cows. In these tales as in many Gardner novels, sex and marriage are economic weapons and combat over money is the order of the day in both home and office. There's a wonderful exchange between Wennick and E.B. Jonathan when the old man discovers Pete has been chasing one of the secretaries. Jonathan: "How are you going to play with fire without getting your fingers burnt?" Wennick: "How the hell am I going to warm my hands over a cold stove?" Jonathan (who is paying alimony to two much younger ex-wives): "You don't need to warm your hands. . . . [Women] will get you in the long run. . . . After the fighting begins, your home will seem like hell. . . . [A]limony, eating into your salary like a cancer. . . . When they see the infatuation waning, they try to find some way of capitalizing."[17] In both "Among Thieves" and "Take It Or Leave It" the police are tools of the politicians who wallow like pigs in graft and corruption and violence. But all the social criticism in the Wennick series is only marginally more important than their legal component. First and foremost is that they're grand tales, told by a superb natural storyteller at the top of his form.

***

Gardner's last series of novels began a few years after the debut of the D.A. series and ran until his death almost a third of a century later.

The protagonists of the 29 books he wrote under the byline of A.A. Fair are an obese irascible private investigator and a savvy young leg man, perhaps vaguely suggestive of Rex Stout's Nero Wolfe and Archie Goodwin but with the difference that fat foul-mouthed money-mad Bertha Cool is a woman and small street-smart Donald Lam is a former lawyer. With his eye for female beauty, genius for constructing elaborate scams, detective skill and zippy first-person narrative style, Donald is not so much an Archie Goodwin clone as Peter Wennick under an alias. And, like virtually every Gardner series character before him, he revels in the Darwinian struggle, seeming (in the words of Frank E. Robbins) "to take chances simply because of the urge to beat the opposition and come out on top."[18]

Gardner was no expert on the history of the kind of fiction he wrote but he clearly knew Melville Davisson Post's "The Corpus Delicti" (1896) and, with full acknowledgment of his source, developed the heart of that story—the lawyer's ability and willingness to advise a client how to commit a cold-blooded murder, admit the deed in open court and walk away free—into *The Bigger They Come* (1939), first and one of the finest of the Cool and Lam novels. Here's the crucial conversation between Lam and his new employer. Cool: "Donald, . . . I know all about your trouble. You were disbarred for violating professional ethics." Lam: "I wasn't disbarred and I didn't violate professional ethics." Cool: "The grievance committee reported that you did." Lam: "The grievance committee were a lot of stuffed shirts. I talked too much, that's all." Cool: "What about, Donald?" Lam: "I did some work for a client. We got to talking about the law. I told him a man could break any law and get away with it if he went about it right." Cool: "That's nothing. Anyone knows that." Lam: "The trouble is I didn't stop there. . . . I don't figure knowledge is any good unless you can apply it. I'd studied out a lot of legal tricks. I knew how to apply them." Cool: "Go on from there. What happened?" Lam: "I told this man it would be possible to commit a murder so there was nothing anyone could do about it. He said I was wrong. I got mad and offered to bet him five hundred dollars I was right, and could prove it. He said he was ready to put up the money any time I'd put up my five hundred bucks. I told him to come back the next day. That night he was arrested. He turned out to be a small-time gangster. He babbled everything he knew to the police. Among other things, he told them that I had agreed to tell him how he could commit a murder and get off scot-free. That he was to pay me five hundred dollars for the information, and then if it looked good to him, he had planned to bump off a rival gangster." Cool: "What happened?" Lam: "The grievance committee went after me hammer and tongs. They revoked my license for a year. They thought I was some sort of a shyster. I told them it was an argument and a bet. Under the circumstances, they didn't believe me. And, naturally, they took the other side of the question—that a man couldn't commit deliberate murder and go unpunished." Cool: "Could he, Donald?" Lam: "Yes." Cool: "And you know how?" Lam: "Yes. . . ." Cool: "And locked inside that head of yours is a plan by which I could kill someone and the law couldn't do a damn thing about it?" Lam: "Yes." Cool: "You mean if I was smart enough so I didn't get caught." Lam: "I don't mean anything of the sort. You'd have to put yourself in my hands and do just as I told you." Cool: "You don't mean that old gag about fixing it so they couldn't find the body?" Lam: "That is the bunk. I'm talking about a loophole in the law itself, something a man could take advantage of to commit a murder." Cool: "Tell me, Donald." Lam [laughing]: "Remember, I've been through that once." (69-71) At the climax Lam demonstrates his own thesis by getting up in a courtroom, confessing to a murder (which in fact he didn't commit) and daring the legal system to touch him for it.[19]

The ambience of this series gave Gardner the opportunity to build novels around the sort of grand scams that previously he had confined to magazine stories. Only rarely does a Lam novel deal centrally with lawyer characters and legal themes, but on those occasions Gardner is at his most Darwinian. In *Beware the Curves* (1956) Lam winds up in Orange County, masterminding the strategy of law school classmate Barney Quinn who is defense counsel at the trial of John Ansel for the six-year-old murder of his employer Karl Endicott. Detective work has convinced Lam that the real murderer was banker Cooper Hale but he has no evidence to prove it. The defense rests without putting on a case. Closing arguments begin and, following Lam's script, Barney Quinn manipulates the district attorney into committing himself to an unequivocal theory of what had happened. "He sketched Ansel, emotionally upset, blowing hot and cold. First he intended to kill Endicott then he intended not to. He had thrown his gun away and had intended to leave [Endicott's] house. Then opportunity had presented itself and he had snatched [a second] gun from the bureau and had killed Endicott." (215) The judge instructs the jury that they can find Ansel guilty of first-degree murder, second-degree murder or manslaughter. Conferring with Quinn after the jury has retired, Lam explains his strategy. "The district attorney walked into the trap. . . . If the killing was committed with the gun lying on the dresser . . . it had to be manslaughter." Quinn: "And suppose the jury convicts him of manslaughter?" Lam: ". . . [T]hen come to the rail for a whispered consultation with me." (217) The jury indeed returns a manslaughter verdict and after the whispered conference with Lam comes a scene reminiscent of Melville Davisson Post's earliest Randolph Mason tales as Quinn moves to set aside the verdict. "The crime of manslaughter outlaws within a period of three years. In other words, there can be no prosecution or conviction for manslaughter after a period of three years has elapsed from the date of the crime. . . . [S]ince the defendant has now been convicted of a manslaughter which was perpetrated more than three years ago, the Court has no alternative but to release him. . . ." (220) The novel ends with the innocent man convicted but released on a technicality and the guilty man, untouchable for the crime he committed, implausibly sentenced to life without parole after being framed by a woman on the periphery of the plot who has a penchant for having sex with men and then charging them with rape. Such breathtaking cynicism would have been unthinkable in a contemporaneous adventure of Perry Mason.

***

In the final years of his middle period as a novelist, Gardner was still living up to the contract with America he had imposed on himself almost twenty years earlier, allowing millions of readers to thrill to Mason's lawyerly hocus-pocus without moral twinges. Indeed he created some of the most ingenious variations on his standard themes in his novels of the early and middle Nineteen Fifties. *The Case of the Hesitant Hostess* (1953) begins in mid-trial and is built almost entirely around Mason's desperate attempts to demolish the testimony of the chief witness against the derelict defendant. In *The Case of the Terrified Typist* (1956) Gardner turns handsprings to keep to his contract despite a jury verdict against Mason's client and despite the fact that the defendant is indeed both guilty and without moral justification.

One of the finest demonstrations of the Gardner contract at work is found in one of the last novels of the period. In *The Case of the Lucky Loser* (1957) an anonymous woman hires Mason over the phone to sit in court during a trial and let her know his conclusions. Wealthy young Ted Balfour is charged with involuntary manslaughter after allegedly getting drunk at a party and driving his car over an unidentifiable drifter whose "skull was smashed like an eggshell." (37) A day of testimony convinces Mason that the chief prosecution witness is lying and that there will probably be a hung jury. In the next morning's paper he reads that the jury had indeed split and that Ted's attorney had then agreed to accept the verdict of the trial judge provided the penalty be limited to a fine and suspended sentence. (This sounds obscene in today's post-MADD era but was not all that shocking in the Fifties.) Later that day Mason is retained by the seductive young wife of Ted's uncle to visit the palatial home of Addison Balfour, the dying tyrant who rules the family with an iron hand, and convince the old man that his grandson is indeed innocent. Addison offers Mason a huge fee if he'll take over Ted's defense from the attorney who brokered the plea bargain. "You're not like most of these criminal lawyers. You don't want just to get a client off. You try to dig out the truth. I like that. . . ." (79-80) Then the police find a bullet in the crushed skull of the drifter and, concluding that Ted deliberately shot the man and then faked the hit-and-run to mutilate the man's face and body, charge him with Murder One. Mason goes into court and argues, with full citation to several California appellate decisions, that Ted can't be tried because, having been found guilty of involuntary manslaughter in the same matter, he's already been once in jeopardy and any further prosecution would violate the Fifth Amendment. This move would remind us irresistibly of how Melville Davisson Post's satanic lawyer Randolph Mason defended the guilty murderer in "The Corpus Delicti"—except that Gardner has made a solemn contract with us and we know Mason is not exerting his wiles on behalf of someone we don't want to see beat the system. Like the jurists in Post's early tales, Judge Cadwell is taken aback by the apparently outrageous legal result demanded by the lawyer named Mason who's arguing before him. "It comes as a shock to the Court to think that a defendant could place himself behind such a barricade of legal technicality." (138) Unlike Post's trial-level judges, Gardner's refuses to let law trump justice. ". . . I feel a higher court should pass on this matter. . . . If I hold the defendant for trial . . . , the matter can be taken to a higher court on a plea of once in jeopardy." (138) Eventually of course Mason sees the truth and exposes one of the most convoluted plots his creator ever dreamed up.

***

A few months after *Lucky Loser* was published, the Perry Mason TV series began its long prime-time run on CBS. The company that made the series, Paisano Productions, was named after Gardner's Rancho del Paisano in Temecula, which in turn was named for El Paisano, one of the dozens of characters Gardner had created for the pulps. Not only did Gardner own a controlling interest in the company, but between 1957 and 1966 he put in long hours closely supervising the scripts.

There is no better index of how far his concept of lawyering had changed since the early 1930s than the memoranda he dictated in his capacity as adviser to the TV series. "[O]ne of the first things to do is to start with some character who is to become Perry Mason's client and to make the audience like that character. . . . Therefore when I see these scripts come in [where, although Gardner doesn't put it this way, the client is a Holmesian 'Bad Man'] I feel that we are selling our character down the river. I want to vomit at the idea of the great Perry Mason with his sense of justice, his basic faith in human nature, descending so low as to be hired to represent a person of that caliber. . . . [I]t is a basic rule of the Perry Mason stories that the audience must want the character to be represented by Perry Mason to come out on top."[20]

During the program's decade-long run Gardner somehow found time to dictate new Perry Mason novels, but to an increasing extent he came to think of them as fodder for the TV series and they soon began showing the marks of the medium's infantile restrictions. The courtroom tiger of the earlier books, evolved into the kinder, gentler lawyer of the middle period, now mutated into a close cousin of the character Raymond Burr was portraying every week on the small screen, a ponderous bureaucrat mindful of the law's niceties. The last ten or twelve years' worth of Mason novels are as chaotic as most of the episodes of the weekly TV episodes. Plot holes left unplugged, ludicrous motivations, mush-witted reasoning, characters who know things they couldn't possibly have known, solutions that don't begin to explain who did what to whom, daisy chains of multiple coincidence, all are found abundantly in late Masons. Even the courtroom sequences are often as wretchedly constructed as their TV-series counterparts: in *The Case of the Daring Divorcee* (1964) Hamilton Burger introduces totally irrelevant evidence just so that certain story elements can be furthered, and in *The Case of the Worried Waitress* (1966) he forgets to present evidence that a crime was even committed.

But even in these sad last years there are a few highlights. *The Case of the Bigamous Spouse* (1961) has a beautifully mounted plot and a variety of sharp comments on everything from sales technique and modern marriage to police lawlessness and the undertaking business. Much of *The Case of the Ice-Cold Hands* (1962) deals not with murder but with an intriguing civil issue: who owns the proceeds when a winning bet at the racetrack is made with embezzled funds? In *The Case of the Phantom Fortune* (1964) Mason all but reverts to his original incarnation, playing fast and loose with the penal law while protecting his client's wife from a blackmailer, then finding himself suspected of trying to hang a felony charge on an innocent party. Mason is given superb cross-examination scenes in *The Case of the Shapely Shadow* (1960), *The Case of the Reluctant Model* (1961), *The Case of the Mischievous Doll* (1963), and *The Case of the Amorous Aunt* (1964), while *The Case of the Troubled Trustee* (1965) is distinguished by Hamilton Burger's savage cross-examination of Mason's client.

At age 75 Gardner seems to have become painfully aware of the ease with which, before subsequent reforms in civil commitment law, unscrupulous relatives with a hired doctor and lawyer in their pockets could railroad a mentally sound senior into a death-trap sanitarium. The result of his concerns was *The Case of the Beautiful Beggar* (1965), the most excitingly inventive and deeply personal of all his late novels. A young woman who claims to be the niece of a wealthy 75-year-old entrepreneur (another Gardner self-portrait?) begs Mason to rescue her uncle from greedy relatives who have had the old man institutionalized and themselves appointed conservators of his property. Mason's conduct of the proceeding over the old man's competency and his gorgeous banking gimmick to get some of the client's money back occupy the first half of the book. Late in the game comes the inevitable murder-and-trial complex which, as in so many late Gardner books, is routine, boring, and punctuated by incredible runs of lucky guesswork on Mason's part.

By the time the Mason TV series ended its run (with a case where the judge was played by Gardner himself), the decisions of the Supreme Court under Earl Warren had almost completely undermined what had always been the premise of the Mason novels: that a defendant menaced by the underhanded tactics of police and prosecutors needed a pyrotechnician like Mason in his or her corner. Once the so-called theory of trial by ambush had become obsolete, once the Court had ruled that convictions obtained by such tactics were unconstitutional and had to be reversed, Mason lost his *raison d'etre*.

The new wave of Court decisions roughly coincided with Gardner's discovery that he had cancer. He responded to both threats in the same way: by carrying on as if nothing had happened. No changes in the American legal system or within his slowly dying body could keep him from doing what he wanted with his own life or the life of the universe he had created.[21] When Mason in *The Case of the Velvet Claws* said: "I fight!" he was speaking for Gardner too. What he had written in *The Case of the Lucky Loser* about Addison Balfour he lived in his own flesh. "Despite the sentence of death which had been pronounced upon him, he continued to be the same old irascible, unpredictable fighter. Disease had ravaged his body, but the belligerency of the man's mind remained unimpaired." (46) He kept on fighting till the end, which came on March 11, 1970.

***

I discovered Perry Mason when I was thirteen and read most of his cases three or four times apiece during my eight years in high school and college. In my senior year, when I signed up to take the Law School Admission Test, it was a blind leap in the dark: all I knew about law I had learned from Gardner's novels. As chance or fate would have it, I performed well enough to receive scholarship offers I couldn't refuse. A year and a half after graduating from New York University School of Law, chance or fate stepped in again and I began corresponding with Gardner, having no idea that he was dying. Near the end of his first and longest letter to me, dated January 22, 1969, he mentioned his declining output of fiction and blamed it on "the terrific influx of mail. I just don't know how to handle this mail. I feel that letters should be answered but there are times when it seems an impossible task. My secretaries counted up one day (which was exceptional) and found I had dictated more than twenty thousand words of correspondence on that day and I was still far from being caught up." We exchanged a number of letters afterwards but I never got around to explaining how in effect he had turned me into a lawyer, or to thank him.

Now at last I've done both.

NOTES

In order to avoid a huge number of redundant endnotes I have adopted the practice of providing relevant information in the text if feasible. Every quotation from a novel by Erle Stanley Gardner is followed by a parenthesized number referring to the page(s) where the quotation is found in the first edition of that novel. Most quotations from Gardner's correspondence and memoranda are followed by a parenthesis with the letters DBH and a number referring to the page(s) where the quotation is found in Dorothy B. Hughes, *Erle Stanley Gardner: The Case of the Real Perry Mason* (Morrow, 1978). My thanks to Jon L. Breen, J. Randolph Cox and Marvin Lachman for a critical reading of this essay; to Lynn Munroe for locating one of the most elusive of Gardner's lawyer stories; to Donald A. Yates for supplying crucial page references; and to the late Mary Dougherty, my own Della Street, who rescued me from many a word-processing blunder.

---

1. Alva Johnston, *The Case of Erle Stanley Gardner* (Morrow, 1947), 58-62.

2. For representative specimens of Gardner's Western stories, see Erle Stanley Gardner, *Whispering Sands: Stories of Gold Fever and the Western Desert*, ed. Charles G. Waugh & Martin H. Greenberg (Morrow, 1981), and Erle Stanley Gardner, *Pay Dirt and Other Whispering Sands Stories*, ed. Charles G. Waugh & Martin H. Greenberg (Morrow, 1983).

3. These were collected in Erle Stanley Gardner, *The Human Zero*, ed. Martin H. Greenberg & Charles G. Waugh (Morrow, 1981).

4. A number of the Jenkins tales are collected in Erle Stanley Gardner, *The Blonde in Lower Six* (Carroll & Graf, 1990), and Erle Stanley Gardner, *Dead Men's Letters* (Carroll & Graf, 1990).

5. For a selection of early Pry adventures from *Gang World*, see Erle Stanley Gardner, *The Adventures of Paul Pry* (Mysterious Press, 1989).

6. An assortment of this character's exploits can be found in Erle Stanley Gardner, *The Amazing Adventures of Lester Leith*, ed. Ellery Queen (Davis Publications, 1981).

7. The entire Corning series is collected in Erle Stanley Gardner, *Honest Money*, ed. Martin H. Greenberg & Charles G. Waugh (Carroll & Graf, 1991).

8. Oliver Wendell Holmes, Jr., "The Path of the Law," 10 Harvard Law Review 457 (1897).

9. See Chapter 2 of this book.

10. For tightly compressed but well-informed and accurate summaries of most of Gardner's novels, see Jon L. Breen, *Novel Verdicts: A Guide to Courtroom Fiction* (Scarecrow Press, 2d ed. 1999), at 62-84.

11. Alva Johnston, note 1 *supra*, at 16.

12. See Chapter 3 of this book.

13. Erle Stanley Gardner, "Among Thieves," *Black Mask*, September 1937, at 8.

14. *Id.* at 10.

15. *Ibid.*

16. *Id.* at 29.

17. *Id.* at 11.

18. Frank E. Robbins, "The Firm of Cool and Lam," in *The Mystery Writer's Art*, ed. Francis M. Nevins (Bowling Green University Popular Press, 1970), 142. This essay was first published in *Michigan Alumnus Quarterly Review*, Spring 1953.

19. The ploy works as follows: A commits a murder in California, then drives across the state line into Arizona where he proceeds to frame himself on a charge of obtaining property under false pretenses, although leaving a legal escape hatch open for himself. He then drives back to California, runs through the quarantine station at the border, is chased and caught by California policemen and locked up in the border town of El Centro. In due course he is legally extradited to Arizona to

face the false pretenses charge. Once he clears himself and that charge is officially dropped, he confesses to the California murder. But when California moves to extradite him, he files a writ of habeas corpus, arguing that on these facts he can't be compelled to return. "The only authority which one state has to take prisoners from another state comes from the organic law which provides that fugitives from justice may be extradited from one sovereign state to another. I am not a fugitive from justice. . . . [A] man is not a fugitive from a state unless he flees from that state. He doesn't flee from that state unless he does so voluntarily and in order to avoid arrest. I did not flee from California. I was dragged from California. I was taken out under legal process to answer for a crime of which I was innocent. I claimed that I was innocent. I came to Arizona and established my innocence. Any time I get good and ready to go back to California, California can arrest me for murder. Until I get good and ready to go back, I can stay here and no power on earth can make me budge." (269-270) [Citing *In re Whittington*, 34 Cal. App. 344, 67 Pac. 404 (1917), and *People v. Jones*, 54 Cal. App. 423, 201 Pac. 944 (1921).] Gardner's friend Dean Wigmore "scoffed" at this device but, after the author had literally written a brief for him on the issue, "admitted that the alleged loophole in the law had greater possibilities than he had at first supposed." Alva Johnston, note 1 *supra*, 16-17. *Jones* involved a man who had fled to Mexico after being convicted of manslaughter in Oklahoma. Mexican officials later took him forcibly across the border into California, where he was arrested by California authorities and held for extradition to Oklahoma. The court held that Jones' contention of an illegal conspiracy between Mexican and U.S. authorities was unsupported by any evidence and that, even if his removal from Mexico were irregular under Mexican law, he couldn't challenge that procedure in the courts of California. This case is easily distinguishable from the situation in *The Bigger They Come*. *Whittington*, which is much closer to the facts in the novel, was all but overruled by the California Supreme Court near the end of Gardner's life. *In re Patterson*, 64 Cal.2d 357, 49 Cal. Rptr. 801, 411 P.2d 897 (1966).

20. Francis L. Fugate & Roberta B. Fugate, *Secrets of the World's Best-Selling Writer: The Storytelling Techniques of Erle Stanley Gardner* (Morrow, 1980), 100.

21. *The Case of the Fabulous Fake* (1969) was the last Mason novel published in Gardner's lifetime and the only one in which he made a concession to the mood of the times. In a sequence unconnected with the main plot, Mason defends his only minority client in the entire canon, a young black man falsely accused of a pawnshop robbery.

CHAPTER 5

When Celluloid Lawyers Started To Speak

By the criteria of quality, quantity and leitmotifs, those movies that take law, lawyers, lawyering and justice as their subjects—a loosely connected assortment of films which I hereby dub juriscinema—enjoyed the first of three golden ages between the dawn of talking films in the late 1920s and the descent of strict self-censorship in Hollywood in mid-1934. Many films of juriscinema's second golden age, which roughly coincides with the flourishing of the Warren Court, and of the third, the post- and anti-Warren Court era that still seems to be with us in the 21st century, and certain individual films that fall between the great ages, have been discussed in a spate of essays and even a few books published over the last several years. Most films of the first golden age have been neglected.

This neglect is unfortunate but far from unaccountable. Discussion of old movies is difficult to say the least when many of the films are all but inaccessible. The videocassette and DVD revolutions have facilitated factually reliable discussion of all sorts of cinematic subjects but juriscinema of the first golden age is not one of them: very few of the important titles in that category have ever been made available in those formats. This is one reason why not a single film from the period is discussed in the leading guide to juriscinema,[1] whose authors restricted themselves to commercially obtainable titles. That a significant number of the films discussed in this chapter are otherwise accessible (at least by those who have cable or satellite) is due largely to Turner Classic Movies, without whose vast resources the chapter could never have been written. Films from studios whose backlog is not owned by TCM must be discussed on the basis of reference sources—an unsatisfactory situation but, thanks mainly to the American Film Institute, not an impossible one.

Much of this chapter consists of capsule summaries of movies, each one intended as a sort of miniature model that will provide an idea both of the film and of the role law, lawyers and/or lawyering play in it. After some discussion of the very earliest Hollywood films of the period with strong juriscinematic interest (all of them dating from 1928-29), we move to the films of this type released between 1930 and mid-1934. The single finest film of legal interest deserves and receives a section all to itself. Many of the rest are treated in affinity groups or according to genre (women's pictures, comedies, Westerns). Films that resist such organization are discussed chronologically in a "potpourri" section. Finally we consider how the first golden age of juriscinema came to an end after the imposition of strict self-censorship. In order to prevent this rather long chapter from becoming a book, films from the so-called Poverty Row studios are (with a handful of exceptions) excluded, as are movies with only peripheral legal significance.

Before descending into the data it may be helpful to offer a few pointers on how to evaluate them. Excluding comedies and Westerns, many of the films we are about to explore can be divided into (1) those focusing on the emotional entanglements of one or more women and (2) those focusing on the personal and professional entanglements of one or more men. Films in the first category were aimed primarily at female viewers and tell the story of a woman who either becomes involved with a lawyer or goes on trial, or both. These so-called "women's pictures" or "weepies" predate the coming of sound but became dominant in the first years of talking pictures when, far more often than in silent days and for obvious reasons, the female lead would find herself in a courtroom. Films in the second category were aimed primarily at a male audience and tell the story of a man who may or may not have a law degree but in one way or another gets caught up in a situation involving lawyers and law. The films aimed at women tend to be slowly paced and full of emotional outbursts, while those aimed at men tend to move like greased lightning, with plenty of crackling dialogue and physical action and a bitingly cynical take on whatever milieu they portray. These two categories are mutually exclusive. But a film in either category or in neither (a comedy, for example, or a Western) may also have one or more lawyer characters whom viewers are clearly meant to despise, and in considering these cinematic lawyers it will be worthwhile to distinguish between those whose perfidy is specific to their profession and those whose profession is unconnected with their villainy. I offer these life preservers in the hope that they'll save readers from drowning in the sea of detail that follows.

***

The early films dealing with law, lawyers, lawyering and justice cannot begin to be understood without a capsule survey of certain aspects of the American scene in the years immediately preceding the birth of talking pictures. We who have lived through the cultural upheavals of the past few decades tend to think of the 1920s as a dead Puritanical time, but those who lived and were young at the time saw it quite differently. In a country theoretically founded on individual freedom, they saw undreamt-of practical freedoms exploding into life all around them. Radical iconoclasts like Theodore Dreiser and Sinclair Lewis were publishing novels that would never have seen print in any earlier decade. Equally radical journalists like H.L. Mencken and Ring Lardner were writing essays and short stories that debunked everything dear to the conventional American heart. Young men and women discarded their parents' inhibitions and joined the sexual revolution that was described almost fifteen years ago by the sardonic centenarian Jacques Barzun (1907-2012), perhaps the longest-lived person who shared memories of that decade with readers.

". . . Lovemaking as an art and the techniques to be mastered for adequate, not to say, professional, performance became a concern of the wider public. Sexology was welcomed to the circle of ologies, while the popularization of Freud led to the belief that suppressing the sexual instinct was dangerous. . . ."[2]

". . . [N]early everywhere the previous requirement of adultery as the sole ground [for divorce] gave way. . . . Those who resisted this great drive to acknowledge copulation as a human right and a subject of constant public interest waged a losing battle."[3]

The insanity of Prohibition inspired a national orgy of alcohol consumption, and the corruption of government at every level that followed in Prohibition's wake and was manifest even to the dimmest observer fueled a vast cynicism about American political institutions and officeholders—and also about lawyers.

Near the end of the decade when the social, political and religious dogmas of previous generations were seen as "a farrago of balderdash"[4] came the technological breakthrough that permitted sound to be recorded directly on film. Inevitably, the first talking movies shared the cultural orientation of their time. Add an insatiable hunger for film stories full of dialogue to be captured by the new technology, and it followed as night follows day that Hollywood would become a sellers' market for (1) stage plays, which by definition were heavy on dialogue, and (2) plays and short stories and novels and original scenarios that collectively would create what I have dubbed juriscinema. For what could offer more in the way of nonstop dialogue than oratorical duels, whether in or out of court, between lawyers?

***

Almost as soon as talking films were feasible at all, their patrons began to see and of course to hear a cycle of courtroom melodramas. "Such movies," says Alexander Walker, "had obvious attractions: they were cheap and quick to make, required few sets, even when obligatory 'flashbacks' from the evidence were involved; and, above all, they gave the studios ample opportunity to do what they had spent many millions equipping themselves for—talk."[5]

Perhaps the first of the breed was *On Trial* (Warner Bros. © 12/29/28), which was directed by Archie Mayo and based on the 1919 stage play of the same name by Elmer Rice, whom we shall encounter again later in this chapter. During the trial of Robert Strickland (Bert Lytell) for the murder of his business associate Gerald Trask (Holmes Herbert), Strickland takes the stand, confesses his guilt and asks for an end to the proceedings. His request is denied and the next witness is the dead man's widow Joan Trask (Pauline Frederick), who describes the events surrounding her husband's murder. (If she's a prosecution witness as she must be, how did the defendant get to testify ahead of her?) The next day Strickland's young daughter Doris (Vondell Darr) is called—by which side once again isn't specified—and testifies that shortly before shooting Trask her father had learned that his wife May Strickland (Lois Wilson) had spent the day with the man. Finally May takes the stand and describes Trask's penchant for lechery and blackmail. On this basis the jury returns a verdict of not guilty! The talking sequences of this film were either recorded or reproduced with a faulty system which, according to *Variety* (21 November 1928), made the actors' lines "no more than muffled sounds, almost indistinct . . . and imperfectly synchronized."[6]

Next out of the can was *The Bellamy Trial* (MGM © 12/10/28), directed by Monta Bell from his own scenario based on the 1927 novel of the same name by Frances Noyes Hart. Stephen Bellamy (Kenneth Thomson) and lovely Sue Ives (Leatrice Joy) are put on trial for the murder of Bellamy's wife Mimi (Margaret Livingston). Both defendants take the stand—whether they knew they had a Constitutional right not to is unclear like all other legal issues in these primitive talkies—and are brutally cross-examined by the District Attorney (Charles Middleton), who repeatedly jabs a knife into a cast of Mimi's bust while questioning them. Despite prosecutorial tactics worthy of Middleton's later Ming the Merciless character in Flash Gordon serials, both defendants are found not guilty. Finally a surprise witness comes forward who saw the murder and clears Bellamy and Ives of the slightest suspicion of guilt.

Third in the cycle came *His Captive Woman* (First National © 2/11/29), directed by George Fitzmaurice from a scenario by Carey Wilson based on Donn Byrne's short story "Changeling" (collected in *Changeling and Other Stories*, 1923). The film opens with cabaret dancer Anna Janssen (Dorothy Mackaill) on trial for murdering her wealthy lover. But once the witness stand is taken by Tom McCarthy (Milton Sills), the stolid policeman who had arrested her and brought her back from the South Seas for trial, we morph from forensic oratory into a long silent flashback depicting how he and Anna had fallen in love after being shipwrecked on a desert island. The judge is so impressed that he sentences the couple to get married and live on that same island for the rest of their lives! *Variety*'s verdict (10 April 1929) was that the filmmakers "have so strained, twisted, pummeled and otherwise mistreated plausibility that the resultant product is pretty silly."[7] Sounds like one of the world's great understatements to me.

Perhaps the best known among the early specimens of juriscinema is *Coquette* (Pickford/United Artists © 3/20/29), which was the first talking film for silent superstar Mary Pickford and the beginning of the end of her career. Sam Taylor directed this adaptation of the 1928 play of the same name by George Abbott and Anne Preston Bridgers. Taking the part played on the stage by Helen Hayes, Pickford played Norma Besant, a flirtatious Southern belle whose latest conquest is the proud but crude hillbilly Michael Jeffery (John Mack Brown). Norma's physician father (John Sainpolis) refuses to let the couple marry, orders Jeffery out of his house and later, learning that they've spent a night together (perhaps under innocent circumstances), shoots the young man down in cold blood. His friend and attorney Robert Wentworth (George Irving) pressures Norma to claim—without either of them ever using the word of course—that Jeffery had raped her.

Wentworth: "Norma, our only chance to save your father is based on the unwritten law—to say that he killed a man who had ruined his daughter's good name. You understand? You've got to say that he has avenged a wrong—that Michael was a beast."

Norma: "A beast. My Michael—a beast?"

Wentworth: "Norma, darling, I know you're innocent and that your father was mistaken. But don't you see, if he was mistaken he had killed an innocent man! And to save his life, you must say he was justified in killing Michael—and that you're proud of him."

Norma: "Pwoud of him? [She delivers all her lines Elmer Fudd style.] I wish I'd never seen him! I hate him! I hate him! He killed the only thing in life I love. He did that to me and I don't care what happens to him now. . . . I'd be glad to see him hang!"

But in the three months between this dialogue and the trial, she changes her mind—exactly why is never made clear—and, on direct examination as a defense witness, perjures herself.

Wentworth: "Did Michael Jeffery make love to you there?"

Norma: "Yes."

Wentworth: "Did you resist him?"

Norma: "Yes."

Wentworth: "But he forced his attentions?"

Norma: "Yes."

Wentworth: "And you could not resist his lovemaking?"

Norma: "No."

Wentworth: "And he made you yield?"

Norma: "Yes."

Wentworth: "He made you yield to an extreme?"

Norma: "Yes."
Wentworth (obviously playing to the jury): "Then he did what would justify any father in killing him!"
Norma: "Yes."

After objecting to the last exchange and being rightly sustained, the prosecutor (Henry Kolker) begins his cross-examination. Norma denies she loves Michael or planned to marry him, claims he was promiscuous ("He was just a—a beast!"), then breaks down on the stand. Dr. Besant approaches her in the witness box and, while every law-trained viewer howls with disbelief, says: "Norma, look me in the eye. . . . Norma, have you been telling the truth about that night?" He asks her forgiveness and kisses her, then turns to the bench and makes an impromptu address to the court.

> "Your Honor, my daughter wishes to retract all of her testimony. What she told you about herself and Michael Jeffery was a sacrifice on her part to save my life. And I cannot accept that sacrifice. My daughter's an innocent girl, and I killed a man who was guilty of no wrong. I'm aware that I owe my life to the state. As a Southern gentleman, sir, I have never failed to pay my debts. And I stand ready now to offer my life for one I've taken."

At this point he goes to the evidence table, takes the murder pistol—which, I kid you not, is still loaded!—and blows his brains out in open court. In the stage play it was Helen Hayes who committed suicide but the filmmakers thought the audience would never accept such an act by sweet little Mary. It defies belief considering the Suth'n-fried-ham emoting by almost everyone in the cast, but Pickford won an Academy Award for her performance in this unintended gigglefest.

Thru Different Eyes (Fox © 4/16/29), directed by John G. Blystone and apparently the first of these courtroom melodramas not based on a pre-existing literary or dramatic work, takes us to the trial of Harvey

Manning (Edmund Lowe) for the murder of his best friend Jack Winfield (Warner Baxter), whose body was found in the Manning home. The prosecution's story, illustrated by flashbacks, is that Manning's wife Viola (Mary Duncan) got him out of the house so she could have a tryst with Winfield but that Manning returned unexpectedly, caught them in flagrante and shot his rival dead. The defense account, also depicted in flashback, is that Viola had been a faithful wife and that Winfield's hopeless passion for her had driven him to suicide. The jury finds Manning guilty but then Viola takes the stand and, in testimony shown in yet more flashbacks, claims that she killed Winfield herself, to get even for his having impregnated and dumped her years before. Which story are we to believe? Clearly what makes *Thru Different Eyes* of greater cinematic and historical interest than its coevals is that to a certain extent it prefigures such classics as *Citizen Kane* and *Rashomon*, depicting key events and characters several times and each time from a different viewpoint.

Silent star Norma Shearer made her talkie debut in *The Trial of Mary Dugan* (MGM © 5/20/29), which was directed by the playwright Bayard Veiller and based on his own 1928 stage drama of the same name. Like few if any movie directors then or now, Veiller rehearsed his cast in front of a live audience for two weeks before shooting began. The prologue shows Shearer as the title character having a fit of hysteria as she's taken from her cell to the courtroom where she is to stand trial for the murder of her wealthy lover, who was found stabbed to death in their love nest. When defense attorney Edmund West (Lewis Stone) does little or nothing to cross-examine prosecution witnesses, Mary's fledgling lawyer brother Jimmy (Raymond Hackett) protests and eventually takes over his sister's defense. He puts her on the stand but is horrified at the gist of her testimony: that she had been the mistress of four different men in order to get the money to put him through law school! Undaunted, Jimmy goes on to prove that the real murderer was none other than Edmund West, first establishing that the murderer was left-handed, then tossing a knife at West which the latter instinctively catches with—well, enough said. Could this be the origin of the device Atticus Finch used in *To Kill a Mockingbird* more than thirty years later to show that *his* client was innocent?

Madame X (MGM © 7/29/29) was directed by the distinguished stage actor Lionel Barrymore, who improved hugely on existing talkie technique when he had the recording microphones put on fishing poles so that the actors could move around during dialogue. The device didn't improve their performances, which are so absurdly hyperemotional that viewers today are more likely to roll on the floor giggling than to break down in tears as intended. Unlike the other films in the cycle, this one was set in France—naturally enough since it was based on a French play by Alexandre Bisson which debuted on the New York stage in 1910 and had been adapted into a silent feature ten years later. The backstory shows Jacqueline Floriot (Ruth Chatterton) leaving her diplomat husband (Lewis Stone) for a playboy. When she returns to care for her sick son, her husband throws her out. Eventually she meets and forms a liaison with the international cardsharp Laroque (Ulrich Haupt). Years later they return penniless to France and in a rage she shoots Laroque when she learns that he plans to blackmail her husband. Since she won't reveal her name to the authorities, and the brand new young attorney (Raymond Hackett) assigned to represent her never volunteers his, neither of them is aware that he is not only her lawyer but her son.

The elder Floriot offers young Raymond advice that will soon break his heart. "It's an old trick in law but it's always been a good one. Whenever you find a woman in grave distress as this one is, you blame everything she is upon some man." As a favor to the former Attorney General of France, who is eager to observe his son's first case, the court makes a place for the older man on the bench. It's from that vantage point that he and "Madame X" recognize each other and the climactic tear-jerking begins.

From her box the defendant addresses the jury, still without identifying herself but claiming she shot Laroque so that her son, whom she also won't identify, wouldn't discover her degrading life.

> "I have said I wouldn't speak but I will. Oh yes, yes, I will! But no one else must. No one!. . . . I'm only trying to stop anyone from trying to help me—from trying to save me. That someone is a boy! A son of mine! Somewhere in this world. . . . That boy thinks I'm dead. Oh, I want him to think it! . . . I killed [Laroque] to keep that boy, who is flesh of my flesh and blood of my blood, from knowing what I was—what I am."

At this point she faints. The prosecutor then asks the jury to impose the death penalty. "She killed a man to save others. Very beautiful. But not as yet legal." Then for the first time the prosecutor mentions the name of her defense counsel. Realizing at long last that her lawyer is also her son, she breaks down. Still unaware that she's his mother, Raymond makes his final plea along the lines his father had suggested. As he orates, the audience becomes aware that in this version of *Madame X* (although apparently not in any of the countless remakes that came later) the title serves not just to provide a convenient tag for the woman who has refused to give her name but also to evoke the cross and present her as a Jesus figure.

> "Here she is, willing to go to her death that others might never feel the shame which they should. . . . This man, this husband of whom she speaks, should not be protected! . . . He should be here on trial and not she! For he is without heart—without soul. . . . The man who is so good, so pure himself, he wouldn't give another creature one more chance! Who is this man? Where does he come from?. . . . It would be well for all men and women in France that we know the name of

this—this paragon who lives amongst us. And the boy of whom she speaks!. . . . The young man who would not pick this poor creature up and take her to his heart and call her mother, in preference to touching the hand of the man who calls himself his father, is no man, and has no right to a mother!. . . . Even now she asks that nothing be done for her. Oh, gentlemen, you must believe, you must feel what I do! . . . Something within my heart here today tells me we are crucifying this woman without understanding her. You cannot convict this woman! You cannot deny her mercy. For mercy is something she has never known."

Raymond then breaks down in tears himself.

While the jury deliberates, the three Floriots are reunited in the woman's holding cell and Madame X speaks to the young man who, being rather dense, never catches on that she's his mother.

"I don't care about anything now that I know that it's you—you, who pleaded for me. Because, you see, after listening to you I know that my son, wherever he is, would treat me as his mother—no matter what I've done—no matter what becomes of me. . . . This boy has just told me what my boy would do. . . . I haven't got anything to pay you with for what you've done for me. But I can give you a mother's—kiss. If—if you'll let me."

She kisses Raymond, who still has no idea who she is, and falls over dead as this orgy of juristic tear-jerking comes to an end.

***

A silent lawyer is a contradiction in terms. This fact alone explains why lawyers acting as lawyers were all but unknown on the silent screen. Conversely, once all-talking films had irrevocably displaced both the silent cinema and the part-talkie hybrids like *On Trial*, it was inevitable that moviegoers would see and, more important, hear an abundance of lawyer characters on the screen.

Approaching the subject from behind a Rawlsian veil of ignorance, one might reasonably assume that in any film with a significant legal component the protagonist—i.e. the character played by the actor top-billed in the credits—would be described as a lawyer *and* would be seen performing lawyerly functions. As we shall see, the assumption is correct in many instances of early juriscinema including *Counsellor at Law* (the only film of its kind so excellent that it deserves a section all its own) and many near-classics. But an essay rigidly confined to movies of this description would not only be less than comprehensive but would require some quite interesting films to be left, as it were, on the cutting-room floor. Therefore readers will also encounter in these pages films (1) where the protagonist is described as a lawyer but is never seen doing a lawyer's work, or (2) where the lawyer character performing lawyerly functions is a significant member of the cast but not the protagonist, or (3) where, as in most of the primitives considered above, no important character is a lawyer but the film climaxes in court. This chapter might have been organized according to the above categories, but a consequence of doing so would have been that films with similar content would be considered in isolation from each other. It seemed sounder to group films with similar content in the same section, with a preliminary admonition to the reader to keep in mind the distinctions drawn above.

Of course, some interesting examples of juriscinema are impossible to pigeonhole neatly: they owe nothing to the infamous William J. Fallon, nor is their protagonist a woman or a person of color, nor do they fall within the genres of the "women's picture," the gangster film, the whodunit, the comedy or the Western. The only feasible approach with such films is to lump them together in chronological order, as I now proceed to do.

The Furies (First National © 3/19/30, directed by Alan Crosland from a screenplay by Forrest Halsey based on Zoe

Akins' 1928 stage play of the same name) begins with Fifi Sands (Lois Wilson) announcing at a dinner party that her husband, a notorious womanizer, has agreed at last to give her a divorce, although she is refusing any alimony. Then Mr. Sands is found murdered and suspicion soon falls on Fifi's childhood sweetheart Owen McDonald (Theodor von Eltz), who still loves her. Fifi prevails upon her late husband's lawyer Oliver Bedlow (H.B. Warner) to represent McDonald but it's a poor choice for at least two reasons beyond the obvious conflict of interest: Bedlow wants Fifi for himself and he's the murderer. At the climax of the film Bedlow locks Fifi in an apartment and reveals the truth to her and, when rescuers come pounding at the door, leaps out a window to his death.

Manslaughter (Paramount © 8/9/30, directed by George Abbott from his own screenplay based on Alice Duer Miller's 1921 novel of the same name) features that rara avis of early juriscinema, a lawyer acting honorably as a lawyer. Spoiled heiress Lydia Thorne (Claudette Colbert) is sweet on crusading district attorney Dan O'Bannon (Fredric March), but when her reckless driving causes the death of a traffic cop who was trying to give her a speeding ticket, he prosecutes her for the film's titular crime and the result of his impassioned no-one's-above-the-law oratory is that she gets sent to prison. She vows to get even with him, but her time behind bars teaches her compassion for the lowly. Released after two years thanks to influential family connections, she finds that O'Bannon has gone into private practice and tries her damndest to get him fired until she realizes that she still loves him. How the film ends is too obvious to need recounting.

Brothers (Columbia © 9/18/30, directed by Walter Lang from a screenplay by John Thomas Neville and Charles R. Condon based on Herbert Ashton Jr.'s 1928 stage play of the same name) starred Bert Lytell as twins who are adopted into different social classes and don't learn of each other's existence until they're adults. Eddie Connolly becomes a piano player in a gin joint while his luckier sibling Bob Naughton is taken into the home of a well-to-do lawyer (Howard Hickman) and himself becomes a brilliant attorney, although one with a drinking problem. The story heats up when Bob gets into a fight with and kills an understandably miffed criminal whose wife had become Bob's mistress after Bob had unsuccessfully defended him. Where does this fight take place? Why, in the gin joint where Eddie Connolly tickles the ivories! The result of course is that Bob's unknown twin brother is identified as the murderer. Bob clears Eddie but then collapses and is taken to a sanitarium, and at the request of Bob's adoptive father Eddie impersonates his twin and comes to live in the Naughton house where he falls in love with Bob's fiancée Norma (Dorothy Sebastian). Just as he's about to do the noble thing—forsake Norma, leave the haunts of the rich and return to his humble origins—word arrives of Bob's death, and he decides to continue as his brother and marry the woman they both loved. One can't help wondering what happened the first time he had to pass as a lawyer.

The Lawyer's Secret (Paramount © 5/6/31, directed by Louis Gasnier and Max Marcin from a screenplay by Lloyd Corrigan and Max Marcin based on an original story by James Hilary Finn) seems to be the only film of the early 1930s that deals with the attorney-client relationship. One night at a sleazy gambling joint, sailor Joe Hart (Richard Arlen) loses heavily and, in order to keep playing, sells his gun to fellow gambler Laurie Roberts (Charles "Buddy" Rogers). After losing his last cent, Joe steals a car to get back to his ship. Meanwhile Laurie, who also lost heavily, is convinced by a gambler known as The Weasel (Francis McDonald) that the wheel was fixed. They break into the joint after hours and are trying to open the safe when they are caught by the proprietor, whom The Weasel kills with the gun Laurie bought from Joe. Laurie returns home late to his sister Kay (Fay Wray), who is engaged to lawyer Drake Norris (Clive Brook), and, under attorney-client privilege, tells him the story. What happens next of course is that poor Joe Hart is charged with the murder, put on trial and sentenced to hang. His girlfriend Beatrice Stevens (Jean Arthur) begs Norris to handle the appeal but, for reasons obvious to the viewer, he refuses. When

Kay begs him to reconsider, he admits that he's been told the truth about the murder in a confidential communication but refuses to identify his client. He urges Laurie to clear Joe but Laurie refuses. When Joe's appeal is denied, Drake goes first to the District Attorney and then to the governor, telling them everything but the name of his client, but to no avail. The night before Joe is to be executed, two of his sailor friends trick The Weasel into a meeting with Laurie Roberts which leads to Laurie blurting out the truth where others can hear it. The Weasel gets the death penalty, Laurie draws a few years in prison and Joe is released.

The lawyer character in *A Free Soul* (MGM © 6/3/31, directed by Clarence Brown from a screenplay by John Meehan and Becky Gardiner based on Adela Rogers St. Johns' 1927 novel and Willard Mack's 1928 stage play of the same name) is Stephen Ashe (Lionel Barrymore), a hard-drinking, free-thinking San Francisco criminal lawyer apparently modeled on Earl Rogers, whose daughter wrote the novel the film was based on. Stephen's free-spirited daughter Jan (Norma Shearer) is the only member of the Ashe family who isn't appalled when he shows up at a family dinner drunk and accompanied by Ace Wilfong (Clark Gable), a gangster he's just gotten off on a murder charge.[8] Attracted by Ace's dangerous quality, Jan leaves her conventional fiancé Dwight Winthrop (Leslie Howard) behind and goes along when her father and Ace walk out of the party. That is the beginning of the affair which, despite Stephen's outrage at her having taken up with a "mongrel," continues until one night father and daughter make a sort of contract: Stephen will give up liquor and Jan will give up Ace. They go off to the mountains for a vacation but resume their bad habits as soon as they're home. While Stephen goes on a binge, Jan returns to Ace but finally sees that he's a swine and dumps him for Dwight Winthrop. When Ace threatens to kill Winthrop and expose Jan's sordid affair with him unless she returns to his bed, Dwight visits his casino and shoots him in cold blood. To keep Ace's relationship with Jan out of the papers, Dwight claims he shot Ace over a gambling debt.

His trial has reached the phase of closing arguments when Stephen lurches out of the gutter, takes over the defense and, with the court's permission, calls one more witness—Jan herself. The ostensible purpose of this tactic is to show that Winthrop killed Ace in a fit of temporary insanity but in fact it establishes Stephen Ashe as juriscinema's next Jesus figure after Madame X. "Don't you see my hands are bleeding where the spikes are being driven through?" he asks the jury before pausing for a quick nip. The prosecutor punctuates Stephen's questions to Jan with not precisely legalistic but totally justified objections: "This is theatrical! Emotional!" After forcing Jan to admit her affair with Wilfong, Stephen makes his final address to the court and jury.

> "I'm going to ask you to listen with your hearts. . . .
> It was through her father that [Jan] met this gambler,
> this beast! Her father endorsed this unholy friendship!
> . . . There's only one breast that you can surely pin the
> responsibility of this crime on. Only one! Stephen Ashe
> is guilty and nobody else. Stephen Ashe!"

In the best *Madame X* manner he then collapses and dies. We never learn the jury's verdict, but the final scene shows Jan leaving San Francisco to do some sort of redemptive work in New York and Dwight promising to follow and make a new life with her.

Soon after appearing in *A Free Soul,* and several months before he won an Oscar for his performance in that film, Barrymore played another lawyer in *Guilty Hands* (MGM © 8/6/31, directed by W.S. Van Dyke from a screenplay by Bayard Veiller), which opens with a fascinating conversation among "strangers on a train" bound from New York to a nameless seaside community. The train is going through a tunnel as we join attorney Richard Grant (Lionel Barrymore) and two fellow passengers.

> P1: "You mean a man has a right to commit
> murder?"

Grant: "Oh, not legally of course."

P1 (shocked): "You can't mean morally!"

Grant: "My dear sir, we haven't morals anymore, just laws. A man isn't punished for committing a murder. We put him in jail for his mistakes, because he's been caught. Of course, it's possible to commit a murder and not be caught."

P1: "Of course! I've read books about that. Detective stories. The perfect murder, the perfect alibi."

Grant: "I'm not talking about books. It's possible to commit a murder and not be caught. I believe that under certain conditions murder is justifiable."

P1: "Speaking as an expert?"

Grant: "Yeah. For ten years I was district attorney of New York, and in that time I sent over fifty men to the electric chair. (Pause while an obsequious black attendant lights cigars for the passengers.) Now that I've retired to private practice, I've kept a hundred of 'em out of it!"

P1: "I Guess I'm old fashioned. It seems all wrong to me. The Bible says 'Thou shalt not commit murder.'"

Grant: "The Bible says 'A life for a life' too, doesn't it? Well, doesn't it?"

P1 (reluctantly): "Yes."

P2: "What I can't understand is you, a lawyer, advocating murder."

Grant: "Oh, now, my dear sir, I didn't say any such thing, no no no no! I simply said that in certain cases murder was justifiable. And I voiced the belief that a clever man in such a case could commit a murder so skillfully—you know what I mean?—so brilliantly, that he could get away with it."

P1: "Mr. Grant, what would you call a justifiable murder?"

Grant: "Justifiable murder?"

P1: "Yeah."

Grant: "Oh—a justifiable murder is a murder that's justifiable. Well, this is my station."

The conversation of course prefigures events to come. Grant is on his way to the lavish island home of a wealthy and compulsively lecherous client (William Bakewell) whom he has saved several times from richly deserved civil and criminal liability. When the lawyer discovers that his own daughter (Madge Evans) is the client's latest sexual target, he decides to commit the perfect and justifiable murder he theorized about on the train. The rest of the film not only has no interest as juriscinema but its third-grade performances and cheesy thunder-and-lightning effects and heavy-handed (in the most literal sense) climactic irony make it all but impossible to sit through except out of a sense of scholarly duty.

Of all the law-related movies of the first golden age, only two were based on novels with a literary reputation, the earlier of the pair being *An American Tragedy* (Paramount © 8/22/31, directed by Josef von Sternberg from a screenplay by Samuel Hoffenstein based on Theodore Dreiser's 1925 novel of the same name). The film follows the broad outlines of the Dreiser novel, which was based on the celebrated Chester Gillette murder trial. Clyde Griffiths (Phillips Holmes), the neglected son of dirt-poor street evangelists, is working as a bellhop in a large Chicago hotel when he happens to meet his prosperous Uncle Samuel (Frederick Burton) and is offered a job in the latter's upstate New York shirt factory. In due course Clyde becomes foreman of a department within the factory and, in defiance of plant rules, begins a furtive affair with newly hired worker Roberta Alden (Sylvia Sidney) but loses all interest in her when he meets and falls for the beautiful and wealthy Sondra Finchley (Frances Dee), whom he sees as his ticket to money and social prestige. Then disaster strikes: Roberta tells him she's pregnant. Clyde devises a plan to take her out on the lake in a canoe and drown her so that her death looks like an accident, but when the two are actually on the lake and out of others' sight he changes his mind (or does he?) and agrees to jettison his plans for social advancement and marry her. Roberta, who can't swim, accidentally overturns the boat. Clyde ignores her screams for help and swims to shore, letting her drown as he had first intended. He's soon arrested and charged with murder, but thanks to his uncle's money he has two lawyers (Emmett Corrigan and Charles Middleton) who are as fine a pair of shysters as a defendant might hope for.

> "And for that reason we've invented this other story about a change of heart. It's not quite as true as yours, but it is true that you did experience a change of heart in that boat. And that's our justification. . . . You're not guilty. You've sworn to me you did not intend to strike her there at the last, whatever you might have been provoked to do at best. And that's enough for me. You're not guilty."[9]

Spectators pack the courtroom for Clyde's trial. Sondra Finchley, whom both sides agree to call Miss X,[10] is not among the 127 prosecution witnesses. All the lawyers rant and rave and strut their oratorical bombast. Finally the prosecution rests and the defense calls Clyde to the stand, hoping to show him guilty of "mental and moral cowardice, and nothing more and nothing less." His own attorneys badger and scream at him as if they were the prosecutors and keep him on the stand for days. Objections fly thick and fast and opposing counsel almost come to blows in open court. District Attorney Orville Mason (Irving Pichel) brings the fatal canoe into court and makes Clyde sit in it as he's cross-examined. "She was drowning as you wanted her to drown! And you let her drown!" A spectator interrupts the proceedings, shouting: "Why not kill the dirty sneak now and be done with it?"—grounds for a mistrial in the real world but not here in the magic kingdom of juriscinema. The case goes to the jury and we are treated to less than a minute of their deliberations. "I don't believe his lawyers would let him lie about it," says one naif before his colleagues shout him down. The verdict of course is Guilty and Clyde is sentenced to death. In the final scene he is visited on death row by his mother (Lucille LaVerne), who blames herself for his plight and urges him to take his punishment like a man.

In the story as Theodore Dreiser told it, Clyde Griffiths was a toad beneath the harrow, victimized by a money- and status-obsessed society. In Josef von Sternberg's version society is never indicted in the least and Clyde, despite his good looks, comes across as a cold, calculating, shifty-eyed opportunist, close cousin to those prime-time murderers of a later generation whose best laid plans were undone regularly by Lieutenant Columbo. Dreiser was so infuriated by the film's message—the system works, all is well—that he sued Paramount for making a distorted version of his novel, harmful to his literary reputation. He lost.[11]

The Woman in Room 13 (Fox © 4/14/32, directed by Henry King from a screenplay by Guy Bolton based on the 1919 stage play of the same name by Samuel Shipman, Max Marcin and Percival Wilde) is a melodrama of love and intrigue that culminates in the murder of philandering concert singer Victor LeGrand (Gilbert Roland) by his scorned mistress Sari Lodar (Myrna Loy) at the same time that Paul Ramsey (Neil Hamilton), who wrongly suspects that his wife Laura (Elissa Landi) has been sleeping with LeGrand, is hammering on the door of the singer's apartment. Caught in the apartment with the murder weapon in his hand and wrongly thinking that it was Laura who killed LeGrand, Paul confesses to the crime himself. At his trial Laura reciprocates, as it were, by falsely testifying that she had indeed been sleeping with LeGrand. Her perjury gives Paul the benefit of the so-called "unwritten law" excuse and the jury, though finding him guilty, spares him the death penalty. Eventually Sari writes Laura a letter confessing the truth and kills herself. The film ends with Paul out of prison and reunited with his wife.

Two Against the World (Warner Bros. © 8/18/32, directed by Archie Mayo from a screenplay by Sheridan Gibney based on an original story by Marion Dix and Jerry Horwin) may not be a great film but it deserves a prize for most idiotic lawyer behavior in an early talkie. Attorney David Norton (Neil Hamilton), a son of privilege sympathetic to the poor, sues the wealthy Hamilton clan over the death of a workman named Polansky. Adell Hamilton (Constance Bennett) develops an interest in David and, as a device to meet him socially, arranges a fender-bender between their cars. As their relationship warms, Adell offers to send Polansky's widow a monthly check until the lawsuit is settled. Later in the film Adell and her brother Bob (Allen Vincent), who is both a compulsive gambler and a drunk, are charged with the murder of upper-class cad Victor Linley (Gavin Gordon), to whom he owed a small fortune in gambling debts and whom he wrongly suspected of being Adell's lover. Being a friend of the Hamiltons, the District Attorney (Oscar Apfel) bows to public pressure not to try the case himself and manipulates, I kid you not, David Norton into becoming special prosecutor! "You can't refuse. I've already informed the press that you've accepted. . . . And if you fail to gain conviction, your goose is cooked. . . . I wish you the best of luck." Adell takes the stand and is caught in a lie—not by Norton, of course, but under questioning by the foreman of the jury. But in order to protect both her brother and her married sister Corinne (Helen Vinson), who was indeed having an affair with Linley, Adell falsely testifies that Bob told her he had shot the man "because he had reason to believe that the honor of my name demanded it." The result of her perjury is a Not Guilty verdict based on the "unwritten law." As the film ends, David tells Adell that he knew she was lying on the stand to shield her sister but, because he loves her, did nothing about it. Small wonder that this cynical gem was never remade in the era of strict censorship!

As the Devil Commands (Columbia © 12/19/32, directed by Roy William Neill from a screenplay by Jo Swerling based on an original story by Keene Thompson) is surely the appropriate title for a film about one of early juriscinema's most diabolical lawyers. Wasting away from an incurable disease, wealthy John Duncan (Charles Sellon) intends to divide his estate between his cousin Robert Waldo (Alan Dinehart), who is a lawyer, and his protégé and caregiver Dr. David Graham (Neil Hamilton), who is in love with Duncan's nurse Jane

Chase (Mae Clarke) and who doesn't know that in fact he's Duncan's son. Waldo however persuades the old man to leave David everything, not out of altruism but as part of an Iagoesque scheme to take both Jane and the entire Duncan estate. After David refuses Duncan's deathbed request to be euthanized, Waldo sneaks into the sickroom and gives the dying man an overdose of the medicine David had prescribed, with the predictable result that David, now the only person with financial motive to kill Duncan, is charged with his murder. Volunteering as defense counsel is Waldo, who of course throws the case. David is sentenced to life imprisonment and divested of the Duncan estate, which now passes by intestate succession to Waldo—except for the valuable real property, which for some unfathomable legal reason he can't take while David is still alive. Waldo therefore unframes his victim by forging and finding a suicide note supposedly signed by John Duncan, with a view to getting David out of prison and then killing him in a death chamber he's prepared in his basement. Jane catches on to the scheme just in time to kill Waldo and save David's life.

Broadway Bad (Fox © 2/7/33, directed by Sidney Lanfield from a screenplay by Arthur Kober and Maude Fulton based on an original story by William R. Lipman and A.W. Pezet) stars Joan Blondell as showgirl Tony Landers, who is lusted after by wealthy stockbroker Craig Cutting (Ricardo Cortez) but is secretly married to college student Bob North (Allen Vincent), the marriage being kept under wraps because Bob would be expelled if it became known. When Bob wrongly accuses Tony of infidelity and sues for divorce, naming Craig as co-respondent, the resulting scandal makes Tony a Broadway star and she and Craig become fond of each other. Four years later the jerk Bob discovers that Tony was pregnant when he divorced her and snatches the boy she'd been secretly raising. The film climaxes at a trial where Tony and Craig testify that Tony was indeed cheating during her marriage and that the child's real father is Craig, defeating Bob's custody demand by brazenly committing perjury albeit of a sort that a simple DNA test would expose today.

The false testimony brands Tony as a slut and her perfectly legitimate child as a bastard, but in Hollywood terms it's a happy ending with the formation of a new family rooted in love.

In *The Woman Accused* (Paramount © 2/16/33, directed by Paul Sloane from a screenplay by Bayard Veiller based on a magazine serial by ten authors—including Irvin S. Cobb and Zane Grey—that was published in *Liberty* magazine early in 1933), Glenda O'Brien (Nancy Carroll) accepts a proposal from New York attorney Jeffrey Baxter (Cary Grant) and the couple make plans to leave immediately for a cruise on which they'll be married. That evening Gladys commits the *faux pas* of seeing her jealous ex-lover Leo Young (Louis Calhern), who threatens to have his gangster friend Little Maxie (Jack LaRue) kill Jeffrey if Glenda doesn't give him up. Glenda brains Leo with a statue, then leaves to meet the cruise ship and Jeffrey. When the murder is discovered and Glenda comes under suspicion, District Attorney Clarke (Irving Pichel) authorizes Leo's friend Stephen Bessemer (John Halliday) to join the cruise and dig up evidence against her. The climax takes place at a shipboard masquerade party where Stephen conducts a mock murder trial with Glenda as defendant. Under the pressure of his questioning she breaks down and confesses, but all the passengers except Stephen think she's acting. Just before being arrested she tells Jeffrey the truth. Back in New York, Jeffrey beats Little Maxie into confessing Leo's plan to kill him, then visits the DA and convinces him that there's not enough evidence to put Glenda on trial. With the case dropped, lawyer and client are free to marry.

Pick-Up (Paramount © 3/28/33, directed by Marion Gering from a screenplay by S.K. Lauren and Agnes Brand Leahy based on the Sidney Lazarus adaptation of Viña Delmar's 1928 short story of the same name) opens with Mary Richards (Sylvia Sidney) sent to prison for the "badger game" racket in which her husband Jim (William Harrigan), also sentenced to prison, forced her to take part. Released after two years, Mary meets and falls for cabdriver Harry Glynn (George Raft), eventually moving in with him and encouraging him to open his own garage. Harry becomes a prosperous entrepreneur and develops an infatuation for socialite Muriel Stevens (Lillian Bond). Mary of course is still married to Jim but learns from a lawyer that she's legally entitled to an annulment on the ground that her husband has been in jail for more than two years. In rapid order she gets her annulment, Harry leaves her for Muriel, and Jim escapes from prison. He's recaptured but gets even with Mary by swearing that she helped him escape. Harry drops Muriel, sells his business to finance her legal defense and the couple end up poor again but together again.

The Kiss Before the Mirror (Universal © 4/3/33, directed by James Whale from a screenplay by William Anthony McGuire based on Ladislaus Farago's 1932 stage play *Der Kuss vor dem Spiegel*) takes place in Vienna but Austrian lawyers too would probably be astounded by its courtroom aspects. Walter Bernsdorf (Frank Morgan), on trial for murdering his unfaithful wife (Gloria Stuart), is being defended by his best friend Paul Held (Paul Lukas), who in the course of the trial discovers that his own wife Maria (Nancy Carroll) is also unfaithful. After following her to a rendezvous with her current lover (Donald Cook), Paul becomes obsessed with the similarity between his own situation and his client's and insists that Maria come to court and hear his final argument on Bernsdorf's behalf. "The more a man loves and the more he is deceived," he orates, "the greater his desire for revenge!" Then he takes a gun from his pocket and aims it at Maria, who screams and faints. Grounds for mistrial in the real world but here in the magic kingdom of juriscinema the court simply takes a recess and the jury starts deliberating. Later, still expecting Paul to kill her, Maria swears that she still loves him and Bernsdorf, having been acquitted, begs his lawyer not to follow in his own footsteps. Paul forgives his erring wife and they embrace.

The second law-related early talkie adapted from a novel by a major American author—albeit one of his lesser works, written when he was desperately in need of money[12]—was *The Story of Temple Drake* (Paramount © 5/11/33, directed by Stephen Roberts from a screenplay by Oliver H.P. Garrett based on William Faulkner's 1931 novel *Sanctuary*), a film so full of sleazy sexuality that it was subjected to industry censorship when most Hollywood movies weren't.[13] Temple (Miriam Hopkins), the uninhibited daughter of a Southern judge (Sir Guy Standing), refuses to marry local lawyer Stephen Benbow (William Gargan) and continues to flirt with and tease countless other men. Then one drunken night in a thunderstorm she's trapped in a remote plantation house occupied by bootlegger Lee Goodwin (Irving Pichel). Goodwin goes away, leaving his feeble-witted hanger-on Tommy (James Eagles) to guard her, but his sadistic henchman Trigger (Jack LaRue) kills the halfwit, rapes Temple in the barn behind the house, then takes her to the brothel run by Miss Reba (Jobyna Howland) and makes her his moll. Goodwin is charged with Tommy's murder but refuses to rat on Trigger to his assigned counsel Stephen Benbow, who eventually visits Miss Reba's place after learning from Goodwin's wife (Florence Eldredge) that Temple is living there with Trigger. To keep the psychotic Trigger from killing Benbow, Temple claims that she's staying at the brothel voluntarily. After Stephen leaves she tries to escape and, to keep from being raped again, shoots Trigger dead. Then she tells Stephen the truth and begs him not to make her testify at Goodwin's trial, which is being presided over of course by her father. Stephen's duty to his client compels him to call her as a witness but he finds himself unable to ask her the crucial questions about Tommy's murder. Temple breaks down and—in censored language that blurs much of what really happened[14]—tearfully confesses the truth. Then she faints and Stephen carries her from the courtroom. "Be proud of her, Judge," he tells her father. "I am."

***

William J. Fallon is little known or remembered today, but in his last decade of life he typified the legal profession like no other attorney of his time and after his death he figured crucially in several key works of early juriscinema. Getting to know Fallon, however, is not an easy task. The only readily available source of information about him is Gene Fowler's *The Great Mouthpiece* (Crown, 1931),[15] a book which Fowler himself called a "life story" of Fallon rather than a biography, and rightly so: it's cast in the mold of what today we call the nonfiction novel, built around real people and places and events but full of incidents and dialogue that clearly do not come intact from real life even when the author seems to be quoting trial transcripts. Unreliable though the book may be, we need to consider it here.

According to Fowler, William Joseph Fallon was born on New York City's West 47th Street on January 23, 1886, the son of a well-to-do Irish contractor who moved the family upstate to Mamaroneck in Westchester County when the boy was ten. (23) Gifted with a near-photographic memory that enabled him to read a book in two hours and "repeat almost word-for-word the entire text . . . ," he graduated from Fordham University in 1906 as valedictorian of his class and with a medal for the highest grade in philosophy. (76) Three years later, after completing Fordham Law School and passing the New York bar, he went to work in the White Plains office of veteran criminal defense lawyer David Hunt. (90) He married the former Agnes Rafter in 1912 and soon became the father of two daughters. (88) Between 1914 and 1916 he served as an Assistant District Attorney in Westchester County. (98)

Gene Fowler devotes little space to Fallon's time as a prosecutor but, near the end of the book, has him recollect one incident worth our attention. "I sent a man to prison for life, on a murder-charge. A year later, I found he was innocent. That's what cured me of wanting to prosecute. I got the Governor to pardon the man. But the damage already was done. . . ." (350-351). We shall see that variations of this incident were to figure largely in the movies inspired by Fallon's life.

On January 12, 1918, Fallon "invaded" New York City. (133) Over the next nine and a half years he devoted his considerable talents to the defense of Manhattan's wealthiest gangsters, bootleggers, con artists and stock swindlers. "Fallon's fees were the first tremendous ones to be paid by captains of modern crime-syndicates for legal advice. He became, in fact, a corporation counsel for the underworld. . . . After a few successes, . . . his services were virtually commanded by men powerful in politics and in criminal circles." (145) "He became the Great Mouthpiece for the grand dukes of Racketland." (148)

Fallon's forensic skills included arranging for incriminating evidence to vanish from prosecutors' offices, lying to and baiting trial judges, making honest and truthful witnesses seem perjurers or fools. He was a genius at "riding over courts and hypnotizing juries. . . ." (313) He "was completely the actor; the dramatic effect of the moment was all-important to him. . . ." (239). So great was his flair that at one point the theatrical impresario David Belasco offered to have a play written for him if he would star in it. (176, 319) He was an expert at playing to the media, which in the 1920s meant the many newspapers that were published daily in New York City. "My clients always are [innocent]. I'd be helpless if they weren't." (168) In any event very few of them were convicted when he was defending them. "If [a Fallon client] were not acquitted, he was reasonably sure of incredible delays or a jury disagreement. . . . It seems incredible how many times Fallon accomplished a hung jury by the count of 1 to 11. Hints of jury-bribing began to travel the court-corridors." (163) In 1924 he was tried in federal court on two counts of bribing a juror named Charles W. Rendigs (337-340) but defended himself with the same vigor and flair and trickiness he sold at top prices to underworld clients and was acquitted. (384) Two years later, when disbarment proceedings were brought against him, he reached into the same bag of tricks and got the charges dismissed. (391-392) When not twisting judges and prosecutors around his little finger he had affairs with countless Broadway showgirls (keeping his wife and daughters discreetly in the background) and, like thousands of others during Prohibition, drank whiskey as if it were water. He died of a gastric hemorrhage and heart attack on April 29, 1927, not long after his 41st birthday and shortly before the silent films of his lifetime were displaced by talkies.

For Gene Fowler, who apparently knew and clearly admired his subject, Fallon was "this impulsive, vain, brilliant, reckless, gay, tragic fellow." (239) Most readers of *The Great Mouthpiece* probably saw him as the shyster incarnate; in any event that was how film-makers saw him. He was "sturdy and handsome. He moved with the grace and sure rhythm of a trained boxer. . . . His erect bearing, his squared shoulders, inflated chest, large head, and the tangle of apricot-colored hair, made him appear six feet two inches, instead of five feet eleven. . . . [He had a] remarkably resonant voice . . . [and] a wit that danced." (139) This description suggests that the perfect actor to have played Fallon in a movie based on his life would have been Spencer Tracy. Hollywood never made such a film, but the legends of Fallon's exploits at the bar, some found in Fowler's book and others in more ephemeral sources, literally created the image of the lawyer in half a dozen movies released in the early 1930s. The Fallonesque lawyer of juriscinema, however, is never conspicuously Irish and hasn't the slightest resemblance to Spencer Tracy, being slender, suave and smooth-voiced and usually sporting a tiny mustache. Unlike their real-world original, Fallon's cinematic avatars invariably reform before the end titles.

The earliest feature to show the Fallon influence, even to gifting its shyster protagonist with a similar name, is *For the Defense* (Paramount © 7/25/30, directed by John Cromwell from a screenplay by Oliver H.P. Garrett based on an original story by Charles Furthman). Shrewd criminal defense lawyer William Foster (William Powell), whose activities are being investigated by police detective Daly (Thomas Jackson), is emotionally involved with actress Irene Manning (Kay Francis) but refuses to commit to her. To make him jealous Irene starts going out with a wealthy waster named Defoe (Scott Kolk). One night the two are driving back from a drinking party with Irene at the wheel when their car runs over and kills a pedestrian. Defoe takes the blame and is tried for manslaughter with Foster as his defense counsel. The trial is going badly for Foster when Irene confesses that she was to blame for the accident and Foster decides that the only way to get both her and Defoe off the hook is by bribing one of the jurors. At this point the film begins to echo the Rendigs jury-bribery scandal: Foster's scheme works but afterwards detective Daly looks into the matter, makes the bribe-taker talk and puts Foster under arrest. Irene is about to confess her own guilt to the District Attorney (William B. Davidson) when Foster saves her from doing so by pleading guilty and is sentenced to five years in prison. Irene promises to be waiting for him when he gets out.

April and May of 1932 must have been the perfect spring for moviegoers who thought of lawyers as the men they loved to hate. Within a span of about six weeks three new films sprang up on the nation's screens, each from a different studio, each with different directors and writers and stars, each built around a shyster with roots in William J. Fallon. *The Mouthpiece* (Warner Bros. © 4/18/32, directed by James Flood and Elliott Nugent from a screenplay by Joseph Jackson and Earl Baldwin based on Frank L. Collins' 1929 stage play of the same name) opens with a sequence that is clearly an intensified version of an incident in Fallon's life: prosecuting attorney Vincent Day (Warren William) obtains a conviction in a murder case, only to discover later— too late to prevent the man's execution—that the defendant was innocent. Ridden with guilt, Day switches sides and soon becomes the city's most prominent and trickiest criminal defense lawyer.

About a third of the way through this film comes a self-contained sequence that for me is the perfect embodiment of early juriscinema's take on lawyers. When auditors begin to go over a bond house's books, cashier Barton (John Wray), who embezzled $90,000 from the firm, comes to Day in desperation, bringing with him a handsome briefcase containing the $40,000 he hasn't already lost on the market and women. Day calls in Smith (Morgan Wallace), the head of the firm, and inveigles him into accepting partial restitution and agreeing not to file charges.

> Day: "Your stock and bond customers—the unfortunate publicity of an embezzlement would naturally affect their confidence in your institution. How much confidence can you afford to lose this year, Mr. Smith?"

Smith: "Day, you're an unmitigated scoundrel."

Day: "Thank you! But I find it much nicer than being just an ordinary one."

As negotiations proceed, Smith's blood begins to boil.

Smith: "Day, you're positively the most unmitigated scoundrel in the world."

Day: "It's comforting to know that I'm progressing so rapidly in your esteem."

Day turns over $30,000 in cash, keeping Barton's briefcase for himself, then brings out his client.

Smith: "Don't speak to me! You've lost the right to talk to honest men!"

Day: "Don't worry, Barton. You can talk to us."

Barton: "I'm sorry, Mr. Smith."

Smith: "Sorry! You steal $90,000 and you're sorry!"

Barton: "But I tried to make restitution."

Smith: "Restitution! A paltry thirty thousand!"

Barton: "I restored forty thousand."

Smith (gesturing at Day): "He said thirty thousand."

Day (smugly): "Naturally there was the attorney's fee."

Smith: "You—you took $10,000 for your part in this criminal affair?"

Day: "I took $10,000 for my advice as a lawyer. . . . I may be able to be of service to you some day, Mr. Smith."

After Smith has stalked out of the office, Day contemptuously kicks his client out to face the Depression economy penniless.

Barton: "But—you're not—you're not going to keep all of my $10,000, are you, Mr. Day?"

Day: "Yours? *You* stole it. *I* earned it."

Barton: "But—but it's all I've got!"

Day: "You haven't got it. You *had* it."

Barton: "But I can't get a job now. What can I do?"

Day: "Go out and jump in the river, you cheap tinhorn crook. Now get out!"

Day's eventual downfall takes the form of a stenographer sent to his firm by an employment agency, and a delightful form it is. Celia Faraday (Sidney Fox) is a teen-age sexpot fresh from Kentucky and a total klutz at secretarial work. Day not only doesn't fire her but lures her to his apartment and propositions her. She turns him down on the ground that she's in love with bank messenger Johnny Morris (William Janney). In time Celia comes to despise Day's legal tricks and quits her job in disgust,[16] but Johnny is arrested for bond theft before the couple can relocate to Kentucky and she's forced to come back and beg the lawyer to use his wiles on her fiancé's behalf. Underworld connections tip Day that the real thief was Joe Garland (Jack LaRue), who is arrested at Day's behest after refusing to confess and clear Johnny. Day resolves to give up shystering, but before he can become an honest lawyer Garland gets out on bail and guns him down.

Early in *Attorney for the Defense* (Columbia © 5/3/32, directed by Irving Cummings from a screenplay by Jo Swerling) comes a scene with marked similarities to the early sequences of *The Mouthpiece* as district attorney William J. Burton (Edmund Lowe) is berated by his secretary Ruth Barry (Constance Cummings) for obtaining a murder conviction and death sentence against James Wallace (Dwight Frye) on purely circumstantial evidence. When Wallace is proven innocent shortly after his execution, Burton seeks to make amends by resigning his office and putting Wallace's son Paul (Donald Dillaway) through law school. Years pass and Burton, now a criminal defense attorney with Paul working in his office, launches a civic crusade against gangster Nick

Quinn (Bradley Page), who in turn has Val Lorraine (Evelyn Brent), his present paramour and Burton's former mistress, make a play for Paul and get him into trouble that can be used against Burton. The sexual intrigue comes to a head when Val gets Paul drunk and phones Burton to come for him. Burton arrives to find her dead and Paul unable to remember what happened. Still feeling responsible for the wrongful execution of Paul's father, Burton sends the young man home and confesses to the murder himself. Ruth Barry, who has followed Burton into private practice as his secretary, tries but fails to borrow money for his defense, then visits him in jail, tells him she loves him and urges him to defend himself at trial. This is all Burton needs to restore his will to live, and his cross-examination of prosecution witnesses generates enough new evidence to pin Val's murder on Nick Quinn.

State's Attorney (RKO © 5/5/32, directed by George Archainbaud from a screenplay by Gene Fowler and Rowland Brown based on an original story by Louis Stevens) was written in part by the author of *The Great Mouthpiece* and clearly betrays the influence of that book: not only is the protagonist a drunk like William J. Fallon (and like John Barrymore during filming), but defendants take the Fifth Amendment in the unusual form that Fowler attributes to Fallon: "I refuse to answer, on the ground that to do so might tend to incriminate or degrade me." (249) But in the film as a whole, Fallon's career is not so much replicated as flipflopped. Tom Cardigan (John Barrymore), hard-drinking mouthpiece for mob boss Vanny Powers (William "Stage" Boyd), has no qualms about using his skills on behalf of what Holmes called "the bad man."[17] "The grocer takes your money, doesn't ask any questions. A criminal lawyer doesn't cross-examine his fees." For a fee of $5000 from Powers he defends and wins an acquittal for prostitute June Perry (Helen Twelvetrees), then takes her out of Powers' stable and makes her his mistress.

After being wounded by a rival gangster, Powers suggests that Cardigan accept an offer to become First Assistant District Attorney and serve in effect as double agent for the mob. Cardigan refuses.

"Vanny, when I'm with you, I'm with you hook, line and sinker. If I go on the other side, I stay there." His ambition to be governor soon leads him to switch and he quickly rises to the position of District Attorney, getting convictions via the same kind of tricks with which he had previously gotten acquittals. "You know, if I was defending that dame, she'd be free tonight," he remarks after winning a murder case. Although still involved with June, Cardigan starts seeing Lillian Ulrich (Jill Esmond), the bloodthirsty daughter of his political patron (Oscar Apfel). Lillian asks Cardigan to marry her and he agrees, but minutes after the ceremony he realizes he's made a huge mistake and, when he tells June what he's done, she moves out of their love nest. Lillian quickly becomes involved with a tenor (Albert Conti) and an annulment of her marriage is arranged, but June is gone.

Time passes and she comes back into his life. She happens to witness Powers murder Duffy, the rival gangster who wounded him, but is warned that both she and Cardigan will be rubbed out if she tells the truth. Cardigan gets June to leave town and himself leads the police team that arrests the gangster chief. "It's a great world," remarks Powers' new shyster (C. Henry Gordon). "Duffy's on a slab. You defended him once. Then you defended Powers." Cardigan replies: "Yeah. Now I'm going to hang him." A little later the medical examiner asks: "Remember the old days, Tom? This would have been an open-and-shut case of self-defense." Cardigan's response echoes his previous exchange with the new shyster: "Remember when I used to send to Milwaukee for the eyewitnesses?" In a nutshell, whether a lawyer stands up for A and smears B or vice versa depends on what's in it for the lawyer. This time of course Cardigan can't use the testimony of the one genuine eyewitness, but at trial June is subpoenaed for the defense: apparently both to support a self-defense claim *and* to testify that Powers was not the shooter! Cardigan waives cross-examination but, when Powers lets out a loud guffaw, he retracts the waiver—"That laugh is going to cost you your neck," he whispers to Powers—and wrings the truth from June on the stand. "All right," she tells him as she steps down, "now go ahead and be governor!" That reproach spurs

Cardigan to do an about-face. Although the case isn't over, he makes an emotional speech to the jury in which he reveals that he and Powers had been in reform school together for burglary, renounces his political ambitions and resigns on the spot. "I shall return to the defense of those unfortunates who, like myself, were reared in the gutter." Leaving his assistants to complete the case against Powers, Cardigan walks out of the courthouse with June at his side.

From an attorney's perspective one of the most unsatisfying of the films indebted to Fallon is *Lawyer Man* (Warner Bros. © 12/28/32, directed by William Dieterle from a screenplay by Rian James and James Seymour based on Max Trell's 1932 novel of the same name). As we follow the career of Anton Adam (William Powell) it soon becomes clear that the people who made this picture know nothing about their subject and couldn't care less: the simplest legal distinctions are ignored and almost all the lawyer work takes place out of the camera's eye. But it's also an exceptionally lively and funny film, with that quintessential WASP William Powell—hopelessly miscast as an ethnic (né Antonio Adamo?) with roots in Manhattan's Lower East Side—loping and leering and waggling his eyebrows and phallic cigars for all the world like Groucho Marx with a real mustache. Adam wins an offstage acquittal (apparently on a murder charge) for petty hoodlum Izzy Levine (Allen Jenkins) and is offered a partnership by his courtroom adversary, prosperous uptown attorney Granville Bentley (Alan Dinehart). Was Izzy innocent or guilty? By what tactics did Adam prevail? How did a big-shot civil lawyer get to be prosecuting a criminal case? As they say on the Lower East Side, dun't esk! With his secretary Olga Michaels (Joan Blondell) in his wake, Adam moves into a palatial office and begins dating his new partner's sister Barbara (Helen Vinson). In another offstage trial he trounces political boss John Gilmurry (David Landau), who offers him a place in "the organization" which Adam refuses. Later he's retained by showgirl Virginia St. Johns (Claire Dodd) to bring a breach of promise suit against Dr. Frank Gresham (Kenneth Thomson), a Gilmurry ally.

The torrid letters from her former lover that Virginia leaves with Adam lead him to anticipate a six-figure settlement and a huge fee for himself, but she and Gresham reconcile before the trial begins, and the results of Adam's demand that she not drop the suit are devastating: the Gresham love letters vanish from his office and Adam is indicted for extortion. That trial, which we glimpse for just a few seconds, ends in a hung jury, but Adam's career in the big leagues is ruined and, in a key sequence, he decides to break with Barbara and, in effect, become a Fallon figure.

> "Look down there. People. Millions. Every guy for himself. Pushing, shoving, trampling each other, sure. City full of them. Crooked streets and crooks. Fight, cheat, deal from the bottom. Boost the guy that's riding high and kick the guy that's down. That's what it takes to make good here. And that's what I'll give them. When they kick you, kick back, only harder. Sock 'em. If they can't take it, that's their hard luck. They made a shyster out of me. Okay. I'll be the biggest, busiest shyster that ever hit this town. If they want rats, I'll be a rat. The daddy of all rats! I'll show them."

After a period as a shyster that whizzes by in about a minute of screen time, Adam stumbles into and accepts a civil case of some sort against Gilmurry. The issues aren't explained and the trial isn't shown but, just before the jury returns with a verdict, Adam bluffs the political boss into settling: $20,000 for the client, $10,000 for himself. On his way out of the courthouse Gilmurry asks a juror how much they awarded the plaintiff. "Oh," the other replies, proving once more that no one involved in this film grasped the simplest legal distinctions, "we found you not guilty."

Gilmurry again offers Adam a place in his organization. This time Adam agrees, but only if he's appointed an Assistant District Attorney. Strange appointment! The lettering on his new office door reads Deputy District Attorney, not Assistant, and he's never assigned any cases to prosecute but simply uses his power to pursue the vendetta against Dr.

Gresham, getting him indicted and convicted for billing the city thousands of dollars for services never performed. Gilmurry retaliates sending gunmen to kill Adam, who counters by bringing in Izzy as his bodyguard. Finally Gilmurry offers Adam a judgeship if he'll lay off, but our hero opts for a rather different career move.

> "I'm going back to my own people, where you don't have to be a rat to succeed. . . . A lawyer's job is like a doctor's. That's what it should be. A guide. A helper. A big brother to a lot of poor trampled slobs who can't hold their own against party bosses like you. Not a trickster and a cheat but a counselor and a friend. That's what I was. And that's what I'm going to be again. And that's why I don't want your judgeship or anything else that you've got to offer. I'm finished, washed up, fed up. With you, and your party, and your politics."

The film ends with Adam back in his Lower East Side Eden, poor but happy and with Olga who has always loved him still at his side.

The protagonist of *The Nuisance* (MGM © 5/18/33, directed by Jack Conway from a screenplay by Bella and Samuel Spewack based on an original story by Chandler Sprague and Howard Emmett Rogers) is lawyer Phineas "Joe" Stevens (Lee Tracy), who—with the help of the drunken quack Prescott (Frank Morgan) and a professional accident victim (Charles Butterworth) and various paid-off witnesses—makes a nice living out of fraudulent lawsuits against the local streetcar company. Finally company attorney John Calhoun (John Miljan) declares war, hiring Dorothy Mason (Madge Evans) to pose as an accident victim and retain Prescott, whose instructions to her on how to fake various injuries she secretly tapes, while Calhoun himself cozies up to Prescott at his favorite speakeasy and is soon privy to his methods of faking X-rays. Joe discovers that Prescott has spilled the beans and, after a vicious tongue-lashing, the doctor walks in front of a passing auto and kills himself.

Ridden by grief and guilt and unaware that Dorothy is part of the plot against him, Joe explains to her that he became a shyster only after the streetcar company used shyster tactics against a genuinely injured client of his. Dorothy refuses to inform further on Joe, with whom she's fallen in love, despite Calhoun's threats to have her charged with perjury. Joe discovers a check from the streetcar company in Dorothy's luggage but what he does about it isn't revealed until the trial, where Calhoun cross-examines Dorothy and is about to make her tell who was behind the phony accident ring when Joe interrupts: Dorothy can't be forced to testify against him because he's just married her! After the trial Joe kicks Dorothy out but, when she's arrested for perjury as Calhoun had threatened, stages a harassment campaign against the streetcar company and Calhoun himself until the charges are dropped. The film ends with Dorothy released from jail and Joe promising to become an honest lawyer.

The Women in His Life (MGM © 12/5/33, directed by George B. Seitz from a screenplay by F. Hugh Herbert) opens with criminal lawyer Barry Barringer (Otto Kruger)—a hard-drinking womanizer who never got over being deserted by his wife—receiving visits from two potential clients. Doris Worthing (Irene Hervey) begs him to represent her father (Samuel S. Hinds), an innocent man charged with murdering his sluttish second wife, and Florence Steele (Irene Franklin), who freely admits that she murdered her husband, asks Barry to get her off. At first Barry accepts the guilty client and rejects the innocent, but when Doris mentions that Florence strongly resembles a modiste she knows, a light bulb goes on in his head and he agrees to represent Worthing too. But after getting Florence acquitted (by bringing the modiste to court and totally confusing the eyewitnesses who identified the defendant) he drops the Worthing case and takes off for a Florida vacation with his girlfriend Catherine Watson (Isabel Jewell). While he's gone, his junior partner Roger McKane (Ben Lyon) develops some leads suggesting that Mrs. Worthing was murdered by gangster Tony Perez (C. Henry Gordon), with whom she'd been having an affair. When Barry returns he sees a photograph of Mrs. Worthing and—gasp!—recognizes her as the ex-wife who had dumped him years before. He goes out on a near-fatal drinking binge and, while he's in the hospital, Worthing is found guilty of murder and sentenced to the electric chair. Barry recuperates and resumes work on the case but so ineptly that McKane first knocks him down and then gets him disbarred, after which he opens a so-called legal consulting firm, with a clientele consisting solely of criminals. But eventually he has a change of heart and, minutes before Worthing's execution, tricks Tony Perez into a confession secretly caught on tape. The film ends with Barry readmitted to the bar and engaged to Catherine while McKane prepares to tie the knot with Doris.

The final film of the first golden age inspired by Fallon's checkered career was *The Defense Rests* (Columbia © 7/18/34, directed by Lambert Hillyer from a screenplay by Jo Swerling). Matthew Mitchell (Jack Holt) is a brilliant shyster with a bottomless bag of legal tricks and a reputation so awesome that newspapers print extras announcing the acquittal of his clients even before the verdicts are in. When Mabel Wilson (Shirley Grey) is tried for the murder of her gambler lover Ballou (J. Carrol Naish), Mitchell gets her acquitted by having her testify—tearfully and with much display of her legs—that she shot the man in self defense while he was drunk and abusing her. In fact, as Mitchell knows, Mabel is innocent. His assistant Joan Hayes (Jean Arthur), a lawyer herself, is disgusted by his tactics and berates him for legal trickery that has let Ballou's real murderer go free, but he defends himself on the ground that he owes no loyalty except to his client. Joan investigates the murder on her own, finds evidence indicating that the real killer was Ballou's partner Gentry (Robert Gleckler), and threatens to have Mitchell arrested for suborning perjury if he doesn't give up shystering, but he refuses to change his ways. His next client is Cooney (John Wray), a gangster charged with the murder of the four-year-old child he had kidnapped even though the family had paid the ransom. Mitchell accepts a $50,000 retainer, employs his usual shyster tricks at the trial, and is winning the case hands-down when the murdered child's mother (Sarah Padden) commits suicide in his office. Suddenly Mitchell is a changed man. When Joan discovers that his $50,000 retainer came from the ransom money, he resigns as Cooney's lawyer and secretly gives the evidence to the district attorney (Arthur Hohl), who uses it to obtain a guilty verdict. As for the Mabel Wilson case, Mitchell tells Joan to file a subornation of perjury charge against him but Joan, who loves him despite his years of shyster practice, has a better idea: if he marries her, she can never be made to testify against him about anything! The murder of Ballou is taken care of extra-legally when his henchmen rub out Gentry.

***

Of all the films discussed in this chapter, the only one that deserves to be called a masterpiece is *Counsellor at Law* (Universal © 12/5/33, directed by William Wyler from a screenplay by Elmer Rice based on his 1931 stage play of the same name). All the events take place in a lavish Art Deco suite of law offices high up in the then new Empire State Building, with not a moment of courtroom action so that we are spared the nonsensical trial sequences that make so many law films of the early 1930s laughable to viewers who are attorneys. Instead Wyler and Rice offer a multi-layered and richly nuanced portrait of the private and professional lives of a manic-depressive workaholic attorney—and of the simultaneous crises in each that drive him to the brink of suicide—as well as incisive sketches of the staff, and of the clients and others who have occasion to enter the offices, and of the various ethnic cultures (Jewish, Irish, Italian, German) whose members are bonded by the experience of steerage and the scorn of their common foe the WASP. "Those guys that came over on the Mayflower don't like to see the boys from Second Avenue sitting in the high places." The cast is so huge, the pacing so brisk and the interplay among characters and storylines so complex that any viewer whose attention wanders even briefly gets lost. Even the people who at first glance seem dispensable—like the blonde receptionist with the glass-shattering voice (Isabel Jewell) and the unbilled walk-on who comes into the suite to shine the partners' shoes—have serious functions to perform in one part of the panoramic story or another.

"The last time I crossed the Atlantic it was in steerage." That was then. "People from old families come and think I'm doing them a favor if I accept their retainers." This is now. George Simon (John Barrymore), senior partner in the New York firm of Simon & Tedesco, has risen from Jewish immigrant origins to great success as an attorney and to social prominence as well, thanks to having married "one of the Four Hundred," a WASP divorcée (Doris Kenyon) with two teen-age children from her first marriage (Richard Quine and Barbara Perry) whom Simon loves as if they were his own even though they may well be the most noxious brats ever seen in a movie. "*Our* father lives in Washington," boasts the male half of the detestable duo. "*He's* not our father!" But he's resisted total assimilation and welcomes his old mother (Clara Langsner) with open arms when, looking as if she'd just stepped off the boat, she visits his plush offices and asks him for a favor. Simon's secretary Rexy Gordon (Bebe Daniels) is constantly being asked out by law clerk Herbert Weinberg (Marvin Kline) and constantly turns him down: not because she's anti-Semitic as Wyler fools us briefly into suspecting but because she's hopelessly in love with another Jew, her married boss. Simon's partner John Tedesco (Onslow Stevens), who by common consent "ain't so hot on the legal end," is nevertheless being considered for a judgeship. "I got a young Harvard boy named Weinberg in here," Simon tells the county clerk (T.H. Manning) who visits him to discuss the matter. "He could be John's secretary. And, believe me, he'll hand down opinions that'll give the Court of Appeals an inferiority complex."

Judging from the variety of its cases and clients, the firm seems to hold itself out as omnicompetent. The curtain rises shortly after Simon has secured an acquittal for Zadorah Chapman (Mayo Methot), who was charged with and almost certainly guilty of her husband's murder. But in the course of a single day we see him handling a breach of promise suit for a gold-digging slut (Thelma Todd), lobbying a U.S. Senator over the phone on behalf of a client, dictating correspondence in a will contest (which his wife pressures him to drop because the party on the other side is a social acquaintance of hers), arbitrarily tripling the fee he charges one of his divorce clients, and making a quick profit in the market from an advance tip on a forthcoming U.S. Supreme Court decision. Like the makers of the films inspired by the career of William J. Fallon, Wyler and Rice see the practice of law through unfooled eyes.

But if George Simon is far from an idealized Atticus Finch prototype, neither is he a shyster. Mrs. Becker (Malka Kornstein), a woman from the old neighborhood, prevails upon him to represent her firebrand son Harry (Vincent Sherman), who was clubbed by police and arrested for making a Communist speech in Union Square. Simon arranges with an assistant DA for a guilty plea and a suspended sentence but Harry refuses the deal.

> Harry: "I don't want your advice or your help or your friendship. You and I have nothing in common. I'm on one side of the class war and you're on the other."
>
> Simon: "Oh, stop talking like an idiot! Do you think I was born with a silver spoon in my mouth? I began life in the same gutter that you did. Why, you wouldn't have the guts to go through one tenth of what I went through to get where I am! You and your Cossacks and your class wars! Do you think I don't know what it means to sweat and go hungry? Don't come around me with any of that half-baked Communistic bull and expect me to fall for it."
>
> Harry: ". . . How did you get where you are? I'll tell you! By betraying your own class, that's how! Getting in right with bourgeois politicians and crooked corporations that feed on the blood and the sweat of the workers. . . . Sitting here in your Fifth Avenue office with a bootblack at your feet and a lot of white-collar slaves running errands for you. You're a renegade and a cheap prostitute, that's what you are! You and your cars and your country estate and your kept parasite of a wife . . . and her two

pampered brats! Comrade Simon of the working classes, who's rolling in wealth and luxury while millions of his brothers starve. You dirty traitor, you!" (Spits and stalks out.)

As the film proceeds, all these threads combine with others to push Simon to the brink. First he discovers that a kind deed he had performed a few years earlier—setting up a phony alibi so that small-time criminal Johan Breitstein (John Qualen), who has since gone straight, will not be sent to prison for life—has come to the attention of Grievance Committee bigwig Francis Clark Baird (Elmer H. Brown) and may soon lead to his disbarment. "Don't you know, whenever you give anybody a helping hand, he always turns around and kicks you in the pants?" The crisis forces him to cancel his plans to sail to Europe with his wife, who refuses his anguished plea to stay with him in his hour of need ("Well, isn't that just a little bit selfish, George?") and insists on going alone. Then Simon learns that Harry Becker has died of his injuries. "In his own eyes he died a hero and a martyr to a cause. That's better than living to be old and ending your days in disgrace." Then, in a moment of defiance, he cries out: "Let 'em disbar me! What do I care? I'll spend the rest of my life enjoying myself." Then after thinking a minute he reverses himself. "I'd go nuts in six months. How am I going to spend the rest of my life? I'm no golf player and I don't know an ace from a king. I don't even know how to get drunk![18] All I know is work. Take work away from me and what am I?.... A living corpse."

In a desperate bid to salvage his career, Simon sends investigator Charlie MacFadden (J. Hammond Dailey) to shadow Baird and find something scandalous in the latter's life. With the help of some offscreen breaking and entering, MacFadden brings back evidence that Baird is supporting a mistress and an illegitimate child and Simon blackmails the hypocritical WASP into dropping the ethics inquiry. He then begins a mad rush to get to the ship before it sails and join his wife, only to discover that she isn't sailing alone but with a companion in the form of suave Roy Darwin (Melvyn Douglas), a man of her own social class to whom Simon had recently lent money. That is what breaks him.

It is night. Simon sits alone in his palatial office suite, then slowly as if in a trance rises and approaches the window and throws it open. For the first time in the film we hear street noises—from dozens of stories below. Simon climbs the sill and is about to jump when the office door opens behind him and Rexy sees him and screams—one of the most intense emotional moments in any movie—and in a fit of manic fury he all but physically attacks her for stopping him. But the moment is past. They sit there in the dark at opposite ends of the office, drained, spent. Suddenly the phone rings. It's the president of a steel company, whose son has just killed his wife. The office lights blaze on and Simon is galvanized into life, flailing about, screaming, chortling with delight and, as the film ends, dashing off with Rexy at his side to save another wealthy guilty client from a murder charge. And we in the audience are delighted to see him recover the will to live.

Almost thirty years after this magnificent film was released, many in my generation were inspired to choose law school by Gregory Peck's performance as Atticus Finch in *To Kill a Mockingbird* (1961). Anyone who would make that choice because of seeing *Counsellor at Law* belongs in an asylum. We can never admire and love George Simon as we love Atticus, but—and in the last analysis this may be more important—we come to understand him as Atticus, seen as he is through an idealized lens, can never be understood.

***

Readers who are not too familiar with the law-related films of the early 1930s but more at home in juriscinema's second golden age, which roughly coincides with the peak years of the Warren Court and which is typified by *To Kill a Mockingbird*, are likely by now to be wondering: Did early talkies produce not a single celluloid Cicero worthy to stand in the same courtroom with Atticus Finch? In fact there are many honorable lawyer characters in films of this period. They function, however, not as lawyers but as players in emotional dramas with female stars and primary appeal to a female audience. This chapter would not be complete without consideration of the roles lawyers played in the kinds of movies known variously as emotional dramas, women's pictures and weepies.

In *Anybody's Woman* (Paramount © 8/31/30, directed by Dorothy Arzner from a screenplay by Zoe Akins and Doris Anderson based on Gouverneur Morris' short story "The Better Wife"), society lawyer Neil Dunlap (Clive Brook) is divorced by his wife and goes on a long drinking binge during which he happens to run into chorus girl Pansy Gray (Ruth Chatterton), whom he had once defended in court on an indecent exposure charge. The next morning he wakes up to find that he and Pansy are married. His family and friends drop him over his union with a commoner but Pansy's love restores him to sobriety and lawyerly competence and—once a client of Neil's (Paul Lukas) who wants Pansy for himself is put in his place—the couple from different worlds make a go of their marriage.

In *The Right of Way* (First National © 2/7/31, directed by Frank Lloyd from a screenplay by Francis Edward Faragoh based on Sir Gilbert Parker's 1901 novel of the same name) Canadian criminal lawyer Charles "Beauty" Steele (Conrad Nagel) accuses his wife (Olive Tell) of having an affair with a former lover while he was away successfully defending Joe Portugais (Fred Kohler) on a murder charge. On the heels of that discovery he learns that, in order to pay gambling debts, his brother-in-law Billy Wantage (William Janney) has stolen a client's money from his safe. A fight breaks out in the gambling house while he's trying to recover the money and Steele is seriously injured but his life is saved by Joe Portugais, who takes him to a remote village where it's discovered that he has amnesia. Calling himself Charles Mallard, Steele starts a new life in the village. Only when he falls in love with Rosalie Evantural (Loretta Young) and they plan to marry does Joe tell him the truth about his past life and his existing wife. Steele tells Rosalie that he must go away for a while and returns to his original home, only to find that his wife has assumed he's been dead all this time and married her former lover. Billy Wantage begs Steele to stay dead and allow his wife to be happy and, when he refuses, follows him into the woods and shoots him, although he lives long enough for a tearful farewell scene with Rosalie.

It's a Wise Child (MGM © 3/26/31, directed by Robert Z. Leonard from a screenplay by Laurence E. Johnson based on his own 1929 stage play of the same name) is set in a gossipy town in dairy country and concerns a young woman who isn't pregnant and the men who are suspected of impregnating her. Joyce Stanton (Marion Davies) and lawyer Steve (Sidney Blackmer), who is keeping to himself the fact that he loves Joyce, are respectively beneficiary and trustee under her late father's testamentary trust. One evening Joyce and her fiancé, bank clerk Roger Baldwin (Lester Vail), happen to see the Stanton housemaid Annie Ostrom (Marie Prevost) being arrested during a police raid on a roadhouse and Joyce's brother Bill (Ben Alexander) fleeing from the scene. Joyce tells a few white lies to get the charges against Annie dismissed and Annie then tells her that she secretly married Bill a few months earlier and is now pregnant. Knowing that the true love of Annie's life is Cool Kelly (James Gleason), Joyce asks Steve to arrange an annulment of the maid's marriage and engages a professional midwife to take care of the child when it's born. She and the midwife are seen together by local gossips and rumors start flying like wildfire that it's Joyce who's expecting, although Joyce has no idea what people are saying about her. Each of the film's male characters denies that he's the father and Steve drops hints to Joyce that she should immediately marry whoever is. Eventually Joyce catches on that everyone thinks she's pregnant but, to protect Annie, refuses to explain why she was with the midwife. When Steve nobly makes a public admission that he's the father of the non-existent fetus, Joyce realizes that he's the only man who really loves her and wedding bells ring.

The Night Angel (Paramount © 7/18/31, directed by Edmund Goulding from his own screenplay) takes place in middle Europe but is cut from the same mold as its congeners with American settings. After prosecuting the tavernkeeper and madam who calls herself Countess von Martini (Alison Skipworth) and getting her sentenced to prison, Prague city attorney Rudek Berkem (Fredric March) saves her daughter Yula (Nancy Carroll) from being sent to the reformatory and begins to fall in love with this proletarienne even though he's already engaged to Theresa Masar (Phoebe Foster), who is of his own social class. Biezl (Alan Hale), a jealous brute who wants Yula for himself, first tries to ruin Rudek's reputation and then threatens to kill him. A fight between the three protagonists in Yula's room at her mother's tavern ends with Rudek stabbing Biezl to death. He is tried for murder but Yula's tearful speech convinces the jury that he acted in self-defense. Theresa nobly bows out and the lovers from two different worlds are reunited.

My Sin (Paramount © 9/26/31, directed by George Abbott from a screenplay by Owen Davis and Adelaide Heilbron based on Abbott's adaptation of Frederick Jackson's 1929 stage play *Her Past)* begins in Panama where the notorious "nightclub hostess" Carlotta (Tallulah Bankhead) is put on trial for the murder of a man she killed in self-defense. Representing her is alcoholic lawyer Dick Grady (Fredric March), who wins an acquittal and, as a result, overcomes his alcohol addiction and is hired by businessman Roger Metcalf (Harry Davenport). Dick goes to Carlotta's apartment to thank her for helping him regain his self-respect, finds her about to kill herself, and uses all the money he has left to help her create a new and respectable identity. Calling herself Ann Trevor, Carlotta moves to New York and becomes an interior decorator. Later Dick too relocates to New York, where he discovers that Carlotta is engaged to wealthy Larry Gordon (Scott Kolk) but doesn't plan to tell him about her past. Attending a reception for "Ann Trevor," Dick finds that one of the guests is his former employer Roger Metcalf—who happens to be Larry's uncle—and tells the Gordon family about his defense of Carlotta, although claiming that the woman killed herself in Panama. At this point "Ann" confesses that she is Carlotta and that's the end of the marriage plans. A year later she and Dick run into each other again and agree to marry.

In *Possessed* (MGM © 11/27/31, directed by Clarence Brown from a screenplay by Lenore Coffee based on Edgar Selwyn's 1920 play *The Mirage*), Marian Martin (Joan Crawford) leaves her job in a small-town paper mill and her boyfriend Al Manning (Wallace Ford) and goes to New York to better herself. There she meets wealthy attorney Mark Whitney (Clark Gable) and they begin a three-year-long affair that brings her sophistication, culture and money. Eventually she asks him to marry her but he refuses, fearing that someday she'll hurt him as his first wife did. They continue their affair, with Marian keeping a separate apartment for appearances' sake and calling herself Mrs. Moreland, until Mark decides to run for governor and, in order to save him political embarrassment, she disappears. But it doesn't help: the opposing candidate sends out hecklers to disrupt Mark's campaign speeches with flyers reading "Who Is Mrs. Moreland?" Then one night at a huge rally Marian speaks out from the audience, describing Mark as an honorable man who once belonged to her but now belongs to them. Sobbing, she runs out into the rain. Mark catches up and, as the film ends, commits to her whatever the political fallout.

Forbidden (Columbia © 1/5/32, directed by Frank Capra from a screenplay by Jo Swerling based on Capra's original story) opens with a vacation cruise on which librarian Lulu Smith (Barbara Stanwyck) begins an affair with politically ambitious lawyer Bob Grover (Adolphe Menjou). Several months into their relationship, Lulu tells Bob that newspaper reporter Al Holland (Ralph Bellamy) has asked her to marry him. Bob confesses that he can't propose to her himself because he already has a wife (Dorothy Peterson), an invalid he can't abandon. Lulu breaks up with Bob without telling him that she's pregnant. Eighteen years pass and Bob, now both a widower and the District Attorney, is reunited with Lulu and meets his teen-age daughter Roberta (Charlotte Henry). They pick up their affair where it left off and Bob goes on to become first a mayor and then a congressman, but when he's nominated for governor, Al Holland comes back into the picture.

To prevent the man who is now city editor of his paper from publishing a story that will ruin Bob's career, Lulu kills him. After serving a short term in prison she receives a pardon from—who else?—Governor Bob! A year later Bob dies. His will leaves Lulu half his wealth but she gallantly tears it up so that Roberta will never learn of her illegitimacy.

Peg o' My Heart (MGM © 5/17/33, directed by Robert Z. Leonard from a screenplay by Frank R. Adams based on Frances Marion's adaptation of J. Hartley Manners' 1912 stage play of the same name) begins with poor Irish widower Patrick O'Connell (J. Farrell MacDonald) being told by London lawyer Sir Jerry Markham (Onslow Stevens) that his daughter Peg (Marion Davies) has just inherited £2,000,000 from her dead mother's family, but only if she lives in England for three years and agrees never to see Patrick again. Keeping the proviso secret from her, Patrick arranges for her to go to England and be educated in the home of snobbish Mrs. Chichester (Irene Browne). After tons of emotional complications without legal aspects, Peg learns about the testamentary Catch-22, renounces her inheritance and returns to Ireland and her father. Sir Jerry then shows up on the O'Connell doorstep and asks her to marry him.

Midnight Mary (MGM © 6/23/33, directed by William Wellman from a screenplay by Gene Markey and Kathryn Scola based on an original story by Anita Loos) is related almost entirely in flashback as Mary Martin (Loretta Young), awaiting the jury's verdict in her trial for murder, tells the story of her life to the court clerk. After serving three years for a theft she hadn't committed, she met gangster Leo Darcy (Ricardo Cortez) and, with no legitimate jobs open to her, became his mistress and partner in crime. While casing a gambling house Leo planned to rob, Mary happened to meet society lawyer Tom Mannering, Jr. (Franchot Tone), who helped her escape when the gang got into a gun battle with the police and then set out to reform her. After graduating from secretarial school she was hired by Tom's law firm. Then one night while she was out with

Tom, one of the cops from the gambling house shootout happened to see her and recognized her as the woman who got away. Mary wound up back in prison and, a year later, Tom married a socialite (Martha Sleeper). After serving her sentence Mary was again unable to find an honest job and had to go back to Leo or starve. One night she happened to run into Tom, discovered that he was miserable in his marriage and started seeing him again. Leo found out and sent men to kill Tom but they gunned down his best friend by mistake. In order to save Tom's life, Mary then killed Leo. At her trial she never mentioned Tom's name. End of flashback. Just as the jury's verdict is read — Guilty — Tom bursts into court, confesses his affair with Mary, demands a new trial and takes over as her lawyer.

Beauty for Sale (MGM © 9/8/33, directed by Richard Boleslawski from a screenplay by Zelda Sears and Eve Greene based on Faith Baldwin's 1933 novel *Beauty*) is about the love lives of several young women who work in an exclusive New York beauty parlor owned by Madame Sonia (Hedda Hopper). Letty Lawson (Madge Evans) is dispatched to a posh mansion to give a manicure to bored socialite Henrietta Sherwood (Alice Brady) and becomes attracted to her lawyer husband (Otto Kruger) after Henrietta's dog chews up her hat and he insists on paying for the damage. There follow some platonic dates between Letty and Sherwood and an emotional scene in which Bill Merrick (Eddie Nugent), who wants Letty himself, tells her she's no better than a gold-digger. Letty joins Sherwood on his yacht while Henrietta spends the summer in Maine, and at season's end the lawyer tells her he loves her and wants to go on seeing her. Terrified by the suicidal ending of a fellow beautician's doomed romance, Letty breaks with Sherwood, begins dating Bill, and is about to marry him when she learns that Mrs. Sherwood has dumped her husband for an architect (John Roche), a development which permits the film to end with Letty and Sherwood reunited.

In *Sadie McKee* (MGM © 5/9/34, directed by Clarence Brown from a screenplay by John Meehan based on Viña Delmar's 1933 magazine serial "Pretty Sadie McKee") Joan Crawford plays a servingmaid in a wealthy home who catches the eye of her employer's son Michael Alderson (Franchot Tone), a lawyer. When Michael defames her boyfriend Tommy Wallace (Gene Raymond) at a dinner party, Sadie denounces the entire Alderson family and takes off with Tommy for New York. They plan to get married but Tommy deserts Sadie at the last minute and joins Dolly Merrick (Esther Ralston) in a traveling club act. Heartbroken, Sadie finds work as a dancer at a nightclub where one evening she meets Jack Brennan (Edward Arnold), a wealthy alcoholic who's doing the town with his best friend— Michael Alderson! Before long Sadie and Brennan are married. Eventually Tommy and Dolly return to New York but Sadie passes up the chance to resume her affair with him and concentrates on saving her husband, who's been told by doctors that he'll die in six months if he doesn't stop drinking. When Brennan is sober and healthy again, Sadie asks him to divorce her so she can have the man she really loves. Brennan nobly agrees and Michael Alderson no less nobly sets out to find Tommy, only to discover that he has tuberculosis. For Sadie's sake Michael gets Tommy admitted to a hospital, but too late. On his deathbed Tommy reveals to Sadie that it was Michael who tried to save him and the film ends with the couple reunited.

***

Women and minority lawyers were almost unknown in the real world of the early 1930s and their counterparts on the screen were correspondingly rare. A grand total of four films from the first golden age have significant female lawyer characters—one of whom we've already encountered in *The Defense Rests* (1934), where Jean Arthur played the assistant to Jack Holt's Fallonesque shyster—and exactly one concerns an attorney of color. Although both the film with the black lawyer and one of the three with a woman were made by bottom-of-the-barrel independent studios whose product in general I've excluded from this chapter, the rarity of such characters and the extent of contemporary interest in their treatment justify an exception to my rule here.

Scarlet Pages (First National © 9/22/30, directed by Ray Enright from a screenplay by Walter Anthony and Maude Fuller based on the 1929 stage play of the same name by Samuel Shipman and John B. Hymer) would have been included in the previous section on "women's pictures" of legal interest except for its unique distinction: the lawyer character is a woman herself. For reasons she won't explain, criminal defense specialist Mary Bancroft (Elsie Ferguson) refuses an offer of marriage from district attorney John Remington (John Halliday). Soon afterwards she agrees to represent dancer Nora Mason (Marion Nixon), who is charged with the murder of her foster father (Wilbur Mack). After the usual courtroom dramatics it comes out that Nora had ample justification: the old man had made her submit sexually to a theatrical promoter (William B. Davidson). After the jury returns a Not Guilty verdict comes the big surprise: Nora is the daughter Mary had left in an orphanage twenty years earlier! The film ends with Nora reconciled with her sweetheart (Grant Withers) and her mother with the DA.

In *Drifting Souls* (Tower, 1932, directed by Louis King from a screenplay by Douglas Z. Doty and Norman Houston based on an original story by Barbara Hunter) a woman lawyer (Lois Wilson) offers her services for a year to anyone who will donate the $5,000 needed for an operation to save her father's life. Her proposition is taken up by a racketeer who has conned a young millionaire into thinking he committed a hit-and-run while drunk. Following the racketeer's script, the lawyer first alibis the young man and later marries him, but when the mark's fortune vanishes in the Depression the racketeer exposes him to the police. At his trial for manslaughter his bride/defense counsel manages to clear him and pin the guilt on the racketeer. The film ends with the married couple actually falling in love.

A woman lawyer is the protagonist of *Ann Carver's Profession* (Columbia © 5/22/33, directed by Edward Buzzell from a screenplay by Robert Riskin) but that doesn't mean the film would appeal to women lawyers today. Ann Carver (Fay Wray) marries singing football hero Bill Graham (Gene Raymond) after they both graduate from college. She passes the bar—for which in this film law school does not seem to be a prerequisite—but opts to keep house for Bill. Then all but inadvertently she goes to court and wins a breach of promise suit for a wealthy playboy, and the result is a meteoric legal career for her while Bill's career as a draftsman stagnates. Eventually he quits his job for a higher-paying crooning gig at a nightclub where alcoholic chanteuse Carole Rogers (Claire Dodd) makes a play for Bill and Ann, mistakenly thinking the two are making music offstage too, publicly humiliates her husband. Unable to handle his wife's success and his own failure, Bill moves out. Carole makes moves to take Ann's place in Bill's life but accidentally chokes herself to death in his apartment while drunk and Bill is charged with murder. His defense counsel of course is Ann, who tells the jury that Bill's troubles are her fault and announces that this will be her last case. The jury finds him not guilty and Ann returns to housewifehood while Bill suddenly finds himself a successful architect.

The first golden age produced one and only movie with an attorney of color as an important character. His law degree however is irrelevant to the film, which was aimed at and seen by no one but black audiences in segregated theaters. Long lost and recently rediscovered, albeit in truncated form, *Veiled Aristocrats* (Micheaux, 1932) was produced, written and directed by Oscar Micheaux (1884-1951), who in many respects was the black counterpart of Ed Wood, an inept enthusiast condemned to zero budgets and lionized after his death in countless books and articles, although unlike Wood he's a crucial figure in the popular culture of his race. The film was based on Charles W. Chesnutt's 1900 novel *The House Behind the Cedars*, from which Micheaux had also made a 1924 silent of the same name, but apparently differs in many respects from both the silent version and the novel. Light-skinned African-American attorney John Walden (Lorenzo Tucker) returns to his family after a never-explained 20-year absence to find that he has a younger sister Rena (Lucille Lewis), whose lover Frank Fowler (Carl Mahon) has skin much darker than that of the Waldens. Determined to gentrify his family, John passes for white, moves to a classier part of town with

Rena and introduces her to a wealthy white man (a light-skinned black actor whose name remains unknown) who, unaware of her race, falls in love with her. In the 1924 silent version, Rena and the white man get married and, on discovering that they have a black daughter-in-law, his parents go to court to get the marriage annulled on racial grounds.[19] Whether this sequence is reprised in the talkie is unclear since only 44 minutes of the latter survive.[20] In any event Rena finally realizes she belongs with Fowler and reunites with him.

***

Comedy movies come in almost as many varieties as Heinz products, and reasonable minds may often differ as to whether a particular film belongs in this genre at all. Of the early talkies that clearly or at least arguably fall into this category, a rather large number involve lawyer characters or legal aspects to a significant degree.

The protagonists of *Queen High* (Paramount © 8/22/30, directed by Fred Newmeyer from a screenplay by Frank Mandel based on the 1926 stage play of the same name by Laurence Schwab, B.G. De Sylva and Lewis Gensler and on Edward Henry Peple's 1916 stage play *A Pair of Sixes*) are partners in the garter manufacturing business. After interminable fussing and feuding, T. Boggs Johns (Charles Ruggles) and George Nettleton (Frank Morgan) take the advice of their lawyer Cyrus Vanderholt (Rudy Cameron) and play a hand of draw poker, the winner to run the business for a year and have the loser serve as his butler. Amid the forgettable songs and jokes, Johns' nephew (Stanley Smith) and Nettleton's niece (Ginger Rogers) fall in love. Eventually the partners discover that their poker pact isn't legally binding and chase the lawyer out of the picture.

Silent screen star Gloria Swanson made her talkie debut in *What a Widow!* (Gloria/United Artists © 9/4/30, directed by Allan Dwan from a screenplay by James Gleason and James Seymour based on an original story by Josephine Lovett) as Tamarind Brooks, a woman made wealthy by her much older husband's death. She sails for Paris in search of romance and finds it with several men on the ship including lawyer Gerry Morgan (Owen Moore). Eventually she drops all the Europeans she's been flirting with and marries Gerry as the plane returning them to the U.S. flies over the Statue of Liberty.

The Naughty Flirt (First National © 12/30/30, directed by Edward F. Cline from a screenplay by Richard Weill and Earl Baldwin) kicks off when Kay Elliott (Alice White), the daughter of a prosperous lawyer (George Irving), throws a wild party that ends in night court. Alan Ward (Paul Page), a young lawyer in her father's office, gives her a tongue-lashing about her behavior, which sparks her into making a play for him. Everything goes Kay's way until Alan overhears someone say she had made a bet that she'd have him eating out of her hand in short order. For trying to make a fool out of him he gives her a sound spanking which instantly reforms her. She takes a secretarial job with her father's firm and she and Alan begin to fall genuinely in love—until her false friend Linda Gregory (Myrna Loy), whose brother Jack (Douglas Gilmore) wants to retrieve the family's Depression-battered fortune by marrying Kay himself, makes it seem that she and Alan are having an affair. This is a romantic comedy so all ends happily for everyone except the viewers, who have had to endure Alice White's screechy Noo Yawk accent for more than an hour. Paul Page's lawyer character is certainly honorable enough, but very little in the film would have needed to be changed if he'd been an accountant or junior executive, and juriscinemaphiles would have been spared his stick-like performance.

The Gang Buster (Paramount © 1/16/31, directed by A. Edward Sutherland from a screenplay by Percy Heath and Joseph L. Mankiewicz) is about Charlie Case (Jack Oakie), a naive and superstitious young man who sells insurance policies protecting against cyclone damage. After inadvertently saving the life of lawyer Andrew Martine (William Morris), Charlie falls in love with the attorney's daughter Sylvia (Jean Arthur) and sells her grateful father a $100,000 life policy—only to discover later that Martine has been targeted for death by one of his former clients, gangster Sudden Mike Slade (William "Stage" Boyd). When Slade snatches Sylvia in a scheme to trade her for some incriminating papers in her father's possession, Charlie endeavors to get her back by informing the gangster that kidnapping is illegal. Needless to say his plan doesn't work, but all ends well anyway.

Billed immediately after the stars of *Don't Bet on Women* (Fox © 1/29/31, directed by William K. Howard from a screenplay by Lynn Starling and Leon Gordon based on an original story by William Anthony McGuire) is Roland Young as smug and self-satisfied lawyer Herbert Drake. After advising his divorced and woman-averse client Roger Fallon (Edmund Lowe) to learn the art of controlling women without their knowledge—an art he himself claims to have mastered—Drake bets $10,000 that Roger can't within 48 hours kiss the first woman who joins them on the veranda. When that woman turns out to be Drake's so-carefully-controlled wife (Jeanette MacDonald), the lawyer insists that the bet is on and romantic complications start multiplying like rabbits, albeit without any legal component.

The main character in *Lonely Wives* (Pathe © 2/22/31, directed by Russell Mack from a screenplay by Walter DeLeon based on a 1912 German vaudeville skit adapted for U.S. vaudeville ten years later) is Richard Smith (Edward Everett Horton), a stern and proper attorney who has both a wife and a habit of womanizing at every opportunity. Learning of his penchant, Diane O'Dare (Laura La Plante) tries to flirt her way into getting him to handle her divorce at a deep discount. As luck would have it, Diane's estranged husband Felix (Edward Everett Horton) is a dead ringer for Richard and, for reasons I won't go into here, is impersonating the lawyer when his lovely wife Madeline (Esther Ralston) returns from a solo vacation itching for amour. The mock-Shakespearean comedy of mistaken identities runs its course with plenty of innuendo but no adultery and with both Madeline and Diane reunited with their look-alike husbands.

The Girl Habit (Paramount © 6/30/31, directed by Edward F. Cline from a screenplay by Owen Davis and Gertrude Purcell based on A.E. Thomas and Clayton Hamilton's 1915 stage play *Thirty Days*) is another of those comedies of errors rich in sexual innuendo that flourished in the early 1930s until self-censorship killed the genre. When wealthy philanderer Charlie Floyd (Charles Ruggles) gets engaged to equally prosperous Lucy Ledyard (Sue Conroy), his lawyer Huntley Palmer (Douglas Gilmore), who wants to marry Lucy for her money, begins pulling all sorts of tricks—like forging risqué letters supposedly written by Charlie to his former mistress Sonya (Tamara Geva), whose present husband Tony Maloney (Allen Jenkins) is a gangster—to break the couple up. This is a comedy so no one gets hurt and all ends well, though not for the lawyer.

Peach-o-Reno (RKO © 12/23/31, directed by William A. Seiter from a screenplay by Ralph Spence, Tim Whelan and Eddie Welch) stars vaudeville comics Bert Wheeler and Robert Woolsey as Wattles & Swift, a pair of divorce lawyers in the city that at the time was the marriage dissolution capital of the United States. The hijinks begin when each partner inadvertently undertakes to represent the spouse of the other's client. Smith arranges for middle-aged Aggie Bruno (Cora Witherspoon) to be caught with a professional co-respondent of the male gender while Wattles is setting the stage for Joe Bruno (Joseph Cawthorn) to be caught with a woman in the same line of business. Then Wattles gets a death threat from an Arizona gambler whose ex-wife he had represented and, in a frantic effort to protect himself, dresses up in women's clothes and poses as the female co-respondent, only to be exposed when his wig catches fire. Eventually there's a divorce trial (broadcast on radio) but the film ends with the Brunos reunited and their daughters Prudence and Pansy (Dorothy Lee and Zelma O'Neal) engaged respectively to Wattles & Swift.

The Heart of New York (Warner Bros. © 3/6/32, directed by Mervyn LeRoy from a screenplay by Arthur Caesar and Houston Branch based on David Freedman's 1929 stage play *Mendel, Inc.*) is the kind of ethnic comedy that even Turner Classic Movies won't show today. Mendel (George Sidney) is a wacky inventor who lives with his wife and three children on (where else?) the Lower East Side. His older daughter Lillian (Ruth Hall) is engaged to Milton (Donald

Cook) who, being at one and the same time a doctor, a dentist and a lawyer, is the perfect (or should that be poifect?) nice Jewish boy for any nice Jewish girl (or should that be goil?). Milton puts on his lawyer hat when the rapacious manufacturer Gassenheim (Oscar Apfel) tries to halt production on Mendel's revolutionary new dishwashing machine.

Love, Honor and Oh, Baby! (Universal © 9/26/33, directed by Edward Buzzell from a screenplay by Norman Krasna and Buzzell himself based on Bertrand Robinson and Howard Lindsay's 1930 stage play *Oh, Promise Me*) seems to be Hollywood's only comedy of the first golden age that deals with a subject most of us associate with much later decades. Struggling small-town lawyer Mark Reed (Slim Summerville) is introduced by his girlfriend Connie Clark (ZaSu Pitts) to her friend Louise (Adrienne Dore), who wants to sue vegetarian banker Jasper B. Ogden (George Barbier) for sexual misconduct. When Mark tells the woman she has insufficient evidence to succeed, Connie decides to take a job at the bank and entrap Ogden in a sex scandal. She encourages the randy banker's advances to the point that on his next business trip out of town he reserves train berths for two. Mark finds out what Connie's up to and substitutes his own trap, manipulating Ogden into sneaking into Connie's bedroom at night with the upshot that the banker is sued for what today we call sexual harassment. Mark's comic variants on William J. Fallon's shyster tricks—like having Connie read on the witness stand from her diary and imply all sorts of sexual connotations in her descriptions of the vegetables Ogden had recommended to her—force the banker to cough up $100,000 in settlement money and stop hitting on his female employees. This may sound like a serious film but it was clearly intended for chuckles.

I'm No Angel (Paramount © 10/16/33, directed by Wesley Ruggles from a screenplay by Mae West) is the story of Tira (Mae West), a circus performer whose star turn gains her fame, wealth and a bevy of well-to-do admirers, the one for whom she falls hardest being Jack Clayton (Cary Grant). The two make plans to get married but the romance sours on the night Jack visits Tira's penthouse while she's out and encounters her jealous former main squeeze Slick Wiley (Ralf Harolde), who pretends he's still her lover. Jack calls off the engagement and Tira, ignorant of how he was fooled by Slick, hires shyster Benny Pinkowitz (Gregory Ratoff), whose motto is "Give me that much loophole and I'm through it like an eel," to sue for breach of contract. On cross-examination, Clayton's lawyer (Irving Pichel) confronts Tira with several of the previous men in her life.

> Lawyer: "And no doubt you recall those five gentlemen seated in the first row, right inside the railing? Mr. Blake, Mr. Larson, Mr. Willard, Mr. Foster and Mr. Harris?"
> Tira: "Well, I do recall their faces but them ain't the names they gave me."

With the case going against her, Tira decides to question witnesses herself. "The plaintiff, not being a practicing attorney, may put her questions as best she can," rules the judge (Walter Walker). Just as she sashays before the twelve good men and horny, His Honor warns the jury not to be "swayed" by the plaintiff's charms. Between questions to witnesses Tira makes side comments like "I'm just askin' good, honest and intelligent people not to take the word of an ex-convict [i.e. Slick Wiley] against a good, honest and innocent woman." Jack interrupts the juristic farce with an offer to settle the case. Later Tira entertains the bug-eyed judge in her penthouse, a tryst which is interrupted by a phone call from the no less smitten Juror Number 4, to whom she addresses the immortal line: "Don't forget, come up and see me sometime." The film ends as Jack learns that he was mistaken about Tira's involvement with Slick and the couple get back together.

In *Tillie and Gus* (Paramount © 10/17/33, directed by Francis Martin from a screenplay by himself and Walter DeLeon based on an original story by Rupert Hughes), genial flimflam artist

Augustus Winterbottom (W.C. Fields) joins forces with his ex-wife Matilda (Alison Skipworth), who is equally skilled at the game, to save their young niece Mary Sheridan (Jacqueline Wells) and her family from wily lawyer Phineas Pratt (Clarence Wilson). After Pratt has swindled the Sheridans out of Mary's inheritance from her father, the family's only remaining possession is a decrepit ferry which Tillie and Gus help them restore to working condition. When Pratt purchases a ferry of his own and tries to put the Sheridans out of business, the issue of who gets the franchise is settled by a Fourth of July race between the boats—which ends with the Sheridans winning and Phineas dunked in the drink.

The protagonists of *Havana Widows* (First National © 11/18/33, directed by Ray Enright from a screenplay by Earl Baldwin) are out-of-work showgirls Mae Knight (Joan Blondell) and Sadie Appleby (Glenda Farrell), who go to Havana on borrowed money and pose as wealthy widows, hoping to entrap rich men they can sue for breach of promise. Mae meets and falls for young Bob Jones (Lyle Talbot) but, when the girls' lawyer Duffy (Frank McHugh) tells them Bob has no money of his own, they decide to target his randy father (Guy Kibbee). Then they meet Deacon Jones' wife (Ruth Donnelly) and, realizing they can't sue a married man for breach of promise, take Duffy's advice to get the old philanderer into a compromising situation and then blackmail him. One comic complication piles atop another but all ends well with Deacon divorced from his shrewish wife and his son Bob married to Mae.

***

One of the most potent and popular genres of the early 1930s was the gangster film. Nothing in that genre requires a lawyer character and in fact there are no such characters in *Little Caesar* (1930) or *The Public Enemy* (1931) or *Scarface* (1932) or any of the other classics of the genre. Yet a number of lesser known gangster films did have a legal component.

In *Bad Company* (RKO © 2/6/31, directed by Tay Garnett from a screenplay by Garnett and Tom Buckingham suggested by Jack Lait's 1930 novel *Put on the Spot*), Helen King (Helen Twelvetrees) agrees to marry lawyer Steve Carlyle (John Garrick) without knowing that Steve's sole client is gang boss Goldie Gorio (Ricardo Cortez) or that her own brother Mark (Frank Conroy) is the head of a rival gang. Gorio, who has his own designs on Helen, finances a lavish wedding for her and Steve and lavishes gifts on the newlyweds. Later the gang boss learns that federal agent McBaine (Harry Carey) is planning to kill him and sends Steve into the G-man's trap, in which he's seriously wounded. Finally Helen understands the truth about her husband and her brother. Gorio wipes out Mark and his gang in a scene inspired by the St. Valentine's Day Massacre, then makes moves on Helen, who encourages him because she knows the only way she can save Steve is by killing the mob leader. The film climaxes with a police raid on the fortified apartment hideaway where Helen is trapped with Gorio and his men. Steve escapes from the hospital and makes his way through the battle lines to the apartment and Helen shoots Gorio down in her husband's presence.

Afraid to Talk (Universal © 10/21/32, directed by Edward L. Cahn from a screenplay by Tom Reed based on the 1932 stage play *Merry-Go-Round* by Albert Maltz and George Sklar) is one of those grim and cynical films of big-city corruption that vanished with strict self-censorship. Bellboy Eddie Martin (Eric Linden) is framed for a gangland murder in his hotel that he happened to witness. After a brutal beating supervised by Assistant District Attorney Wade (Louis Calhern), he confesses. The outraged doctor who treats the young man calls in criminal lawyer Harry Berger (Gustav von Seyffertitz). Despite his efforts Eddie is sent to prison, but because he still knows too much, Wade sends some thugs to kill Eddie in his cell and make it look like suicide. The plot is thwarted (though not by Berger) and some of the corrupt politicians in the city are brought to justice but Wade remains unscathed and, as the film ends, issues a press release claiming that the city has been totally cleaned up.

20,000 Years in Sing Sing (First National © 12/23/32, directed by Michael Curtiz from a screenplay by Wilson Mizner and Brown Holmes based on an adaptation by Courteney Terrett and Robert

Lord of Warden Lewis E. Lawes' 1932 memoir of the same name) is a gritty little picture featuring one of the slimiest attorneys in early juriscinema. Soon after gangster Tommy Connors (Spencer Tracy) is sent to Sing Sing, his lawyer Joe Finn (Louis Calhern) tries and fails to get special privileges for his client by bribing the enlightened and progressive prison warden (Arthur Byron). Later during an automobile drive Finn makes moves on Tommy's girlfriend Fay Wilson (Bette Davis), who is seriously injured jumping from the car to escape him. The warden allows Tommy to visit her. When he learns how she was hurt, the two of them go to have it out with Finn. The confrontation ends with Fay shooting the lawyer to death but Tommy takes the blame and the radically downbeat final scene shows him about to be electrocuted.

The Mad Game (Fox © 10/9/33, directed by Irving Cummings from a screenplay by William Conselman and Henry Johnson based on Conselman's original story) takes place as Prohibition is coming to an end. Bootlegger Edward Carson (Spencer Tracy) is prevailed upon by his lawyer William Bennett (John Miljan) to plead guilty to a federal income-tax evasion charge for which, the fix supposedly being in, he'll receive only a fine and a suspended sentence. Actually there is no fix — Bennett wants Carson put away so he can take up with his client's mistress Marilyn Kirk (Kathleen Burke) — and Judge Penfield (Ralph Morgan) sentences Carson to five years in prison. Chopper Allen (J. Carrol Naish) takes over Carson's mob, has Bennett and Marilyn bumped off, and launches a series of kidnappings-for-ransom which terrorize the nation. Carson, whose wife and daughter had been murdered by kidnappers years before, offers the authorities a deal: if he's paroled, he'll undergo plastic surgery and infiltrate the mob in order to destroy it. At the violent climax he gives his life to save Judge Penfield's kidnapped son.

In *Sleepers East* (Fox © 1/16/34, directed by Kenneth MacKenna from a screenplay by Lester Cole based on Frederick Nebel's 1933 novel of the same name), parolee Lena Karelson (Wynne Gibson) meets Jack Wentworth (Howard Lally), the mayor's son, and foolishly accompanies him to a gambling club where after losing heavily he kills the club's owner in Lena's presence. When the police pin the crime on a gangster who was also about to kill the gambler, Lena promises Jack that she'll keep her mouth shut and leaves town. Martin Knox (Harvey Stephens), the accused gangster's lawyer, trails her to Toledo and threatens to get her put back in prison as a parole violator if she doesn't come back and testify for the defense. As the train returning them passes through Lena's old home town, her childhood sweetheart Jason Everett (Preston Foster) comes on board. Then political operator Carl Izzard (J. Carrol Naish) takes Lena aside and tells her that if she testifies for the defense she'll be tried as an accessory to the gambler's murder. The film climaxes of course in the courtroom. With great reluctance Lena testifies to the truth and is about to identify Jack as the killer when he stands up in court and shoots himself. Jason and Lena are reunited at the fade-out.

***

Throughout the Nineteen Thirties and Forties one of Hollywood's most popular genres was the detective film, centering on the protagonist's solution of one or more crimes, almost invariably murders. Lawyers were no more necessary in this genre than they were in gangster films, but in fact they appeared in several whodunits in a variety of roles: as detectives, as victims, as suspects and, needless to say, as murderers.

The earliest lawyer character to function as a cinematic sleuth seems to have been Andrew Bullivant, whose irascibility has earned him the nickname Grumpy. This juristic curmudgeon, who may well be the spiritual grandfather of John Mortimer's Rumpole of the Bailey, was reportedly portrayed on stage by English actor Cyril Maude more than 1400 times before he was brought to the screen in *Grumpy* (Paramount © 8/22/30, directed by George Cukor and Cyril Gardner from a screenplay by Doris Anderson based on the 1920 stage play of the same name by Horace Hodges and Thomas Wigney Percyval). Bullivant (Cyril Maude) is living in retirement on his country estate with his granddaughter Virginia (Frances Dade) and house guest Chamberlain Jarvis (Paul Cavanagh) when Virginia's boyfriend Ernest Heron (Phillips Holmes) shows up for a visit, bringing with him a valuable diamond that he was commissioned to carry from South Africa to England. Ernest is attacked in the Bullivant library on the night of his arrival and the diamond is stolen and replaced by a camellia. Suspecting that the culprit is Jarvis, Grumpy follows him to London and begins to accumulate evidence that in due course leads to a confession and the return of the stone.

Charlie Chan, the protagonist of six detective novels by Earl Derr Biggers (1884-1933) and more than forty films plus radio and TV series, was not a lawyer but encountered lawyers now and then in the course of his sleuthing, for instance in *Charlie Chan Carries On* (Fox © 2/11/31, directed by Hamilton MacFadden from a screenplay by Philip Klein and Barry Conners based on Earl Derr Biggers' 1930 novel of the same name). The film opens in London with the murder of one of the members of a round-the-world tour. When Inspector Duff of Scotland Yard (Peter Gawthorne) is unable to solve the crime before the travelers leave London, he joins the party, which includes elderly criminal lawyer Patrick Tait (William Holden). More murders take place as the tour proceeds around the world. In Honolulu Duff comes too close to the answer and is himself shot, leaving his old friend Chan (Warner Oland) to carry on with the cruise and find the killer—who turns out not to be the lawyer.

The Trial of Vivienne Ware (Fox © 4/5/32, directed by William K. Howard from a screenplay by Philip Klein and Barry Connors based on Kenneth M. Ellis' 1931 novel of the same name) bears certain similarities to Erle Stanley Gardner's Perry Mason novels, which began appearing the year after this film's release, but there are also significant differences. While Gardner in his early novels allows us to see only what happens in Mason's presence, the film makes us privy to the events leading up to the trial. Vivienne Ware (Joan Bennett) and her fiancé, architect Damon Fenwick (Jameson Thomas), go to the Silver Bowl nightclub where Vivienne is insulted by singer Dolores Divine (Lilian Bond), Fenwick's former lover. After taking Vivienne home,

Fenwick returns to the club to pick up Dolores. The next day Vivienne sends Fenwick a letter she'll soon regret. Several hours later the police arrest her for his murder. Representing her is attorney John Sutherland (Donald Cook), who is also in love with her—another element one never finds in a Perry Mason. The trial, perhaps the most swift-paced in any film, begins with a mountain of evidence against Vivienne. One: on the morning after the nightclub scene she walked in on Dolores in sexy pajamas eating breakfast with Fenwick in his house and stalked out furious. Two: immediately afterwards she sent Fenwick a letter which might be construed as threatening. Three: her handkerchief was found near Fenwick's body. Four: a neighbor claims to have seen her entering Fenwick's house that night. Vivienne denies being anywhere near the house at the time of the murder but Sutherland doesn't believe her. Nevertheless he puts her on the stand and she testifies as follows. One: her letter to Fenwick was meant to break their engagement, not threaten him. Two: she must have dropped her handkerchief during her breakfast visit to Fenwick's house. Three: at the time of the murder she was at a hockey game which she left early because she felt ill. The district attorney (Alan Dinehart) cross-examines Vivienne so ruthlessly that she breaks down, sobbing that even her own lawyer doesn't believe her. At this point we find ourselves in the juristic cloudcuckooland that most Hollywood law films sooner or later enter: the prosecutor calls the defense lawyer as a witness! Changing Vivienne's plea from not guilty to self-defense, Sutherland testifies that he attended the hockey match with her and, when she left early, followed her to Fenwick's house. The next day Sutherland proceeds as if his client were still pleading not guilty. First he calls witnesses who put Dolores Divine at Fenwick's house at the time of the murder, then he calls Dolores herself, who testifies—as dozens of characters in Perry Mason novels would do after her—that she found the body and said nothing about it but isn't the murderer. (Apparently Vivienne, like countless clients of Perry Mason, had done the same thing.) Dolores also testifies that

218

she saw the real killer leaving the scene, and that it was either her jealous boss, nightclub owner Angelo Peroni (Noel Madison), or his look-alike cousin Joe Garson (Noel Madison?). Peroni shoots Garson as he's about to testify and is himself shot down by the police and Garson's dying confession implicates both cousins. Spectators roar, flashbulbs blaze, lawyer and client embrace, the verdict is not guilty. All this in less than 60 minutes!

In *Miss Pinkerton* (First National © 7/7/32, directed by Lloyd Bacon from a screenplay by Niven Busch and Lillie Hayward based on Mary Roberts Rinehart's 1932 novel of the same name), Nurse Hilda Adams (Joan Blondell) is hired to care for wealthy Julia Mitchell (Elizabeth Patterson), whose nephew Herbert Wynne (Allan Lane) was recently murdered. The person who murdered Wynne and later kills Aunt Julia too turns out to be the family lawyer (Holmes Herbert).

Penguin Pool Murder (RKO © 12/19/32, directed by George Archainbaud from a screenplay by Willis Goldbeck based on Stuart Palmer's 1931 novel of the same name) was the first of six detective films about Palmer's spinster schoolteacher character Hildegarde Withers. Miss Withers (Edna May Oliver) is touring New York's Battery Park Aquarium with her class when the body of stockbroker Gerald Parker (Guy Usher) plops into the penguin tank. Inspector Oscar Piper (James Gleason) soon establishes that the murder weapon was a hatpin stolen from Miss Withers and driven through Parker's right ear, but at her suggestion he tells reporters that the weapon went through the dead man's left ear. Eventually Parker's wife Gwen (Mae Clarke) and her former lover Philip Seymour (Donald Cook) are charged with the murder and put on trial. Their defense counsel is Barry Costello (Robert Armstrong), who was visiting the aquarium at the time of the murder. Costello puts Miss Withers on the stand as a defense witness and, defying a cardinal rule of evidence, starts cross-examining her savagely, trying to make the jury think she killed Parker herself.

"You didn't notice the defendant in this case, Mr. Seymour, drag the unconscious body of the man you had

JUDGES & JUSTICE & LAWYERS & LAW

once loved and then hated behind the tanks and then come out? You didn't . . . steal behind the tanks with your deadly stiletto of a hatpin and drive it most cruelly and foully into the right ear of the unconscious man? (Miss Withers sits silent.) Your Honor, I have finished with this witness."

"You may be finished with the witness, Mr. Barry Costello," Withers retorts, "but the witness is not finished with you! So Gerald Parker was stabbed in the *right* ear, was he?" Within another minute, living the fantasy of anyone who's faced hostile questions in a courtroom, she exposes the lawyer as the murderer.

Charlie Chan's Greatest Case (Fox © 8/29/33, directed by Hamilton MacFadden from a screenplay by Lester Cole and Marion Orth based on Earl Derr Biggers' 1925 novel *The House Without a Key*) is set in Honolulu and involves a series of murders and other crimes in the wealthy family headed by Dan Winterslip (Robert Warwick), who is the first victim. Chan in due course pins the villainy on Dan's fortune-hunting lawyer Harry Jennison (Walter Byron).

Penthouse (MGM © 9/5/33, directed by W.S. Van Dyke from a screenplay by Frances Goodrich and Albert Hackett based on Arthur Somers Roche's 1935 novel of the same name) begins with attorney Jackson Durant (Warner Baxter) getting gangster Tony Gazotti (Leo Carrillo) acquitted on murder charges and then paying a price for his zealous advocacy: his partners kick him out of the firm and his socialite fiancée Sue Leonard (Martha Sleeper) breaks their engagement. The legal component of the film ends here. As Durant consoles himself with liquor, Sue accepts a marriage proposal from Tom Siddall (Phillips Holmes), who dumps his mistress Mimi Montagne (Mae Clarke), who makes up with her former lover, racketeer Jim Crelliman (C. Henry Gordon), who throws a party at his apartment for the express purpose of hearing Mimi tell Tom that they're through. The former lovers go out on Crelliman's balcony, a shot is heard, Mimi is found dead and Siddall, who like an idiot picked up the murder weapon, is promptly arrested. Sue begs Durant to represent her fiancé but what he does on Siddall's behalf is hardly lawyerlike. With help from Mimi's roommate Gertie Waxted (Myrna Loy) and from Tony Gazotti's underworld connections, Durant eventually pins the murder on hit man Murtoch (George E. Stone), who on Crelliman's orders shot Mimi from her own penthouse apartment and then threw the gun onto Crelliman's balcony. In a burst of offstage gunfire Gazotti dies shooting it out with Crelliman and his men. The film ends as Siddall reunites with Sue and Durant proposes to Gertie.

Two of the last mystery films made at MGM before the coming of self-censorship differ widely not only in quality but in the function of the attorney character. *The Thin Man* (MGM © 5/24/34, directed by W.S. Van Dyke from a screenplay by Albert Hackett and Frances Goodrich based on Dashiell Hammett's 1934 novel of the same name) is the high-spirited (pardon the double entendre) classic that kicked off the cinematic exploits of Nick and Nora Charles (William Powell and Myrna Loy), those madcap amateur sleuths never without cocktails in their hands who in their unique manner investigate the disappearance of wealthy inventor Clyde Wynant (Edward Ellis) and the murder of his mistress Julia Wolf (Natalie Moorhead). At the climax they give a dinner party for all the suspects and expose Wynant's lawyer Macaulay (Porter Hall) as a double murderer.

About a month later came *Murder in the Private Car* (MGM © 6/27/34, directed by Harry Beaumont from a screenplay by Ralph Spence, Edgar Allan Woolf and Al Boasberg based on Harvey Thew's adaptation of Edward E. Rose's 1922 stage play *The Rear Car*), which kicks off with attorney Alden Murray (Porter Hall) informing Los Angeles telephone operator Ruth Raymond (Mary Carlisle) that she's the long-lost daughter of railroad magnate Luke Carson (Berton Churchill). Most of this inane comedy-melodrama takes place as Ruth and Murray and eccentric sleuth Godfrey D. Scott (Charlie Ruggles) and an assortment of others are traveling to New York in Carson's de luxe private railroad car. The passengers encounter an escaped gorilla from a circus train, mysterious radio messages, a few murders including that of lawyer Murray, and an imminent collision with another choo-choo.

***

The coming of sound offered huge opportunities for certain forms of American film and made possible the first wave of movies dealing with law, lawyers, lawyering and justice but seemed for a while to be the death knell for that peculiarly American genre, the Western, which had flourished through most of the 1920s but came to a dead halt late in the decade. When Hollywood's new gurus, the sound technicians, insisted that it was impossible to record sound except indoors under tightly controlled conditions, it became the accepted wisdom that the Western, which depended on rugged outdoor action and spectacular stunts, was doomed. Between 1928 and 1930 all the major studios dropped their profitable Western stars.

Exactly who was first to prove that sound could be recorded outdoors remains in dispute. John Ford, a contract director at Fox during these crisis years, claimed the credit for himself,[21] but so did Raoul Walsh who was also directing at Fox at the time.[22] Whether credit rightly belongs to one or the other or both or neither, the floodgates were soon opened wide to talking Westerns and most of the big stars of the Twenties found homes on the range once more. Most of Hollywood's studios large and small joined in the new Western boom, bringing back stars from the Twenties like Buck Jones and launching the careers of newcomers including a brawny Iowan who called himself John Wayne.

Shoot-em-ups and juriscinema would seem at first glance too antithetical to have interfaced, and indeed the juristic component in early Westerns is usually minor in nature where it exists at all. The sprawling epic *Cimarron* (RKO © 12/31/30, directed by Wesley Ruggles from a screenplay by Howard Estabrook based on Edna Ferber's 1930 novel of the same name) starred Richard Dix as freewheeling lawyer and newspaper editor Yancey Cravat, who persuades his Eastern-born wife Sabra (Irene Dunne) to come west and settle with him in the newly-opened Oklahoma territory.

Among the episodes in this film's 40-year time span is one of legal interest: Yancey returns from the Spanish-American War to put on his lawyer hat and defend his old friend Dixie Lee (Estelle Taylor), who is being tried as a "public nuisance," i.e. a hooker. This is one of the few instances in a film of the first golden age where a lawyer character is shown doing something both lawyerly and admirable.

One of the same studio's 60-minute quickie Westerns, released about nine months after *Cimarron*, is much more typical of the interface. In *Sundown Trail* (RKO © 9/11/31, directed and written by Robert F. Hill) ranch manager Buck Sawyer (Tom Keene) falls in love with his late employer's daughter (Marion Shilling) when she comes West to take over her father's spread. Accompanying her is a greedy lawyer (Hooper Atchley) who warns her against Buck, but the principal badguys in this low-budget oater are a crooked neighboring rancher (Stanley Blystone) and his gang.

***

Most 60-minute Westerns of the early Thirties that engage the desperation of the time do so only in relatively simple ways but a few penetrate deeper, portraying the conflict between the simple sense of decency in a community and the legal system founded on the sanctity of property and of its own rules legitimizing economic exploitation. The finest such film is *One Man Law* (Columbia © 1/11/32), the fourteenth in a series of 28 Westerns, roughly an hour in length apiece, which shoot-em-up superstar Buck Jones[23] made at the studio between 1930 and 1934. Like several others in the series, this one was both written and directed by Lambert Hillyer, a top specialist in films of the sort.[24] None of his other films, however, centrally engages legal themes as *One Man Law* does. Hillyer's acid contempt for a system that employs property concepts to enforce exploitation permeates almost every aspect of this extraordinary little picture.

The film opens at a sort of field day in Grass Valley County, featuring events like a turkey shoot and a horse race. The finest marksman in the valley is Brand Thompson (Buck Jones), who wins all the turkeys offered as prizes and gives them away to neighbors as fast as he receives them. That he's the most admired and trusted man in the community is clear both to us in the audience and to entrepreneur Jonathan P. Streeter (Robert Ellis), who observes Thompson as he demonstrates his shooting skills and disarms a menacing drunk. Streeter, we soon learn, has plans for Thompson's future.

Stubb (Ernie Adams), a weasel-faced outsider in Streeter's pay, approaches Thompson and manipulates him into betting that his beloved gray stallion Silver can beat Stubb's black in the day's horse race. The loser agrees to give the winner a "complete outfit," a term which, as Thompson realizes only belatedly, includes his horse. What he doesn't know is that Stubb's black is not a cow pony but a trained racehorse. The race itself, a highlight of the film and a fine demonstration of Hillyer's skill as an action director, ends as expected, with Silver losing to the black by a head. Weeping, feeling not that he's lost something he owns but that he's betrayed his partner and best friend, Thompson hands over his horse to Stubb. Watching these events from the stands is Grace Duncan (Shirley Grey).

The next day Streeter invites Thompson to his luxurious ranch house, returns everything Thompson lost in the bet, including Silver, and—although careful not to tie the gift to this proposal—asks Thompson to become Grass Valley's new sheriff. Not that he expects any special favors. "Pay me by upholding the law," he says, "the very letter of the law." An ecstatic Thompson agrees and the stage is set for the film's central conflict.

Streeter and his Eastern partners own title to much of the land in the valley and Streeter has leased it out in parcels to dozens of small ranchers who have spent years improving the property but without the security of legal ownership, which Streeter has often promised but never delivered. Now his Eastern associates have sold these parcels of land to people who want to resettle in the West.[25] When the newcomers arrive with their deeds, they demand possession of the land to which they have clear title under the rules of property law. This is when Thompson learns that he's legally required to evict his friends and neighbors.

> Streeter: "Yes. It's the law. An unfortunate case, but nevertheless the law."
> Thompson:"Why, that's robbery!"
> Streeter:"It may seem so. But it's legal. And it's your duty to enforce it."
> Thompson: "It's inhuman and I won't do it!"

Wise old Judge Cooper (Edward J. Le Saint) confirms Streeter's view of the legal issue and tells Thompson that his only chance of helping his friends and neighbors is to perform his legal duty.

> Thompson: "Do you think I'd keep a job that forces me to drive my friends, people who have trusted me, off the land they've really earned?"
> Cooper: "Son, if you and I are going to have any chance to save those people, you've got to do that."

So the reluctant law man begins betraying the community's common sense of decency, enforcing legalized robbery. "Those deeds stand," he tells the cheated ranchers. "And after tomorrow the owners will have to be given legal possession." "There is a law in this country after all," one newcomer mutters happily. Thompson's deputies quit their positions in disgust as he begins to dispossess his former friends. "Grimm, these folks have a legal right to this place and it's up to me to see that they get it. . . . I'm coming in, Ed, and I don't much care whether you shoot or not."

Despised by everyone in the valley, forced to defend Streeter against threats of lynching from outraged homeless ranchers, Thompson once again consults with Judge Cooper.

> Thompson: "I tell you I can't stand it any more!"

> Cooper: "You've got to! . . . The law is his weapon
> and we've got to turn it back on him somehow. . . .
> He's got to be *forced* to give back that land *willingly!*"

If a single line in the film captures its thrust with precision, that line of Judge Cooper's is it.

At this exact moment the golden opportunity turns up in the person of weasel-faced Stubb who, having no idea that the man he took Silver from is now the sheriff of Grass Valley, comes to Judge Cooper's office to make a criminal complaint.

> Thompson: "Judge! Judge, here's the answer to our prayer! Streeter stole his horse!"
> Cooper: "What's he worth?"
> Stubb: "Nine hundred."
> Cooper: "Grand larceny!"
> Stubb: "He wanted me to sell, and when I wouldn't, he hit me over the head."
> Cooper: "Assault and battery!"
> Stubb: "He hit me over the head with a tin money box. See?"
> Cooper: "With a deadly weapon!"

By this time Streeter has sold his ranch and is about to leave the state. While a ranchers' lynch mob forms outside of town, Thompson rushes out to serve the judge's warrant before Streeter can remove himself from the jurisdiction. Riding Silver, he reaches the ranch just as Streeter is heading for the border on the black racehorse and the mob is approaching from another direction. Hillyer has brought the film around full circle to climax with another race between the same horses that competed at the beginning. After a well-directed chase scene, Thompson bulldogs Streeter off the black just a few feet beyond the state line marker and, in yet another gesture of contempt for rules of law, drags him back inside the jurisdiction and serves him with the warrant.

The film's final scene takes place back in the jailhouse, with Streeter, not Thompson, now in a cell.

> Streeter: "But I tell you, Thompson, I've got to get out of here. I want to post bail."
>
> Thompson: "Can't find Judge Cooper. He sets the amount." (Cut to a shot of the judge, sitting in Thompson's office and silently chuckling.)
>
> Streeter: "That's ridiculous!"
>
> Thompson: "No, it's the law."
>
> Streeter: "I'm not a criminal!"
>
> Thompson: "That warrant says you broke the law."
>
> Streeter: "But I'm in danger! Suppose those ranchers find out I'm here?"
>
> Thompson: "They know it by now."
>
> Streeter: "But you can't protect me alone!"
>
> Thompson: "I'm not going to try, Streeter. I think too much of my neck. Besides, I'm resigning as soon as Judge Cooper gets here." . . .
>
> Streeter: ". . . I'll give you five thousand dollars to let me out of here!"
>
> Thompson: "That wouldn't be legal."

Ultimately a deal is struck. In return for not being lynched, Streeter will give the ranchers deeds to the property that by rights should be theirs and will reimburse all the newcomers what they paid for the land plus a bonus for their time and trouble. On this note Hillyer closes the legal aspects of *One Man Law*. Of course, if any of the newcomers had decided not to take back their money but instead to keep the land they legally owned, the stage would have been set for a sequel film, without villains, and built around a genuinely tragic situation in which right clashes with right. Such a film would seem to have been beyond Lambert Hillyer's genuine but not unlimited gifts. He continued to direct low-budget features throughout the Nineteen Thirties and

Forties, then began directing 30-minute episodes of early 1950s TV series like *The Cisco Kid*—in which he occasionally recycled sequences and whole storylines from *One Man Law* and other Westerns he'd made with Buck Jones at Columbia more than twenty years before.

***

No lawyer characters appear in *Cornered* (Columbia © 8/10/32, directed by B. Reeves Eason from a screenplay by Ruth Todd based on William Colt MacDonald's 1931 novelet "Long Loop Laramie") but there is a trial sequence, shot for economy reasons on a set obviously designed for 1930s-type courtroom dramas. Sheriff Tim Laramie (Tim McCoy) acts as defense attorney for ranch foreman Moody Pearson (Niles Welch), to whom he owes his life, when Moody is charged with the murder of his boss, the father of Jane Herrick (Shirley Grey), with whom both Tim and Moody are in love. Moody is convicted but Tim lets him escape, then turns in his badge and follows the fugitive to a distant county where he encounters Laughing Red Slavens (Noah Beery), the real killer and perhaps the juiciest psychotic in any Western.

The title of *The Cowboy Counsellor* (Allied © 10/10/32, directed by George Melford from a screenplay by Jack Natteford) suggests a full-fledged piece of frontier juriscinema but appearances are misleading. Former rodeo champ Hoot Gibson stars as Dan Alton, a book salesman who roams the West hawking copies of a tome entitled *The Ranchman's Own Lawyer*. When Luke Avery (Fred Gilman) is charged with a stagecoach robbery, Dan becomes attracted to the defendant's sister Ruth (Sheila Mannors) and agrees to "represent" him. Some lawyer! First, suspecting that the real holdup man was Ruth's neighbor Bill Clary (Jack Rutherford), he ransacks Clary's house in a vain search for incriminating evidence. Then he "borrows" from the sheriff's office the Mexican scarf worn by the bandit and, conspicuously wearing it around his neck, holds up the coach bringing the judge and the state's attorney to town. Once the trial begins and the jurymen learn of this incident, they develop a reasonable doubt and find Luke not guilty. At this point the judge recognizes Alton as the man who stopped his coach and orders him arrested but Dan escapes and captures Clary with money from the original robbery on him. At the conclusion of this lighthearted romp Dan and Ruth ask the judge to marry them but, when His Honor admits that he's forgotten the words for the ceremony, Dan reverts to his original status and tries to sell the jurist a copy of *The Ranchman's Own Lawyer*.

Fighting for Justice (Columbia © 10/24/32, directed by Otto Brower from a screenplay by Robert Quigley based on an original story by Gladwell Richardson) tells of Tim Keane (Tim McCoy) and his fight to regain the family ranch, which was sold out from under them after the odious Mr. Trout (Hooper Atchley) kept the money the old man had given him to pay the back taxes on the property. No one will be surprised to learn that Trout is a lawyer.

Renegades of the West (RKO © 11/11/32, directed by Casey Robinson from a screenplay by Albert Shelby LeVino based on Frank Richardson Pierce's 1921 magazine story "The Miracle Baby") starred Tom Keene as a young man who, while serving a six-month prison sentence on trumped-up charges, picked up some leads from a cellmate about the truth behind his father's murder. The only function of the lawyer character (Joseph Girard) is to listen while Tom tells him the film's backstory. The murderer turns out to be not the attorney but that most hated of all villains in Westerns of the early Depression years, the town banker.

The Mysterious Rider (Paramount © 1/19/33, directed by Fred Allen from a screenplay by Harvey Gates and Robert N. Lee based on Zane Grey's 1921 novel of the same name) boasts one of the slimiest lawyer characters in a Western. Cliff Harkness (Irving Pichel) begins by falsely claiming legal ownership of ranchland that is about to skyrocket in value thanks to a dam project. After selling their own property back to Wade Benton (Kent Taylor) and his neighbors, Harkness sells the same land to Mark King (Berton Churchill). Then he steals the receipt he gave Benton and claims never to have been paid at all, so that Benton's outraged neighbors have the poor guy thrown in jail for stealing the money with which he was supposed to have repurchased the property. The ranchers are about to be evicted when a "mysterious rider" begins harassing Harkness and his cohorts. The masked hero turns out of course to be Benton, who knows a secret way out of his jail cell.

In *Silent Men* (Columbia © 2/23/33, directed by D. Ross Lederman from a screenplay by Stuart Anthony based on an original story by Walt Coburn), Tim Richards (Tim McCoy) gets a job on a ranch whose owner is in the middle of a feud with another rancher. After the usual riding and shooting he discovers that the feud is being manipulated by the foreman of one ranch (Mathew Betz), the local sheriff (Lloyd Ingraham), and the lawyer for the Cattlemen's Association (William V. Mong).

Legal advice is much more central to *Rainbow Ranch* (Monogram © 8/3/33, directed by Harry Fraser from his own screenplay). Seaman Ed Randall (Rex Bell) is granted leave to help his widowed aunt (Vane Calvert) protect the ranch of the title from land pirate Marvin Black (Bob Kortman), who has built a dam on his own property to deprive her of water. In due course Ed is told by attorney Wilbur Hall (Phil Dunham) that his late uncle bought Rainbow Ranch complete with perpetual water rights, meaning—at least in this juristic neverneverland—that whatever Ed may do to get the water back is legal. Hall is murdered before he can say more and Ed is jailed for the crime but escapes to blow up the dam and pin both his uncle's murder and the lawyer's on Black.

In *The Last Trail* (Fox © 8/8/33, directed by James Tinling from a screenplay by Stuart Anthony very loosely based on Zane Grey's 1909 novel of the same name), Tom Daley (George O'Brien) comes to Arizona to take over his late uncle's valuable ranch. What he doesn't know is that his uncle's lawyer John Ross (J. Carrol Naish) is looking for an impostor to pose as Tom and take over the spread. Tom shows up incognito and winds up being hired by Ross to impersonate himself, with the lawyer's accomplice Patricia Carter (Claire Trevor) passing as Tom's wife. His real identity is exposed just as the will is being settled and the rest of the film plays itself out in standard shoot-em-up fashion with Ross biting the dust and Tom and Pat agreeing to become man and wife for real.

The Last Round-Up (Paramount © 1/25/34, directed by Henry Hathaway from a screenplay by Jack Cunningham based on Zane Grey's 1916 novel *The Border Legion*) stars Randolph Scott as Jim Cleve, who is falsely accused of the murder of an old miner and is about to be convicted by Judge Savin (Richard Carle) when he is rescued by outlaw leader Jack Kells (Monte Blue) and out of gratitude joins Kells' gang, the Border Legion. Eventually Jim and Kells become rivals for the affections of saloon singer Joan Randall (Barbara Fritchie). The film ends with Kells and his treacherous henchman Sam Gulden (Fred Kohler) killing each other, leaving Jim and Joan to start a new life together. The film is mentioned here only because Jim's sidekick Bunko McKee (Fuzzy Knight), who is killed before the end titles, is a disbarred lawyer.

***

For anyone interested in how and why strict self-censorship came to Hollywood and in what respects the new regime changed movies, the book to read is Thomas Doherty's *Pre-Code Hollywood: Sex, Immorality, and Insurrection in American Cinema, 1930-1934* (Columbia University Press, 1999). The so-called Motion Picture Production Code had been in effect since 1930 but, as Doherty's book makes clear, was almost completely ignored during the early Thirties and had much the same effect on American films of the period that Prohibition had had on liquor consumption. Then came the reaction. As Doherty puts it: "After four years of gun-toting gangsters and smart-mouthed convicts, adulterous wives and promiscuous chorines, irreverence from the lower orders and incompetence from above, the immoral and insurrectionist impulses on the Hollywood screen were beaten back by forces dedicated to public restraint and social control."[26]

The prime mover behind the strict enforcement of the Code was the Roman Catholic church, whose leadership "embarked upon a nationwide crusade to lead parishioners away from Hollywood's temptations."[27] Late in 1933 the hierarchy formed a National Legion of

Decency, whose aim was to clean up "the pest hole that infects the entire country with its obscene and lascivious moving pictures."[28] Catholics were made to recite the Legion pledge at Sunday mass. In a "command binding in all conscience under pain of sin,"[29] Cardinal Dougherty of Philadelphia ordered his entire flock to boycott not just "obscene and lascivious" films but all movies. Other religious groups quickly boarded the bandwagon, and at the same time the FDR administration in Washington began making noises about content regulation for the film industry, which according to the Supreme Court had no rights under the First Amendment.[30] "The whole world has gotten the idea that Hollywood is Hell's home office . . . ," said one theater manager.[31]

In order to avert both a nationwide religious boycott and the threat of Federal censorship, the industry resolved to censor itself, bringing in Joseph I. Breen, a prominent Catholic layman, as head of the Production Code Administration. "I am the Code," Breen announced.[32] Clearly he did not mean to claim plenary power over movies. Just as it is the function of a federal or state administrative agency to interpret and enforce its enabling legislation, Breen's function was to interpret and enforce the Production Code, the 1930 document whose principal drafter was a Jesuit priest and which with its Amendments is reproduced in Appendixes 1-3 of Doherty's book.

Even a casual reading of the Code establishes that its principal targets were the celebration of sexual freedom and the glorification of crime. If Breen and his cohorts ruled that a film dealt improperly or too explicitly with seduction or pre-marital hanky-panky or prostitution or adultery, or that women in the cast were exposing or wiggling the wrong parts of their bodies, they demanded cuts, or the rewriting and reshooting of offending scenes. The kind of "women's pictures" that were characteristic of the early 1930s was promptly demolished. What the Code's sexual proscriptions outlawed was the sympathetic portrayal of female characters who enjoyed sex either before or outside of marriage. But, by abolishing one of the most fruitful venues for presenting lawyer characters (always male) who tended to behave more honorably than their counterparts in other film genres, the banning of such films caused a great deal of collateral damage to juriscinema.

The Breen office also demanded cuts and revisions in any film that was deemed to glorify crime and criminals. "Law . . . shall not be ridiculed, nor shall sympathy be created for its violation."[33] This and similar provisions of the Code were clearly aimed at banning the classic gangster films of the early Thirties, which probably would have died out anyway once Prohibition was repealed. But they too inflicted much collateral damage on juriscinema, ruling out films like 1932's *One Man Law*, which had no lawyer characters but was built around sympathy for the legally dispossessed and boundless contempt for rules of law, and all but outlawing the cycle of pre-1934 films whose lawyer protagonist was modeled on William J. Fallon.

Nowhere does the Code say that lawyers may not be ridiculed or portrayed in a negative light. Yet from shortly after the coming of strict Code enforcement until its slow dissolution beginning more than twenty years later, the kinds of films considered in this chapter became rare. When such a film was made, it lacked life and bite. Even when a law film from the early Thirties was remade, as many of them were,[34] the remake was almost always a pale imitation of its original. The Code put an end to the first golden age of juriscinema indirectly, by suffocating the unfooled, sexually and intellectually liberated environment that early talkies had imported from the cultural climate of the 1920s. We can see and feel the difference when we consider two films released very shortly after the Code began to be strictly enforced.

The protagonist of *Crime Without Passion* (Paramount © 8/21/34, directed by Ben Hecht and Charles MacArthur from their own screenplay based on Ben Hecht's 1933 magazine story "Caballero of the Law") is attorney Lee Gentry (Claude Rains), who defends guilty criminals and uses shyster tactics to get them acquitted and winds up suffering the fate of James M. Cain's protagonist in *The Postman Always Rings Twice* (1934). Gentry accidentally shoots fiery-tempered Spanish dancer Carmen Brown (Margo) while trying to break up with her and, convinced that he killed her, pulls out all the stops trying to set up an alibi for himself. Eventually he discovers that Carmen's friend Della (Greta Granstedt) happened to see him under circumstances that destroy his phony alibi. Then he gets into a fight with Della's boyfriend Eddie White (Stanley Ridges) and shoots him in self-defense but under circumstances that make the act seem like cold-blooded murder. As the police lead him away, Gentry discovers that Carmen isn't dead after all. Here we have a textbook example of what happened to a film about a lawyer after the Breen Office monkeyed with it.[35] The miracle is that, compulsory retribution and all, it's still a fascinating movie.

So too is *The Case of the Howling Dog* (Warner Bros. © 9/22/34, directed by Alan Crosland from a screenplay by Ben Markson based on Erle Stanley Gardner's 1934 novel of the same name), which starred Warren William in the first of a six-film series about lawyer-detective Perry Mason. In Gardner's novel Mason represents Bessie Forbes on the charge that she murdered her husband, who had dumped her for another man's wife. What makes *Howling Dog* unique among the 82 Mason novels is that this time Mason's client is guilty, and he knows it when he gets her acquitted so that she can never be tried again. ". . . I am not a judge; nor am I a jury. . . . I have never heard the story of Bessie Forbes; nor has any one else. It may have been that anything she did was done in self-defense. . . . But I acted only as her lawyer."[36] Every moment of the novel is seen from Mason's point of view and nothing happens outside his presence. In the film we witness enough of the murder scene so that we can be certain that Bessie (Mary Astor) did indeed act in self defense. Prior to strict enforcement of the Code that alteration would not have been necessary.

Under the strictly enforced Code "cinematic space was a patrolled landscape with secure perimeters and well-defined borders."[37] But the years of strict enforcement were far from a cinematic wasteland: indeed they were precisely the years that saw

Stagecoach (1939), *The Grapes of Wrath* (1940), *Citizen Kane* (1941), *Casablanca* (1942), all the classics of what Thomas Doherty calls "Hollywood's vaunted 'golden age' . . . [a]n artistic flowering of incalculable cultural impact."[38] "The fractures of American life, still less the open embrace of sex, did not close up when the Code clamped down. No matter how rigid the body cast, Hollywood cinema is too supple and expressive an art to constrain [sexual energy or social protest]. . . . [I]n the hidden recesses of the cinematic subtext, under the surface of avowed morality and happy endings, Hollywood under the Code is fraught with defiance of Code authority."[39]

The Code clearly did not put an end to lawyer characters or legal themes in films but it surely ended the first golden age of juriscinema. Between the second half of 1934 and the beginning of the breakdown of censorship twenty-odd years later, Hollywood offered relatively few films with a legal component. Most of the post-Code law films were not as rewarding as their counterparts from the early Thirties and even the best of them, like John Ford's *Young Mr. Lincoln* (1939), were not connected by leitmotifs as so many pre-Code law films were connected by the cultural forces sketched at the beginning of this chapter. It was not until the years that coincided with both the breakdown of the Code and the rise of the Warren Court that film-makers launched juriscinema's second golden age. But that, as Scheherazade might have said, is another story.

NOTES

1. Paul Bergman & Michael Asimow, *Reel Justice: The Courtroom Goes to the Movies* (Andrews & McMeel, 1996). For commentary on this book, see Francis M. Nevins, Book Review, 20 *Legal Studies Forum* 145 (1996).
2. Jacques Barzun, *From Dawn to Decadence* (Harper Collins, 2000), 734.
3. *Id.* at 735.

4· This elegant euphemism for an earthier phrase at which most law publishers would look askance comes from Edmund Wilson, *The Dead Sea Scrolls* (Oxford University Press, 1969), 281.

5. Alexander Walker, *The Shattered Silents: How the Talkies Came to Stay* (Morrow, 1979), 139.

6. Quoted in Alexander Walker, *supra* note 5, at 121.

7. Quoted in Alexander Walker, *supra* note 5, at 139.

8. A hat with Wilfong's initials was found beside the body of the victim, a rival gangster, and around the time of the crime witnesses saw Ace leaving the scene hatless. In the only part of the trial we see, Ashe gives the hat to Wilfong, who grimaces comically for the cackling jury as he tries to jam the all-too-small fedora down on his head. One can almost hear Ashe's closing argument: "If the hat don't fit, you must acquit!" We are never told whether he arranged for a substitution of chapeaus in order to get an acquittal for a client he knew was guilty, but most viewers will have their suspicions.

9. This language, which is a condensed version of the seventh paragraph in Book Three, Chapter XIX of Dreiser's novel, demonstrates how closely the film-makers followed the book when and where they could.

10. The film-makers took this designation from Book Three, Chapter XX of Dreiser's novel. But where did Dreiser get it from? Most likely from Alexandre Bisson's play *Madame X*, which was first staged in New York in 1910, or from the 1920 silent movie based on the play. Of course it's also possible that Dreiser contrived the name independently, without ever having seen the play or the film. Either way, for the adamantly unreligious Dreiser the X had no Christian significance.

11. For an account of the litigation, see W.A. Swanberg, *Dreiser* (Scribner, 1965), 369-372, 376-378.

---

12. See 1 Joseph Blotner, *Faulkner: A Biography* (Random House, 1974), 605. Blotner defends *Sanctuary*'s merits as literature despite Faulkner's statements.

13. For excerpts from some of the documents pertaining to censorship of this film, see the entry on *The Story of Temple Drake* in *The American Film Institute Catalog of Motion Pictures Produced in the United States: Feature Films, 1931-1940* (University of California Press, 1993), 2063-2064.

14. "He attacked me—Trigger did," Temple sobs on the witness stand. "I went to the city with Trigger and stayed with him until this week." Her father the judge interposes a question from the bench: "And stayed there a prisoner, you mean?" Actually she stayed with him voluntarily because—this is the big secret the film-makers couldn't reveal—being raped gave her orgasms. "I killed him!" Temple cries. Then she faints, leaving the question unanswered. See Thomas Doherty, *Pre-Code Hollywood: Sex, Immorality and Insurrection in American Cinema*, 1930-1934 (Columbia University Press, 1999), 114-118.

15. In order to avoid a slew of footnotes identical except for page numbers, all references to Fowler's book in this section are cited in the text.

16. As a going-away present Day gives her a check for $100 which he was paid, so he says, by the American Journal of Law for a recently published article. In order to prove that the gift doesn't come from his shystering activities he shows her a copy of the article, which we see is entitled "Contracts and Torts: An Analysis." As if any law journal would publish an article on such a gargantuan topic, written by an attorney whose practice is exclusively criminal, and pay him a then huge sum for it to boot!

17. Oliver Wendell Holmes, Jr., "The Path of the Law," 10 *Harvard Law Review* 457, 459 (1897).

18. This line is particularly ironic in view of the fact that John Barrymore was a compulsive alcoholic whose absences from the set and inability to remember lines caused long delays in production. For an account of the

filming of *Counsellor at Law*, see Jan Herman, *A Talent for Trouble: The Life of Hollywood's Most Acclaimed Director, William Wyler* (Putnam, 1995), 114-119.

19. See Larry Richards, *African American Films Through 1959: A Comprehensive, Illustrated Filmography* (McFarland, 1998), 179.

20. My account is based on Richard Corliss' three-part article "An Oscar for Micheaux," *Time*, online edition, 6 June 2002 (www.time.com/time/sampler/article/0,8599,260216-1,00 et seq.)

21. "They said it couldn't be done," Ford told Peter Bogdanovich in the late 1960s, "and I said, 'Why the hell can't it be done?' They said,'Well, you can't because—' and they gave me a lot of Master's Degree talk. So I said, 'Well, let's try it.'" Ford contended that his 22-minute short *Napoleon's Barber* (1928) was "the first time anyone ever went outside with a sound system." Peter Bogdanovich, *John Ford* (University of California Press, 1968), 50.

22. Walsh lived almost twenty years longer than Ford and, in his late eighties, wrote the engaging but hopelessly unreliable memoir *Each Man in His Time* (Farrar, Straus & Giroux, 1974). By his account, studio head Winfield Sheehan frantically summoned Walsh back from a Mexican vacation and sent him to see his first talking picture. As he was leaving the theater he heard a burst of sound from a Fox Movietone newsreel dealing with a dockworkers' strike, felt a rush of inspiration, and went back to Sheehan's office with the announcement: "I'm going to make the first outdoor sound feature." *Id.* at 219. The film he made, or rather started to make as both director and leading man until he lost one eye in a freak accident, was *In Old Arizona* (1929), which proved immensely popular and earned Warner Baxter an Academy Award for his performance as the Cisco Kid. But Walsh's memoir is so full of gaps and outright mistakes that it would be foolish on the basis of his book alone to conclude that he was the first to prove that sound could be recorded outdoors. For fuller discussion of the defects in Walsh's account, see Francis M. Nevins, *The Cisco Kid: American Hero, Hispanic Roots* (Arizona State University Bilingual Press, 2008), 38-39.

23. Jones was born Charles Gebhard at Vincennes, Indiana in 1891 and became a headlined rodeo rider and roper in his early twenties. He found his way into the movies after World War I, starring in more than sixty features for the Fox studio, most of them Westerns, between 1920 and 1927. His directors at Fox included John Ford, William Wellman and Lambert Hillyer, about whom more in the following note. During the Thirties and early Forties Jones starred in Western series at Columbia (1930-34), Universal (1934-37) and smaller studios. In November 1942, while on a war bond tour, he burned to death in the disastrous Cocoanut Grove fire. More than 70 years later he is still considered one of the foremost screen cowboys. See Buck Rainey, *The Life and Films of Buck Jones: The Silent Era* (World of Yesterday Publications, 1988) and *The Life and Films of Buck Jones: The Sound Era* (World of Yesterday Publications, 1991).

24. Hillyer, like Jones, was born in Indiana, sometime between 1888 and 1895 depending on which reference book one consults. He began directing Westerns starring William S. Hart in 1917. The features he made during the Twenties were a mixed bag but included three films with Tom Mix and five with Buck Jones, all for the Fox studio. Between 1931 and 1935 he worked exclusively at Columbia and for the first half of this stint he directed nothing but Buck Jones Westerns. His best-known non-Westerns are the two horror films he made at Universal, *The Invisible Ray* (1935) and *Dracula's Daughter* (1936). During the Forties he directed dozens more 60-minute Westerns, first at Columbia, later at Monogram, then when television began displacing the quickie features that were his stock in trade he signed a contract with Ziv Studios and made episodes of early TV series like *I Led Three Lives* and *The Cisco Kid*. He died in July 1969, a few days before his 76th birthday.

25. Hillyer subtly flubs his plotting at this point in the film. When Streeter manipulates Thompson into accepting the sheriff's badge, he expects to be long gone by the time the newcomers reach Grass Valley with their deeds and therefore he has no real reason to want in office

someone who will enforce "the very letter of the law." According to the film, Streeter's Eastern associates sold the land prematurely and the sale of his own ranch in Grass Valley was somehow held up so that he is still around to feel the original ranchers' wrath when the new settlers arrive. But he couldn't have anticipated any of this at the time he rigged the horse race.

26. Thomas J. Doherty, *supra* note 11, at 319.

27. *Id.* at 320.

28. *Ibid.*

29. *Id.* at 321.

30. During and for almost twenty years after the first golden age of juriscinema, the leading U.S. Supreme Court case on this subject was *Mutual Film Corp. v. Industrial Commission of Ohio*, 236 U.S. 230 (1915), which had held that movies were not protected under the First Amendment. That decision was not overruled until *Joseph Burstyn, Inc. v. Wilson*, 343 U.S. 495 (1952). For a comprehensive overview, see Edward de Grazia & Roger K. Newman, *Banned Films: Movies, Censors & the First Amendment* (Bowker, 1982).

31. Thomas J. Doherty, *supra* note 11, at 325.

32. *Id.* at 327.

33. *Id.* at 361.

34. *A Free Soul* was remade as *The Girl Who Had Everything* (MGM © 2/27/53, directed by Richard Thorpe from a screenplay by Art Cohn), starring Elizabeth Taylor, Fernando Lamas and William Powell. The Josef von Sternberg version of Dreiser's *American Tragedy* was superseded by the Oscar-winning *A Place in the Sun* (Paramount © 9/2/51, directed by George Stevens from a screenplay by Michael Wilson and Harry Brown), starring Montgomery Clift, Elizabeth Taylor and Shelley Winters. *State's Attorney* was remade as *Criminal Lawyer* (RKO © 1/19/37, directed by Christy Cabanne from a screenplay by G.V. Atwater and Thomas Lennon), which starred Lee Tracy, Margot Grahame and Eduardo Ciannelli. With its setting changed from middle Europe to the

United States, *The Kiss Before the Mirror* was remade by its original director as *Wives Under Suspicion* (Universal © 6/4/38, directed by James Whale from a screenplay by Myles Connolly) with Warren William, Gail Patrick and Constance Moore. *The Nuisance* returned to the screen as *The Chaser* (MGM © 7/26/38, directed by Edwin L. Marin from a screenplay by Everett Freeman, Harry Ruskin, and Bella and Samuel Spewack), starring Dennis O'Keefe, Ann Morriss and Lewis Stone. *Penthouse* was reincarnated as *Society Lawyer* (MGM © 3/31/39, directed by Edwin L. Marin from a screenplay by Leon Gordon and Hugo Butler) with Walter Pidgeon, Virginia Bruce and, reprising his role in the original version, Leo Carrillo. *The Mouthpiece* was remade twice: as *The Man Who Talked Too Much* (Warner Bros. © 7/6/40, directed by Vincent Sherman from a screenplay by Walter DeLeon and Earl Baldwin), starring George Brent, Virginia Bruce and Brenda Marshall, and as the much better *Illegal* (Warner Bros. © 10/15/55, directed by Lewis Allen from a screenplay by W.R. Burnett and James R. Webb), starring Edward G. Robinson, Nina Foch and Hugh Marlowe.

35. For excerpts from some of the documents pertaining to the censorship of this film see the American Film Institute Catalog, *supra* note 10, at 424-425.

36. Erle Stanley Gardner, *The Case of the Howling Dog* (Morrow, 1934), 294.

37. Thomas Doherty, *supra* note 11, at 1.

38. *Ibid*.

39. *Id*. at 3.

CHAPTER 6

Through the Post-Code Thirties on Horseback

From Western films we can learn precious little about the historic American West but often a great deal about the time when a particular film was made. An intimate connection between a Western or for that matter any other kind of movie and the themes and turmoil of its period adds to the film, as it does to any work of fiction, a dimension of interest that tends to grow as the work itself ages. After a generation or two, thanks to miracles of technology like DVD, teachers can use older movies almost as a form of time travel, as an introduction for students to some of the social and emotional shape of a time when even their parents were not yet born.

The first decade of talking films was perennially in need of story material that was rich in both emotional conflict and dialogue. Courtroom drama for this reason became a staple item on every studio's menu, and films of this sort that predate the Production Code are discussed in detail in Chapter 5.[1] A few of these pictures are still esteemed today from a cinematic perspective, notably *Fury* (MGM, 1936), which was directed by Fritz Lang shortly after his escape from Nazi Germany and resettlement in Hollywood. Most of them, however—whether still accessible on cable or satellite or surviving only in ancient vaults and as entries in comprehensive encyclopedias[2]—have little to recommend them purely as movies and are burdened with melodramatic plots and acting styles and wildly ill-informed notions of courtroom procedure that make them laughable to the legal community today and useless in a seminar like mine.[3] The major exception to this generalization and in my judgment the finest law-related film of the decade is William Wyler's *Counsellor at Law*. As we saw in Chapter Five, the absence of conventional courtroom sequences enabled Wyler to dodge the bullet that maimed or killed most lawyer movies of the time and to portray the practice in a manner still vivid and compelling more than eighty years later. Curiously enough, the same holds true for law-related 1930s Westerns: those with little or no courtroom action are precisely the ones that offer the most interesting treatments of the themes of law, lawyers and justice.

Even after the Code, what most decisively shaped American films of the 1930s was the Depression, which brought a bleakness, cynicism and despair to movies of all sorts including some of the critically invisible 60-minute Westerns.[4] Any members of the younger generations who bothered to watch such pictures in quantity might have been amused or puzzled by how often they dealt with a greedy banker who was about to foreclose the mortgage on some young woman's ranch; but there was nothing amusing or escapist in these films to the people who were watching them in unpretentious small-town theaters at the time the pictures were made. In the thirties, losing one's home to a bank was not an exotic menace but a credible threat and all too often a grim reality. Although many 60-minute Westerns of the decade engaged the desperation of the time only in relatively simple ways of this sort, a few like *One Man Law* penetrated deeper, portraying the conflict between the simple sense of decency in a community and the legal system founded on the sanctity of property and of its own rules legitimizing economic exploitation. That communitarian and populist tradition remained very little affected during the regime of strict Production Code enforcement that began in mid-1934. In these films the unscrupulous banker or businessman is typically the only member of the cast who wears a suit, while the common folk dress in farmers' and ranch hands' garb—basically the same dress code one finds in the seminal Soviet films of the

1920s. These little Westerns, made *by* people without much money and *for* people with far less, were hugely popular but never taken seriously or even noticed by those who followed what was happening on the nation's theater screens. Even today most film scholars continue to believe that no talking Westerns worth a moment of their attention were made until John Ford's *Stagecoach* set out across the salt flats in 1939, dismissing unseen the dozens of 60-minute shoot-em-ups in which John Wayne starred before Ford cast him as The Ringo Kid. One of those pictures, the only one that deals centrally with legal themes, is the next film we shall consider here.

Wayne played the lead in six "B" Westerns for Warners (1932-33) and sixteen for Monogram (1933-35), a small studio which included a contract for his services among its assets when, in the summer of 1935, it merged with several other Poverty Row operations into the newly formed Republic Pictures. During the 1935-36 season Wayne starred in eight more "B" Westerns,[5] three of them directed by Joseph Kane (1894-1975), a former film editor who had taken up this new career only a year before.[6] By far the best of Kane's trio with Wayne was *King of the Pecos* (1936), which resembles *One Man Law* in being constructed around the conflict between law that exploits the people and law that serves the people but breaks new ground in placing two lawyer characters at the heart of the conflict.

***

The film opens with a close-up of a rotating wagon wheel as a band of newcomers with a cattle herd wearily cross a desert landscape. But Kane quickly shows us that these aren't the heroic pioneers of Western myth; they are exploiters, social Darwinians, bad men in every sense of the term including that of Holmes in "The Path of the Law." They are led by a sort of troika, each of whose three members stands for something exceptionally evocative for audiences during the Depression and is represented by an exceptionally appropriate physical object. The obese capitalist Alexander Stiles (Cy Kendall), whose symbol is reserved for later in the film; his tame lawyer Brewster (J. Frank Glendon), whose symbol

244

is the lawbook; his tame killer Ash (Jack Clifford), represented of course by the gun; these are the evil trinity here.

Two hundred miles from the river of the title, Stiles halts his party and announces: "Boys, I claim this land by right of discovery. We'll locate here." That night over the campfire he confers with his attorney.

> "Stiles, your right of discovery may not hold in the future. Being your lawyer, I suggest that you let me draw up the proper legal papers. You can buy up the land with a pile of dirt-cheap land scrip."
>
> "We won't have to do that, Brewster. All we have to do is control the waterholes. You file on them, and Ash and his men will hold the land for me with their guns. . . . What do you suppose our little empire'll survey?"
>
> "Oh, about a million acres."
>
> "Not bad for a start."

Studying a map of the territory, Stiles recognizes the strategic importance of the waterhole at a remote location called Sweetwater.

> "Put Sweetwater down, Brewster. When they start driving Texas cattle to the Kansas markets, that's going to be the key to our empire."
>
> "Might be trouble about Sweetwater. Man by the name of Clayborn's already settled there."
>
> "Oh? Well, that's all right. I'll buy him out fair and square."
>
> "What if he refuses to sell?"
>
> "Brewster, you learned your law from Blackstone. Ash learned his from Judge Colt's. If Blackstone loses, I'm counting on Colt's to win."

Stiles pays a visit to John Clayborn (John Beck), who with his wife

(Mary MacLaren) and teenage son (Bradley Metcalfe) is making a new home in the wilderness.

> "I'll give you five hundred dollars for your land and your shanty just as they stand. You can take your cattle and move on to a new range."
>
> "This place isn't for sale, Stiles."
>
> "I'll be more than fair. A thousand."
>
> "I'm not sellin'!"
>
> "We're buying up this country with land scrip. You'd better take the thousand."
>
> "I've held my homestead against Comanches. Reckon I can hold it against land thieves. Get out."
>
> "I'm sorry, Clayborn. A thousand dollars is a heap of money when all you've got to do is call your dog and move on."

Cut to Stiles and his gunmen attacking the Clayborn cabin from the hills around it. Young John's parents are murdered and the boy is brutally beaten by Ash and left for dead. A split second of screen time later—no one ever accused Joe Kane of boring transitions—the boy has become a man (John Wayne), a lawyer and, as we see, a crack shot. Dialogue between the relative that raised him and another rancher tells us that ten years have passed since his parents were slaughtered.

> "Well, Henry, I see the boy's still at it. What's he plannin' to be, a lawyer or a gunman?"
>
> "Looks like both."
>
> "Well, when you hang your shingle you'll get my business. You oughta be right smart at collectin'."
>
> "Thanks, Bill. But there's one case I've got to take care of first. John Clayborn versus Alexander Stiles."

The stagecoach on which Clayborn travels to the Texas town of Cottonwood which is the center of Stiles' million-acre kingdom is also carrying Eli Jackson (Edward Hearn) and his lovely daughter Belle (Muriel Evans), who have bought property from Stiles by mail, and a huge safe imported by Stiles from St. Louis as a secure home for his money. The head of the film's evil trinity has found his symbol. When the coach reaches Cottonwood and the safe is unloaded, Stiles describes it to his men.

> "They call her a Salamander because she can go through the hottest fire and never melt."
> "They got nothing on you, Stiles. I ain't never seen anything make you melt either."

This is how John Clayborn, who has shortened his name to Clay, identifies his target. He approaches Stiles and introduces himself as an attorney intending to start a practice in Cottonwood.

> "I'm afraid you've come to the wrong town, Mr. Clay. We already have one lawyer here. That's plenty."
> "I'll take a chance on that."

Local ranchers Hank Matthews (Arthur Aylesworth) and Josh Billings (Herbert Heywood) are passing by during this exchange. A minute or two later they take Clayborn to their cabin and explain to him how Stiles has become king of the Pecos.

> "Let me get this straight. Stiles buys your cattle, pays you back with these notes which he refuses to honor."
> "You're dang tootin'. The only way we can get anything out of 'em is discount 'em in half and take 'em out in trade at his store."
> "Why do you sell him your cattle?"

"We gotta or he won't give us no more water. He owns every drop in the country. . . ."

"Sounds like a polite form of cattle rustling to me. I'll take your case, Hank."

Meanwhile back in Cottonwood, Ash, Brewster and Stiles are discussing their latest victim.

"Did you give that fella Jackson fifty head of stock?"

"He signed our usual sales contract. He has the utmost confidence in Mr. Stiles."

"Yeah. He's working for me now and doesn't know it."

When Clayborn comes into Stiles' office and serves him with a summons and complaint, Stiles tears them up. On the day scheduled for the hearing, with the county courthouse packed, the sheriff bulls his way in and pounds the judge's bench with his gun butt. "Court's open." He pounds again. "Court's adjourned." There is a huge belly laugh at Clayborn's expense. "Where's the judge?" he demands. "He wasn't able to get here," the sheriff chuckles. As the scene ends, Clayborn and Stiles briefly exchange pleasantries.

"Don't be discouraged, Clay. This court may open most any time in the next twenty years."

"This court will be open Monday morning, Stiles. You'll be here."

Having had his eyes opened to one of the film's central themes, that law is an empty shell without the armed support of the people, Clayborn calls a secret night meeting of the small ranchers under Stiles' heel. "Stiles claims all the water rights around here. As a lawyer I'm here to tell you that those claims wouldn't be recognized by any court in the Union. . . . We can prove that [the water rights] are in the public domain and open for you men to file on. Now here's how we'll go about it."

On Monday morning Judge Dunlap rides into Cottonwood, surrounded by an armed escort party of ranchers. Under the aegis of their firepower he opens court and makes a speech of gratitude. "I am thankful to you citizens for offering the court the protection it has lacked in the past. You have made it possible for me to render justice impartially." Then he calls the case. Kane has no interest in legal technicalities but the courtroom scene gives him the opportunity to contrast the oral styles of Clayborn the servant of the people and Brewster the servant of power.

> "Your Honor, I represent the independent cattle owners of the section. They've come here to petition the court for the right to water their herds. For years they've been paying toll to the defendant, Alexander Stiles, for the use of water which is in public domain. I wish to submit evidence proving the defendant has no ownership of these water rights."
>
> "In rebuttal I offer these documents for the defendant, Alexander Stiles, showing that the aforesaid Alexander Stiles has filed on and is legal owner of said water rights in question before this court."

The judge orders a two-hour recess while he studies the papers. Stiles conducts a quick conference with Brewster which is followed by an ironic exchange with Clayborn.

> "I've run this country for the past ten years fair and square, and there isn't a living soul that can say a word against me."
>
> "That's right. Dead men tell no tales."

Ash picks up one of Brewster's lawbooks, follows Clayborn out to the street and literally throws the book at him. Clayborn knocks Ash down—reversing the scene early in the film where he'd been beaten by Ash and left for dead—but the gun duel between them that seems inevitable is postponed when Judge Dunlap returns to the bench with his decision. "And the evidence before the court proves conclusively that while the defendant Alexander Stiles has filed on all these rights, he is entitled to only one claim in accordance with the homestead laws of this nation. Therefore it becomes the duty of this court to declare the aforementioned water rights are in public domain, open for filing." There's a mad scramble out of the courtroom as everyone goes off to file claims, which apparently requires a long ride to a distant town. As he leaves the courtroom, Clayborn has a final word for Stiles. "I beat you in a civil case, Stiles, but I specialize in criminal law. Particularly murder." As soon as Clayborn is out of the room, Stiles turns to his tame killer. "Ash, this calls for your kind of law now."

Roughly thirty minutes of screen time has elapsed to this point. From here on, law is literally out of the picture as Kane concentrates on action. "I doubt if there was anybody in the business who could move people any better in action films than Joe," one of the stuntmen who worked with Kane said many years later. "He might kill you in the process, but he always got the job done on time and on budget."[7] Ash and his gunmen take cover in the hills and prepare to shoot down the ranchers as they ride past, while Stiles' proxies, who are wearing white armbands, will be allowed through the gauntlet. Clayborn frustrates the plot by stealing a pile of women's underwear from Stiles' store and improvising white armbands for the ranchers. He is wounded in the gun battle between factions but escapes through a cave with two exits. Later in Cottonwood, Stiles fires Brewster for losing the water litigation, then sends Ash out to murder his former lawyer and recover his share of their profits.

The film's climax is precipitated when the Texas Pacific Railroad reaches Abilene and the new Kansas shipping point raises the price of Texas cattle from three dollars a head to twenty.

Suddenly the small ranchers' herds are worth a fortune. "Round up every head of stock on the ranches I still control," Stiles orders Ash. "If they don't want to give 'em to you, take 'em." The gunmen seize as many cattle as they can, killing Eli Jackson in the process. Clayborn calls another meeting of ranchers and organizes a massive cattle drive which, as Stiles had predicted years before, must stop on the way to Abilene at the waterhole he had taken by murdering Clayborn's parents. "Load the Salamander safe on a wagon. I'm heading for Sweetwater."

Clayborn and the ranchers reach Sweetwater with their herd and, as they expected, find it occupied and fortified. There is a final exchange of dialogue in which Stiles demands half the cattle in exchange for opening the gate and giving them access to water.

> "Stiles, you have no right to block this trail."
> "No? Well, this is one piece of property I have a legal deed for."
> "And I know where you got it. . . . I'm John Clayborn. Stiles, I want you and Ash to surrender. You're going back to Cottonwood and stand trial for murder."

Stiles of course refuses and the final conflict breaks out as Clayborn and the ranchers take basically the same positions Stiles and his men had taken in the hills above Sweetwater ten years before and besiege the cabin with a hail of lead. The siege is broken when Clayborn uses improvised flaming arrows to set fire to the cabin containing Stiles, his men and the Salamander so that we are reminded of the joke about nothing melting either the fat man or his safe. Many of Stiles' gunfighters are cut down while trying to escape from the burning cabin and load the safe on the wagon. Stiles, Ash and the remnants of his gang flee across the desert with the ranchers in hot pursuit, a furious action sequence that ends with something that looks more like a horrible accident than a planned stunt. The four horses pulling Stiles' wagon stumble over one another and the wagon with Stiles and the safe goes over a cliff. As Clayborn and his men ride up, Kane gives us a powerful close-up of the fat capitalist lying dead on the dry earth and his emblematic safe lying on its side next to him, just as dead. Clayborn completes his revenge by chasing Ash into the rocks and, in their long-delayed but inevitable gun duel, shooting him down.

I never met Joseph Kane but back in the early 1970s, when I was a young professor and he was almost eighty, we had some phone conversations and a little correspondence. On one occasion, perhaps a year or two after the 1972 presidential election, he mentioned that he still kept a McGovern bumper sticker on his car. This is precisely what one would expect from the man who, almost forty years before, had directed this rich little film about the connections among economic power, brute force and the law. How I wish he'd lived long enough to address one of my seminars!

***

By the end of the thirties, political dictatorship and the coming war in Europe had largely taken over the roles that economic injustice and the Depression had played in American life and popular culture for most of the decade.[8] The cycle of lawyer films set in the present petered out with pictures like *The Spellbinder* (1939) and *The Man Who Talked Too Much* (1940), which were inferior remakes respectively of *State's Attorney* and *The Mouthpiece* from 1932. The cycle of law-related Westerns, however, ended on a brighter note.

Made in the last months of 1939 and released in the first week of 1940, *Legion of the Lawless* was the twelfth in a group of sixteen Westerns made at RKO between 1938 and 1940 starring George O'Brien[9] and (with two exceptions) directed by David Howard.[10] All sixteen are well worth seeing but *Legion of the Lawless* is the only one in which O'Brien plays a lawyer. What makes this film a distinct rarity is that it presents an overwhelmingly positive picture of what lawyers are and do.

Wearing a neat suit, Jeff Toland (George O'Brien) is riding past a sign that places him a few miles from the communities of Ivestown and East Ivestown when a peddler on a wagon (Horace Murphy) is chased by gunmen across the bridge that divides those locations. He explains to Toland that he was turned back by force while on his way to deliver supplies to Lafe Barton, the owner of East Ivestown's general store. Toland suggests that he sue the people who stopped him and identifies himself as an attorney intending to practice in the area. The peddler discourages him. "Ivestown doesn't crave strangers. East Ivestown, you'd starve to death."

Toland rides on into Ivestown anyway, and the people on the street turn their backs to him as he dismounts and enters the El Dorado saloon. The bartender (Rychard Cramer) won't talk to him and the only customer, Doc Denton (Herbert Heywood), the town drunk, can't. A brutally beaten Lafe Barton (Eddy Waller) staggers into the saloon and falls over. While Toland plays Good Samaritan and tries to take care of the injured storekeeper, Les Harper (Norman Willis), who was responsible for the beating, comes in and tosses Barton out and back across the line into East Ivestown where he belongs. Later a sobered-up Doc Denton explains to Toland that Harper is *de facto* head of the masked vigilante organization originally formed by his brother-in-law Henry Ives to maintain law and order in Ivestown. Its main function at present is to keep the have-nots in their place on the east side.

Not long afterwards, Toland meets Ives' daughter Ellen (Virginia Vale) and tells her he's hanging up his shingle in the community.

> "But lawyers have to have courts to practice in, sheriffs, and judges. We haven't any of those in Ivestown."
>
> "Oh, but you will. Ivestown's growing up. The railroad's coming through here. That's why I'm here. . . ."

Doc Denton expresses the same lack of enthusiasm for Toland's law practice, telling him: "The only law here is the vigilantes."

No sooner has Toland opened his office than he is visited by Henry

Ives (Hugh Sothern), a gunman named Borden (Monte Montague), and Les Harper. "We don't need any lawyers in this town, Toland," Harper snarls. "That might be a matter of opinion, Harper," Toland replies. Unlike his brother-in-law, Ives is willing to debate the question, and his dialogue with Toland is from a legal perspective the most crucial in the film.

"Let me remind you that the history of the West is a history of violence and bloodshed. Every new settlement has been overrun with the worst type of lawbreaker, outlaw and murderer. Because I was determined that Ivestown should be a city of homes and happy prosperous families, I took steps to see that such riffraff had no chance to take root here."

"So you formed the vigilantes."

"Exactly. With the full approval of our territorial governor. I tell you, ruffians give us a wide berth. If they don't, we know how to take care of them."

"Primitive and dangerous. Every man has the right to a public trial. Supposing your vigilante committee should make a mistake? What chance has that man to get justice?"

"Every case is considered fairly. We never make a move till we're positive we're right."

"A good theory—for a small community. But Ivestown's growing up. The railroad's coming through this far. There will be a great many problems that your vigilante committee won't be able to settle."

Harper breaks into the discussion with a threat to give Toland the kind of beating Lafe Barton got. Toland has a brawl with Borden after the gunman kicks the teenage boy (William Benedict) who was sweeping the sidewalk in front of the law office. Harper is about to shoot Toland in the back during the fight when Ellen Ives stops him.

Later Toland and Ellen have a talk of the same sort he had with her father, only without a violent conclusion.

> "The kind of peace I hate, Miss Ellen, is the one that is forced on people by abusing and terrorizing them. And that's what you're going to have here, just as long as your so-called vigilantes keep out organized law and order."
>
> "You don't know what you're talking about, Mr. Toland. This is the best-run town in the territory."
>
> "I don't doubt there's some good in the Committee. But with the wrong man at the head of it, it becomes a dangerous weapon. Just as it is here."

As in other series Westerns of the late 1930s,[11] the masked vigilantes are intended to evoke their contemporary counterpart, the Ku Klux Klan.

As Dave Marden (Delmar Watson) and a team of railroad surveyors arrive in Ivestown, Henry Ives ponders the changes in the world around him and contemplates calling a meeting of the vigilantes to discuss whether they should disband. Meanwhile Harper starts buying up the property in Ivestown that he thinks the railroad will want and sends his goons to ransack Toland's office and scare him out of town. Believing that his best hope of changing Ives' mind is through his daughter, Toland persuades Ellen to visit East Ivestown with him and see how the other half lives. Lafe Barton's small son throws a rock at Ellen's horse as she's crossing the bridge into the ghetto. Toland asks Lafe to make a list of the crimes committed by the vigilantes but, lacking all faith in the promise of a legal system, the storekeeper refuses to co-operate.

A week later, chief surveyor Marden asks Toland to notarize his report and reveals that the railroad is going to go through East Ivestown. "The folks in East Ivestown are finally going to get a break," Toland exults as he gets Doc Denton to sign the report as a witness. Harper and his men get the doctor so drunk that he tells them the news, then they ransack Marden's papers and read the report for themselves. Toland knows that trouble will follow.

That night he follows Harper and a group of vigilantes as they ride across the bridge into East Ivestown, force a Mexican blacksmith (Martin Garralaga) to sign over his property, then move on to Lafe Barton's store and make him the same sort of "offer he can't refuse": take fifty dollars for the property and get out of town within 48 hours or die. Toland breaks in, a gunbattle erupts and Barton's son is seriously wounded, though not before pulling a heart-shaped ornament from the gunbelt of the masked vigilante who shot him. The assailants escape but leave behind bills of sale for every piece of property in East Ivestown, with the purchaser identified simply as "Bearer."

Armed with this evidence, Toland visits Ives and finally persuades him to call an immediate meeting and disband the vigilantes, but Harper and his faction kill Ives on the trail and Toland finds the body. Harper then takes over the meeting, which is being held at the El Dorado, announces that the railroad will bypass Ivestown completely and, over the objections of the responsible members of the group, organizes the vigilantes to take over East Ivestown by force. Doc Denton eavesdrops on the meeting, rides off to warn Toland, who has gone to tell Ellen Ives of her father's murder, and confesses that it was his fault that Harper learned of the railroad's plans.

That night Toland gets to East Ivestown ahead of the vigilantes and organizes the oppressed into a self-defense force. The downtrodden hold an instant plebiscite and vote to secede from Ivestown and appoint Toland their sheriff. When the vigilantes ride into the ghetto they are surprised by the defenders and Harper is unmasked. "Les Harper, I arrest you for attempted murder," Toland says. Barton and the outraged residents of East Ivestown want to lynch their prisoner on the spot. "We'll do this legally, Lafe," Toland replies, and they find a building where Harper can be locked up. Meanwhile the vigilantes regroup, set fire to East Ivestown and free their leader. The people of East Ivestown are ready to set fires of their own in retaliation but Toland resists this move on the ground that "Most of the vigilantes don't belong to Harper's gang" and bargains for thirty minutes to bring Harper back. He finds the gang barricaded in the El Dorado, shoots it out with them—the fact that Ivestown is outside his jurisdiction being conveniently overlooked by all hands—and kills Harper just as the East Ivestown people march on the saloon and complete the mopping up. The governor disbands what's left of the vigilantes and Toland prepares to marry Ellen and settle down to a peaceful law practice as the film ends.

***

With the movement from the anguish of the Depression to the agony of the war, legal themes both in Westerns and in American movies as a whole tended to recede into the background,[12] as witness the fact that when *Legion of the Lawless* was remade less than three years later as *Pirates of the Prairie* (RKO, 1942, directed by Howard Bretherton and starring Tim Holt), the protagonist was no longer a lawyer but a gunsmith. Cinematic interest in legal motifs didn't return in full force until the war was over and the McCarthy-HUAC reign of cultural terror in the early Fifties had run its course.[13] The period that extends roughly from 1957 through 1965 and more or less coincides with the great years of the Warren Court is often considered the golden age of American films on the subject of law, lawyers and justice,[14] not only because of the sheer number of excellent movies the period generated—*12 Angry Men* (1957), *Anatomy of a Murder* (1959), *Inherit the Wind* (1960), *Judgment at Nuremberg* (1961), *To Kill a Mockingbird* (1962) and the unsung *Man in the Middle* (1963), to name a few—but also because so many films of the time, not to mention TV series like *Perry Mason* (1957-66) and *The Defenders* (1961-65), presented lawyers and the legal system in idealistic if not idealized terms.[15] If there is any bridge leading back from this period to the law-related Westerns of the Depression, it's that unpretentious little picture *Legion of the Lawless*, where George O'Brien portrays virtually an Atticus Finch on horseback and where the lawyer's function is to overthrow injustice and exploitation by subjecting them to a regime of rules. Someday perhaps such portrayals will be credible again.

NOTES

1. Among the films of this sort that postdate the Code are *Evelyn Prentice* (MGM, 1934, directed by William K. Howard, with William Powell playing the attorney as he had in 1932's *Lawyer Man*); *Bordertown* (Warner Bros., 1934, directed by Archie Mayo, starring Paul Muni as a Latino lawyer); *The Witness Chair* (RKO, 1936, directed by George Nicholls, Jr., with Ann Harding and, as the attorney, Walter Abel); *Criminal Lawyer* (RKO, 1937, directed by Christy Cabanne, with Lee Tracy in the title role); and *The Spellbinder* (RKO, 1939, a remake of the 1931 *State's Attorney*, directed by Jack Hively and with Lee Tracy in the John Barrymore part). All of these and many more, for example the six-picture Perry Mason series released by Warner Bros. between 1934 and 1937, have been shown in recent years on cable and satellite.

2. Browsing at random through a multi-volume work like *The Motion Picture Guide* (1986), edited by Jay Robert Nash and Stanley Ralph Ross, one finds all sorts of little-known and rarely-seen films that bear on the cinematic treatment of legal themes. How many times have I read or been told that *Adam's Rib* (MGM, 1949, directed by George Cukor, starring Spencer Tracy and Katharine Hepburn) was the first movie about a woman lawyer? Much earlier pictures with a female attorney in the leading role, such as *Ann Carver's Profession* (Columbia, 1933, directed by Edward Buzzell, starring Fay Wray) and *Portia on Trial* (Republic, 1937, directed by George Nicholls, Jr., with Frieda Inescort as the Portia) have rarely if ever been on videocassette or cable and therefore never existed. The publication of *The American Film Institute Catalog: Feature Films* 1931-1940 (University of California Press, 1993) finally gave us a reference work with a decent subject guide to law-related movies from the talkies' first decade. Similar films from the

Forties however remain inaccessible in reference works, leaving most law students totally ignorant of pictures like *Smart Woman* (Allied Artists, 1948, directed by Edward A. Blatt, starring Constance Bennett and Brian Aherne), which dealt with a pair of feuding lawyers married to each other: the same situation as in *Adam's Rib* but played seriously, not for laughs.

3. Powerful though it is when judged purely in cinematic terms, Lang's *Fury* would be a disaster in a law-school seminar. In the trial of 22 members of the lynch mob that burned down a small-town jail and allegedly incinerated the innocent prisoner within (Spencer Tracy), the prosecutor never presents any evidence of a dead body—not surprising since Tracy in fact escaped alive—and opens his case by putting on the stand various townspeople who swear to alibis for various defendants and then pillorying each of his own witnesses! If Lang consulted any lawyers before making this picture they must have been admitted to the bar of Cloud Cuckoo Land.

4. Nearly a thousand such films were released between 1930 and 1939. For titles, credits and other information, see Les Adams & Buck Rainey, *Shoot-em-Ups* (1978).

5. Most books on Wayne give these films short shrift. For fuller discussions than usual, see Don Miller, *Hollywood Corral* (1976), ch. 6, and Allen Eyles, *John Wayne* (2d ed. 1979), pp. 31-55.

6. For a substantial essay on Kane's career, see Harry Sanford, "Joseph Kane," in *Close Up: The Contract Director* (Jon Tuska ed. 1976), pp. 143-187.

7. Quoted in Sanford, *supra* note 6, at 143.

8. Beginning in 1938, one can find covert references to Hitler within the structure of series Westerns, cliffhanger serials and other types of popular film as robber-baron capitalists like Streeter in *One Man Law* and Stiles in *King of the Pecos* are phased out of the villain roles and replaced by political tyrants commanding uniformed legions of killers. It was not by chance that Stanley Andrews, who played the fuehrer of

Texas in Republic's 15-chapter serial *The Lone Ranger* (1938), looked so much like Hitler; nor that Killer Kane, the Capone-like interplanetary gangster of the Buck Rogers science-fiction comic strip, was transformed into "The Leader Kane" in Universal's 12-chapter serial *Buck Rogers* (1939), starring Buster Crabbe and with a storyline clearly reflecting contemporary events in Europe; nor that the evil Emperor Ming from earlier Flash Gordon cliffhangers lost his similarity to Dr. Fu Manchu and was given a military uniform, the motto "I am the universe" and the title The Dictator Ming in Universal's 12-chapter *Flash Gordon Conquers the Universe* (1940), with Buster Crabbe again in the lead. Two of the best Hitler-inspired 60-minute Westerns from the same period are *The Night Riders* (1939) and *The Kansas Terrors* (1939), both entries in Republic's long-running Three Mesquiteers series. But even after the United States entered the war, an occasional Western still pitted the hero against a Thirties-style economic exploiter. In *Texas Masquerade* (United Artists, 1943) the economic exploiter is also a lawyer and Hopalong Cassidy (William Boyd) poses as an attorney to thwart him.

9. O'Brien was born in 1900 and became a major star at the Fox studio during the 1920's, perhaps his best known silents being John Ford's *The Iron Horse* (1924) and F.W. Murnau's *Sunrise* (1927). In the Thirties he starred almost exclusively in Westerns, first at Fox, later at RKO. After Pearl Harbor he joined the Navy and made it his second career, although fellow naval officer John Ford occasionally arranged for him to be released from duty for roles in Ford films such as *Fort Apache* (1948), *She Wore a Yellow Ribbon* (1949) and *Cheyenne Autumn* (1964). When I met O'Brien he was eighty years old (though looking at least thirty years younger) and seemed to have a total recall of everything that had ever happened to him. He suffered a massive stroke a year or so later and died in a nursing home in 1985.

10. Born in Philadelphia in 1896, Howard worked from 1917 until the end of the silent era as an assistant to D. W. Griffith, King Vidor, Rex Ingram and other top directors. His own directorial career began with

Spanish-language versions of early Fox talkies. The vast majority of his English-language features were Westerns starring George O'Brien. He died in 1941, a week after Pearl Harbor.

11. In *The Mystery of the Hooded Horsemen* (1937), starring Tex Ritter, the group is simply a gang of hoodlums led by a hidden mastermind of the sort common in cliffhanger serials. In *The Fighting Texan* (1937), starring Kermit Maynard, a Klan-like group pops up for no reason at all in one sequence and then vanishes from the film. The series Western most clearly inspired by the Klan is Republic's *The Purple Vigilantes* (1938), a Three Mesquiteers adventure which anticipates *Legion of the Lawless* in treating its hooded terrorist organization as originally serving a legitimate purpose but corrupted over time. Preceding all of these Westerns by a few years and perhaps in a sense inspiring them were contemporary "social consciousness" thrillers clearly intended to conjure up thoughts of the Klan, such as Warners' *Black Legion* (1936, directed by Archie Mayo and starring Humphrey Bogart).

12. Curiously enough, the transition years between Depression and war gave birth to three of American prose fiction's enduring classics on legal themes: Walter Van Tilburg Clark's *The Ox-Bow Incident* (1940), Richard Wright's *Native Son* (1940), and James Gould Cozzens' *The Just and the Unjust* (1942).

13. The most interesting law-related works reflecting the witch hunt are Arthur Miller's play *The Crucible* (1953) and Ellery Queen's novel *The Glass Village* (Little Brown, 1954). One of the few movies of the time that dealt with the reign of terror in a legal perspective is *Count the Hours* (RKO, 1954), directed by Don Siegel and starring Macdonald Carey as an attorney, aptly named Douglas Madison, who is ostracized by the community after he's assigned to defend an unpopular client.

14. See Thomas J. Harris, *Courtroom's Finest Hour in American Cinema* (Scarecrow, 1987).

15. Deeply negative takes on the system are offered in two of the period's finest law-related films: Hitchcock's *The Wrong Man* (1957) and the first version of *Cape Fear* (Universal, 1962). As we shall see in

Chapter Eight, the final minutes of the latter film cheat outrageously in order to close with an affirmation of unearned faith in the legal system's efficacy.

Arthur Train (above) concluded from his days as a prosecutor that neither the legal system nor life itself offered justice. His fictional Ephraim Tutt was "a protagonist of real Justice."

The early stories of Melville Davisson Post (above) portray the quintessential lawyer for his times when social Darwinism was in the air everyone breathed. His amoral Randolph Mason uses his knowledge of the law's technicalities to help crminals get away with their crimes. Later Post created Uncle Abner in stories that focused on divine law standing above man's puny structures of justice.

William Joseph Fallon (right) was a prosecutor who became a mouthpiece for gangsters. His exploits, which included making prosecutors' evidence disappear, inspired a number of early films.

Law and justice, three perspectives: (clockwise from top) Erle Stanley Gardner's Perry Mason battled for clients in a legal system that favored the state and permitted "ambush prosecutions." John D. MacDonald's novel *The Executioners*, twice filmed as *Cape Fear*, viewed law as a social convenience to be abandoned as ineffective in dealing with primitive threats to survival. Howard Fast's morally complex novel *The Winston Affair* inspired *Man in the Middle*, an unsung classic film of the Warren Court era.

Frontier justice, 1932. Among the 60-minute westerns of the early 1930s, *One Man Law* stands out for its portrayal of the conflict between the simple sense of decency in a community and a legal system employing sanctity of property to legitimize economic exploitation. Lawman Buck Jones (above) is forced to evict ranchers from their long-worked properties in favor of legal title-holders. (Photo courtesy of WesternClippings.com.)

Lawyer John Wayne and Arthur Aylesworth (above) serve a subpoena in *King of the Pecos* (1936). The film, thematically similar to *One Man Law*, breaks new ground in putting two lawyers at the heart of the conflict. Lawyer George O'Brien and a group of citizens confront vigilante leader Norman Willis in *Legion of the Lawless* (1940) below. The film is a rarity in that it presents an overwhelmingly positive picture of what lawyers are and do. (Photos courtesy of WesternClippings.com.)

CHAPTER 7

Telejuriscinema, Frontier Style

This chapter will and must be selective and illustrative, not comprehensive. The reason why is not far to seek.

The first Western series made for television was *The Lone Ranger* (1949-57), which consists of 221 episodes running approximately 30 minutes apiece. Its instant success at the dawn of the TV age inspired a huge number of other 30-minute Western series aimed at a juvenile audience: *The Cisco Kid* (1950-56, 156 episodes), *The Gene Autry Show* (1950-55, 91 episodes), *The Range Rider* (1950-53, 78 episodes), *The Adventures of Kit Carson* (1951-54, 104 episodes), *The Roy Rogers Show* (1951-57, 100 episodes), *Wild Bill Hickok* (1951-58, 114 episodes), and *Hopalong Cassidy* (1952-54, 40 episodes), to name some of the better-known. That's more than 450 hours of viewing—assuming one can find copies of these episodes—and these are by no means all the shoot-em-up series that made up the TV Western's first wave! Now add in some of the better-known 30-minute "adult" Western series like *Gunsmoke* (1955-61, 233 episodes), *The Life and Legend of Wyatt Earp* (1955-61, 266 episodes), *Have Gun—Will Travel* (1957-63, 225 episodes), *Trackdown* (1957-59, 72 episodes), *The Rifleman* (1958-63, 168 episodes), *Lawman* (1958-62, 156 episodes), and *Wanted: Dead Or Alive* (1958-61, 94 episodes). That's another 600-plus hours of viewing time. Now add in a handful of the most fondly remembered 60-minute series, such as

263

Cheyenne (1955-62, 107 episodes), *Wagon Train* (1957-63 and l964-65, 251 episodes), *Maverick* (1957-62, 124 episodes), *Rawhide* (1957-65, 217 episodes), *Sugarfoot* (1957-61, 69 episodes), *Bronco* (1958-62, 68 episodes), *Bonanza* (1959-73, 440 episodes), the expanded version of *Gunsmoke* (1961-75, 403 episodes), and *The Big Valley* (1965-69, 112 episodes). The result is almost 1800 hours of additional viewing time. Factor in the 90-minute series like *The Virginian* (1962-70, 225 episodes), the expanded version of *Wagon Train* (1963-64, 32 episodes) and *Cimarron Strip* (1967-68, 26 episodes). Another 420 hours of viewing time. And we haven't even mentioned the 30-minute anthology series like *Death Valley Days* (1953-70, 532 episodes) and *Zane Grey Theatre* (1956-61, 146 episodes), or any of the dozens of series that didn't last long enough to become household names! Considering the enormity of the source material, can justice be done to the subject in a chapter?

Perhaps.

I happen to have been born at just the right time to become a shoot-em-up fan when the early juvenile-oriented series dominated the small screen. My parents bought their first set in time for me to begin watching episodes of those series again and again in the early to middle 1950s. Soon after my tenth birthday and for no particular reason that I can recall, I began squirreling away each week's issue of *TV Guide* after the current week was over so that I was inadvertently accumulating a detailed history of the medium, complete with casts and descriptions of most of the episodes of every series ever broadcast. When the juvenile-oriented shoot-em-up was displaced by the so-called adult Western, I was old enough to make the transition too. As an adult I learned how to use the Copyright Office motion picture catalogues, which contain a wealth of information about episodic television unknown even to many specialists. I picked up further expertise through the abundant TV reference books published in the last few decades—books which run the gamut from excellent to abysmally ignorant but which, when used by an informed reader, are priceless—and, more recently, through imperfect but invaluable Web sources like the Classic TV Archive. Equally important, I still enjoy Westerns enough to *want* to write this chapter, and to address the question: How have the makers of TV Western series dealt with the perennial themes of law, lawyers and justice?

***

The TV Western and the treatment of legal themes within it share the same starting point, in the fall of 1949 when *The Lone Ranger* made its debut. Within its first few months the series offered superb illustrations of a dichotomy in presentation of legal themes that would characterize virtually all of the first wave of TV Westerns.

The first three episodes—"Enter the Lone Ranger" (15 September 1949), "The Lone Ranger Fights On" (22 September 1949) and "The Lone Ranger's Triumph" (29 September 1949)—were all written and directed by George B. Seitz, Jr. (1915-2002), son of the director George B. Seitz (1888-1944), who had helmed silent cliffhanger serials for Pathe in the 1920s and ended his career at MGM as director of the Andy Hardy family comedy films. The three episodes form a continuing story and indeed the first ends with a cliffhanger as if Seitz Jr. were paying tribute to his father. The first half of what cumulatively might be considered the first TV movie retold the familiar origin story: the ambush of Captain Reid's Texas Ranger patrol and the survival of one man, the captain's younger brother John Reid (Clayton Moore), who is nursed back to health by his boyhood Indian friend Tonto (Jay Silverheels), then assumes the mask and identity of The Lone Ranger. Although his first item of business is to track down the gang that killed his brother and the other Rangers, his ultimate objective is broader. "For every one of those men I'm going to bring a hundred lawbreakers to justice. I'll make the Cavendish gang, and every criminal that I can find for that matter, regret the day those Rangers were killed." But he vows to bring in his quarry not draped over their saddles but alive to stand trial. "If a man must die it's up to the law to decide that, not the person behind the six-shooter." To which Tonto replies: "That right. . . . Me want law here too, for all." Although never an official representative of the legal system, the masked rider of the plains is as devoted to law-and-order as the most fervent priest to his faith, and we are clearly meant to agree that his cause is right.

Yet whenever a lawyer character appears in a subsequent episode, he's invariably a swine.

In "Spanish Gold" (1 June 1950; directed by Seitz from a teleplay by Herb Meadow and Milton M. Raison based on a 1949 radio play by Ralph Goll) the adversary figure for the first time in the series is an attorney. James P. Hague (Bruce Hamilton) and deputy sheriff Gil Jackson (Kenneth Tobey) commit a cold-blooded murder for which they frame Tug Spencer (Steve Clark). Hague represents Spencer at his trial but, as another character later comments, "Most of the time he didn't seem to know which side was paying him." Hague throws the case so that the old man is convicted and hanged. Later he and the corrupt deputy confer in Hague's office and divide the profits from their crime. "One third for you," Hague says, "the rest for me." When the deputy asks what entitles him to two-thirds, the attorney replies: "If anyone else had defended Tug Spencer, would he have been hanged for a killing you did? That's another third." A minute or so later comes another marvelous exchange between these men.

> Hague: "Are you consulting me professionally?"
> Deputy: "Not me. . . . I want to go on living."

The Lone Ranger learns of the outrage from the young man who was Spencer's cellmate before his execution and sets out to bring Hague to justice.

As far as I can determine, no more lawyer characters appear in the series until near its end several years later. In "The Too Perfect Signature" (31 March 1955; directed by William J. Thiele from a teleplay by Harry Poppe, Jr.) the masked man and Tonto try to prove that unscrupulous attorney Henry Stacy (Stacy Keach, Sr.) and his accomplice have been forging deeds to ranchers' land. And in the series' final season, when producer Jack Wrather took over and had the final cycle of 39 segments shot in color and on relatively high budgets, came one of the finest episodes in the entire 221. In "Quicksand" (1 November 1956; directed by Earl Bellamy from a teleplay by Walker Tompkins and Robert Leslie Bellem) a renegade Indian and his white lawyer accomplice (Denver Pyle) ambush the Ranger and Tonto and leave them to die in a quicksand bog.

In these three episodes of *The Lone Ranger* we notice an interesting dichotomy. What makes James P. Hague of "Spanish Gold" the vilest of the lawyer villains is precisely that his form of villainy is possible only for a lawyer, whereas in the other episodes the corrupt lawyers could have belonged to any profession or none and the stories would have been exactly the same. This distinction between essential and accidental lawyer chicanery is also found in other TV Western series of the first wave.

The first series to reach the small screen after *The Lone Ranger* was *The Cisco Kid* (1950-56), starring Duncan Renaldo as the romantic rogue character familiar to Western fans from the long-running Cisco Kid movies and Leo Carrillo as his language-mangling compañero Pancho. The similarities between the series concepts are obvious: two men roaming the old West, frequently mistaken for outlaws, setting things to rights wherever they go. And several of the situations they set to rights involve slimy lawyers.

Among the 26 episodes that made up the first season of the series, three consecutive segments pitted our heroes against a scumbag with a law license. In "Uncle Disinherits Niece" (13 February 1951; directed by Paul Landres from a teleplay by Betty Burbridge) crooked lawyer Sam Foster (Bill Kennedy) murders a rancher who had threatened to disinherit his niece if she didn't stop seeing her boy friend. Cisco and Pancho try to clear the young man. In "Phoney Heiress" (13 February 1951; directed by Landres from a teleplay by J. Benton Cheney) our heroes try to save a young woman's inherited property from crooked lawyer George Holden (Jack Reynolds), who has hired an impostor to pose as the rightful owner. And in "Water Rights" (20 February 1951;

directed by Albert Herman from a teleplay by Raymond L. Schrock) Cisco and Pancho go up against a banker and his lawyer partner (Tristram Coffin) who are scheming to sabotage the ranchers' water project and then foist their own project on the valley. Included in the 26 episodes of the second season was "Quicksilver Murder" (12 February 1952; directed by Paul Landres from a teleplay by J. Benton Cheney), where the chief adversary is a public prosecutor (Hugh Prosser) who is stealing quicksilver shipments and using chemical means to commit murder when threatened with exposure.

Episodes from later seasons continued on occasion to make use of lawyer characters and themes but without lawyer villains. The third season"s "Fear" (22 February 1953; directed by Eddie Davis from a teleplay by J. Benton Cheney) was an "old dark house" mystery about a dead man's ghost terrorizing the heirs who are required by his will to live on his ranch. One of the ghost's victims is attorney T. Thomas Trimble (John Hamilton), a blustering idiot but certainly no worse. The fourth season's "The Raccoon Story" (17 December 1953; directed by Paul Landres from a teleplay by Warren Wilson) involved Cisco and Pancho with an old prospector whose will left all his property to his dog. (Apparently no one could find a raccoon who could do what the script required.) In "Not Guilty" (31 January 1954; directed by Landres from a teleplay by Barney A. Sarecky) a jailed killer's friend plots to abort justice by impersonating the circuit judge (Lyle Talbot). And "New Evidence" (8 January 1955; directed by Lambert Hillyer from a teleplay by Ande Lamb) contains one of the few courtroom sequences in the first wave of TV Westerns but the principal plot device is lifted bodily from the trial sequence in John Ford's classic *Young Mr. Lincoln* (20th Century-Fox, 1939, starring Henry Fonda).

The first star of feature-length Westerns who recognized that TV would shape the genre's future was Gene Autry (1907-1999), who in 1950 formed Flying A Productions for the purpose of making not only a 30-minute TV series starring himself (*The Gene Autry Show*,

1950-55) but other series with actors he hoped to develop into the next generation of shoot-em-up stars. The first of these to go into production was *The Range Rider* (1950-53), starring Jack (later Jock) Mahoney and Dick Jones as a pair of drifters who go about the old West helping decent folks and fighting bad guys, a certain number of whom are lawyers. In one of the earliest episodes, "Gunslinger in Paradise" (19 February 1951; directed by George Archainbaud from a teleplay by Sherman Lowe), our heroes find the bodies of a man and woman who were left to die of thirst on the desert. It turns out that the killers are a corrupt lawyer (Denver Pyle) and a client of his (Dick Curtis) who will inherit a huge estate in case of the deaths of the couple and their child (Jerry Hunter). In an episode from the second season, "The Fatal Bullet" (28 December 1951; directed by Archainbaud from a teleplay by J. Benton Cheney), Mahoney and Jones prove that a man convicted of murder and awaiting execution (Tom London) was framed by his own defense counsel (James Griffith).

The Adventes of Kit Carson (1951-54), starring Bill Williams as the California scout and Don Diamond as his perennially lovelorn comic sidekick El Toro, offered nothing special but survived for 104 episodes, a few of which included a legal component. "Enemies of the West" (1951; directed by Lew Landers from a teleplay by Eric Taylor) even featured a sympathetic lawyer (Davison Clark) whom Kit and El Toro are escorting to the state prison with a pardon for a man wrongly convicted of murder. In time we learn that the lawyer agreed to serve as appointed counsel for the defendant despite being the best friend of the judge who was murdered, but this absurdity turns out to have no bearing on the plot. Most of the attorney characters encountered by Kit and El Toro are cut from darker cloth. In "Ventura Feud" (1951; directed by Landers from a teleplay by Luci Ward) the lawyer villain (William Tannen) forges a Spanish land grant and uses it as the basis of a suit to dispossess the rightful owners of a huge tract of California land. And in "The Range Master" (1951; directed by Landers from a teleplay by Ward) we find an attorney (Kenneth MacDonald) who not only devises a cattle swindle to cheat his rancher client but kills the rancher's foreman, frames the rancher and then represents him at trial and on appeal, both of which of course he loses.

The Roy Rogers Show (1951-57) was the first TV shoot-em-up to be set in the contemporary West rather than frontier times but was just as rich in despicable lawyer characters as were series set in the past. Like *The Cisco Kid* and *The Range Rider* and many another early TV Western series, the *Roy Rogers* episodes were shot in groups of two, three or four by the same director using overlapping casts. In the debut episode "Jailbreak" (30 December 1951; directed by John English from a teleplay by Albert DeMond and Ray Wilson), Roy and his real-world wife Dale Evans investigate an attempt on the life of young Tom Lee (Rand Brooks), who's in the Mineral City jail awaiting trial for the murder of the local banker, and soon discover that Tom was framed for the crime by his own attorney (Douglas Evans). Shot back-to-back with this segment but not broadcast until two months later was "The Desert Fugitive" (24 February 1952; directed by English from a teleplay by DeMond and Wilson), in which Roy and Dale become involved with the twin brother of an escaped convict (Rand Brooks) who was murdered by his lawyer and accomplice in crime (Stephen Chase) after breaking out of prison. Near the end of the first season, in "The Mayor of Ghost Town" (30 November 1952; directed by Robert G. Walker from a teleplay by Milton M. Raison), Roy and Dale take hands in a title dispute with both an eccentric mining engineer (Hal Price) and a crooked lawyer (Zon Murray) claiming to own a deserted community. As far as I can determine the only non-corrupt holder of a law license in any of the 100 episodes of this series is the attorney in "Ambush" (15 January 1956; directed by George Blair from a teleplay by Dwight Cummins) who offers Roy and Dale some information as they hunt for the person who shot and wounded an old prospector. The lawyer's role is so minute that the actor who played the part isn't named in the credits.

Another series set in the New West was *Sky King* (1952, 1956-59), starring Kirby Grant as the aviation-loving owner of the Flying

Crown ranch, with Gloria Winters as his niece Penny and, in the early episodes, Ron Hagerthy as his nephew Clipper. In "Designing Woman" (14 June 1952; directed by John H. Morse from a teleplay by Curtis Kenyon) the three are returning from an aerial survey when Sky's plane the Songbird is flagged down by a woman (Angela Greene) claiming to be the niece of a local rancher who died mysteriously. She turns out of course to be an impostor in the pay of the attorney for the estate (Robert Shayne). We've seen that the same plot had been used eighteen months earlier with an Old West setting in the *Cisco Kid* episode "Phoney Heiress."

Was there something about the early 1950s that attracted the writers and directors of TV Westerns to evil lawyers? *Wild Bill Hickok* (1951-58), starring Guy Madison as the buckskin-clad marshal and gravel-voiced Andy Devine as his sidekick Jingles, pitted its heroes against a fine specimen of the breed in "Blacksmith Story" (10 February 1952; directed by Frank McDonald from a teleplay by Bill Raynor), where they match wits with a greedy attorney (Robert Livingston) who gets a sadistic blacksmith (Richard Alexander) to beat up ranchers in order to drive them off their property. Near the end of the same year, the relatively short-lived *Hopalong Cassidy* series (1952-54), starring William Boyd in the role he'd made famous in movies between 1935 and 1948, offered a variation on this plot in "Alien Range" (1 October 1952; directed by Thomas Carr from a teleplay by Sherman L. Lowe). This time the victims are immigrant settlers and it's not a blacksmith but a rancher (Glenn Strange) who conspires with the evil lawyer (James Griffith) in the scheme to dispossess them. A taste for family resemblances is part of the job description for whoever wants to study the TV Western.

But why were attorneys so uniformly presented as toads? It's hard to believe that so many of the writers and directors who specialized in this type of film-making had grudges against the profession, and in any event these early series were aimed at youngsters who often had only the vaguest notion of what lawyers were. My suggestion is that the negative portrayal of lawyers stems from the all but invariable tendency of these series to make no distinction between lawful behavior and "doing the right thing." The juvenile-oriented TV Western takes place in a Cloud Cuckoo Land where, as Gene Autry's theme song puts it, "the only law is Right." In this simplistic universe the heroes, who by definition are the good guys, subsume every positive role that a lawyer could possibly perform, leaving nothing for the lawyer characters to be but bad guys. A more diverse and realistic exploration of lawyer characters and legal themes had to await the coming of the so-called adult Western, which freed writers and directors to deal with the chasm that so often separates law and justice.

***

Conventional wisdom has it that the Hoppy-Gene-and-Roy type of TV Western was displaced almost overnight in the fall of 1955 by the simultaneous debut of *Cheyenne*, *Frontier*, *Gunsmoke* and *The Life and Legend of Wyatt Earp*. A glance at the chronology blows two huge holes in this thesis. On the one hand, the juvenile type of series co-existed with the adult variety for several years: *Annie Oakley*, *The Lone Ranger* and *The Roy Rogers Show* continued to air new episodes until the spring of 1957, *Wild Bill Hickok* until the spring of 1958, *Sky King* and *Adventures of Rin-Tin-Tin* until the spring of 1959. On the other hand, adult Westerns could be seen on the small screen quite a while before *Gunsmoke* and its congeners.

An early foreshadowing of the TV Western's future was offered by various 30-minute anthology series like *Ford Theatre* (1952-57), *Schlitz Playhouse of Stars* (1952-59) and *General Electric Theatre* (1953-62) that occasionally featured Western segments, where action and stunts were minimal to nil and emphasis was placed on dramatic conflict, featuring stars like Dane Clark, Broderick Crawford and Ronald Reagan who had never appealed to juvenile audiences. These programs were soon joined by the longest-running anthology series of them all, *Death Valley Days* (1953-70), which was devoted exclusively to Westerns but without continuing characters or shoot-em-up storylines.

Even those who confined themselves to programs with the same stars every week might have sensed something in the wind before the fall of 1955. *Cowboy G-Men*, a 39-episode syndicated series from 1952, with B Western hero Russell Hayden and former silent child star Jackie Coogan getting into lots of fights and chases as Federal agents operating on the frontier, superficially seemed aimed at fans of Rogers, Autry and the like. But the scripts tended to be quite offtrail, with strong and bizarre roles for women and for excellent actors like Jim Davis and Morris Ankrum and, usually playing psychotic gunmen of a sort never encountered by Hoppy-Gene-or-Roy, a wild-eyed wolf-faced young man named Timothy Carey who a few years later would join director Stanley Kubrick's floating stock company. The lawyers involved in *G-Men* plots were invariably crooks. In "Salted Mines" (directed by Lesley Selander from a teleplay by William R. Cox, Brown Holmes and Buckley Angell) a mine broker (Kenneth MacDonald) unknowingly sells worthless claims to customers who are then assured by his secret partner (Archie Twitchell), the only attorney in town, that they have no grounds to sue. In "Ozark Gold" (directed by Leslie H. Martinson from a teleplay by Angell) the villain is a U.S. Attorney (Richard Travis) who, when caught, offers to make a pile of money for himself and fellow federal agent Hayden by arresting innocent people and then taking bribes not to prosecute them. But if the bar was fair game in telefilms of the early Fifties, the bench remained sacrosanct. In "Hang the Jury" (directed by Reg T. Browne from a teleplay by Orville H. Hampton) Hayden and Coogan go after a judge (Morris Ankrum) who's been conspiring with outlaws to collect the rewards for their own capture but soon find that the real judge has been killed and replaced by his corrupt twin brother. And in "Gypsy Traders" (directed by Donald McDougall from a teleplay by Buckley Angell) they ride into territorial Montana with a writ of habeas corpus to release a federal judge (Gregg Barton) who, just before ruling in favor of some gypsies in a dispute over copper-rich land, was framed for murder by the town marshal (Harry Hickox) and the gypsies' own lawyer (James Seay), who wants the land for himself.

Since its formation in 1935 the premier studio specializing in 60-

minute Western features had been Republic Pictures, whose executives recognized by the early 1950s that this type of movie was dying and therefore began producing Western series for the small screen. *Stories of the Century* (1954-55, 39 episodes) was something of a cross between the anthology and the single-character series. Each 30-minute segment centered around a genuine Western outlaw but with historic events reshaped so that Jim Davis as hard-bitten railroad detective Matt Clark played a major role in bringing the person to justice. The first 30 episodes were directed by William Witney (1915-2002), the Hitchcock of the low-budget action film, and among the soon to be prominent actors he cast as badman of the week were Lee Van Cleef (as Jesse James), Fess Parker (as one of the Dalton brothers), Jack Elam (as Black Jack Ketchum) and Jack Kelly (as Clay Allison). Witney's dynamic visual genius makes much of the series still eminently watchable today but the only episode of legal significance is "John Wesley Hardin" (9 April 1954; directed by Witney from a teleplay by Milton M. Raison), in which Matt Clark and his assistant Frankie Adams (Mary Castle) go after the gunman (Richard Webb) who killed forty people, then became a lawyer and finally resumed a life of crime. Distinction without a difference?

During the same season that saw the debut of *Gunsmoke*, Russell Hayden returned as both producer and occasional guest star of a syndicated series that was nowhere near as interesting as *Cowboy G-Men* but seemed likewise split between juvenile and adult elements. *Judge Roy Bean* (1955-56, 39 episodes) starred Edgar Buchanan as the whiskered grouch in a silk hat who called himself "the law west of the Pecos," with Jack Beutel and (every so often) Hayden himself as Texas Rangers who help him keep order. But this can hardly be considered the first TV Western series with a protagonist trained in the law: Buchanan's Judge Roy is a jurist purely by his own appointment, and when he bangs his gavel and turns his general store into an improvised courtroom, nothing much of a legal nature happens. The only exception I've discovered is "The Defense Rests" (1 June 1956; directed by Reg T. Browne from a teleplay by

Buckley Angell), where the climax takes place in a formal court with Beutel charged with robbery and Buchanan acting as defense counsel.

***

In the fall of 1955 not one but two varieties of so-called adult Western series with continuing characters debuted on network TV. In many respects the similarities between the two types outweighed the differences, but for simplicity's sake this chapter will treat them separately.

Foremost among all 30-minute adult Western series was CBS' *Gunsmoke*, starring James Arness as Marshal Matt Dillon, which was a 30-minute show between 1955 and 1961, then expanded to 60 minutes and lasted in that format till the spring of 1975. Most students of TV Westerns would probably agree that among 30-minute series only *Have Gun—Will Travel* (CBS, 1957-63), with Richard Boone as the black-garbed intellectual gunfighter Paladin, was as consistently excellent as early *Gunsmoke*. But many others also had long runs and are fondly remembered: *The Life and Legend of Wyatt Earp* (ABC, 1955-61), with Hugh O'Brian in the title role; *Tales of Wells Fargo* (NBC, 1957-61), starring Dale Robertson as Wells Fargo agent Jim Hardie; *Lawman* (ABC, 1958-62), with John Russell as vaguely Dillonesque Marshal Dan Troop; and *The Rifleman* (ABC, 1958-63), starring Chuck Connors as rancher and single parent Lucas McCain. Among the series that enjoyed respectable two- or three-year runs were *Broken Arrow* (ABC, 1956-58), with John Lupton and Michael Ansara as Indian agent Tom Jeffords and Apache chief Cochise; *Man Without a Gun* (syndicated, 1957-59), starring Rex Reason as frontier newspaper editor Adam MacLean; *The Restless Gun* (NBC, 1957-59), with John Payne as wandering gunslinger Vint Bonner; *Trackdown* (CBS, 1957-59), with Robert Culp as Texas Ranger Hoby Gilman; *The Texan* (CBS, 1958-60), starring Rory Calhoun as Bill Longley; *Wanted: Dead Or Alive* (CBS, 1958-61), with Steve McQueen as bounty hunter Josh Randall; *The Deputy* (NBC, 1959-61), starring Henry Fonda as Marshal Simon Fry; *The Rebel* (ABC, 1959-61), with Nick Adams as Confederate veteran Johnny Yuma; and *Shotgun Slade* (syndicated, 1959-61), with Scott Brady playing a cross between a

Westerner and a Fifties private eye. The success of the better known series led to a glut of competitors, many of them cancelled after one season or less: *Buckskin* (NBC, 1958-59), *The Rough Riders* (ABC, 1958-59), *Hotel de Paree* (CBS, 1959-60), *Johnny Ringo* (CBS, 1959-60), *Man from Blackhawk* (ABC, 1959-60), and the NBC offerings *Tate* and *Wrangler*, which were seen during the summer of 1960 but never made it into the fall. Among the commercial failures were at least two gems: *Law of the Plainsman* (NBC, 1959-60), with Michael Ansara as Harvard-educated Apache deputy marshal Sam Buckhart, and Sam Peckinpah's quickly axed cult favorite *The Westerner* (NBC, 1960), starring Brian Keith as drifter Dave Blassingame. Within a few years the 30-minute Western had been displaced by the 60- and 90-minute varieties but there were still some series in the shorter format including *Branded* (NBC, 1965-66), starring Chuck Connors as disgraced ex-cavalryman Jason McCord; *The Legend of Jesse James* (ABC, 1965-66), with Christopher Jones in the title role; *The Loner* (CBS, 1965-66), with Lloyd Bridges as nomadic Civil War veteran William Colton; *A Man Called Shenandoah* (ABC, 1965-66), with Robert Horton as an amnesic drifter hunting his lost self; and *The Guns of Will Sonnett* (ABC, 1967-69), starring Walter Brennan and Dack Rambo as the father and son of a gunfighter on the run.

The profuse dates in the previous paragraph are not inserted to show off erudition but to make a point, namely that the years in which the adult Western flourished happened to coincide with three events outside the genre: (1) the golden age of the Warren Court; (2) the idealized if not idealistic presentation of lawyer protagonists in movies like *Inherit the Wind* and *To Kill a Mockingbird*; and (3) the heyday of TV lawyer series set in the present like *Perry Mason* (CBS, 1957-66) and *The Defenders* (CBS, 1960-63). This conjunction had a profound impact on the way legal themes and lawyer characters were presented in TV Westerns.

That the strongest and most enduring of the 30-minute adult Western series were *Gunsmoke* and *Have Gun—Will Travel* is due to any number of factors: expert directors, superb scripts (with John

Meston, John Dunkel and the young Sam Peckinpah writing for *Gunsmoke* and Harry Julian Fink and Gene Roddenberry for *Have Gun*), haunting background music (much of it by the never-credited Bernard Herrmann), and the powerful performances of James Arness and Richard Boone as protagonists of their respective series. That every episode of *Gunsmoke* during its first few seasons was adapted from a script by John Meston for the earlier *Gunsmoke* radio series, which starred William Conrad as Marshal Dillon, perhaps accounts for the fact that several law-related segments of the series dealt with the same subject, the edges of the concept of lawfulness. In at least three episodes—"The Killer" (26 May 1956; directed by Robert Stevenson from a teleplay by John Dunkel), "Who Lives by the Sword" (18 May 1957; directed by Andrew V. McLaglen from a teleplay by Meston), and "There Never Was a Horse" (15 May 1959; directed by McLaglen from a Meston teleplay)—Marshal Dillon is pitted against a sociopathic gunman (sometimes wearing a badge) who evades the law by provoking others into drawing first so he can kill them and claim self-defense. But other segments, also adapted from John Meston radio scripts, offered somewhat different takes on legal themes. In "Bloody Hands" (16 February 1957; directed by McLaglen from a Meston teleplay) Dillon turns in his badge after being forced in the name of the law to do something he detests. In "The Bureaucrat" (16 March 1957; directed by Ted Post from a teleplay by William F. Leicester) a Washington politician (John Hoyt) takes over the law enforcement function in Dodge City against Dillon's warnings and soon finds an angry mob rebelling against his dictatorial methods. In "Born to Hang" (2 November 1957; directed by Buzz Kulik from a Meston teleplay) Dillon encounters a drifter (Anthony Caruso) who was miraculously saved from being lynched and is planning a legal revenge against the men who tried to hang him. In "Letter of the Law" (10 October 1958; directed by Richard Whorf from a teleplay by Les Crutchfield) Dillon in obedience to a court order tries to evict reformed gunman Brandon Teek (Clifton James) and his wife (Mary Carver) from their home, but when Teek threatens violence, Dillon rides to Wichita to appeal to the court on Teek's behalf. In the rare episode featuring a character who has a law license, that person usually turns out to be as warty a toad as the lawyers in the Hoppy-Gene-and-Roy Westerns to which *Gunsmoke* supposedly was the antithesis. In "Print Asper" (22 May 1959; directed by Ted Post from a Meston teleplay), Dillon takes a hand when an attorney (Ted Knight), hired by a rancher (J. Pat O'Malley) to draw up a deed conveying the family property to his sons, phrases the document so that title vests in the attorney himself.

The character of Paladin in *Have Gun—Will Travel* had no law degree but his range of intellectual skills and interests was broad as the prairie and Richard Boone, gifted with perhaps the most magnificent voice in the history of television, could outperform any licensed attorney when the occasion called for oratorical power. "The Five Books of Owen Deaver" (25 April 1958; directed by Lamont Johnson from a teleplay by Sam Rolfe) pits Paladin against a moronic sheriff (James Olson) who rules a frontier town by enforcing to the letter every provision in a five-volume statutory code intended for the city of Philadelphia. In "Incident at Borrasca Bend" (20 March 1959; directed by Andrew V. McLaglen from a teleplay by Jay Simms) Paladin rides into a makeshift town to return a pouch of gold to its owner and suddenly finds himself standing trial for murder in a kangaroo court. The magic of Boone's voice and the imagination of various directors and writers made possible some episodes built around legal problems of the present, such as the violent juvenile offender. In "The Prisoner" (17 December 1960; directed by Buzz Kulik from a teleplay by Robert E. Thompson) Paladin tries to save a young outlaw (Buzz Martin) who was imprisoned at age 13 and sentenced to hang on his 21st birthday, which as the story unfolds is only a few days off.

Three months later the theme was revisited in the stunning "Fandango" (4 March 1961; directed by Richard Boone from a teleplay by Harry Julian Fink). Paladin volunteers to help a Civil War comrade who is now sheriff of a Western town (Robert Gist) recapture two youths (Andrew Prine and Jerry Summers) who broke jail after being sentenced to hang for a brutal murder. While the two men and their prisoners are on their way back to town, Paladin learns that the victim's brother Lloyd Petty (Karl Swenson) is bent on private vengeance. "He wants to cut the heart out of those boys just like he was an Apache Indian," the gunfighter says after an encounter with Petty on the trail. Boone and Fink skillfully orchestrate the film to evoke sympathy for the doomed boys—until the jailhouse deathwatch before the hanging at dawn when the sheriff reads from the opening address of the county prosecutor at the youths' trial.

> "On the night of August 23, 1876, the defendants James Horton and Robert Olson did with malice aforethought beat Thomas Petty, age 19, to death with clubs, fists and a metal chain, one quarter inch in thickness and four feet in length. The deceased crawled for one mile during a period of five hours before lapsing into a coma. He died two days later of concussion and internal hemorrhages. The defense will contend that this brutal murder began as a fandango; that the defendants meant only to frighten the deceased and that there was no intent to kill. The defense will point out to you the youthfulness of the defendants. They'll play upon your sympathies. They will demand your understanding and indulgence for murder. The defense will point up the background of these boys, one of low mentality and doubtful parentage, the other the only son of an honest widow, lacking a father's firm hand. But I tell you that there is no mitigation for murder. There is no excuse for murder. I tell you that no one, no matter what his age and no matter what his condition, has the right to kill another human being and ask for our indulgence."

With our reactions split down the middle the film reaches its climax. Lloyd Petty and his gunmen dynamite the jail minutes before the hanging and the explosion blows a hole in the cell wall through which one of the two boys manages to escape. Paladin has a chance to stop the youth but holsters his gun and lets him go.

> Sheriff (injured): "You made a mistake."
> Paladin: "No. No, I made a judgment."
> Sheriff: "He'll kill another man tomorrow, or the day after, or the day after that. It'll happen."
> Paladin: "Maybe you're right, Ernie. Maybe."
> Sheriff: "Well, I've still got a prisoner and I'm going to do what the law prescribes."

This grim episode ends with bodies littering the half demolished jail, the unluckier of the young murderers about to be taken to the gallows, and—in a radical innovation for series TV—not the slightest assurance that the protagonist's judgment was right.

One of the finest TV Western segments built around a legal concept is "El Paso Stage" (15 April 1961; directed by Robert Butler from a teleplay by Gene Roddenberry). On a stagecoach journey to the Texas town of Brackettville, Paladin has a conversation with a young attorney (Jeremy Slate) about a point of contract law.

> Attorney: "You see, in this case an employee finds that his job requires him to commit certain legal but immoral transactions so he sues to break the contract and collect all money due him. But his employer contends that any requirement that a job meet individual moral standards was a conditional acceptance and therefore no contract exists. See? To put it simply, can we superimpose our own standards on our business arrangements?"
> Paladin: "If those standards are usual, common and ordinary, employee wins and collects." (Citing an 1853 Supreme Court case called *McAdams v. United States* that does not seem to exist.)

Later the attorney describes conditions in Brackettville.

> Attorney: "They just hired a new marshal last month. Those idiots there, the businessmen, think they can buy peace and order with a sixgun. They've hired a killer."
>
> Paladin: "I take it you don't approve."
>
> Attorney: "We've a few people left with sense. We're fighting it. . . . With law. I can see you obviously don't agree with that method."
>
> Paladin: "On the contrary. I have the highest regard for the statutes. Including some you won't find in that book there. One of them—survival—if you lose on that count, friend, there's no appeal."

Once the coach reaches Brackettville and Paladin meets saloonkeeper Sam DeWitt (Karl Swenson) and the sadistic marshal Elmo Crane (Buddy Ebsen), this hypothetical becomes real as the gunfighter discovers he's been hired to do something perhaps just barely legal but against his code of ethics.

> Paladin: "Mr. DeWitt, The Brackettville Courier a few weeks ago ran an item stating that your son was involved in certain dangerous and reckless activities."
>
> Sam: "Well, he's a good boy but I just want him curbed a bit."
>
> Paladin: "I wrote suggesting a thousand dollars and you wired agreement."
>
> DeWitt: "That's right, and I have the money all counted out here."
>
> Paladin: "I gathered from the article that the boy had been a little wild, a little reckless, but that he had committed no serious crime as yet."
>
> Crane: "Mister, DeWitt hired you to do a simple job. It

don't require a lot of explanations. Understand? . . . We'll arrange for DeWitt's kid to be riding out of town after dark. You grab him and take him over to Laredo. We got friends there who'll sit on him for a while till he cools down a bit."

Paladin (aghast): "Marshal, you want me to kidnap the boy?"

DeWitt: "One thousand dollars. Take it or leave it."

Paladin (counting out money from DeWitt's cashbox): "I'll take one, two, three, four, five hundred dollars for my time and trouble in getting here."

Marshal Crane clubs the gunfighter and is ready to shoot him down but DeWitt intervenes, stuffs $25 in Paladin's pocket and orders him to leave town on the next coach. "Easy to make a marshal, DeWitt," Crane growls. "Awful hard to unmake one. Don't meddle in my job again." Paladin, stunned but not cowed, uses the $25 to win $1000 in one play at DeWitt's crooked roulette wheel, but before he can leave the saloon Crane draws his gun on him. "You tampered with the wheel," DeWitt says. "Put the money back." Paladin crouches, prepares to draw. "He's the marshal," DeWitt reminds him. "If you outdraw him they'll hang you. You can't win." Paladin backs down, holsters his weapon and is followed to the street by the young lawyer from the stagecoach journey.

Attorney: "That took a lot of courage. Moral courage."

Paladin: "No, that was an exercise in the law I told you about. Survival. Survival and patience."

The lawyer then introduces himself as Frank DeWitt, the man Paladin was brought to Brackettville to kidnap.

Paladin: "Your father told me that you were

reckless, a troublemaker. I had a different picture in mind."

Attorney: "I am a troublemaker. I object to marked decks and watered whiskey and fear and shotgun justice and Crane and my father and their kind of clean government!"

Paladin: "You're reckless all right."

With some time left before the next stage leaves, young DeWitt introduces Paladin to Judge Robbins (Hank Patterson), who explains the legal situation.

Frank: "This document has the effect of removing Crane from office."

Judge: "A writ of injunction."

Frank: "We've been able to cite five instances of unjustifiable homicide committed by Crane. We can move in on him now."

Judge: "The writ empowers me to appoint someone to relieve him of his badge and hold him for investigation. . . ."

Frank: "I thought you might like the job. . . . We're filing it by telegraph. If you stay here in the office out of Crane's way till we get back, the judge can swear you in then."

But Paladin never gets legal authority to act. While he's cloistered in the judge's office, Crane shoots Frank down on the street, challenges anyone to say he didn't kill the young lawyer in self-defense, burns the writ and shoves Paladin on the four o'clock stage.

That night the gunfighter comes back and corners Sam DeWitt in his saloon office, where there's another contract negotiation as the saloonkeeper, devastated by the cold-blooded murder of his son, tries to hire Paladin to "unmake" the marshal with his pistol.

Sam: "Can you kill him? I still have the thousand dollars. It's yours. He tried to kill you. You'll just be protecting yourself. . . . Two thousand."

Paladin: "He wears a badge."

Sam: "Three thousand."

Paladin: "He ordered me to leave town. The courts would just assume that I was trying to resist arrest."

Sam: "Four thousand. That's every cent I have."

Paladin: "And he might outdraw me anyway. The risk alone is worth five."

Sam: "I don't have that kind of money."

Paladin: "Good night, Mr. DeWitt."

Sam: "No, wait! Do you promise you'll kill him?"

Paladin: "I promise I'll settle my score with him. I promise I'll defend myself. . . . Take it or leave it."

As DeWitt is getting the money from his wall safe, Crane comes by from outside, shoots the saloonkeeper in the back, then climbs into the darkened office and stalks Paladin, planning to frame him for the murder. The cat-and-mouse between the two, shot amid the chiaroscuro of the darkened saloon, climaxes with Paladin luring Crane out of town and over the border into Mexico, where the social contract that gives his badge meaning doesn't apply and where Paladin at last can shoot him down without legal or moral qualms.

No other 30-minute series offered the scope for treatment of legal themes as *Gunsmoke* and *Have Gun—Will Travel* but occasional attempts were made. *Jefferson Drum* (NBC, 1958-59), a short-lived series starring Jeff Richards as a frontier newspaper editor, went off the air after 26 unmemorable weeks with "Simon Pitt" (11 December 1958; director and writer unknown), in which Drum goes to purchase newsprint in a neighboring town where he's threatened by the local political boss and befriended by the title character, an attorney (Michael Connors). Clearly the segment was intended as the pilot for a new series with a Western lawyer hero. No one expressed any interest. But with as many as two dozen Western shows a week on network TV, it was inevitable that sooner or later would come a series whose protagonist had a law degree, and indeed a number of attempts at just such a series were aired on one of TV's best known Western anthology shows.

Four Star's *Zane Grey Theatre* (CBS, 1956-61) was hosted by one of the production company's owners, Dick Powell, who each week would introduce a story having nothing to do with Zane Grey and featuring actors not usually identified with Westerns. Precisely because it lacked continuing characters, the series had the potential to offer strong stories of all types, including some of legal interest like "Time of Decision" (18 January 1957; directed by Harold Schuster from a teleplay by Sidney Morse). In the town of Sand Rock, Nevada, farmer Sam Townley (Bill Erwin) comes into the saloon for a drink and is attacked by Ted Curtis (Tommy Cook), son of the area's most powerful rancher. In a fit of rage Ted draws on the unarmed Townley and threatens to shoot him down in cold blood. Townley is forced to kill young Curtis in self-defense but two of the three others in the saloon—Curtis ranch foreman Bart Miller (Mort Mills) and storekeeper Dan Slater (Walter Sande)—charge the hapless farmer with murder. Townley is locked up and clearly has no more chance of acquittal than Tom Robinson was to have a few years later in *To Kill a Mockingbird*. There are only two lawyers in Sand Rock and one of them works for the dead man's wealthy father, Jed Curtis (Trevor Bardette). The other, Evan Tapper (Lloyd Bridges), is begged by Townley's wife (Jean Howell) to act as defense counsel even though he's never handled a murder trial before. Knowing what taking on the case will mean to his attempt to build a practice in the community, Tapper refuses to represent the doomed outsider. "If Jed Curtis said the sun wasn't shining you'd try to hide your shadow," a disgusted and despairing Mrs. Townley tells him. Tapper's wife Nancy (Diane Brewster) presses him to reconsider: "Why would you be jeopardizing our future defending a man's life? . . . I always thought being a lawyer must be a wonderful thing, like being a doctor or a minister. Someone who'd always be there when you needed help. . . . You always told me a man deserved a fair trial, innocent or guilty."

To placate his wife Tapper drops in at the saloon and questions the bartender (Regis Toomey), who tells the lawyer what we in the audience know to be a lie: that he doesn't know what happened. As word spreads that Tapper may represent Townley, pressure builds on him to turn the case down. Bart Miller threatens to shoot his nose off. His wife and daughter are terrorized until Mrs. Tapper begs Evan to stay out of the case. Jed Curtis offers to give Tapper his lucrative legal business if Tapper doesn't represent Townley. At last Tapper visits the jail to talk to the farmer himself.

> Tapper: "I'm mighty upset about not being able to help you."
> Townley: "Don't feel bad. A man does what he's gotta do. Thanks for coming by."

After Miller and one of the Curtis goons give Tapper a brutal beating, the lawyer's wife begs him to move the family out of Sand Rock. "I can't," he replies. "I just can't. I don't know if I can tell you why. . . . We live here. This is our home. If we start running now, where will we stop? . . . I'm no hero, sweetheart, but I've got to stay here and fight. Just something I've got to do." At this point the storekeeper Slater, moved by Tapper's courage under fire, secretly visits the attorney and confirms Townsley's self-defense claim. This is how the film ends: not with the optimistic fadeout TV usually demanded (the innocent defendant's acquittal and the attorney's enshrinement as hero of the town) nor with the implacably downbeat courtroom climax of *To Kill a Mockingbird* but rather with a moral decision, rooted not in any idealistic view of the lawyer's duty but in something much closer to machismo. The only note of hope at the end is a curiously muted one: "It may not be as lonely as we think."

A year and a half later the same series presented "Threat of Violence" (23 May 1958; directed by Robert Gordon from a teleplay by John McGreevey), in which gunfighter Clay Culhane (Chris

Alcaide) tires of dealing death, hangs up his weapons and tries to make a new life for himself as an attorney but finds his reputation hindering him until he defends a Hispanic (Cesar Romero) whose past record makes him the prime suspect in a murder case. This segment served as the pilot for Four Star's *Black Saddle* series (NBC, 1959-60), with Peter Breck replacing Chris Alcaide as the gunman turned lawyer. Many segments of the series pit Culhane's earlier career against his present vocation and are structured to assure us that the legal system offers a way of settling disputes as far above self-help violence as humankind is above the wild beasts. In "Client: McQueen" (24 January 1959; directed by John English from a teleplay by Robert Yale Libott) Culhane, retained by a once wealthy rancher (Basil Ruysdael) who was dispossessed of his property by members of his family, discovers that he's expected to use his gunfighting skills in his client's service. Almost exactly a year later, in "Means to an End" (29 January 1960; director and writer unknown) the same storyline recurs as Culhane is hired by a woman (Patricia Donahue) with precisely the same expectation. In "The Apprentice" (11 March 1960; directed by David Lowell Rich from a teleplay by John McGreevey) the client hires a gunman (Buddy Ebsen) and his protégé (Richard Rust) to settle his legal problems the easy way and Culhane tries to persuade the pistoleros to leave town even though the senior of the two is the man who first taught him to kill effectively. As was standard in TV Western series with no lawyer character, going outside the law is never justified. In "Change of Venue" (11 December 1959; directed by William Dario Faralla from a teleplay by John McGreevey) Culhane has to defend a man accused of his girlfriend's murder (Dean Harens) not only in court but against the threats of the dead woman's sister and brother-in-law (Patricia Medina and Willard Sage) to hang the defendant before the trial. Of course the series creators tended to make things easy for themselves by usually having Culhane represent the innocent and expose the guilty (although with more gunplay at the denouements) just as Raymond Burr's Perry Mason was doing every Saturday evening over at CBS. But once in a while the *Black Saddle* storylines were more offtrail. In "Client: Mowery"

(28 March 1959; directed by David Lowell Rich from a teleplay by Frederic Louis Fox) a dying rancher (Simon Oakland) who was shot by the town marshal (Russell Johnson) asks Culhane to draft a will that leaves his property either to the marshal or to two outlaws, survivor take all. In "Client: Frome" (25 April 1959; directed by John English from a teleplay by Frederic Louis Fox) Culhane represents a man (Adam Williams) who returned to town after a long period of amnesia only to find that he's been declared legally dead and his wife (Mary La Roche) has remarried. In "Apache Trial" (20 November 1959; directed by William Dario Faralla from a teleplay by Joe Stone and Paul King) Culhane finds himself representing a hated Indian agent before a tribal court. And in "Letter of Death" (8 January 1960; director and writer unknown) the frontier lawyer brings and wins a civil suit for false imprisonment and then sets out to prove that his client (Adam Williams) was guilty. Perhaps someday *Black Saddle* will be revived on cable or satellite and we can see whether these segments are in fact as daring as they sound.

TV Westerns rarely owed anything to the great works of European literature, but Kafka's *The Trial* might well have been the inspiration for a segment of *The Rebel* in which law and outrage are one. In "The Legacy" (13 November 1960; directed by Bernard McEveety from a teleplay by Frank D. Gilroy), Confederate veteran Johnny Yuma (Nick Adams) is arrested, taken to a town he never set foot in, put on trial for the murder of someone he never heard of, quickly convicted and sentenced to hang. Needless to add that McEveety and Gilroy rationalize the Kafkaesque situation—which turns out to stem from a conspiracy involving the judge (Jon Lormer) and his three sons who are respectively the prosecutor, defense attorney and sheriff—or that, unlike Joseph K, Yuma survives.

***

The 60-minute adult Western began at the same time as its 30-minute counterpart, in the fall of 1955. *Cheyenne* (ABC, 1955-63), starring Clint Walker as trail scout Cheyenne Bodie, marked the entry of the Warner Bros. studio into the TV Western market. Two years later came the debut of the long-running *Wagon Train* (NBC, 1957-63, 1964-65). The success of *Cheyenne* led Warners to launch two more Western series in a somewhat lighter vein: *Maverick* (ABC, 1957-62), starring James Garner as Bret Maverick, gambler, devout coward and gleeful scammer of the ungodly, and *Sugarfoot* (ABC, 1957-61), with Will Hutchins as bumptious drifter Tom Brewster. The high ratings of those series in turn led Warners to offer *Bronco* (ABC, 1958-62), starring Ty Hardin as drifter Bronco Layne. Midway through the 1958-59 season came the legendary *Rawhide* (CBS, 1959-66), with Eric Fleming as trail boss Gil Favor and the young Clint Eastwood as his ramrod Rowdy Yates. *Bonanza* (NBC, 1959-73) introduced the family or dynasty Western, with Lorne Greene as Ben Cartwright, patriarch of the Ponderosa, and (originally) Pernell Roberts, Dan Blocker and Michael Landon as his sons by three different wives. Its 14-year run was topped only by *Gunsmoke*, which expanded from 30 to 60 minutes in the fall of 1961 and stayed on the air in that format until 1975, a full two decades after its TV debut. Among the other 60-minute series that enjoyed some success were *Laramie* (NBC, 1959-63), *The Outlaws* (ABC, 1960-62), *The Big Valley* (ABC, 1965-69) with Barbara Stanwyck as matriarch of another dynastic frontier empire, the often wildly amusing *Laredo* (NBC, 1965-67), *The Wild Wild West* (CBS, 1965-69) which attempted to fuse Western action with the James Bond type of thriller, the railroading Western *The Iron Horse* (ABC, 1966-68), and the dynastic *Lancer* (CBS, 1968-70). Hour-long series that fell by the wayside after one year or less include *Stagecoach West* (ABC, 1960-61), *Gunslinger* (CBS, Spring 1961), *The Dakotas* (ABC, Spring 1963), *The Road West* (NBC, 1966-67), *Hondo* (ABC, Fall 1967), *The Legend of Custer* (ABC, Fall 1967), and *The Outcasts* (ABC, 1968-69).

What this chronology indicates is that the peak years of the 60-minute Western series coincided roughly with the peak years of their 30-minute counterparts—and also of course with the flourishing of the Warren court, with the release of a number of now classic theatrical films that showed American lawyers and the American legal system at their finest, and with the heyday of such "good lawyer" TV series as *Perry Mason* and *The Defenders*. As we shall see, 60-minute Westerns were as strongly affected by all three influences as were their shorter and tighter counterparts.

One of the first feature films identified with the Warren Court era was *12 Angry Men* (1957), and within several months its influence began permeating the TV Western. An early episode of *Maverick*, "Rope of Cards" (19 January 1958; directed by Richard L. Bare from a teleplay by R. Wright Campbell based on an original story by Robert Ormond Case) puts good-humored gambler Bret Maverick (James Garner) in a situation obviously derived from that of Henry Fonda in *12 Angry Men*: he's dragooned onto a jury hearing the case of a young man accused of killing a local rancher and quickly discovers that the jury is packed with the victim's cronies who are predetermined to bring in a verdict of Guilty.

Neither Warners nor any other company making 60-minute TV Westerns in the late Fifties and early Sixties offered a series with a lawyer as central character but Tom Brewster (Will Hutchins), the protagonist of Warners' *Sugarfoot*, was perpetually taking correspondence courses in how to be an attorney: "jogging along/With a heart full of song/And a rifle and a volume of the law." This premise, so Will Hutchins wrote me, was not due to anyone's awareness that the first golden age of law-related movies and TV series was about to begin.

> "It was decided to make my character an itinerant mail-order law student because that's just what Will Rogers Jr. was in *The Boy from Oklahoma* (Warner Bros., 1953), the feature from which *Sugarfoot* was adapted. . . . I always thought Sugarfoot was a cop-out. He rides with his gun in one saddlebag and his law book in the other—the balance of justice—but he always resorted to gun play. Moral: the law doesn't work very well, does it?"

Hutchins' comments illuminate a classic *Sugarfoot* episode broadcast just a month after *Maverick*'s "Rope of Cards" and likewise taking off from the premise of *12 Angry Men*. The defendant in "Deadlock" (4 February 1958; directed by Franklin Adreon from a teleplay by James O'Hanlon) is Calvin Williams (Herbert Heyes), who's been charged by political boss Victor Valla (John Vivyan) with large-scale cattle rustling. Brewster, who has a temporary job sweeping out Valla's saloon, is a newcomer with no knowledge of local affairs and therefore gets dragooned onto the jury, along with a Mexican (Martin Garralaga) and an Indian (Rico Alaniz) who are legally ineligible to serve and nine other men who in one way or another are under Valla's thumb. A neat exchange during the voir dire shows Brewster's naive idealism about legal matters.

> Brewster: "Well, according to the law you've gotta believe a man's innocent till he's proved guilty."
> Defense counsel: "You understand the law. The question is, will you support it?"
> Brewster (taken aback): "Doesn't everybody?"

The evidence against Williams seems flimsy to say the least, but in his closing argument the puppet prosecutor demands that the jury sentence him to death and confiscate all his property. As the chosen twelve file into a private room, they find that Valla has generously supplied all of them except the Indian with cigars and fine whiskey to lubricate their deliberations. The rush by all his colleagues to an instant verdict of guilty at last tips Brewster to the truth.

> "The man is innocent and you know it! You're railroading him! . . . No one actually stole those cattle. They were deliberately blotted and planted in the Williams herd by Valla himself. This is a frame-up. Valla's trying to destroy Williams and take the ranch. And you're helping him! . . . You're all in on the same ticket. This jury's rigged from top to bottom. Now you go out there in that box and present that verdict and I'll

repudiate it. I'll expose the whole rotten frame! All right, try it!"

The other jurors however have families or roots in the community and are subject to pressures that the footloose Brewster doesn't face.

> One juror: "We do what we have to do."
> Another: "You can't fight it. The man's a devil."
> A third: "This is his town, Brewster. What he wants, he takes. And what he doesn't want, he gets rid of."
> A fourth: "Hang this jury, Brewster, and you're writing your own death warrant. Now, how are you going to vote?"

Brewster manages to persuade the others that the decision should be made by secret ballot. Result: eleven votes for conviction and one for acquittal. The deadlock is then announced in court. "One clean man in a colony of lepers!" the defendant Williams cries out. ". . . Eleven of you are sneaking, stinking bootlicks. But because of one, I don't know who to hate. To that one, God bless you."

The furious Valla sets out to uncover the identity of the one juror with integrity by terrorizing each of the twelve in turn until one of them talks. He cuts off the whisky supply of the alcoholic on the jury, has others beaten and whipped. In an implausible but characteristic demonstration of the TV Western's idealism, the "stinking bootlicks" behave like heroic hostages of the Nazis in a World War II film and stand together in solidarity, refusing to betray their comrade, and the unheroic Brewster does nothing to help the others. Imagine what Clint Walker would have done if this had been an episode of *Cheyenne*!

Finally Valla has one of the recalcitrant jurors (Sam Buffington) shot in the back on the town's main street, and to

Brewster's horror the sheriff refuses to do anything about the cold-blooded murder.

> Brewster: "The law's got to be upheld!"
> Sheriff: "What is the law, Brewster? It's the will of the people. You know what this [badge] is supposed to say? It's supposed to say the people of this town want law and order, and they've elected me to see that they get it. That I represent their collective power, and that any challenge to my authority is a challenge to theirs. This jail has three windows and two doors. Find me in this town five men with the courage to guard 'em and I'll not only arrest Valla, I'll hang him. Valla'll be dead of old age before you find one."
> Brewster: "Yeah, I guess so."

Valla continues to pressure the surviving eleven to identify who deadlocked the jury, but even under torture no one cracks. Finally, as Valla's goons (including a young Dan Blocker, soon to become *Bonanza*'s Hoss Cartwright) are giving Brewster a brutal beating, the other jurors and the townspeople as a whole take up arms and start shooting their oppressors. The uprising climaxes in a slam-bang fistfight between Valla and Brewster, who at last gets a chance to do what Clint Walker would have done long before, and as the episode ends law and order are restored.

The fact that Will Hutchins' character is studying law by correspondence course is irrelevant to most episodes of *Sugarfoot*, and in the overtly legal segments he usually operates as a sort of frontier Perry Mason, defending some innocent party and pinning the guilt on the real criminal. In "The Trial of the Canary Kid" (15 September 1959; directed by Montgomery Pittman from a teleplay by Catherine Kuttner based on an original story by Pittman) Hutchins portrays both defender and defendant as Brewster's aunt forces him at gunpoint to represent his outlaw cousin and identical double at a murder trial.

His client in "The Gaucho" (22 December 1959; directed by Paul

Guilfoyle from a teleplay by Edmund Morris) is a young Latino (Carlos Rivas) who is falsely charged with murder after romancing a young Anglo woman over her father's opposition. In "Vinegarroon" (29 March 1960; directed by William J. Hole, Jr. from a teleplay by Warren Douglas) Brewster himself is convicted of murder and sentenced to hang by the notorious Judge Roy Bean (Frank Ferguson) and tries to save his neck not through any legal ploy but by taking advantage of the judge's fondness for the famous actress Lily Langtry. "Toothy Thompson" (16 January 1961; directed by Lee Sholem from a teleplay by Warren Douglas) finds him representing a chronic troublemaker (Jack Elam) who's charged with attempting to kill a man investigating political corruption. And in the final episode of the series, "Trouble at Sand Springs" (17 April 1961; directed by Herbert L. Strock from a teleplay by Paul Leslie Peil and Leo Gordon) he's appointed defense counsel for two brothers (former *Lassie* star Tommy Rettig and Craig Hill) accused of murder.

The main reason why *12 Angry Men* proved so useful to TV Western series is that, with the action confined to the jury room, no attorney was ever seen. Therefore the film's premise was adaptable not just to series with a lawyer or quasi-lawyer protagonist like *Sugarfoot* but indeed to virtually any series on the air: not just *Maverick* but also the classic cattle-drive series *Rawhide*. "Incident of the 13th Man" (23 October 1959; directed by Jesse Hibbs from a teleplay by Fred Freiberger based on an original story by Endre Bohem) offers not one but two stand-ins for Henry Fonda as ramrod Rowdy Yates (Clint Eastwood) and trail cook Wishbone (Paul Brinegar) ride into the town of Blanton so Wishbone can see a dentist and are drafted onto the jury in a murder case where their colleagues are once again dead set on finding the defendant guilty. It's anyone's guess how many other series of the time included an episode spinning off from *12 Angry Men* but my hunch is at least half a dozen.

Only a small number of the countless Western feature films

made since the dawn of talkies dealt centrally with legal themes, but one that left an enduring mark on other Western features and on Western TV series was *The Ox-Bow Incident* (20th Century-Fox, 1942), the anti-lynching classic directed by William Wellman and starring Henry Fonda. In the thirty years between *Ox-Bow* and *Dirty Harry* (1971; directed by Don Siegel and starring Clint Eastwood) it was an axiom in Westerns, questioned about as often as the existence of God is questioned within the four walls of a church, that due process of law is sacred; that taking the law into one's own hands via lynch mob or vigilante organization or by any other means was never justified no matter what the situation or provocation. One of the unique aspects of *Maverick* was its delight in parodying other Western features and TV series, and perhaps its finest hour in this vein is "Bolt from the Blue" (27 November 1960; directed and written by Robert Altman), in which the satiric target is *Ox-Bow* itself. Beauregard Maverick (Roger Moore) catches a sly old man named Eben Bolt (Tim Graham) trying to horsenap his mighty stallion Gumlegs but then they're both captured by a mob of ranchers and townsmen chasing Bolt and his elusive partner Benson January, who have "dehorsed the countryside." Starky (Charles Fredericks) and the rest of the mob take Maverick to be January and are about to lynch both men on the spot when the party is interrupted by a bumptious youth (Will Hutchins) who never gives his name but can only be Tom Brewster from *Sugarfoot*.

> Lawyer: "Who's their counsel?"
> Starky: "There ain't gonna be no counsel. We caught 'em, we're gonna hang 'em.
> Lawyer: "Without a trial?"
> Starky: ". . . They're horse thieves and that's trial enough for me."
> Lawyer: "Now look, Starky, I am a lawyer and I know the law and the law says. . . ."
> Starky: "We didn't come here to listen to no speeches, young man."

Lawyer: "They're entitled to a trial even if they're guilty."

Starky: Who says?"

Lawyer: "The law of the land. You seem to forget I am a lawyer."

Starky: "Nobody can forget you bein' a lawyer. You've been runnin' around town for months tryin' to stir up a case for yourself."

When mob member Bradley (Percy Helton) begins to get queasy about lynching the prisoners, Starky decides to resolve the issue democratically.

Starky: "All right, boys, looks like it goes to a vote. All in favor of hangin' say Aye."

Everyone in the mob except Bradley: "Aye!"

Starky: "All in favor of a trial. . . ."

Maverick and Bolt (at the top of their lungs): "AYE!"

Lawyer: "The second bunch of ayes have it."

But before the circuit judge can be sent for there has to be a conference beween attorney and client.

Maverick: ". . . Just convince them they've got the wrong man, will you?"

Lawyer (hands over ears): "Tuttuttuttuttut! It isn't ethical for me to listen to evidence until I'm hired."

Maverick: "Oh. All right, well, you're hired."

Lawyer: "That'll be one hundred dollars in advance and another hundred if I get you off."

Bolt (who earlier had noticed that Maverick was carrying a roll of bills): "It's a deal! The money's in the saddlebag."

> Lawyer: "I'm only going to take a hundred, Mr. January. If you don't hang I'll trust you for the rest."
> Bolt: "Mr. Lawyer, I ain't trying to tell you how to run your case, but if you want to win this one for sure, just cut these ropes and let us git!"
> Lawyer: "You'll get a proper trial, old man. You too, Mr. January."
> Maverick: "I'm not January!"
> Lawyer: "Mr. January, let me decide the proper line of defense. I'm the lawyer."

After the lawyer has ridden off to find the circuit judge, Maverick takes aside the youngest member of the lynch mob (Arnold Merritt).

> Maverick: "Hey, Junior. That lawyer. Is he any good?"
> Junior: "Hasn't lost a case yet."
> Bolt: "That's encouragin'."
> Junior: "Hasn't had a case yet. You'll be the first."

But when we get to meet Judge Hookstratten (Richard Hale), who's just finishing up a trial in town, we wonder whether Maverick might not do better without him. "It is the duty of the law to protect as well as to prosecute. It's our function to work for the accused, look after his interests as well as convict him. Now with these values firmly in mind, I now pronounce the defendant—GUILTY! HANG HIM!" The young lawyer rides into town soon after Hookstratten has left but in time to meet Angelica Garland (Fay Spain), who has just gotten off the stagecoach and has been hunting for the man who had left her waiting at the altar in St. Louis—Benson January. The two catch up with Hookstratten on the trail.

> Lawyer: "Your Honor, I am a lawyer and there is a trial you are needed for. . . ."
> Hookstratten: "What kind?"
> Lawyer: "Horse stealing."

Hookstratten (smacking his lips): "That's a *hanging* crime!"

They arrive just in time to stop the impatient lynch mob from hanging Maverick and Bolt and Altman's version of a "proper trial" gets underway, with no one sworn in, no one cross-examined, and Angelica not only identifying Maverick as Benson January but trying to shoot him where he stands. The mob serves as jury and deliberates for roughly a nanosecond.

> Starky (as jury foreman): "Your Honor, we figger we made a mistake about that nice old fella. But January, he's guilty as sin."
> Hookstratten: "You're acquitted, old man. January, you're sentenced to hang. That'll be twenty-five dollars."

Bolt, "out of gratitude and due respect for the law," pays the judge's fee out of Maverick's bankroll and, preparing to ride off, happens to mention that it's Sunday.

> Maverick: "Sunday! It's Sunday? Why, you can't hang a man on Sunday!"
> Starky: "You just watch us."
> Lawyer: "He's right. . . . According to law you can't hang a man on Sunday."
> Hookstratten (who hanged his last defendant a few hours ago): "By golly, Counselor is right! You have to wait till after midnight. . . . That's the law, you've got to wait till then. Not a minute before."
> Starky: "All right, tie him up, boys, and break out the bottles."

We are still only about halfway through the film, and Altman continues to pile twist upon comic twist and character upon bizarre character much as he would do on the big screen a decade later in *M*A*S*H* (1970), leaving us with perhaps the only TV Western episode that uses legal themes as the basis for anarchic farce.

One of the feature films from the Warren Court era that proved particularly fruitful for TV Westerns was *Witness for the Prosecution* (1958), which was totally different from *12 Angry Men* except for one aspect: since nothing in the core of its story required a lawyer character, its surprise climax could be transposed to virtually any TV Western series and indeed was transposed to most. As a teen-age junkie of the genre in the late Fifties and early Sixties I quickly caught on that, whenever the main character was begged by a friend or stranger to prove him innocent of a murder in which he was prime suspect, the guy would turn out to be guilty. But precisely because these episodes decoupled the plot gimmick from the legal environment in which it was originally played out, they're worth little more than passing mention here.

When the first attempt was made to produce an hour-long Western series with the main character an attorney in the formal sense, the venture quickly failed. *Temple Houston* (NBC, 1963-64) starred Jeffrey Hunter as a frontier lawyer and the son of Texas founding father Sam Houston, with Jack Elam as his gunwise buddy Marshal George Taggart. In the unaired pilot film, *The Man from Galveston* (1963; directed by William Conrad from a teleplay by Dean Riesner and Michael Zagor based on Philip Lonergan's story "Galahad of Texas City"), Houston's client, like so many of the TV Perry Mason's, was a woman (Joanna Moore) falsely accused of murder. Featured in the cast were Preston Foster and James Coburn. What happened next was recounted decades later by producer James Lydon.

> "Jack Webb [of *Dragnet* fame] was the head of Warner Brothers television. . . . When Webb called us into his office, he said: 'Fellas, I just sold *Temple Houston*. We gotta be on the air in four weeks, we can't use the pilot, we have no scripts, no nothing—do it!' And we said 'Yessir' but were panicking because it was impossible to have scripts

written and then shoot them, score them, dub them and deliver them to the network in four weeks. So we called some very, very fast writers. . . . They agreed and delivered us shootable scripts the following Friday. We put them into the mill right away and were shooting it Monday morning. We did all the pre-production work Saturday and Sunday. We shot two episodes together. . . . It was the wildest thing I've ever been involved in. We worked day and night . . . with preproduction, production, cutting, scoring, looping— everything. . . . Bill Conrad [the overweight actor who had played Matt Dillon on radio's *Gunsmoke* and would later star in such TV series as *Cannon* and *Nero Wolfe*] directed two scripts simultaneously on two different soundstages at Warners. We bicycled Jeff and Elam between the two companies and Bill shot 'em both in four and a half days. Two complete one-hour shows!"

The series debuted with "The Twisted Rope" (19 September 1963; directed by Abner Biberman from a teleplay by Jack Turley based on James Warner Bellah's short story "Two Murders at Noon"), in which Houston is hired by Dorrie Chevenix (Collin Wilcox) to defend her half-brothers (Richard Evans and Anthony Coll), who are charged with the murder of a lawman and threatened by a lynch mob. Clearly the concept here is Perry Mason out West: the final scenes take place in court, the prosecutor apes Hamilton Burger by accusing Houston of "prolonging this trial with a lot of dramatic nonsense," there's a courtroom reconstruction of the crime scene and even a surprise witness whom Houston gets to confess on the stand. But two strikingly unusual aspects commend this otherwise routine Westernization of the *Perry Mason* formula to our attention. The first is found early in the story when Houston proclaims to Marshal Taggart that "justice is not necessarily just a brief pause between getting caught and getting hung. It includes a fair trial—with counsel." These lines, written less than five months after the Supreme Court's landmark decision in *Gideon v. Wainwright,* furnish a superb illustration of how real-world jurisprudence impacts on the popular culture. The second and even more striking aspect of "The Twisted Rope" is that, contrary to the vast majority of lawyer films in the Warren Court years, this one shows the "good lawyer" figure behaving as the sleazy lawyer characters behave again and again in the films of our own post- and anti-Warren Court era. The Chevenix brothers defended by Houston, although innocent of this particular crime, are scumbags who have been abusing their illegitimate half-sister for years, and when Houston makes Dorrie confess on the stand, this sympathetic character is traumatized into mental breakdown. "Winning a case doesn't mean the lawyer has to be happy about it," Houston tells Taggart at the fadeout.

Later episodes of *Temple Houston* tend to fall into the conventional frontier lawyer-detective pattern. In "Find Angel Chavez" (26 September 1963; directed by Herman Hoffman from a teleplay by John Hawkins and Steve McNeil) Houston's client is his sidekick Marshal Taggart, who killed a man in a shootout but can't prove it was self-defense because someone stole his adversary's gun after the duel was over. In "Toll the Bell Slowly" (17 October 1963; directed by Gerd Oswald from a teleplay by Carey Wilber and Robert Leslie Bellem) Houston finds that he can't clear his client without first clearing the key witness, who has himself been sentenced to hang for murder. "Gallows in Galilee" (31 October 1963; directed by Robert Totten from a teleplay by E.M. Parsons) finds Houston appearing before a notorious hanging judge to defend a man charged with murder for a death that in fact was accidental. Feminists will be especially interested in "Thy Name Is Woman" (9 January 1964; directed by William Conrad from a teleplay by Ken Pettus), in which Houston enlists a woman lawyer to help him defend a saloon hostess charged with a murder she insists was self-defense.

Later episodes of the series tended to keep the legal component to a minimum and put the stress on raucous comedy. In "The Law and Big Annie" (16 January 1964; directed by Charles Rondeau from a teleplay by Charles B. Smith) Houston finds a huge problem on his hands when his buddy Taggart inherits a 4-ton elephant. In "The Last Full Moon" (27 February 1964; directed by Leslie H. Martinson from a teleplay by Robert Sabaroff) an Indian chief whose son has been accused of horse theft decides to retain Houston as defense counsel rather than follow the usual routine and bribe the local Indian agent to set the youth free. The supporting casts in this 26-episode series included Victor Jory, Gene Evans, Victor French, Everett Sloane, Noah Beery, Royal Dano, Robert Lansing, John Dehner, Anne Francis, Ray Danton, Connie Stevens and Robert Conrad.

While the series was in its short-lived first run the pilot film, *The Man from Galveston*, was released to theaters as a 57-minute feature, with the soundtrack unaccountably altered so that the protagonist's name became Timothy Higgins. One reference book describes the picture as a "simple-minded court-room drama" and an "undramatic waste of time. . . ." In retrospect Jeffrey Hunter regretted the whole *Temple Houston* project. "Things went wrong from the start. It was conceived in humor and delivered in dead seriousness. Then about halfway through the season NBC decided to return to the tongue-in-cheek approach. By that time it was too late. The big joke around town was, the series was about a synagogue in Texas."

After its cancellation *Temple Houston* was briefly resurrected on another series in a form that captures the raucous flavor of its comic side. In the *Laredo* episode "Hey Diddle Diddle" (24 February 1967; directed by William Witney from a teleplay by *Houston* scriptwriter Gerry Day) there's a saloon sequence where Cotton Buckmeister (Claude Akins) tells his Texas Ranger colleagues about the time when Houston was trying to get a killer acquitted on the ground that he was drunk at the time he committed the murder. After the jury brought in a guilty verdict and the defendant was hanged, somebody said to Houston: "I told that boozer someday he'd take a drop too many!"

In one sense the most successful 60-minute series with a lawyer protagonist was *The Big Valley* (ABC, 1965-69), for among the three male leads (two as Barbara Stanwyck's sons and one as her late husband's illegitimate son by another woman) the oldest and least dependent on machismo was Jarrod (Richard Long), whose background as a lawyer served as premise for a substantial number of episodes. To cite a few just from the series' first season, in "My Son, My Son" (19 October 1965; directed by Paul Henreid from a teleplay by Paul Schneider) Stanwyck as matriarch Victoria Barkley is threatened with a murder charge when she shoots the son of a neighboring rancher (Robert Walker) who was harassing her daughter Audra (Linda Evans), and Jarrod clears his mother by exposing the victim's covered-up sociopathic past. In "The Murdered Party" (17 November 1965; directed by Virgil W. Vogel from a teleplay by Jack Curtis) the patriarch of a Barkley-hating family asks Jarrod to represent his son (Warren Oates) at a murder trial despite the fact that Jarrod's half-brother Heath (Lee Majors) witnessed the killing. This is one of the myriad of *Witness for the Prosecution* wannabees in which the defendant turns out to be guilty as hell. "A Time to Kill" (19 January 1966; directed by Bernard McEveety from a teleplay by Peter Packer) finds Jarrod investigating whether a friend from law school days (William Shatner) is, as the Secret Service suspects, involved with a counterfeiting ring. And in "Under a Dark Star" (9 February 1966; directed by Michael Ritchie from a teleplay by Ken Trevey) Jarrod tries to help a bitter convict (Albert Salmi) whom he prosecuted but who after nine years in prison has been proved innocent. The legal background of Richard Long's character likewise generated storylines for a number of episodes in subsequent seasons; and since *The Big Valley* survived four years in prime time, in a limited but genuine sense it was the foremost TV Western with a lawyer protagonist.

Far less success was enjoyed by *Dundee and the Culhane* (CBS, Fall 1967), starring British actor John Mills as a transplanted barrister and Sean Garrison as his gunwise apprentice. Although the title of each episode followed a common pattern in the Perry Mason tradition, the series was not so much a Western lawyer-detective show as a traditional adult Western with Sixties values and often ingenious law-related storylines played out at somewhat irregular trials. "The Vasquez Brief" (13 September 1967; directed by Richard Benedict from a teleplay by Fred de Corter) finds Dundee and Culhane using their legal wiles to prevent the summary execution of a land baron's son who's on trial for the brutal acts of his father. In "The Murderer Stallion Brief" (27 September 1967; directed by Alf Kjellin from a teleplay by George Kirgo based on an original story by Dan Ullman) they represent a horse accused of trampling to death the son of the town tyrant. "The 1000 Feet Deep Brief" (25 October 1967; directed by Charles Rondeau from a teleplay by Ken Trevey) sends the legal duo underground to appear for a mine owner whose men blame him for the deaths of seven miners. "The Death of a Warrior Brief" (15 November 1967; directed by Jeffrey Hayden from a teleplay by Jack Miller) pits the series characters against each other in an impromptu court presided over by an old Indian chief with Dundee prosecuting and Culhane defending a prospector charged with the murder of a member of the tribe. In some episodes Mills and Garrison could easily have been replaced by nonlawyer heroes from almost any other TV Western, but the most distinctive segments were generally those with the strongest legal component. The supporting casts included Warren Oates, John Drew Barrymore, Charles Bronson, John McIntire, Sally Kellerman, Dabney Coleman, Ralph Meeker, Carroll O'Connor, George Coulouris, James Dunn, William Windom and Dana Wynter. The series failed to find an audience and was axed after thirteen weeks.

The TV Western declined in popularity in the 1970s but at least a few of the 60-minute series that survived offered some interesting perspectives on legal or metalegal themes, especially as the anguish over the civil rights struggle and the Viet Nam war penetrated this traditionally escapist medium. As far back as the early Sixties a number of Western series had offered episodes in which the protagonist befriends and saves an innocent tormented black man, but perhaps the finest treatment of the theme and certainly from the perspective of this chapter one of the richest was the *Gunsmoke* episode "Jesse" (19 February 1973; directed by Bernard McEveety from a teleplay by Jim Byrnes). Precisely because James Arness is such a towering embodiment of moral authority, he has only a small role in this gem of moral ambivalence and the true protagonist is Marshal Dillon's good-hearted yokel deputy Festus Haggen (Ken Curtis). In a brawling cowtown Festus happens to meet ex-slave Jesse Dillard (Brock Peters), an old friend he hasn't seen in years, who works as trail cook for rancher Dave Carpenter (Jim Davis). Like most black characters in episodic TV of the Civil Rights years, Jesse is so perfect one almost expects to see him walk on water: generous, compassionate, peace-loving, revered by all who know him, and the finest cook in the West to boot. But the reunion between Festus and Jesse is ruined by a U.S. marshal (Regis Cordic) who has a poster offering $500 reward for the black man's arrest, and it soon develops that Jesse had escaped from prison after being sentenced to ten years for killing a white man who had had him whipped. Two hotheaded young drovers (Don Stroud and Robert Pine) to whom Jesse is a father figure ambush and mortally wound the marshal on the trail in an abortive attempt to set the cook free, and the lawman imposes on Festus the obligation to deliver his friend back to the prison where he will surely die. The climax takes place in the aptly named town of Lovelock where Festus finds himself in a Hegelian tragic collision: trapped in the hotel by Carpenter and his men, who are determined to release Jesse and spirit him over the border to Mexico even if it means burning the town down, Festus knows that Jesse is morally innocent and desperately wants to free him but also knows he has a legal obligation to return the black man to his unjust prison sentence even if it means a gun battle with the cowhands whose feelings towards Jesse he totally shares. The tragic dilemma is resolved when Jesse, selflessly thinking not of his own freedom but only of preventing bloodshed, takes a gun smuggled into his room and makes a break, only to be shot in the back by the weaselly hotel clerk (Leonard

Stone) who supplied the gun precisely so that he could kill the black man while escaping and claim the $500 reward. Bernard McEveety directs Jesse's death scene so that viewers with any knowledge of art history will be reminded of Michelangelo's Pieta.

One of the last Western series of TV's first quarter century and arguably the most unusual was *Kung Fu* (ABC, 1972-75), starring David Carradine as half-Chinese Buddhist priest and martial arts expert Kwai Chang Caine. At least once this philosophically inclined shoot-em-up (would chop-em-up be closer to *le mot juste*?) ventured into something like jurisprudence. In "The Book," also known as "Empty Pages of a Dead Book" (10 January 1974; directed by John Llewellyn Moxey from a teleplay by Charles A. McDaniel), Caine and a law-obsessed Texas Ranger named McNelly (Robert Foxworth) are tried and sentenced to death for the accidental killing of a man (James Storm) who was trying to protect his brother (Slim Pickens), a fugitive from Texas justice. "I always thought the law was the most important thing," McNelly tells Caine in their cell. "Now it's going to kill me for something I didn't even do. And it's legal! The trial was legal! The judge did what he thought was right. All together it's the law. I lived by it. I sure don't want to die by it." The two men break jail but the sheriff is badly injured pursuing them, and Caine convinces McNelly that they must save his life even if it means they'll be recaptured and unjustly hanged. The judge brings about the usual TV happy ending by reversing himself and ordering Caine and McNelly released.

***

The success of 30-minute TV Westerns led to the proliferation of 60-minute series whose success in turn led to series that ran a full 90 minutes (including, of course, commercial time). The first of these and the only one to enjoy a long run was *The Virginian* (NBC, 1962-71), which centered on a vast Ponderosa-like spread but without *Bonanza*'s family dynasty aspect. James Drury starred as the anonymous foreman of the Shiloh ranch (imagine more than 200 90-minute films where no one could address or refer to the main

306

character by a normal name!) and Doug McClure played his sidekick Trampas, with a huge assortment of regulars weaving in and out of the series over the years. In the first four seasons (1962-66) Shiloh was owned by retired judge Henry Garth (Lee J. Cobb), whose earlier careers occasionally gave rise to an episode of some legal interest. In "It Tolls for Thee" (21 November 1962; directed and written by Samuel Fuller) Garth is kidnapped and tortured by Martin Kalig (Lee Marvin), a sadistic sociopath he had once sentenced to prison. The Virginian and the men from Shiloh ride after him and finally wipe out the gang in an ambush. Judge Garth grabs a gun and comes within a split second of shooting down the cornered Kalig like a mad dog but in a magnificent if implausible display of self-restraint (especially hard to swallow in a Sam Fuller picture) he brings the man in alive to be dealt with according to law.

In "A Time Remembered" (11 December 1963; directed by William Witney from a teleplay by Peter Germano) Cobb gets to play frontier Perry Mason. When an opera singer (Yvonne de Carlo) with whom he'd had an affair shoots and kills her business manager (Paul Comi) and her claim that he was sexually attacking her turns out to be a lie, she's put on trial for murder, with Garth as her lawyer defending her as Mason so often defended innocent clients who were lying to him. The Mason formula blends with the *Witness for the Prosecution* surprise twist when it turns out that DeCarlo's character is guilty but justified: the dead man was making a sexual attack not on DeCarlo but on her young secretary (Melinda Plowman), who is actually her daughter—perhaps by Garth. This heavy-handed soaper gives Witney no chance to enliven things with the eye-popping action sequences that were his trademark.

The Virginian's success led its production company Universal to expand the 60-minute *Wagon Train* series to 90 minutes for one season (1963-64), after which it reverted to the tighter hour-length format. A few years later CBS launched *Cimarron Strip* (1967-68), a lavishly budgeted 90-minute series more or less on the *Gunsmoke* model, starring Stuart Whitman as hard-bitten marshal Ben Crown, which failed to attract an audience and left the air after one season. At the end of the

Sixties *The Virginian* itself ran out of steam and was retooled under a new title, *The Men from Shiloh* (NBC, 1970-71). When it too failed after one season, the 90-minute Western came to an end and only a few hardy perennials of the 60-minute variety, like *Bonanza* and *Gunmoke*, were still in the saddle. The cancellation of *Gunsmoke* at the end of the 1974-75 season, after an astonishing run of twenty years, brought an end to the golden age of the TV Western. The few series that came later and the pale imitations of recent vintage like *Dr. Quinn, Medicine Woman* are so different from what TV offered in its first quarter century that they need not be considered here.

***

The subject of legal themes and lawyer characters in TV Western series could easily fill a book; if, that is, anyone were around with the knowledge, interest, patience and access to countless hours of film that would be necessary to treat the topic comprehensively. The survey I've attempted here offers only a cross-section. But I will have done what I set out to do, and all that a chapter of this length can do, if my cross-section fairly represents the whole and also suggests how complex is the skein of family resemblances and differences in the segments of such series that undertook to deal with the themes of law, lawyers and justice.

Appendix

The research sources and methods used in law school are useless when one is seeking information on legal themes in TV Westerns, or for that matter on any other aspect of series television. In view of the growing interest in how law and popular culture interact, some brief remarks on how I researched this chapter may be helpful.

Raw data on almost any TV series—during what years and in what time slots it ran, how many episodes it lasted, what were its premises, who were the principals in front of and behind the camera—can be gleaned from two generally reliable sources. The more readable and manageable guide is Tim Brooks & Earle Marsh, *The Complete Directory to Prime Time Network TV Shows, 1946-Present* (Ballantine Books, 6th ed. 1995). Fuller information on behind-the-cameras personnel such as directors and scriptwriters can be found in Vincent Terrace, *Encyclopedia of Television: Series, Pilots and Specials* (New York Zoetrope, 1985-86, 3 volumes). Although nowhere near comprehensive or error-free, the best reference books specifically on Western series are by Harris M. Lentz III: *Western and Frontier Films and Television Credits, 1903-1995* (McFarland & Co., 1995, 2 volumes), and *Television Westerns Episode Guide* (McFarland & Co., 1997). Relatively few cultural studies on the TV Western have yet been published but by far the most knowledgeable is Gary A. Yoggy's *Riding the Video Range: The Rise and Fall of the Western on Television* (McFarland & Co., 1995), which offers more than 600 closely printed pages of well-informed text and a lengthy bibliography listing the vast majority of other source material relevant to the TV Western.

Even with the help of these reference works it's all but impossible to write about series TV without personal experience of the medium and access to an extensive TV archive. Thanks to accidents of birth I was equipped with the former and thanks to Boyd Magers, who is blessed with a virtually photographic memory of TV's first decades and with a treasure trove of over 7,000 cassettes, I was supplied with the latter. His newsletter *Western Clippings* is a priceless assortment of material on Western films in all their forms from early silents through the TV series surveyed in this chapter to recent movies made for cable or satellite. Sitting glued to the tube as I was during much of my adolescence is no substitute for talking with people who worked in series TV day in and day out, and my friendships with a number of the directors who specialized in Westerns—including Thomas Carr (1907-1997), Paul Landres (1912-2001), Joseph H. Lewis (1907-2000) and William Witney (1915-2002)—have given me insights into the making of the kind of films I discuss here that no published source can offer. I am indebted to Will Hutchins for valuable information on the *Sugarfoot* series in which he starred and to Glenn Mosley, who is working on a biography of *Temple Houston* star Jeffrey Hunter, for a copy of the script for "The Twisted Rope."

CHAPTER 8

Cape Fear Dead Ahead

In the real world the Cape Fear river flows in east central North Carolina. It is 202 miles long, the longest river entirely within that state, and during this country's colonial period was a main route into the interior. Formed by the junction of the Deep and Haw rivers at Haywood, it flows southeast past Lillington, Fayetteville, Elizabethtown and Wilmington, where it turns south as an estuary and, three miles west of the cape that shares its name, enters the Atlantic.[1] In the world of the imagination the name Cape Fear has come to stand for three versions of the same fundamental story about law, lawyers and our legal system; a story whose similarities and differences are the subject of this chapter.

***

John D(ann) MacDonald was born in Sharon, Pennsylvania on July 24, 1916, the son of a strong-willed workaholic who rose Alger-like from humble origins to become a top executive at a firearms company in Utica, New York. A near-fatal attack of mastoiditis and scarlet fever at age 12 confined young John to bed for a year, and lack of anything else to do in those days before radio and TV and computers virtually forced him to read or have his mother read to him huge quantities of books. Once back on his feet he began haunting the public library and compulsively devouring every book on its shelves.

MacDonald graduated from the Utica Free Academy in 1933, and from Syracuse University five years later with a B.S. in Business Administration and a fellow Syracuse grad as his wife. In June 1939 he received an M.B.A. from Harvard Business School. After a year of working at jobs he hated, he accepted a lieutenant's commission in the Army and was assigned to procurement work in Rochester, N.Y. until mid-1943 when he was sent to Staff Headquarters at New Delhi, India. A year later he transferred to the OSS, serving in Ceylon as branch commander of an Intelligence detachment and rising to Lieutenant Colonel's rank. During idle times, instead of writing his wife letters he knew would be censored, MacDonald began writing and sending her short stories. One of these she sold. "I can't describe what it was like," he said near the end of his life, "when I found out that my words had actually sold. . . . I felt as if I were a fraud, . . . as if I were trying to be something that I wasn't. Then I thought, my goodness, maybe I could actually be one."

At the end of the war MacDonald was entitled to four months of stateside terminal leave with pay before his discharge. He spent those months behind the typewriter, working 80 hours a week, cranking out 800,000 words worth of short stories and beginning to sell some of them. For the next several years most of the family's income came from magazines, primarily the pulps whose gaudy and lurid covers could be seen on every newsstand in those immediate postwar years. In 1950 he began publishing novels, most of them softcover originals, and through that decade and most of the Sixties he wrote paperbacks so prolifically and well that he forced critics and intelligent readers to take notice of a new book-publishing medium that they might otherwise have dismissed as trash. Most years he also produced one novel for hardcover publication. In 1958 that novel was *The Executioners*, which takes place nowhere near the Cape Fear river but was the starting point for the two later movies that did.

***

It begins quietly on an early summer afternoon with attorney

Sam Bowden, his wife Carol and their three children—the oldest a 14-year-old daughter on the brink of womanhood—relaxing on the beach of a tiny island in a lake near the town of New Essex, which is apparently in upstate New York. Amid banter between the couple Sam recounts to Carol an incident that happened a few days earlier, an incident whose roots date back to World War II, approximately fifteen years earlier, when late one night on a dark street in Melbourne, Australia Lieutenant Bowden came upon the brutal rape of a 14-year-old girl by 25-year-old staff sergeant Max Cady. Bowden had managed to subdue Cady, who was court-martialed and sentenced to life at hard labor. But now, Sam tells Carol, Cady is out—and accosted him outside his law office in New Essex a few days before, ending the encounter with the words "Give my best to the wife and kids, Lieutenant." (9) Carol then reveals that several days earlier she had noticed a stranger at the edge of the Bowden property who fits her husband's description of Cady. Sam goes on to describe how he had talked to the New Essex city attorney and had been told that the police would roust Cady until he left the area. When Carol asks why they don't simply lock the man up, Sam offers a mini-essay in conventional jurisprudence.

"... My God, it would be nice if you could do that, wouldn't it? An entirely new legal system. Jail people for what they might do. . . . I believe in the law. It's a creaking, shambling, infuriating structure. There are inequities in it. . . . But at its base, it's an ethical structure. It is based on the inviolability of the freedom of every citizen. . . . And I like it. I live it. . . . So maybe it is the essence of my philosophy that this Cady thing has to be handled within the law. If the law can't protect us, then I'm dedicated to a myth, and I'd better wake up." (13-14)

The presentation not only of this chapter but the entire novel from Sam Bowden's viewpoint generates a huge technical challenge: MacDonald has to keep us in a state of constant tension while denying us all sorts of powerful scenes that can only be described to the viewpoint character after they happen. Learning that Max Cady has money from the sale of his dead parents' home and is therefore relatively roustproof, Bowden in Chapter Two hires private detective

Charlie Sievers to spy on Cady and warns his two older children of the potential danger. In Chapter Three Sievers, the savviest private eye in the area, admits to Bowden that Cady is savvier. "He's awake every minute. He's cute and he's good. He can see in all directions at once. . . . You're wasting your money. He expected to be covered. . . . [A]ny time he wants to shake loose, he'll figure out a way. . . ." (35-36) When Bowden asks how he can protect his family, Sievers replies: "Don't quote me. I'd make some contacts. Bounce him into a hospital a couple of times, he gets the point. Work him over with some bicycle chain." Bowden: "I'm sorry, Sievers. . . . I can't operate outside the law. The law is my business. I believe in due process." Sievers: ". . . A type like that is an animal. So you fight like an animal. Anyway, I would. . . ." (36-37)

Late that Friday afternoon Bowden gets a frantic call at work from Carol: the family dog has been poisoned and died horribly in front of all three Bowden children. When Sam points out that there is no evidence Cady did it, Carol says: "*I have proof it was Cady. . . . No evidence. No testimony. Nothing legalistic. I just know*. What kind of a man are you? This is your *family. . . .* Are you going to look up all the precedents and prepare a brief?" (43)

Next morning the Bowdens and all three children take turns shooting at targets with Sam's .22 automatic. That afternoon at the local boat yard while Sam and 14-year-old Nancy are making repairs to the Bowden vessel's hull, Cady appears for the first and virtually the only time in the novel. After gazing lustfully at Nancy in her bikini and piously denying he poisoned the dog, Cady tells Bowden how his wife divorced him and remarried while he was in military prison, and how after his release he visited her.

> "I had to bust open the screen door to get to talk to her. . . . I drove her over [to a town fifty miles away] . . . and that night . . . I had her [call home] and say she was taking a little vacation from [her present husband, a plumber] and the kids. . . . I made her write me a love

note and date it. . . . I made her write it full of dirty words.
. . . When I had enough of her, I told her that if she ever
tried to yell cop, I'd mail a photostat of the note to the
plumber. And I'd come around and see if I could throw a
couple of the plumber's kids under some delivery trucks.
She was impressed. I had to put damn near a whole fifth
of liquor into her before she passed out. Then I [left her in
the wilderness without clothes and] give her a good
chance to work her way home." (64-65)

On Monday morning Bowden presents his problem with Cady to
detective captain Mark Dutton, who admits he has used extra-legal
methods in the past "to avert a definite threat to the whole city" but
refuses to do so for "just one individual." (87) Then Sam confides in Bill
Stetch, his firm's senior partner, who tells him:

"Mike Dorrity and I are a pair of licensed pirates. We
needed a balance wheel. . . . But there's some parts of this
business you can't handle . . . Mike and I dirty our hands
with that. . . . You are a good man who believes in himself
and what he is doing. Every law firm ought to have at
least one in the shop. Too few do. So pay no attention to a
cynical old bandit. . . . But don't get too appalled at yourself
when you ask the police for an extralegal favor. . . ." (90-91)

Alone, Bowden berates himself for his legalistic scruples. "Cady
shoots your kids while you cry onto your diploma and look through all
the dusty books for a way to slap his wrist legally" (91). Then he calls
Charlie Sievers and agrees to pay $300 cash in return for an
arrangement the private eye will make.

"I've got a friend. He's got the right contacts. He'll put
three of them on him. . . . They'll beat hell out of him. With
a couple of pieces of pipe and a bicycle chain, they'll do a

professional job. A hospital job. . . . There isn't one man out of fifty . . . who is ever worth a damn after a thorough professional beating. They have rabbit blood for the rest their lives. You're doing the right thing." (93-94)

Even now Bowden isn't convinced. ". . . It's wrong that it should be possible to do a thing like this," he tells Carol that night. ". . . It makes the world sound like a jungle. There's supposed to be law and order." She replies: ". . . Darling, maybe it is a jungle. And we know there's an animal in the jungle." (95) But he still feels a deep sense of guilt over what he has done.

A few days later Captain Dutton calls with news about Cady.

"We got him for disorderly conduct, disturbing the peace and resisting arrest. He got into a fight last night. . . . Three local punks jumped him. They marked him up pretty good before he got untracked. One got away and two are in the hospital. . . . They laid his cheek open with a bike chain and thumped him around the eyes with a hunk of pipe. . . . He was dazed, I guess, . . . and he swung on a policeman when he came running across the yard and gave him a nose as flat as a sheet of paper. The second patrolman dropped him with a night stick and they took him in and got his face sewed and threw him in the tank. . . . He's yelling for a lawyer." (98-99)

In due course Cady pleads guilty and is sentenced to thirty days in the city jail so that the Bowden family is given "thirty days of grace. Thirty days without fear. And thirty days of anticipation of the fear to come." (102)

During the month's respite the school year ends and the Bowdens make the usual arrangements for their daughter and older son to spend several weeks in adjoining summer camps a few hours' drive from home, only this time making sure that the camp managers are aware of the possible threat to the Bowden kids once Cady is free. About two weeks before the release date Charlie Sievers' agency unexpectedly transfers the private eye to its California office so that he can do nothing to arrange a second and more professional beating for Cady except give Sam Bowden the name of his contact person, a small-timer in the local underworld. Then as chance would have it that man dies of a heart attack before Bowden can see him, and the naive and dismayed lawyer makes a fool of himself going around to bars in the rough part of town and trying in vain to find out how a beating might be arranged. With only a few days left to make plans before Cady's release, Sam decides to send Carol and their six-year-old son Bucky to a distant vacation resort while he himself moves into a hotel in town and waits for Cady's release. ". . . I think he'll make a move and I think he'll make it at me, and I'm going to make certain it will be unsuccessful, and if he does, then we'll have the evidence that will send him back for a long time." To which Carol sensibly replies: "Oh, yes. For a year, or three years, and then we can have such a fine time planning just what we'll do when they let him out again. . . ." (129- 130) With a pistol permit from Captain Dutton and a short-barreled revolver, Sam puts in hours at target practice but doubts his ability to use the weapon against a human being. ". . . I don't know. . . . I think I could. I've got to make this so much a part of me that pulling the trigger is a part of the total action. . . . Then if I can start, I can go through it all the way. I hope. . . . [I feel like] a white mouse in a snake pit." (135-136)

After several days of nothing happening, Bowden finds that Cady has vanished after his release. He happens upon a blowsy bar girl whom Cady had taken up with and then beaten, and after a few drinks she repeats to Sam what Cady had said about him. ". . . One time he said . . . to show you how much he liked you, he was going to kill you six times. . . . He said something like by the time I get around to [Sam], I'll be doing him a favor. He'll be begging for it." (153) Even after Bowden tells her how Cady had poisoned the dog and that he intends to kill Carol and his three children before snuffing out Sam himself, she refuses to repeat her statement to the police. ". . . [I]t's a cruel world and I'm sorry if you got problems, but that's the way the ball bounces." (154)

More days go by without incident. Then on the last day of his older son Jamie's summer camp, Bowden gets a call: a sniper has shot the boy in the arm. There is a frantic family reunion at the local hospital and the county sheriff reports on his investigation of the scene. ". . . Nobody was trying to scare the boy. They made a pretty good try at killing him. If he'd put his slug two and a half inches further to his right, that boy would have been dead before he could fall all the way down." (161) When Sam explains why Jamie was shot, the sheriff concludes that Cady is probably in a secure hideout but that even if he were to be found "I don't know any good way to hold him, under the law." (162) His deputy offers a more positive suggestion. ". . . Think of him like he's a tiger. You want to get him in out of the brush. So you stake out a goat and you hide in a tree." (165) Sam angrily rejects the suggestion since the goat he has in mind is Carol or one of the children.

All five Bowdens set out in a two-car caravan for the vacation resort where Carol and Bucky have been staying when, on a curving mountain road, the left front wheel comes off the station wagon and Carol, Jamie and Bucky are almost killed. "Somebody loosened the nuts." (174) The doctor who attends the three warns Sam that his wife is near the breaking point.

It is this incident that gives birth to Bowden's decision. "The concept was so alien to his nature as to revolt him. It meant a reversal of all his values, of all the things he lived by." (178) Alone with Carol, he explains. ". . . I want to kill Cady. . . . [L]ay a trap and kill him and dispose of the body. I want to commit murder, and I think I know how it can be done." Her reply gives the novel its title: "Not murder. Execution." Sam: "Don't help me rationalize. Murder. . . . Have you got guts enough to help me?" (179)

His plan stems from the deputy's suggestion about staking out a goat. The three children are to be left at the vacation resort with Nancy in charge while their parents return home and arrange a trap,

Sam holing up in the barn behind their house while Carol pretends to be alone and draws Cady in close for the execution. "They said no more to each other than was necessary, and they both avoided looking into each other's eyes. It was as though they had embarked on some project that shamed them." (185) After the stage has been set, Sam is overcome by lawyerly scruples and confides his plan to Captain Dutton, who improves on it by loaning the Bowdens a young cop named Andy Kersek who is a Korean War combat veteran and a crack shot. The Bowdens smuggle Kersek into their house and hide him in their basement so that, in the event Cady attacks, he can protect Carol while Sam is running across from the barn.

A long night and the next day pass quietly before the novel's climax. Cady penetrates the house and beats Carol and prepares to rape her and Sam falls and tears up his ankle rushing to save her and he and Cady collide in the yard but he manages to hold onto his pistol and shoots wildly at the fleeing psychopath before stumbling into the house and discovering Kersek in the hall. "Blood ran from a corner of his mouth. The leather grip of a hunting knife protruded grotesquely from his side. . . . His nose was pulped flat against his face." (200)

Now that Cady has killed a cop the police pull out all stops to track him down, and the next day they bring in his body. "We started finding blood halfway up the hill. . . . One of your shots must have hit him. . . . Tore an artery open. He climbed another three hundred feet before he ran out of blood." (208) Bowden's reaction?

> ". . . He had killed this man. He had turned this elemental and merciless force into clay, into dissolution. He searched through himself, looking for guilt, for a sense of shame.
>
> "And found only a sense of savage satisfaction, a feeling of strong and primitive fulfillment. All the neat and careful layers of civilized instincts and behavior were peeled back to reveal an intense exultation over the death of an enemy." (208-209)

In the thirteenth and final chapter we return to the peaceful island where the novel began and listen to the Bowdens discuss how their nightmare has changed them. Carol: "I'm not such an idiot about myself and my tight little world, Sam. I thought it was my absolute right, my unalterable heritage, to be happy. . . . [I had an] enormous and infantile trust that this world was made to be happy in. . . ." Sam: "Isn't it?" Carol: "Only with luck, my darling. Only with the greatest of good fortune. There are black things loose in the world. Cady was one of them. A patch of ice on a curve can be one of them. A germ can be one of them. . . . [Now] I know that everything we have is balanced on such a delicate web of incidence and coincidence." (213) Her words are clearly meant to remind us of Dashiell Hammett's *The Maltese Falcon* and the parable of the falling beams that gave timeless form to the world-view we have come to call *noir*.[2] Sam then describes how he himself has changed. "I was idealizing my profession, and leaning on it too heavily. Now I know it's just a tool. You use it like any other tool. Use it wisely and it can help you. And when it's of no use to you, you take a course of action that will be of use." (214) It's almost as if we are being warned in advance against the idealization of law and lawyering that from the early 1960s into the 21st century has become identified with *To Kill a Mockingbird*.

***

Throughout the 1950s and until his death the dean of crime-fiction critics was Anthony Boucher (1911-1968), who conducted the weekly "Criminals at Large" column for the *New York Times Book Review*. His discussion of *The Executioners* is notable for its insight, enthusiasm and, for a master of compression like Boucher, great length. He set the novel squarely in the tradition we now call *noir*, in which the protagonist is menaced by a "blind inimical force . . . governed by compulsions we cannot understand. . . ."

"What do you do when you know your family is threatened with destruction by a sadist, and yet have no proof that you can offer to the law? And, moreover, you respect that law too much to take the direct course of removing that threat yourself? MacDonald not only tells, with quiet realism, a powerful and frightening story; he takes a deeper look than most suspense novelists at the problem of private and public justice—even if his ending does avoid some of the questions he has raised."[3]

Whether Boucher's review helped clinch the sale of movie rights in the novel is unknown, but three years after its publication *The Executioners* became the basis for the film *Cape Fear* (1961). Its director, J. Lee Thompson, was born in Bristol, England on August 1, 1914 and attended Dover College. "When I was very young," he told me during a phone interview a few years before his death in 2002, "I wrote a play called *Murder Happens* which was put on at the Croydon Repertory in 1933. Then I wrote *Double Error*, which was put on at the Fortune Theatre in 1935. [Film rights to this play] were bought by Associated British, and they also hired me as the scriptwriter. Then came the war in 1939, and I joined the RAF in 1940. During that time I rewrote pretty considerably *Double Error* and called it *Murder Without Crime*, and that was put on at the Comedy Theatre in London and was a big success.[4] Associated British filmed it in 1950 and offered it to me to direct." By the end of the decade he had directed a variety of movies for British studios—perhaps the best of which was *Tiger Bay* (1959)—and had developed a reputation as the most exciting new filmmaker in England. His big break came with the international megahit *The Guns of Navarone* (1961), starring Gregory Peck, David Niven and Anthony Quinn. He continued directing films (more often than not action thrillers starring Charles Bronson as a violent avenger operating outside the law) until 1990, when at age 75 he retired. Ten years later he remained in good health, spending the cooler months at his home in Beverly Hills and summers in British Columbia at his house on Vancouver Island.

In a phone conversation with me around that time[5] Thompson explained how he became involved with the subject of this chapter.

"*Cape Fear* was offered to me by Greg Peck, who owned [the movie rights to John D. MacDonald's novel] *The Executioners*. This was while I was directing him in *The Guns of Navarone*. James Webb wrote the script, came over to London, and we went through his script and again we worked in Paris, and then I came over to L.A. and made my first American film." It was shot on location in Savannah, Georgia in 1961. Almost forty years later Thompson explained to me how he had visualized the picture.

"I realized at the start that it was a fairly ordinary thriller and that it would have to depend a lot on mood and getting the right characterizations, the right actors to portray the lead parts. So I was very lucky in getting a wonderful cinematographer [Samuel Leavitt], and my vision was to make it moody and to emphasize the characterizations. Greg[ory Peck] was extremely unselfish, because when he gave me this script he said that the part of Cady of course would steal every scene, and he put up a wonderful performance against Robert Mitchum. Of course, Robert Mitchum excelled himself.

"To begin with I was interested in playing Telly Savalas as the villain, and I did a test of him and he was absolutely brilliant, he was wonderful. But then I met Mitchum and we went through some scenes together and there wasn't any doubt that he would be an absolutely wonderful Cady, and of course he was a big boxoffice star at the time. Telly Savalas was wonderful in recognizing all this, and of course he played a smaller part, which I was very grateful to him for. We had—I was going to say difficulty but it wasn't really difficulty. But the truth is that Robert Mitchum completely lived the part of Cady, and you know he was quite a handful on the set. He . . .at one time was sentenced to a chain gang there, and he hadn't forgotten that, he was very hostile in the surroundings[6], and this helped in the part, his inner rage came out and — it was very interesting to work with a man who was so into the part."

Thompson's *Cape Fear* was enhanced by a fine supporting cast — Polly Bergen as Bowden's wife Peggy, Telly Savalas as private eye Charlie Sievers, Martin Balsam as police chief Mark Dutton — and even more by a Bernard Herrmann music score that rivals his best work for the films of Alfred Hitchcock.

Does the movie tell the same story as MacDonald's novel? One can reply only with the infuriating answer to which lawyers are regularly doomed: yes and no. Yes in the sense that enough is taken from the novel so that if movie rights had not been purchased from MacDonald before the film was made he could have sued for copyright infringement and won in a walk; No in the sense that Thompson and Webb altered a great deal of MacDonald's storyline and added many innovations of their own so that the film is not only substantially similar to the novel but also substantially different.

In terms of time the movie is set in the early Sixties rather than the middle-to-late Fifties and the characters and events have not the slightest connection with World War II. Mitchum mockingly addresses Peck not as Lieutenant as in the novel but as Counselor, and the real-world events with which the film connects are the civil rights movement and the revolution in criminal procedure that was about to be launched by the Warren Court. In terms of locale the movie is set not in upstate New York like the novel but in the South, essentially the same region which was home to the Atticus Finch character Peck was to play a year later in *To Kill a Mockingbird*, and a host of elements we associate with the later film are also found in this one. The film-makers shrink the Bowden family from three children to one (the pubescent daughter Nancy, played by Lori Martin), shrink the elapsed time from several weeks to an unspecified but much shorter period, devise many scenes in which Gregory Peck is not even present, and put Robert Mitchum on the screen to project directly the sociopathic menace that MacDonald, whose Cady character appears on the printed page hardly at all, had evoked indirectly.

One of the film's most significant additions to MacDonald's novel is that the cinematic Cady is not just a sadistic psychopath out to destroy the Bowden family as in the novel but one who has a lawyer, knows the law, and uses it as a weapon. This innovation permits the filmmakers to ask a question which at most is only hinted at in the novel: Has our legal system vested the sociopaths among us with such a panoply of rights that we are no longer safe? But an even more striking innovation in the film is that the story material from *The Executioners* is merged into a complex structure with no counterpart in MacDonald's novel: a descent from legality at its best to the law of the jungle.

We first see shots of a quiet Southern city, average people on the streets, facades of public buildings—and Max Cady, whose cigar and Panama hat and body language as he lopes along and into the courthouse evoke a feral creature invading civilized space. In an atmosphere of decorum where civilized people are resolving their differences rationally with voices lowered, Sam Bowden is trying a case. At the afternoon adjournment Cady follows Bowden to the parking lot, reaches in and pulls out the attorney's car keys, replicating the incident that in *The Executioners* Bowden narrated to his wife a few days later, concluding with: "Give my love to the family, Counselor. I'll be seeing you." That evening while Bowden is out bowling with Peggy and Nancy, he sees Cady watching them. Later he visits and explains the situation to police chief Mark Dutton (Martin Balsam), who has Cady picked up and taken in.

"I didn't spend eight years in the can studying law for nothing," Cady says while being harassed in Dutton's office. "I've got a legal right to. . . . Or didn't you boys know that?" Dutton has Cady strip-searched in Bowden's presence, finds a bankbook in his wallet, and asks where he got the money. Cady says nothing. Dutton's next words instantly evoke Southern police chiefs and civil rights demonstrators in the early Sixties: "I asked you where you got it, boy!" Cady: "Well now, that could be my business, couldn't it?" Then, to Bowden: "Would you advise me to answer a question like that, Counselor?" Outmaneuvered and forced to release Cady, Dutton turns to Bowden and says: "There are legal ways to convince Mr. Cady that this can be a pretty poor place to live in." In the midst of a systematic official campaign to roust Cady, the Bowdens' dog is poisoned as in the novel. The incident forces Sam to explain to Peggy and Nancy why all three are in danger. Then comes a brief exchange that again evokes the burning issue in the South of the early 1960s. Peggy: "A man like that doesn't deserve civil rights." Sam: "You can't put a man in jail for what he *might* do. Thank heavens for that."

Once again Cady is arrested and brought in but this time he has with him his own lawyer, Dave Grafton (Jack Kruschen). "He's one of these ardent types," Dutton tells Bowden as if Sam had never before heard of a fellow attorney in the same community. "You slap a cigarette out of some hoodlum's mouth and five minutes later he's down in the mayor's office yelling police brutality, rallying the bleeding hearts squad." In Dutton's office and Bowden's presence, Grafton summarizes the harassment of Cady. Bowden: "Don't the police have a right to interrogate a suspect any more?" Grafton: "You know, if anybody had told me a week ago that you were capable of a remark like that. . . ." The clear implication is that Bowden is on the side of civil rights except when they become inconvenient for him. Turning to Chief Dutton, Grafton says: "And isn't it also a fact that with manpower as short as you say it is, that officers are assigned day and night to guarding the premises of one private individual who happens to be a friend of yours? And this without any evidence of danger!"

Dutton is compelled not only to release Cady and end the harassment but to deny the Bowdens any extraordinary protection. "You show me a law that prevents crime. All we can do is act after the fact. You remember the Hoffman murder? Before she was killed, Mrs. Hoffman came up here week after week telling us that her husband was going to do it, and I believed her. But I couldn't arrest the man for something that might be in his mind. That's dictatorship. Now Sam, you're a citizen. Would you want it any other way?" Then: "It's a hell of a note, isn't it? Either we have too many laws or not enough." Bowden then hires private eye Charlie Sievers (Telly Savalas).

What follows is not well integrated with the main storyline but carries forward the theme of evolutionary regress. Knowing he's being shadowed by Sievers, Cady goes for a drive with Diane Taylor (Barrie Chase), a bar girl he's taken up with. "You're just an animal," she murmurs in a half-drunk stupor. "Coarse, muscled, barbaric. . . . What I like about you is, you're rock bottom. . . . It's a great comfort for a girl to know she could not possibly sink any lower." Cady gives her a brutal beating, apparently for no other reason than to impress Bowden. When Sievers and the police find her, Cady is gone and she is too terrified of retaliation to press charges. "A man like that has no right to walk around free," Sievers tells her as she packs and prepares to leave town. She remains unconvinced even when Bowden shows up and asks her to stay. After her departure Sievers says to Bowden almost precisely what his counterpart in the novel had said: "A type like that is an animal. So you've gotta fight him like an animal." Whether he is right is the central question in this version of the story.

The next scene stems from the one in the novel where the Bowdens are at the dock working on their boat, but Thompson and Webb add some jokes that enrich the film's main theme. "You represent a giant stride in evolution," Sam tells Nancy. As in the novel, Cady is spying on them and leers at the teen-age girl. In the next sequences, which have no counterparts in the novel, Nancy while leaving school is terror-stricken when she sees Cady on the street. She races back into the empty building, then narrowly escapes death when she dashes outside and into the path of a car. Bowden takes a gun out of his desk and goes off to shoot Cady down, then has second thoughts and offers him $20,000 if he'll go away and never bother them again. "Counselor," Cady scoffs, "I don't believe you've heard of the Minimum Wage Act." Then: "You know, when I was in the bucket, all I could think about was busting out and killing somebody. I wanted to kill him with my bare hands. Slow. Every single night for seven years I killed that man. And on the eighth year I said, oh no, that's too easy, that's too fast. You know the Chinese death of a thousand cuts? First they cut off a little toe, then a piece of your finger, a piece of your ear, your nose? I like that better." Bowden: "You're the lowest. It makes me sick to breathe the same air."

Convinced that Nancy is Cady's real target, Bowden thrashes out various scenarios with his wife in a scene that once again presents lawful options as worthless.

> Sam: "What would you do if she were—attacked?" Have him arrested?. . . . Would you have him tried? Pull him into court? Naturally he'd deny the whole thing. That means that Nancy would have to testify. You've never watched a child testify in such a case. Thank God you haven't. It's—it's the clinical reports. And the questions. And the detailed answers that she'd have to give. She'd have to give them, all right, because he'd deny it and we'd have to prove his guilt."
>
> Peggy: "A beast like that! Who'd believe him?"
>
> Sam: "No one. No one at all. But that wouldn't spare her the questions. And Cady knows that. He knows that we'd never put her through an ordeal like that."
>
> Peggy: "There's got to be something we can do. There just has to be."
>
> Sam: "There is. There is."

The next moment we see the three waterfront thugs whose employment Sievers had recommended, beating Cady with bicycle chains. But he turns out to be tougher than all three of them and chases them away, putting one in the hospital. Then, bloody but victorious, he calls Bowden at home. "Counselor, you really stepped on it this time, didn't you? I don't know what the bar association thinks about its members compounding a felony but I do know what the law thinks about it. You just put the law in my hands. And I'm going to break your heart with it."

This is when the Bowdens decide that Cady must be murdered. "I can't believe we're standing here talking about killing a man," Peggy says. Their plan is at bottom the same as the staked-goat trap in the novel: trick Cady into thinking that Peggy and Nancy have been sent for safety's sake to the Bowdens' remote cabin in the swamps, then lure him into the killing ground.[8] Before they can take any action the hospitalized waterfront goon reveals who hired him. Dave Grafton files disbarment proceedings against Bowden and, in a moment guaranteed to leave lawyer viewers laughing, the matter is scheduled for hearing in the state capital the very next day. Bowden decides to take advantage of this development: fly to Atlanta, double back at once and join Peggy and Nancy in the swamp cabin. As in the novel, he reveals his scheme to Dutton, who has a deputy named Kersek (Page Slattery) join the Bowdens in the swamp.[9]

We have come from bright daylight and calm discussion in a courthouse to night in the jungle, and to make the descent more vivid Thompson shoots the rest of the film virtually without dialogue. Cady makes his move but catches on that it's a trap and silently kills Kersek. Then he traps Peggy on the houseboat moored beside the cabin[10] and explains that he's about to rape her—legally. "And you a lawyer's wife? Don't you understand? That with consent there's no charges against me. . . . I was going to go for Nancy. But I can always make it with Nancy, you know, next week, next month. . . . You proposition me. You instead of Nancy. And I'll agree never to see you again. . . . Unless of course you want it. Now that's how you give your consent." With what is left of her common sense she makes what would seem the obvious point: "That's not consent, it's blackmail." Cady replies: "The reason don't make any difference. You look that up." Outrageous though it sounds today, his statement is a fairly accurate characterization of Georgia law at the time.[11] Within the movie of course its function is to intensify further our sense that the legal system has gone insane.

The film's last and most violent confrontation takes place back at the cabin when Cady grabs the now unprotected Nancy and is about to rape her when Bowden bursts upon the scene. It's such a viscerally powerful sequence that we almost forget that we've already seen Mitchum overcome three goons with bicycle chains, and that his adversary this time is a lawyer whose only form of physical activity has been bowling. The two roll into the water, Cady holds Bowden's head under and we are almost convinced he's killed him until Bowden finds a rock beneath the surface and pounds Cady with it. Ninety-nine viewers out of a hundred want Peck to keep slamming that rock against Mitchum's skull until it's mush. But he doesn't, and the *mano a mano* continues until Bowden dives for his gun—which has been in the water with him both when he swam to the houseboat and when he swam back—and shoots Cady in the side.

Why did J. Lee Thompson pass up what would have been the perfect ending for this film? "I was in favor of Peck actually killing him," he told me in one of our phone conversations, "and that the film would end right there in the swamp. And of course at that time . . .the studio was anxious for a more happy ending, and so in the end we all went along with that." The actual end of the film is not really happy but just silly. Cady, wounded and lying helpless at Bowden's feet, says: "Go ahead. Go ahead, I just don't give a damn." Bowden replies:

> "No. No! That would be letting you off too easy. Too fast. . . . Oh no. We're going to take good care of you. Going to nurse you back to health. . . . You're going to live a long life, Cady. In a cage! . . . And this time for life! Bang your head against the walls. Count the years. The months. The hours. Until the day you rot!"

If a prize were offered for the movie whose last moments are most radically at odds with everything that has gone before, Peck's profession of unearned faith in a legal system whose impotence has been thrust in our faces for close to two hours would win that award for *Cape Fear* in a walk. But its incongruity within the world of the film and its dependence on the firing of a waterlogged gun are not the only problems with the climax. What Thompson's powerful images and Bernard Herrmann's music almost makes us forget is that Mitchum is in the control position: if he doesn't want to rot in a cage, he has only to go for the gun and force Peck to kill him. After the freeze-frame that follows Peck's words we see over the end credits the blank-faced Bowdens in their boat emerging from the swamp into open water, but whether we are to infer that Peck did indeed gun Mitchum down is anyone's guess. And if any viewer trained in law is wondering about that disbarment hearing Peck failed to show up for, Thompson leaves this a puzzlement too.

***

In the fall of 1978 the University of South Florida organized a conference dealing with John D. MacDonald and I was invited to be one of the speakers. As part of the conference the university wanted to screen a MacDonald-based movie and asked me to recommend a title. I had not seen *Cape Fear* since its first release seventeen years before but remembered it as an excellent suspense picture. Later I learned that MacDonald had agreed with the choice but only because he thought it the least bad of an undistinguished lot. During the time I spent with him at USF I asked why he didn't care for it. His reply, as best I can reconstruct it more than twenty years later, was that the film depended on just the conventional elements of suspense and menace that he had worked so hard to keep out of his novel. Anyone who knows MacDonald's reputation for strong opinions forcefully expressed[12] might expect that he would have been even more upset by Gregory Peck's final speech, which enshrines law and legality as all-but-sacred institutions, and which is so completely at odds with the pragmatic (some would say cynical) view of law Sam Bowden expressed at the end of *The Executioners*, but I can't recall a word from him on that subject. If only I had probed further! If only I had been carrying a cassette recorder! MacDonald died in 1985, but in view of his reaction to the first movie based on *The Executioners* he might well have had a Max Cady fit over the second.

***

The remake, released in 1991, was directed by Martin Scorsese, the former seminarian turned film scholar and, in the view of many, the greatest American filmmaker of his generation.[13] The new screenplay was the work of Wesley Strick, a former rock journalist who had previously scripted the legal thriller *True Believer* (1989, directed by Joseph Ruben and starring James Woods and Robert Downey, Jr.). "They sent me the original movie," Strick said in an interview on the *Cape Fear* set in 1991, "and I didn't like it very much. I thought it wasn't very interesting. It seemed like sort of a failed Hitchcock, which doesn't really turn me on. And also I didn't like the vigilante implications of the story—you know, there comes a point when a man's gotta be a man with a gun and shoot this guy down."[14] In fact the earlier film had ended with a ringing declaration by Gregory Peck that the studio had demanded precisely in order to defuse any vigilante implications. However wrongly Strick recollected the J. Lee Thompson version, it's clear that he was determined to keep the new *Cape Fear* from turning into a close cousin of the Charles Bronson avenger flicks like *Murphy's Law* (1986) and *Death Wish 4: The Crackdown* (1988) and *Kinjite: Forbidden Subjects* (1990) which Thompson had recently been directing. "I mean, that was my real fear, that it would be like *Death Wish*, and I certainly didn't want to promote the idea that guns ultimately solve problems."

The 1991 version starred Nick Nolte and Robert DeNiro in the roles originated by Peck and Mitchum, both of whom appear in cameo parts. The Bernard Herrmann score was retained (reorchestrated by Elmer Bernstein and so drastically rearranged that hardly a scene with roots in the first version is backed with the same themes), but otherwise the 1991 film differs radically from its forerunner: saturated in color, soaked in extreme violence, its storyline so far removed from *The Executioners* that, had it been made without authorization and had John D. MacDonald's estate sued for copyright infringement, the plaintiffs might not have been able to establish substantial similarity between the novel and the new film. Indeed except for a few details not in the first film that come straight from the novel—for example, the city where the Bowdens live is called New Essex—one would be hard put to establish that Scorsese and Strick had read MacDonald at all.

Some of the second film's structural changes were made to cover flaws in the construction of the first, others were to update the story from the early 1960s to the early 1990s and to stamp it with Scorsese's characteristic overtones of religion. In the first category, the Nick Nolte version of Sam Bowden is much more physical than the Gregory Peck version: having seen him play a savage game of racquetball early on and having been told that he used to box, we don't roll our eyes in disbelief when later he holds his own in hand-to-hand combat with DeNiro. His domestic circle is not the cozy family stereotypical in films and TV series of the late Fifties and early Sixties but the dysfunctional menage common in the media during the Eighties and Nineties, his wife Leigh (Jessica Lange) a chain-smoking commercial artist with a wicked temper and their daughter Danielle or Dani (Juliette Lewis) a knowing-eyed nymphet who dresses provocatively and smokes pot. Scorsese's Max Cady is not at all the credible sociopath of the first version. "He's from the hills, Pentecostal crackers, you know." Greasy-haired, a huge cigar burning between his lips, doing sit-ups in front of a photographic shrine that features Stalin and Robert E. Lee and (I think) St. Sebastian, a huge cross with a Bible and a scales of justice hanging from its arms tattooed on him, pious mottos festooned all over him ("Vengeance is mine," "My time is at hand," "The Lord is my avenger," "My time is not yet full come"), gifted with a cat's nine lives and with The Shadow's power to make himself invisible at will—everything about this Cady screams METAPHYSICAL SYMBOL OF EVIL! The woman who corresponds to Diane Taylor in the middle sequence of the film is not a total stranger as in the first version but Bowden's soon-to-be-mistress, so that when DeNiro bites a piece out of her cheek and then beats and rapes her it serves as a much more powerful demonstration of what this version of Cady has in store for everyone Bowden cares about. The scene where Nancy runs in terror through the basement of the empty school building with Cady apparently stalking her is replaced with a much subtler and psychologically more disturbing sequence: Cady, posing as Dani's new drama teacher, lures her into the school auditorium and uses his perverse charisma on her until, even though she now knows who he is, she kisses him and sucks his thumb. Charlie Sievers and deputy Kersek from Thompson's version are merged into a single character (Joe Don Baker), a private eye whom Bowden hires to protect the family. Scorsese scraps the preposterous notion of the Bowdens having a vacation retreat in the middle of a mosquito-ridden swamp and instead has them frantically try to escape up the Cape Fear River in their houseboat. Since the second film is rooted not in the idealistic Warren Court era but in the cynical age that is ours today, the unearned declaration of faith in the system with which the first ended is replaced with a thematically appropriate but brutal and interminable struggle.

From the law-trained viewer's perspective the most important change Scorsese made is in the relation between the antagonists. In both the novel and the first film, Sam Bowden came upon Cady raping a teen-age girl and was the principal witness against him. What Scorsese moves to center stage is the attorney-client relationship, which played no role whatever in the novel and the earlier film. We learn this film's backstory as Bowden tells it to Tom Broadbent (Fred Dalton Thompson), senior partner in the firm Sam works for.

> Bowden: "Fourteen years ago, in this case, I had a report on the victim. . . . [It was a case of] rape and aggravated sexual battery. Anyway I had a report on this victim and it came back that she was promiscuous. And I buried it. . . . I didn't show it to the client, I didn't show it to the prosecution. But if you had seen what this guy had done to this girl. . . ."
>
> Broadbent: "'In every criminal prosecution the

accused shall have the assistance of counsel for his defense.'"

Bowden: "I know the Sixth Amendment, I believe in the Sixth Amendment. I mean that's why I left the Public Defender's office. There was no way to serve the law in that capacity."

Broadbent: "Some folks just don't have the right to the best defense, eh, Sam?"

Bowden: "Of course they deserve the best defense! But I mean if you had seen what he did to this girl. . . ."

Broadbent: "You buried the report."

Bowden: "I mean if it was your own daughter, Tom. . . ."

Broadbent: "You buried the report. Jesus, Sam, I. . . . Oh God."

In this dialogue we encounter for the first time an aspect of Scorsese's film that becomes pervasive as his version of the tale progresses: the law as expounded by his characters is flat-out wrong. Traditionally, when a man was charged with rape, all information about the woman's prior sexual activity was admissible either to show consent or to impeach her credibility as a witness. She could be cross-examined about sexual contact with the defendant or any third party, previous sexual partners could testify about their own affairs with her, and the defendant could introduce evidence as to her sexual reputation within the community.[15] But in the 1970s, during the heyday of the women's liberation movement, pressure mounted for the enactment of so-called rape shield laws restricting the admissibility of evidence concerning an alleged rape victim's past sex life. Michigan passed the first such statute in 1974, and by 1976 rape shield legislation in one form or another had been enacted in more than half the states.[16] One of those states was Georgia, where in 1977 Scorsese's Max Cady had been tried for rape and Scorsese's Sam Bowden had buried the report on his victim's promiscuity.[17]

Any competent Georgia lawyer could have told Scorsese that the legal premise behind his film's backstory was nonsense. But from this nonsense we can learn much.

Soon after the dialogue between Bowden and Broadbent, there is an encounter on the street between Bowden and Cady himself.

> Bowden: "Why me? Look, I was your lawyer, I defended you. Why not badger the DA or the judge? . . ."
>
> Cady: "Best I remember, they was just doin' right by their jobs."
>
> Bowden: "I didn't do my job, is that right? Look, I pleaded you out to a lesser included offense. You could have gotten rape instead of battery."
>
> Cady: "I'd have been up for parole either way in seven years according to the Georgia Penal Code."[18]
>
> Bowden: "Rape is a capital offense. I mean, you know, you could have got life, you could have got death. You could be sitting on death row right now."[19]
>
> Cady: "I learned to read during my stretch. . . . Did you know that after I discharged you I acted as my own attorney? Applied seven times for an appeal. . . . So here we are, two lawyers for all practical purposes, talking shop."

How are we to evaluate the moral conflict that is at the center of this version? There are three templates that one might employ in telling this tale. (1) A conflict between good and evil with Nolte in the former role and DeNiro in the latter. From this perspective, when Nolte betrayed DeNiro he was doing the right thing. A number of law-trained commentators who personally find this perspective disgusting have read the film in this way. "Ironically, the lawyer-protagonist-hero is effectively lauded for betraying his scurrilous, murdering, immoral client. In a broader culture that rewards loyalty, criminal defense lawyers can become heroes when they betray their *guilty* clients."[20] (2) A conflict between good and evil with DeNiro in the former role and Nolte in the latter. From this perspective, we are meant to empathize with Cady and despise Bowden.[21] (3) A sort of Hegelian tragic collision in which right contends with right or wrong with wrong.[22]

Which of these perspectives does the film support? Wesley Strick in his 1991 interview seemed to opt for all three at once.

> "If you could tell the story with another kind of sensibility it would just be more ironic and sort of full of dread, and more a fable of the thin veneer of civilization. It's almost like a black comedy . . . where things just get worse and worse for this perfectly decent guy. He has committed an ethical transgression, but in a sense it's the decent thing. It was wrong, it shouldn't have happened. . . . It's not even good versus evil, it's just decency versus evil. . . . [I wanted] to create a Cady who by his own lights was fighting a holy war, [who] was just. . . . I think Marty [Scorsese] really does see Cady's point of view. . . . He can let his vision extend to the most black part of his character."

Scorsese was shooting the film at the time Strick made these remarks, but the finished picture clearly adopts the first and only the first of the three perspectives. DeNiro's Cady is totally evil, so much so that, unlike Mitchum's Cady, he ceases to be a recognizable human being. Bowden did right to betray him, and the story Scorsese tells is that of a good deed not going unpunished.

In view of the director's religious roots it can't be by chance that in one scene Bowden finds Cady reading the Bible and is told to look up the book between Esther and Psalms. Like most viewers of the film (and readers of this book?), Bowden doesn't know which book Cady is referring to but finds out that night that it's the book of Job. In an interview more or less contemporaneous with making his film, Scorsese emphasized this point. The Bowdens, he said, "are

CAPE FEAR DEAD AHEAD

representative, for me, of humanity. They're basically good people who have had some hard times and are trying to go through them and piece their lives together. Now they're being tested, like Job, by Max. . . ."[23] Which would seem to suggest that Cady for Scorsese is an incarnation of the Biblical God—and that a really juicy blasphemy requires a seminarian.

If we were meant to see DeNiro as an injured innocent and Nolte as a Judas, or to think both antagonists were somewhat in the right and somewhat in the wrong, why did Scorsese tell the story as he did? What Nolte suppressed at DeNiro's rape trial was that his victim had been promiscuous. Any marginally informed viewer in 1991 would have known that rape shield laws had become all but universal in the United States.[24] Assuming that Scorsese knew this, why didn't he have DeNiro claim that the woman had had consensual sex with him, or even better that she had identified the wrong man? Obviously because such changes would have generated an empathy with DeNiro that the director did not want in his film.

Just before Cady is beaten by the hired goons, the camera pans over the rear bumper of his red convertible with its "Pentecostal Cracker" slogans ("You're a VIP on Earth, I'm a VIP in Heaven" and "American by birth, Southern by the grace of God") and a license plate issued by the state of North Carolina. This and a casual mention earlier in the film that the Bowdens had moved from their original home—apparently in hopes of putting an end to Sam's womanizing—are the only indications that the present story and the backstory are set in two different states. Cady is banged up by the goons but, as befits a metaphysical symbol of evil, not seriously injured, so that Kersek remarks: "That son of a bitch could survive a nuclear strike."

At the hearing on Bowden's motion for a restraining order, Cady's lawyer Lee Heller, portrayed by none other than Gregory Peck, gets the judge to forbid Sam from going within 500 yards of his battered client. Heller then announces: "I've petitioned the ABA for his [Bowden's] disbarment on grounds of moral turpitude." No one involved with the film seems to have known that the real-world American Bar Association has no power to disbar anyone. "Oh Jesus," Bowden says later. "It's all fucked up, Kersek. I mean, the law considers me more of a loose cannon than Max Cady. Some big shit attorney's whipped the ABA's ethics committee into a frenzy. There's an emergency session in Raleigh over the assault." The reference to the capital of North Carolina, site of the real-world Cape Fear river, shows that, though ignorant of the functions of the ABA, Scorsese is aware that only the backstory of his film takes place in Georgia.

As in the 1962 version, Bowden pretends to fly to the hearing but doubles back and, as in MacDonald's novel, sets the death trap for Cady in his own house. "If Cady breaks into your home," Kersek tells Bowden, "he can be killed. Justifiably." Among the many dead wrong legal statements which pockmark the film, this one at least has some basis.[25] Later however Bowden questions the thesis: "It's premeditated. It makes me an accomplice, an accessory, an abettor. It's also excessive force." Kersek replies: "Sam, the only thing excessive we could do to Cady would be to gut him and eat his liver. Now that might be excessive."

The booby trap of course backfires. Kersek has rigged the house with all sorts of alarms but Cady inexplicably gets past them and, disguised as the Bowdens' housekeeper, strangles the private eye with piano wire he had taken from the house in an earlier preternatural incursion.[26] The Bowdens flee in terror to their houseboat but Cady has secured himself with belts to the undercarriage of their car and is their unseen passenger for the next few hours, making countless viewers roar with incredulous laughter when they see him slither out at the boat landing. Then in his own craft he pursues them up the Cape Fear River, taking over their houseboat in the middle of a fierce night storm. After a long and sadistic scene where he terrorizes the Bowdens, Dani manages to douse his face with lighter fluid. Screaming and aflame, Cady plunges into the river. But, like the Freddy Kruger figure into which Scorsese has let him mutate, he comes back and again overpowers the Bowdens, while the houseboat is being whirled around in a maelstrom. Now the antagonists have their final legal discussion; and if the bare dialogue on the printed page may hint that Cady has some right on his side, any such suggestion is nullified by DeNiro's wildly over-the-top reading.

Cady [holding the family at gunpoint]: "The people call Samuel J. Bowden. Do you swear to tell the truth and nothing but the truth so help you God?" [Then, when Dani screams what most of us would like to scream at Scorsese, in effect that this quasi-courtroom denouement is ludicrous]: "Don't you make light of your civic duty, daughter. You're the jury."

Bowden: "All right, all right, okay, I swear to tell the truth. What do you want to know?"

Cady: "Was a prior sexual history ever prepared in connection with my defense? [Silence. Cady screams the question a second time, then pistol-whips Bowden, then turns to the women]: "I'm sorry, your honor, I agree, that was argumentative." [To Bowden]: "An investigator did prepare a prior sexual history on the alleged victim, true?" [To the women]: "I can ask leading questions, your honor, he is a hostile witness." [To Bowden]: "And would you care to tell the court what the gist was of this report?"

Bowden: "It was fourteen years ago, I can't remember that. . . ."

Cady [hitting him again, then turning once more to the women to justify the action]: "Because he perjured himself, your honor, he knows damn well exactly what it said, don't you?"

Bowden: "It said that she was promiscuous. It said that she had three different lovers in one month."

Cady: "*At least* three! *At least* three! And did you show this report to the DA?"

Bowden: "No. No."

Cady: " . . . I only discovered it when I began to represent myself, six years into my sentence. But there it was in the court file. But back in '77 you buried it, Counselor. Would you care to tell the jury why? Would you care to tell the court why?"

Bowden [to the women]: "Because I know he brutally raped her and he beat her."

Cady: "Talk to me! I'm standing here!" [Hits him again.]

Bowden: "Just because she was promiscuous didn't give you the right to rape her. Did you brag to me that you'd beaten two prior aggravated rapes? You were a menace!"

Cady: "YOU WERE MY LAWYER! YOU WERE MY LAWYER! That report would have saved me fourteen years! . . . I'm Vergil, Counselor, and I've gotten you through the gates of hell. We are now in the ninth circle. The circle of traitors. Traitors to country. Traitors to fellow man. Traitors to God. You, sir, are charged with betraying the principles of our trade. Can you please quote to me the American Bar Association's Rules of Professional Conduct, Canon 7?"

Bowden: "'A lawyer shall represent his client. . . .'"

Cady: "'Shall *zealously* represent his client within the bounds of the law.'[27] And I find you guilty, Counselor! Guilty of betraying your fellow man! Guilty of betraying your country! Guilty of abrogating your oath! Guilty of judging me and selling me out! And with the power vested in me by the kingdom of God, I sentence you to the ninth circle of hell! There you will learn about loss. Loss of freedom. Loss of humanity. Now you and I will truly be the same, Counselor." [Then, after screaming at the women to take off their clothes, obviously intending to rape and slaughter them in front of each other and Bowden]: "Tonight you're going to learn to be an animal. To live like one and to die like one."

Now the houseboat begins to break up on the rocks and the women manage to leap overboard into the wild river while Bowden and Cady stay behind for the final duel, interrupted by a few more ludicrous lines from DeNiro: "Forget about that restraining order, Counselor? You're well within five hundred yards. . . . Well, here we are, Counselor, just two lawyers working it out." As if to tweak J. Lee Thompson's nose for missing what should have been the ending to the struggle in the first *Cape Fear*, Scorsese has Nolte pick up a huge boulder and crush DeNiro's head with it. Or does he? "There [Bowden] stands," writes one commentator, "with a rock heaved above his head, ready to smash it down on Cady's face, crushing bone and brain. And so things would have turned out but for the fact that the wind changes, the river's currents shift, and the fragment of the houseboat to which Cady has been handcuffed is suddenly dragged away, out of Sam's reach."[28] What makes this reading somewhat plausible is that when we see Cady's face as the current drags him away it hardly seems to have been crushed in; but then neither did it show much evidence of having been set aflame a few minutes earlier. In any event our preternatural symbol of evil begins babbling in tongues as, his ankle cuffed to the houseboat, he sinks into the depths for what, thank heaven, turns out to be the last time. Whether Bowden got to keep his law license, and what the ethics committee thought of his failure to show up at the disbarment hearing, remains as much a mystery in this film as in Thompson's.

***

The story John D. MacDonald first told fifty years ago has proved adaptable to widely different takes on the themes of law, lawyers, lawyering and justice. Especially since the release of Scorsese's film in 1991, the Cape Fear story has all but spawned a Cape Fear industry. On the nonfiction side, it has inspired several analyses in legal periodicals.[29]

It lies at the heart of at least one notable short story[30] and of at least one big-budget film.[31]

To my mind the secret of its fertility is its flexibility. Looking back on MacDonald's novel, we see that it's not really centered on law and that nothing important in it would be changed if his Sam Bowden were a businessman or accountant. The final chapter, with its stress on the absurdity of attributing to law any more than a pragmatic and instrumental value in this savagely random world, is not so much a juristic perspective as a corollary to the dark presuppositions of *roman noir*. By transforming Max Cady into a sociopath equipped with a lawyer and knowledge of law, J. Lee Thompson's film emphasizes legal themes that were peripheral in MacDonald's novel but remains squarely in the *noir* tradition—until those last moments when Gregory Peck's Sam Bowden reaffirms a faith in legality which almost foreshadows his very next movie role, as Atticus Finch in *To Kill a Mockingbird*, but which is radically at odds with everything Thompson has shown us before. Martin Scorsese's film de-emphasizes legal themes and concentrates on religious and psychological dimensions which in the previous versions were nonexistent. But he also adds a new dimension of law and especially of legal ethics to the core story by transforming Sam Bowden from witness against Cady to his lawyer. With the plot altered so that what precipitates the nightmare events is the attorney betraying professional ethics in order to keep his sociopath client from going free, Scorsese's film joins the roster of movies which radically condemn the legal system by hinging on acts which are justified dramatically, morally, indeed every way in the world except under the law.[32]

So, you might ask, which of the three versions of the Cape Fear story to date got it right? But this is like asking which of the characters in *Rashomon* told the truth about the murder. There are no answers, only perspectives.

NOTES

1. *The Columbia Gazetteer of the World*, ed. Saul B. Cohen (Columbia University Press, 1998), Vol. 1, at 530.

2. In Hammett's classic novel *The Maltese Falcon*, Sam Spade tells his treacherous client Brigid O'Shaughnessy that he had once been hired to locate a prosperous realtor named Flitcraft who had left his office to go to lunch one day and never returned. Five years later, Spade says, he found the man and discovered why he had vanished. On his way to lunch that day Flitcraft had happened to pass beneath a building under construction. "A beam or something fell eight or ten stories down and smacked the sidewalk alongside him." The brush with death had made Flitcraft feel as if "somebody had taken the lid off life and let him look at the works. . . . The life he knew was a clean orderly sane responsible affair. Now a falling beam had shown him that life was fundamentally none of these things. . . . He knew then that men died at haphazard like that, and lived only while blind chance spared them." Dashiell Hammett, *The Maltese Falcon* (Knopf, 1930), ch. VII. Again and again in subsequent novels and movies this parable is quoted, alluded to, varied, expanded upon and played with as John D. MacDonald does at the end of *The Executioners*.

3. Anthony Boucher, Book Review, *New York Times Book Review*, 1 June 1958, at 17.

4. It also played at New York's Cort Theatre but closed after 37 performances. Among the audience at one of those performances was visiting San Franciscan Anthony Boucher, who fifteen years later was to review John D. MacDonald's *The Executioners* for the New York *Times*. Boucher's enthusiastic comments on the Thompson melodrama deserve to be excerpted here. "*Murder Without Crime* is a tautly written, economical play with a cast of only four characters—almost a chamber study in murder. It tells of Stephen, young-man-about-London, who quarrels with his mistress over the return of his estranged wife. In a

scuffle he accidentally stabs the mistress, then gets panicky and attempts the amateur's clumsy cover-up, only to realize that his landlord, Matthew, has discovered his secret. It is Matthew who makes the play. A subtle, decadent, sadistic specimen of the impoverished aristocrat, he seems at first a trifle over-written. . . . Gradually, however, the script exposes and analyzes his motives until you finally come to accept him as repellent and vicious but evilly fascinating and thoroughly believable. . . . Matthew has his own quality, his own individual tone, particularly apparent in his vein of morbid and macabre humor. . . . [Actor Henry Daniell's] consummate effortlessness [in the role of Matthew] is more entrancing to watch than all the tricks in the bags of the most pyrotechnic display artists. Bretaigne Windust's direction held the taut mood admirably and succeeded even in imparting perfect pace to the difficult scenes where laughs at once broke and heightened the tension. . . . [A]ny [West] Coast producer who would like to try his luck with a small cast, one-set show with a great star might be wise to get in touch promptly with J. Lee Thompson and Henry Daniell." Anthony Boucher, "Murder Wreaks Havoc on Old Broadway," San Francisco *Chronicle*, 26 September 1943, This World section, at 26. I quote this notice at such length because it makes me wonder to what extent Thompson's Matthew and his game of cat and mouse with Stephen might be considered a forerunner of the Thompson version of Max Cady and *his* game of cat and mouse with Sam Bowden.

5. My taped phone conversations with Thompson took place on 21 April and 9 June 2000.

6. Arriving on location the first day, Mitchum kept singing "How dear to my heart are the scenes of my childhood/When fond recollection presents them to view." When Thompson asked him about the song, Mitchum explained about his time on a Savannah chain gang. "These are the scenes of my childhood, man, and they are very dear, very dear indeed, to my heart." George Eells, *Robert Mitchum* (Franklin Watts, 1984), at 222.

7. While the film was in production, columnist Army Archerd reported in *Variety*: "The spoken word rape has been entirely removed from *Cape Fear*, and Greg Peck and cohorts have substituted 'attack' at all points in the film which could be one of the year's controversial epics." Quoted in George Eells, note 6 *supra*, at 221.

8. Thematically this dank, mosquito-ridden hellhole is essential to the last forty-odd minutes of the film, but even though I ran the picture in my seminar once a year for more than two decades it has never occurred to any of my students, and didn't strike me until I was working on the law journal version of this chapter, that no one with a shred of sanity would ever have chosen such a spot for a vacation retreat. This is one measure of the visceral power of J. Lee Thompson's images and Bernard Herrmann's music.

9. Since the film was shot in Georgia not North Carolina, the "Cape Fear River" signs that we see during the last forty-five minutes had to be specially manufactured to Thompson's order.

10. This is what Thompson in our conversation called "the famous egg scene on the boat, where suddenly Mitchum cracked two eggs and smeared them over the breasts of Polly Bergen. It was something that I suddenly decided on at the last moment. I was on the set and we were shooting the scene and I suddenly said: 'Bring me a bowl of eggs.' Mitchum thought it was a wonderful idea. Unfortunately the censor didn't, and a lot of the scene was cut."

11. Suppose that Peggy had yielded to this threat and that Cady had later been caught alive and charged with rape. To make things easier for the prosecution, suppose further that Cady admits having said and done precisely what the film shows him saying and doing. It still would not have been terribly difficult for his lawyer Dave Grafton to get him off. Georgia case law defined rape as "the carnal knowledge of a female forcibly and against her will." *Mathews v. State*, 29 S.E. 424, 426 (Ga. 1897). The first of the two elements that made up the crime was "force upon the part of the accused, exercised against the female." *Davis v. State*, 110 S.E. 18, 21 (Ga. 1921). The second was that the "unlawful

carnal knowledge shall be against her will," i.e. that the victim "must resist, and her resistance must not be a mere pretense, but must be in good faith." *Id.* at 22. Consent by the victim was fatal to the charge of rape. "Against her will is the equivalent of without her consent; that, if the female at any time yielded her consent to the act, the defendant(s) could not be convicted." *Epps v. State,* 118 S.E.2d 574, 579 (Ga. 1961).

Georgia courts seemed to be congenitally skeptical of rape allegations. In *Davis v. State* the state's highest court remarked that during sex "there may be slight physical resistance even though there is a mental willingness to submit. Physical pain would naturally produce some manifestation of this kind; or it might be indicative merely of maidenly shame or coyness." The court then said: "[A]lthough the woman never said yes, nay more, although she constantly said no, and kept up a decent show of resistance to the last, it may still be that she more than half consented to the ravishment. Her negative may have been so irresolute and undecided, and she may have made such a feeble fight as was calculated to encourage, rather than repel the attack." *Id.* at 22 [quoting *People v. Hulse,* 3 Hill (N.Y.) 309, 316 (Sup. Ct. 1842)].

Consent could be expressed in words or implied by the woman's actions. "If the female consent to the sexual intercourse, it is not rape, and she may express her consent by her conduct at the time of the intercourse." *Davis v. State,* 110 S.E. at 21 (Ga. 1921). Even consent given reluctantly was held in Georgia to be valid. "[T]hough the man use force, if eventually the woman consent there is no rape." *Morrow v. State,* 79 S.E. 63, 65 (Ga. 1913). "[I]n order that the offense might constitute rape, she must have resisted with all her power and kept up that resistance as long as she had strength. Opposition to the sexual act by mere words is not sufficient. Any consent of the woman, however reluctant, is fatal to a conviction for rape. The passive policy will not do." *Welch v. State,* 198 S.E. 810, 811 (Ga. 1938). The state had to show that her resistance was not "a mere pretext, the result of womanly reluctance to consent to the intercourse, but the resistance must be up to the point where it is overpowered by actual force; and any fact tending to the inference that there was not the utmost reluctance and the utmost resistance should be always received by the jury as illustrating the question as to force." *Morrow v. State*, 79 S.E. 65.

Georgia courts did recognize that consent "obtained by force and violence does not prevent the sexual act from being one of rape." *Johnson v. State*, 111 S.E.2d 45, 49 (Ga. 1959). However, a threat to the woman seems to have counted as negativing consent only if it gave rise to a "present and immediate fear of serious bodily injury to the female involved . . . which overpowers the female and causes her to yield against her will." *Id.* at 49.

Consent was not deemed valid if it was induced by fear and intimidation. *Willingham v. State*, 39 S.E.2d 751 (Ga. 1946). "In considering the question of consent and fear upon the part of the female, it is proper also to take into consideration her age, mental capacity and relation if any to the accused." *Davis v. State*, 110 S.E. at 22. These exceptions to the consent requirement would not have helped convict Cady since when he confronted Peggy on the houseboat he had no weapon and didn't threaten to harm her personally. The prosecution could argue that Cady's statements about Nancy were meant to induce fear and intimidation in her. But the defense could argue that Cady's words were no more than a lewd proposition. Since Peggy was an intelligent, healthy adult woman in possession of all her faculties at the time, her failure to resist would make it difficult for her to convince the jury that she had had sexual intercourse with Cady against her will.

Georgia also required evidence other than the victim's testimony to prove a rape had occurred. *Strickland v. State*, 61 S.E.2d 118, 120 (Ga. 1950). However, determination of the sufficiency and extent of the corroboration was a question for the jury. *Id.* at 121. In *Dorsey v. State*, 49 S.E.2d 886, 888 (Ga. 1948), the court reiterated the standing rule that "there can be no conviction of any rape unless the testimony of the female is corroborated. . . . [T]here are certain facts and circumstances which our courts have recognized as indicia of corroboration." Such circumstances included whether the victim made an outcry, or told of the injury promptly, or had torn or disarranged clothing or signs of violence on her person. *Id.* at 888. Any rape claim without such indicia the courts considered dubious. "[I]f no marks are left upon the person or clothing, and no complaint is made at the first opportunity, a doubt is thrown upon the whole charge." *Mathews v. State,* 29 S.E. 424, 426 (Ga. 1897). If Peggy Bowden had simply acquiesced because of Cady's threat to Nancy, the absence of injury to her body and clothing would have created another obstacle to Cady's conviction for rape.

12. His colleague Robert Bloch, the author of *Psycho*, once quipped that anyone who thinks God is dead never got a letter from John D.

13. From among the vast secondary literature on Scorsese, I have found most useful David Thompson & Ian Christie, ed., *Scorsese on Scorsese* (Faber, 1989) and Les Keyser, *Martin Scorsese* (Twayne, 1992). See also Marion Weiss, *Martin Scorsese: A Guide to References and Resources* (G.K. Hall, 1987).

14. Interview, Wesley Strick, *Wide Angle Closeup* [http://members.aol.-com/morgands1/closeup/text/cfstrick.htm].

15. See Cassia C. Spohn, The Rape Reform Movement: The Traditional Common Law and Rape Law, 39 Jurimetrics Journal 119, 126-127 (1999).

16. See Harriet R. Galvin, Shielding Rape Victims in the State and Federal Courts: A Proposal for the Second Decade, 70 Minnesota Law Review 763, 765 (1986).

17. In Georgia an alleged rape victim's prior sexual history is generally inadmissible. Ga. Code Ann. § 24-2-3(a) (1999). It may be admitted, however, if after an in camera hearing the court determines that the evidence offered by the defendant comes within the exception created by § 24-2-3(c), which deals with past sexual encounters between the alleged victim and the defendant. In Scorsese's *Cape Fear* there were no such encounters.

18. In fact Cady would have been eligible for parole much sooner than he thinks. Georgia law defines a felony as a crime punishable by death, life imprisonment or imprisonment for more than 12 months. Ga. Code

Ann. §16-1-3(5) (1999). Until the statute was amended in 1997, rape was punishable by death, life imprisonment, or imprisonment for "not less than one nor more than 20 years." Ga. Code Ann. §16-6-1(B) (1999). Therefore rape was a felony under Georgia law if the sentence imposed was more than one year. According to the Georgia Penal Code, an inmate serving a felony sentence is eligible for parole after the "expiration of nine months of his or her sentence or one-third of the time of the sentence, whichever is greater." Ga. Code Ann. §42-9-45(B) (1999).

A Georgia inmate serving a sentence for aggravated battery cannot be granted parole "unless said inmate has served on good behavior seven years of imprisonment or one-third of the prison term imposed by the sentencing court for the violent crime, whichever occurs first." Ga. Code Ann. §42-9-45(F) (1999). Since Cady received a fourteen-year sentence for his crime, he would have served only one-third or approximately four years and seven months of his sentence before he was eligible for parole whether convicted of rape or battery.

Was the number seven pulled out of thin air? Perhaps not. The Georgia provision which deals with inmates serving felony sentences such as those for rape ends with the statement that "inmates serving sentences aggregating 21 years or more shall become eligible for consideration for parole upon completion of the service of seven years." Ga. Code Ann. §42-9-45(B) (1999). A later subsection of the same statute sets forth a list of crimes including aggravated battery and then provides: "[N]o inmate serving a sentence imposed for any of the crimes listed in this subsection shall be granted release on parole until and unless said inmate has served on good behavior seven years of imprisonment or one-third of the prison term imposed by the sentencing court, whichsoever first occurs." Ga. Code Ann. §42-9-45(F) (1999). These provisions may have been the source of the seven-year figure DeNiro offers, although it's more likely that the number was chosen without research and at random.

In any event this mistake by the filmmakers is rather academic since in a conversation between the private eye Kersek and Sam Bowden we learn why Cady served his full sentence. "Cady had a job in the kitchen. There was this other inmate workin' in there with him. He was an obstinate s.o.b., hated Cady's cigar smoke and he was always bitchin' and moanin' about it. Well, one day they found him with his neck broke, his tongue bit off. . . . They never could place Cady at the scene of the accident, if you want to call it that. At least not out loud. But the parole board, they kept him in for another seven years."

19. Bowden is also dead wrong. Precisely fourteen years before the year this version of *Cape Fear* was made, and as chance would have it in a case arising in Georgia where the backstory of Scorsese's film is set, the U.S. Supreme Court held that imposing the death penalty for rape is grossly disproportionate to the crime and therefore a violation of the Eighth Amendment. *Coker v. Georgia*, 433 U.S. 584 (1977).

20. Raymond M. Brown, A Plan to Preserve an Endangered Species: The Zealous Criminal Defense Lawyer, 30 Loyola of Los Angeles Law Review 21, 30 (1996).

21. One film reference book describes Nolte's Sam Bowden as "a mean-spirited womanizer" who "railroaded" DeNiro's Cady into prison. Jay Robert Nash & Stanley Ralph Ross, 1992 Motion Picture Guide Annual, at 47.

22. This view is espoused by the author of one of the leading books on Scorsese. "Scorsese's basic approach to re-working *Cape Fear* eliminated the white hats and the black hats, the good guys versus bad guys dualism." Les Keyser, note 13 *supra*, at 215. This view, like the view that for Scorsese Cady is the sinned against and Bowden the sinner, requires systematic falsification of the two characters as Scorsese presents them. Keyser follows through beautifully when he describes Bowden as "an attorney prone to cutting corners for powerful clients, cheating on his wife, and alternately ignoring then abusing his adolescent daughter." *Ibid*. In fact the only powerful client we see in Bowden's professional life is Tom Broadbent, the senior partner in Bowden's firm. Sam, who is

representing Broadbent's daughter in a bitter divorce case, categorically refuses to suborn perjury at his boss's behest. The last time Sam cheated on Leigh was long before the film begins, although admittedly he is tempted by Lori Davis (Illeana Douglas). And it's absurd to speak of Scorsese's Bowden as abusing Dani. Keyser goes on to whitewash Scorsese's Max Cady, whom he describes as having been "cheated" by Bowden's suppression of "exculpatory" evidence in the rape case, as if this sociopath had been framed or something. *Ibid.*

A similar view is offered by the author of perhaps the most provocative journal article on Scorsese's film. See Richard K. Sherwin, *Cape Fear*: Law's Inversion and Cathartic Justice, 30 University of San Francisco Law Review 1023 (1996). Sherwin sees Scorsese's Max Cady as the "dark double" who embodies all the dysfunctionalities within the Bowden family but in Sherwin's discussion of the backstory Cady morphs into something close to an injured innocent and Bowden into something close to a swine: "Sam's imperious act of vigilantism, his decision to assume the role of judge, condemning his client when he should have been his client's most zealous advocate, has unleashed an even more violent force of vigilantism." *Id.* at 1041. "Sam does not kill Cady at the end, but . . . if he did kill the secured Cady when no threat was then apparent, is this not an unjustified form of homicide?" *Id.* at 1042.

23. David Rensin, "The Raging Talent of Martin Scorsese: A Playboy Interview," *Playboy*, April 1991, at 64.

24. By 1985 almost every state had passed some form of rape shield law. Cassia C. Spohn, note 15 *supra*, at 127. By 1998 the only state that had not enacted such a statute was Arizona. Christopher Bobst, Rape Shield Laws & Prior False Accusations of Rape: The Need for Meaningful Legislative Reform, 24 Journal of Legislation 125, 132 (1998). However, with some exceptions the Arizona Supreme Court has prohibited character evidence of unchastity either to impeach the credibility of a complainant or for substantive purposes on the issue of consent. *State ex. rel. Pope v. Superior Court*, 545 P.2d 946, 953 (Ariz. 1976).

25. Had Cady been killed either while breaking into or after having broken into the Bowdens' home, the killing would probably have come within North Carolina's self-defense doctrine, which is based on the "principle that one does not have to retreat regardless of the nature of the assault upon him when he is in his own home and acting in defense of himself, his family, and his habitation. . . ." *State v. McCombs*, 253 S.E.2d 906, 910 (N.C. 1979). To prove defense of habitation the homeowner must show that he or she was trying to prevent the intruder from making a "forcible entry into the habitation under such circumstances that the occupant reasonably apprehends death or great bodily harm to himself or other occupants at the hands of the assailant or believes that the assailant intends to commit a felony." *Id.* at 910. Whether or not the homeowner used excessive force is a question for the jury. *State v. Roberson*, 368 S.E.2d 3, 6 (N.C. 1988). In view of Cady's previous behavior towards the Bowdens it would not have been hard for Sam to convince a jury that he reasonably believed Cady planned to harm him and his family.

However, once an intruder in North Carolina actually "gains entry into an occupied dwelling, the usual rules of self-defense replace the rules governing defense of habitation." *State v. Roberson, supra* at 6. The right to kill in self-defense is "based on the necessity, real or reasonably apparent, of killing an unlawful aggressor to save oneself from imminent death or great bodily harm at his hands." *State v. Norman*, 378 S.E.2d 8, 12 (N.C. 1989). North Carolina recognizes both perfect and imperfect self-defense. If Cady had been shot to death after entering the Bowdens' home, Sam could invoke the right of perfect self-defense if he showed: (1) that he believed killing the intruder was the only way to save himself from death or great bodily harm; (2) that under the circumstances his belief was reasonable; (3) that he himself was not the aggressor in the deadly confrontation; and (4) that he did not use excessive force. *State v. Webster*, 378 S.E.2d 748, 752 (N.C. 1989). It seems unlikely that a North Carolina jury would convict Bowden of anything under the circumstances. But if it found that he had used excessive force, he could invoke the right of imperfect self-defense but might still be convicted of voluntary manslaughter. *Ibid.*

26. At least four times before the murder of Kersek, Scorsese's Cady has displayed this Shadowesque power: when he vanished from sight while following the Bowdens to the ice cream parlor, when he vanished from their boundary wall, when he stole the piano wire and when he poisoned the Bowdens' dog.

27. An accurate quotation, but once again the attribution to the ABA is wrong. See Model Code of Professional Responsibility, Canon 7 (1991). Ironically, by 1991 a large number of states had removed the language of "zeal" from their versions of the Canon. Raymond M. Brown, note 20 *supra*, at 30.

28. Richard K. Sherwin, note 22 *supra*, at 1042.

29. In addition to the essays cited *supra*, see Anthony J. Sebok, Does an Objective Theory of Self-Defense Demand Too Much?, 57 University of Pittsburgh Law Review 725. "*Cape Fear* is a frightening movie because it reveals that there is a gap between the risks that society demands we accept and the amount of protection that society is capable of providing. The imminence rule of self-defense demands that regardless of [Bowden's] certitude that [Cady] will do something horrible to him and his family, [he] must not go outside the law to prevent those terrible things from happening. But the law cannot offer enough protection to insure that, as a result of its demand that [Bowden] do nothing, [Cady] will not succeed anyway." If a person is found criminally liable for taking the law into his own hands under these circumstances, the court is proclaiming "that the gap is simply part of the social contract and it is an irreducible part of living in a free society." *Id.* at 744-745.

30. See Madison Smartt Bell, "Witness" [collected in Madison Smartt Bell, *The Barking Man and Other Stories* (Ticknor & Fields, 1990), and anthologized in Jay Wishingrad, ed., *Legal Fictions: Short Stories About Lawyers and the Law* (Overlook Press, 1992)].

31. In *Just Cause* (1995, starring Sean Connery, Laurence Fishburne and Kate Capshaw), director Arne Glimcher offers a climax that fuses the *mano a mano* in the swamp from J. Lee Thompson's *Cape Fear* and the surprise twist from Billy Wilder's (and Agatha Christie's) *Witness for the Prosecution*.

32. This tradition begins with the crucial scene in *Dirty Harry* (1971) where Clint Eastwood as Harry tortures the wounded and helpless Scorpio (Andy Robinson) in order to make him tell where he's buried a teen-age girl alive. In his opening statement in *. . . And Justice for All* (1979) Al Pacino as David Kirkland cries out to the jury that the sadistic judge he's been forced to defend on a rape charge is guilty as hell. Gary Oldman's character in *Criminal Law* (1989) tries to atone for securing the acquittal of a psychopathic serial killer (Kevin Bacon) by befriending the man and betraying his confidential communications to the police. In *Presumed Innocent* (1990) criminal lawyer Alejandro Stern (Raul Julia) can get an acquittal for the innocent Rusty Sabich (Harrison Ford) only by blackmailing the corrupt judge (Paul Winfield) into making rulings favorable to the defense. In *The Bonfire of the Vanities* (1990) Tom Hanks as Sherman McCoy temporarily escapes the politically correct lynch mob in charge of the Brooklyn judicial system by committing perjury. What makes Scorsese's *Cape Fear* slightly different from the above films although still within their ambit is that the crucial scene is never shown but only described many years later.

CHAPTER 9

An Unsung Classic of the Warren Court

Among all the American movies that take law and lawyers as their subject, the ones that are most familiar to and admired by attorneys and laypersons alike are the established classics of the years that roughly coincide with the golden age of the Warren court, such as *12 Angry Men* (1957), *Anatomy of a Murder* (1959), *Inherit the Wind* (1960), and *To Kill a Mockingbird* (1961). But just about everyone interested in the law-film interface seems to have overlooked one superb movie from that era whose title is far from a household name, which has never been released on video or DVD and is rarely seen on cable or satellite, but which richly deserves the attention of everyone interested in the creative use of legal material.

Man in the Middle (Pennebaker-Belmont/20th Century-Fox, 1963). Producer: Walter Seltzer. Cinematographer: Wilkie Cooper. Music score: John Barry (with theme music by Lionel Bart). Screenplay: Keith Waterhouse, Willis Hall. Source novel: Howard Fast, *The Winston Affair* (Crown, 1959). Director: Guy Hamilton. Principal cast: Robert Mitchum (Lieutenant Colonel Barney Adams), France Nuyen (Kate Davray), Barry Sullivan (General Kempton), Trevor Howard (Major Kensington), Keenan Wynn (Lieutenant Charles Winston), Sam Wanamaker (Major Kaufman), Alexander Knox (Colonel Burton).

In several senses this film is not a product of the Warren years nor even an American work at all. Its story unfolds in India during World War II and most of it was shot on an estate not far from London.[1] The director, Guy Hamilton (1922-), is an Englishman born in Paris.[2] The screenwriters, the cinematographer, the composers, two of the principal actors (Trevor Howard and Alexander Knox), and countless subordinate actors and technicians were British. But in a genuine sense this film captures the spirit and ethos of the Warren Court more compellingly than any movie made in the United States—including *To Kill a Mockingbird*.

If you asked a hundred well-informed people to name the fictional lawyer character who most perfectly embodies the idealism of the Warren years, ninety or more would likely give the same answer: Atticus Finch. But despite all the excellences of both Harper Lee's 1960 novel and the 1961 movie starring Gregory Peck, Atticus never faces a moral crisis or develops as a person in the course of the story. He is from the start and remains to the end the soul of decency as both lawyer and human being, and the client he tries to save is a black man who on the facts can't possibly have committed the rape he's being tried for. In *Man in the Middle* the protagonist faces a very real moral crisis, one that forces him to decide whether his obligation to his client requires him to destroy his own career in order to save a person who clearly isn't worth the sacrifice, and his development as a person hinges on how he resolves this dilemma.

Like *To Kill a Mockingbird*, *Man in the Middle* is based on a novel. The most fruitful approach to understanding the film is to begin with the book and its author.

Howard Fast was born in New York City on November 11, 1914, graduated from George Washington High in 1931, and began his long and productive life as a writer with the novel *Two Valleys* (1933), published when he was eighteen. His best known mainstream novels deal either with American history (*Conceived in Liberty*, 1939; *Citizen Tom Paine*, 1943; *Freedom Road*, 1944), or ancient history (*Spartacus*, 1951), or the American Jewish experience (*The Immigrants*, 1977; *Second Generation*, 1978). Under the pseudonym of

E.V. Cunningham he also turned out more than twenty novels of crime and suspense. But writing well over ninety books did not exhaust Fast's energies. He joined the Communist party, served a prison term in 1947 for contempt of Congress, became a victim of the blacklist, started his own publishing house to release the books he wrote during the McCarthy years that his fellow victim Dalton Trumbo has called "the time of the toad,"[3] ran for Congress on the American Labor Party ticket, and picked up enough awards to fill a cabinet. As the blacklist eased in the late Fifties his books were again issued by an established house, Crown Publishers, beginning with the historical novel *Moses, Prince of Egypt* (1958) and, a year later, *The Winston Affair* (1959). He died on March 12, 2003.

"I spent two weeks the summer before it was published at a resort in the Adirondacks," Fast wrote me in 1996, "sitting at a table with the psychiatrist who testified at the actual trial. I got part of the story from him, and he never quite forgave me for not making him the hero of the book. . . . He felt that he with his testimony deserved that honor."[4]

There are huge differences between Fast's novel and the movie version of four years later but they share a core story which will help us understand the filmmakers' innovations. Both works take place during World War II and are set in India, which Fast had covered while serving as a war correspondent for *Esquire* and *Coronet* magazines in 1945. Large numbers of British and U.S. troops are serving in the area side by side and tension between the two armies is running high. Barney Adams, a West Point graduate and wounded combat veteran whom his superiors expect to rise high and fast up the chain of command, is assigned by theater commander General Kempton as defense counsel at a court-martial. The defendant, Lieutenant Charles Winston, is a middle-aged misfit who at a military outpost in the boondocks cold-bloodedly shot to death a sergeant in the British army named Quinn in full view of several witnesses. In order to restore unity with their British allies, the American commanders are determined that Winston be tried promptly and hanged. But since the defendant's brother-in-law happens to be a Congressman, the court-martial must be conducted not in the drumhead style of Melville's *Billy Budd* but in a seemly manner with the facade of due process preserved. Although never issuing Adams a direct order, General Kempton makes clear that this is a show trial and that the defense is not to press the only theory available: that Winston was and still is insane. With only a few days to prepare, Adams visits the huge military hospital where Winston was taken for diagnosis after he was arrested. There he encounters Colonel Burton, the ruthless hospital commander; Major Kaufman, the psychiatrist in charge of the neuro-psychopathic ward; and a nurse named Kate who worships Kaufman but begins to fall in love with Adams. Visiting the isolated outpost where the murder took place, Adams interviews Major Kensington, a psychiatrist in the British army. Everyone with professional expertise admits privately to Adams that his client is insane but a "lunacy board" of military doctors with no psychiatric experience has ruled to the contrary. At a press conference before the trial, Adams responds to an Indian journalist's question with the statement that might does not make right and justice can only exist apart from power. Once the court-martial begins he jumps the reservation and goes all out to establish an insanity defense, clearly destroying his own military career in the process.

So much for the similarities between novel and movie. If rights to *The Winston Affair* had not been purchased from Fast before the film was made, he could have sued for copyright infringement and certainly would have won. But much of what makes *Man in the Middle* so fascinating comes not at all from the novel but from the filmmakers' often radical alterations, which affected everything from overall tone and thrust to dozens of details.

The great virtue of *The Winston Affair* is that, unlike most fiction set in the past, it avoids anachronism. Having spent part of 1945 as a Far East war correspondent, Fast knew what India looked and smelled and felt like in that time when it was crowded with U.S. and British troops. His local color rings true and he organizes his novel around then current social issues, conflicts and perceptions, without any discernible influx of story material from the late 1950s when he wrote the book. The great deficiency of *The Winston Affair* is that, like so much "socially conscious" fiction, it's heavy on earnest rhetoric and light on drama. Conversely, one of the prime strengths of *Man in the Middle* is that Fast's Debate on Great Issues tone is either scrapped or, where kept, is made subordinate to story and character. But while Fast studiously avoided anachronisms, the movie hinges on them.

What specific aspects of *The Winston Affair* were dropped or altered in *Man in the Middle*, why were those changes made and how did the alterations affect the meaning of the movie? Answering these questions reveals much of what makes each work tick to a different rhythm than the other.

The most sensible place to begin is with the first few paragraphs of the novel and the first minute or so of the movie. These are the only moments of either work in which Barney Adams is not present, but aside from that they have not a thing in common. Howard Fast opens the novel with a banal exchange of dialogue between General Kempton and his sergeant. Guy Hamilton opens the movie with a stunning pre-credits sequence of quiet calm and graphic violence as we watch Winston stride from his quarters to the tent barracks, walk into Sergeant Quinn's canvas cubicle, take out a pistol and pump four bullets into him. In the novel we never see the murder at all.

Barney Adams of course is the main character in both the novel and the film but his biography differs sharply in the two works. Fast's protagonist is 28 years old, six years out of West Point, and a Captain. He "ranked first in military law at West Point . . . and . . . graduated from Harvard Law School with honors." (13) The Barney Adams of the movie is much older, from his looks one would say in his middle forties as Robert Mitchum was when he played the role, and accordingly holds the higher rank of Lieutenant Colonel. Mitchum's character is also a West Point graduate and a wounded combat veteran but knows next to nothing about military law and certainly never went to a civilian law school. This version of Adams has invested much more of himself in his career as a soldier, and if he sacrifices that career trying to save his pathetic and disgusting client, the stakes are much higher than they are for his counterpart in Fast's novel. This alteration also makes the movie far more dramatic.

Intertwined with these divergent backgrounds are differences in characterization. One reviewer of *The Winston Affair* called the novel's Barney Adams "little more real than Hawkeye or Sir Galahad. . . ."[5] and another described the character as "so attractive, in fact, that it is a pity no one like him has ever existed."[6] Fast himself more than once compares Adams to a Boy Scout but the protagonist of the novel is at root an East Coast aristocrat, thoughtful, introspective, usually soft-spoken, a man who, even though a professional soldier, would not be out of place in a Wall Street law firm or a Louis Auchincloss novel. Robert Mitchum makes this character both more realistic and more dramatically interesting by portraying him as a sort of Philip Marlowe in khaki. The jeep driver assigned to Fast's protagonist is Corporal Baxter, a 23-year-old Tennessee redneck. Driving Adams through the teeming streets of the city in India where the novel is set, Baxter refers to the natives as "waugs" and then explains: "A waug is a nigger, local variety." (27). This is the book's only reference to blacks or, to use the politically correct term of the time, Negroes. In the film, which is also set during the war years when the armed forces were still segregated, Mitchum's driver is still called Corporal Baxter but has become black. This is an anachronism since the film like the novel takes place in a segregated army, but it's linked to one of the main elements that renders the film far more dramatic than the novel both in terms of 1963 and of today.

"I could not run this hospital for a day without discipline. And I damn well could not run the Jews in it without discipline. . . . Has it ever occurred to you to wonder how they all manage the medical degrees and the safe berths?" (43) The speaker is Colonel Burton, commander of the general hospital, first but by no means last of the villains in *The Winston Affair* who are characterized by their anti-Semitism. Adams in the novel responds like any good liberal of the time. "I had six Jews in my [infantry] company, but four of them were killed in action and the other two were shot up. . . ." (43) Later that day, before ever talking with Winston, Adams discusses his client with the British psychiatrist Major Kensington and learns that Winston was a paranoiac who believed he was being plotted against by "international Jewry, the Elders of Zion, the whole kit and kaboodle of Nazi filth." (61) Then, during a prison-cell interview with Adams, Winston calls Major Kaufman "that lousy Jew bastard" and claims that he killed Sergeant Quinn under orders from God, who is not on but literally in his side. "He stays here and burns." (69) The next day, discussing the case with Adams, Kaufman describes Winston as exhibiting "a pattern of latent homosexuality" and the murdered Sergeant Quinn as "a homosexual, without any question . . . [who] used [Winston] opportunistically and sadistically." (78) Later, over lunch with Adams, Kaufman calls Winston a man "whose twisted life process revolved around a maniacal hatred of Jews, who is a decaying cesspool of every vile chauvinism and hatred ever invented . . . who spat in my face and called me a kike and a sheeny. . . ." (86) In *Man in the Middle* Winston gets no messages from God and refers to the psychiatrist only as "that Doctor Creepy Kaufman . . . always sniveling around." Directed by Guy Hamilton and superbly portrayed by Keenan Wynn, Winston is neither a latent homosexual nor an anti-Semite. He's still paranoid to the point of psychosis but his sickness is rooted almost exclusively in what the film-makers deemed more dramatic and relevant in 1963: hatred of blacks and of minorities in general.

When Adams in the novel is having his first prison-cell interview with his client, Winston asks him: "God damn it to hell, mister, what are you? A lousy kike in disguise?" (69) At the exact same point in the movie, Keenan Wynn screams at Mitchum: "What are you, a lousy wog-lover?" Except for one or two very brief anti- Semitic outbursts, the Winston of Fast's novel is portrayed as a passive character, and both before and during the trial Major Kaufman assures us that the defendant is a man "whose soul is warped and corroded beyond repair, whose mind is decaying and dying. . . ." (86-87) "Even if prevented from suicide, this disintegration will continue and the soul will die." (195) The Winston of the movie is far more aggressive, his disease more menacing; not just because we have seen him commit a vicious murder but because of his diatribes in the prison-cell interviews with Mitchum's Barney Adams.

"The war is nothing. It's what's going to happen after that counts. It's going to start here in Asia. East against West. Black against white. Sergeant Quinn was not on our side, he was on the other. He was a bad influence. He was spreading sedition. He was altogether an evil man. He'd sit and spout democracy, then he'd go out. . . . Up into the hills, one of these native villages. He had women up there. Black women. I saw him! And then he'd come back and tell us about this brave new world that he and his black brothers were going to make after the war was over. I mean, Colonel, I can only take so much of that."

"I watched him. This was no sudden decision, Colonel. I watched him for months. I followed him. He never knew it. I used to follow him up that hill and watch him with those black witches up there. He was defiling the race, Colonel. He was defiling the white race. He wasn't fit to live in a white man's world."

These maniacal outbursts have no counterpart in the novel, nor has the powerful scene where after the last of these conversations Wynn demands that Mitchum get out of his cell. "Nigger! Nigger! You cotton-picking jigaboo!" he screams at his black jailer, then with a look of utter contempt at Mitchum: "Take your brother out of here." In the corridor, Mitchum has the following dialogue with the black MP sergeant.

"Does he do that often?"

"He does it."
"You don't let it bother you?"
"Nah. The poor fella's crazy."

As Mitchum is leaving, the sergeant takes Wynn out for his daily exercise. Guy Hamilton places us with Mitchum, looking down into the sunken prison yard, watching Wynn pace back and forth in an enclosed stone cube that is a perfect visual correlative for his racism. From Fast's perspective the "flaw in the filming was that they omitted anti-Semitism. . . . The film producers were simply unwilling to deal with it."[7] From 40-odd years' distance, however, Hamilton's and the screenwriters' substitution of one form of vicious prejudice for another seems designed not so much to evade controversy as to intensify it.

The two psychiatrist characters play prominent roles in both novel and movie, but except for the fact that privately they both agree that Winston is hopelessly insane their functions in the two works are quite different. Major Kensington as Fast wrote him serves little dramatic purpose beyond providing non-American and therefore in terms of the storyline non-biased confirmation of Winston's insanity. In his first interview with Kensington, which takes place very early in the novel, Adams demands that the British major testify as a defense witness but Kensington is subsequently ordered by his own superiors not to appear at the court-martial and in fact he doesn't. The Kensington of the movie (Trevor Howard) volunteers his testimony and is the only witness Adams calls to establish Winston's insanity. In the novel Adams shames Major Kaufman into turning over the report on Winston's sanity which Kaufman had prepared and Colonel Burton had suppressed, while in the movie the report reaches Adams by other means discussed below. At the court-martial according to Fast, Kaufman testifies as a defense witness and is later punished for it by being sent to a hellhole in the jungle. The Kaufman of the movie (Sam Wanamaker) is transferred *before* the trial to a remote outpost so that he can't testify and is killed in a jeep accident while racing to get back and appear for the defense. In a nutshell, the film version of the struggle to save the worthless Winston carries a higher price tag than the loss of a decent person's career.

In *The Winston Affair* the nurse who works under Kaufman and falls in love with Adams is Lieutenant Kate Sorenson, an officer in the U.S. Army. In *Man in the Middle* she is Kate Davray (France Nuyen), a civilian, whose mixed blood involves her in the film's central issues as Fast never involves her pale counterpart in the novel. "Look at me, Barney. Look at me! I am part French, part Chinese. Can't you imagine how much I despise the Winstons of this world? But I couldn't be his executioner." The Kate character's contribution to Adams' efforts to save Winston takes quite different forms in the two works. During the lunch break on the first day of the novel's court-martial she slips Adams a clearly insane letter Winston wrote to her while a patient in the psycho ward. Later she takes the stand to testify for the defense and her evidence is confirmed by Professor Chatterjee, a local authority on graphology, who utters his expert opinion that the handwriting of the letter is that of an insane person. Since no such letter exists in the film, Chatterjee isn't a character at all and Kate never appears as a witness but instead makes her contribution to the defense in a more intensely dramatic way: she steals from the hospital a carbon of Kaufman's suppressed report on Winston's sanity and then has sex with Adams in order to induce him to take the stolen report and use it.

Radical as all these changes are, they pale by comparison with the changes at the climax of each work. In the novel the panel of nine judges ranging in rank from Captain to Colonel finds Winston not guilty by reason of insanity, the decision turns out not to exacerbate but rather to relieve the ill feeling between Yanks and Brits and, so that joy reigns all around, on his way back to a stateside mental hospital Winston slashes his wrists and kills himself. As one underwhelmed reviewer put it, "Readers may be reassured to find that right is absolutely O.K. and, in the end, wins."[8] Guy Hamilton and the screenwriters vastly improved on the novel's ending by reversing, complicating and darkening it—if indeed that is what they did. In the film there literally is no verdict scene, we are left to figure out for ourselves what the court decided, and the two clues we are given leave more than a little room for doubt. In the final scene where he's saying goodbye to France Nuyen, Mitchum remarks: "Just because you can't lick them, that doesn't mean you have to join them." The clear implication is that Winston has been found guilty and hanged. Except that the noses of the big brass have been rubbed in their own hypocritical filth, the destruction of Adams' career and his separation from the woman he's come to love and the loss of Major Kaufman's life have accomplished nothing. But Mitchum's very last words to Nuyen —"They'll make out all right"—may mean that, just as at the end of Howard Fast's novel, Anglo-American unity remains as strong as ever despite the fact that the court found Winston not guilty by reason of insanity. The final moments of the film are compatible with either view: we see American and British troops parading proudly side by side to the blare of martial music while Adams in the jeep with the black driver goes off in the opposite direction, alone.

But what in the world motivated him? Why does Barney Adams ruin his career in what seems a foredoomed attempt to save a pathetic and disgusting murderer? A quick reading of *The Winston Affair* suggests that Fast's answer is: because he's a Boy Scout at heart and it's the right thing to do. A closer reading hints at another possibility. In the depth of the night between the two days of the trial, Adams thinks back to the day when at age ten "he left for military school for the first time. At the door of their house he clung to his mother, his face pressed against her, his arms around her. He thought to himself then: They'll have to tear me away from her. They'll have to tear my arms off." (175-176) His father says to him: "Be a man now, Barney. That will be expected of you now at all times. You are the son of a soldier and the grandson of a soldier, and you are now going to learn to be a soldier yourself." (176) Is his committed defense of Winston a form of subtle revenge against the military life to which family tradition had condemned him? In any event he's an honors grad of Harvard Law and will certainly have no trouble as a civilian attorney once the war is over.

For Robert Mitchum's Adams, who has no law degree and knows nothing but a soldier's life, the future will be bleaker assuming he survives the war at all. Why did this version of the character throw it all away in what not only seems to be but clearly is from the start (unless you interpret "They'll make out all right" to mean the court found Winston insane) a foredoomed struggle to save the defendant's life? By what steps did he reach the decision to destroy his career on Winston's behalf? Guy Hamilton and the screenwriters make it clear that Mitchum's Adams begins as a good soldier, saluting smartly and doing his commanders' bidding, content to play his role in the coming show trial and get a promotion as his reward. When the junior defense team members, who are lawyers in civilian life, propose that he move to disqualify various members of the court-martial panel, Mitchum flatly refuses to consider the option. "You men are civilian lawyers. You've got a living to go back to. I make my living right here in the army, gentlemen. Can't you just see me challenging a senior officer on the ground that he's a birdbrain?" When Trevor Howard as Major Kensington offers a cynical take on the forthcoming trial, Mitchum says very little to make us disagree with the major's perspective.

> "You've got to go through the motions, don't you? . . .
> Oh, come off it, I know the score. You can plead anything
> for Winston except insanity because if he's insane he's
> not guilty. Right? But he's got to be found guilty because
> he's to hang. And he's got to hang, if only to save the
> American command a good deal of embarrassment."
> "He's got to hang because he's a murderer."
> "He's mad all the same. The man is a paranoiac.
> He's an incurable psychopath."

When France Nuyen as Kate Davray offers him the carbon of Kaufman's report, he is indignant at her for having stolen it; and when he finds it waiting for him in her living room after he has spent the night with her, he tosses it down and stalks out. Even as late as the press conference on the morning before the trial, we are left in doubt whether Mitchum really believes his own reply to the Indian journalist's question. "Justice exists only in its own right. It exists apart from power and apart from might. Expedience can have no part in justice." Certainly his fellow officers think the latter and congratulate him for it. "You know that's a good line? Expedience can have no part in justice. Good quote!"

Within the universe of the film, Mitchum's decision to go all out in Winston's defense is explained, to the extent it's explained at all, in nonlegal terms: he's moved by the unanimous consent of the professional psychiatrists Kaufman and Kensington and of minority characters like Kate and the black MP, and he's outraged at the unsubtle scheming of Colonel Burton and General Kempton to sabotage an insanity defense he had no intent of seriously pressing until their heavyhanded moves got him angry. But everything in the movie pushes us to supplement this internal account, to go outside the film and into the real world, not of 1944 but of 1963, where we find implied an additional answer that reverberates with echoes from the Warren court. Mitchum sacrifices himself because he is *de facto* a lawyer and this is his obligation to his client, regardless of the cost to others or himself.

In the typical lawyer films of the 1930s — *The Mouthpiece* (1932), *Lawyer Man* (1932), *Counsellor at Law* (1933) and a host of others — the attorney protagonist's clients were usually portrayed as incarnations of what Holmes in seeking to distinguish law from morality called the "bad man,"[9] and the prevailing tone towards the profession was an overwhelming cynicism. Such typical films of our own generation as . . . *And Justice for All* (1979), *The Penalty Phase* (1986) and *Criminal Law* (1989) are, if anything, even more cynical and hostile towards the legal enterprise than their counterparts from the talkies' first decade. But the lawyer films from the Fifties and early Sixties tend to be far more idealistic and to feature attorney protagonists who represent unpopular clients or causes, not only without fee but often at great personal and professional cost. One thinks of Macdonald Carey as the aptly named

Douglas Madison in Don Siegel's *Count the Hours* (1953) representing a migrant farmer (John Craven) charged with the brutal murders of the man and woman he worked for; of Glenn Ford as the quixotic law professor defending an innocent Chicano youth (Rafael Campos) in *Trial* (1955); of Anthony Quayle in Alfred Hitchcock's *The Wrong Man* (1956) going to court for the wrongly accused Henry Fonda; of Paul Newman abandoning his lucrative tax practice to represent the innocent Robert Vaughn in *The Young Philadelphians* (1959); of Spencer Tracy defending Dick York's right to teach evolution in *Inherit the Wind* (1960); and of Gregory Peck as Atticus Finch in *To Kill a Mockingbird* (1961) defying his town's racism in a hopeless attempt to save the falsely accused black man played by Brock Peters. Robert Mitchum as Barney Adams in *Man in the Middle* stands squarely in this idealistic if not idealized tradition and may indeed culminate it: his client is a guilty monster, his cause is far from noble and he pays a much higher price for his lawyerlike loyalty to what in the last analysis is much closer to Holmes' "bad man" than to the typical clients and causes of lawyers in the films that roughly coincide with the Warren years. "It's easy to fight for the innocent but when you fight for the sick, for the warped, for the lost, then you've got justice." Beyond this point, where could the tradition go?

Just as Mitchum paid the price for representing Keenan Wynn, so the movie pays for the power it generates. The storyline is conspicuously dependent on anachronisms, and the crucial leap that the film asks viewers to make—from the murder of an English NCO for consorting with native women in the India of 1944 to the civil rights struggles in the American South of almost twenty years later—might have fazed a Nijinski. The British director too often gives American roles to actors with strong British accents (most noticeably Alexander Knox as Colonel Burton) and, even where the characters are played by Americans, too often has them speak in British locutions. Mitchum's assistants, who are supposed to have been New York lawyers in civilian life, are given lines like "We worked twice round the clock on that one" and "I guess he reckons you'll fill the bill." Another nominal American says of Mitchum: "He seems to enjoy this standing up on his hind legs and saying just what he's been told to say." Asked by Trevor Howard if he'd like water in his tot of gin, Mitchum himself replies: "I'll take it neat." The film's unrealistic portrayal of certain military law matters may pass muster with younger viewers but stand out vividly to those dwindling few who served in a legal capacity during World War II and were still alive when I first started work on this chapter.[10]

The film was poorly received on its first release[11] and remains little known and underappreciated today[12] but I hope in this essay to have persuaded readers to seek it out nevertheless. My enthusiasm for this powerful and evocative picture is due in large part to the fact that, whatever its debt to Howard Fast's novel and Warren Court jurisprudence, it owes *To Kill a Mockingbird* far more. Both Harper Lee's novel (1960) and the classic film version with Gregory Peck (1961) came out between *The Winston Affair* in 1959 and *Man in the Middle* in 1963, and the lasting significance of Guy Hamilton's movie is that it does what Fast's novel, for the simple reason that it came out too soon, could not possibly have done. Mitchum's portrayal of Barney Adams creates a new type of Atticus Finch figure: tough and laconic where Atticus was loving and compassionate; representing a guilty white racist where Atticus defended a sympathetic and indisputably innocent black man in the South of the 1930s; lacking a license to practice law but offering a more challenging and far less reassuring incarnation of the lawyerly ethos that is permanently linked with the Warren years.

NOTES

1. According to Howard Fast, on whose novel the film was based, most of the shooting took place "on Lord Somethingorother's estate about ten miles out of London. I was in London with my family and I watched a

good bit of the filming. Bob Mitchum was wonderful. For me he was the best film actor of his time. Each day he sat quietly on the set, slowly putting away a quart of whisky. When his scene came he never flubbed a word, while the British actors were flubbing all over the place. They never had to do a second take because of Mitchum. . . . I was awed by the ability of the British film makers to reproduce an Indian setting there near London." Howard Fast, letter to Francis M. Nevins, 24 February 1996.

2. Hamilton began his career as assistant to the French director Julien Duvivier. The first several films he directed on his own were detective or adventure thrillers, made in Britain with British casts in the early 1950s. By the end of the decade he had graduated to megabudgeted international co-productions like *The Devil's Disciple* (1959), starring Burt Lancaster, Kirk Douglas and Laurence Olivier, and *A Touch of Larceny* (1960) with James Mason, George Sanders and Vera Miles. Immediately after *Man in the Middle* came the film for which Hamilton is perhaps most fondly remembered, *Goldfinger* (1964), third of the James Bond series with Sean Connery. In the Seventies he came back to direct Roger Moore's first two outings as 007, *Live and Let Die* (1973) and *The Man with the Golden Gun* (1974). Other Hamilton titles include *Funeral in Berlin* (1966), starring Michael Caine as Len Deighton's diffident spy Harry Palmer; *The Mirror Crack'd* (1980), with Angela Lansbury as Agatha Christie's spinster sleuth Miss Marple; and *Evil Under the Sun* (1982), with Peter Ustinov as Christie's Hercule Poirot. He seems to have been retired since 1985.

3. Dalton Trumbo, *The Time of the Toad: A Study of Inquisition in America by One of the Hollywood Ten* (privately printed, 1949). For an account of the entertainment-world blacklist in general, see Victor S. Navasky, *Naming Names* (Viking Press, 1980).

4. Howard Fast, letter to Francis M. Nevins, note 1 *supra*.

5. Karl Nyren, book review, 84 Library Journal 2520 (1 September 1959).

6. Book Review, 35 The New Yorker 225 (17 October 1959).

7. Howard Fast, letter to Francis M. Nevins, note 1 *supra*.

8. Book Review, note 6 *supra*.

9. Oliver Wendell Holmes, Jr., "The Path of the Law," 10 Harvard Law Review 457, 459 (1897).

10. A professor emeritus at St. Louis University School of Law and former career JAG officer criticizes the film on three major points. First, he says, "the basic premise [which is also that of Fast's novel] was unreal: the assumption that in order to maintain good relations with the British it was necessary to find Winston guilty and to hang him even if he was as mad as a hatter. The British were realists and they would have accepted a finding of insanity unless they had reason to believe that such finding was obviously unwarranted and had been reached solely in order to save a murderer merely because he was an American and the victim was British. Had I been the American general's Staff Judge Advocate [which is analogous to a corporate CEO's General Counsel] I would have advised him to seek the cooperation of the British commander and to direct the hospital commander to establish a lunacy commission consisting of an equal number of qualified British and American psychiatrists." Further, he says, some of the procedure at the film's court-martial seems a product of the director's and screenwriters' imaginations. "The applicable military rules of evidence [under the Articles of War in effect during World War II] were essentially the same as the civilian rules on that subject. I don't believe that an unidentified, unsigned carbon copy of a document would be admitted in evidence in any court. Of course, if the hospital commander, Colonel Burton, had admitted that he recognized it as a copy of Major Kaufman's report, the original of which had been destroyed, it could and would have been admitted even though unsigned and a carbon copy." Finally, he suggests, the film may exaggerate the extent to which a military lawyer who went against his commander's wishes would suffer retaliation. "Command influence existed. . . . When as a new second lieutenant . . . I was appointed Trial Judge Advocate (TJA) (prosecutor) of a special court-martial . . . , the

colonel called the members of the new court and the TJA into his office and told us that when he sent a case to the court the accused was guilty and deserved the maximum sentence (which was six months). As a very recent civilian lawyer I almost fainted; as a second lieutenant I kept my mouth shut but when it came to decisions on punishment at the trials I recommended what I considered to be appropriate—and never had any repercussions. . . ." Howard S. Levie (1907-2007), letter to Francis M. Nevins, 10 February 1996.

11. Typical of contemporary reviews was that of Bosley Crowther in the New York *Times*. "The format of the courtroom drama has seldom been used to contain a less taut and engrossing test of justice. . . . [The film consists of] a slow, lethargic series of confrontations between Army men, growling and snarling at one another, and a lot of pushing papers around before the matter is finally settled (at least, I think it is settled) in a clearly irregular and tedious trial. . . . In addition to being slow and unconvincing, the show is also sluggishly played. . . . Mr. Mitchum comes on sleepwalking, grumbling and looking tough, and he stays more or less in that mood all the way through the film. . . . The fate of the poor insane man is not made clear at the end. . . ." Bosley Crowther, film review, New York *Times*, 5 March 1964, at 36. The last quoted sentence is just about the only point Crowther got right.

12. "With such a situation, there should have been more fireworks, but Mitchum's sleepy way negated that, and the picture, which might have been a powerhouse, fizzles somewhat but still has enough innate drama to make it worth your watching." 5 Jay Robert Nash & Stanley Ralph Ross, *The Motion Picture Guide*, at 1841 (Cinebooks, 1986). The account of the film in the Nash & Ross encyclopedia is full of errors and closes with the demonstrably wrong assertion that at the end of the court-martial Keenan Wynn's character "is sent to a hospital rather than a gallows." *Id.*

CHAPTER 10

Judging the Judge

The night of Tuesday, 18 November 1986 was just like most nights for more than fifteen years before in that at least one of the major networks aired a new made-for-TV movie. That particular night CBS broadcast the latest film directed by Tony Richardson. No sooner was it seen by those with the wit or luck to be watching CBS that evening than it got lost amid the thousand-odd movies that had debuted on the small screen since its infancy.[1] A quick release on video and an occasional unheralded rerun on a cable channel have done virtually nothing to make the film better known. Richardson's posthumously published autobiography[2] doesn't mention the film at all (for the understandable reason that the manuscript was completed several years before his death and before the film was made), and the only book about the director published so far[3] lists *The Penalty Phase* only in its filmography, with not a word of discussion anywhere. In this chapter I'll argue that this film is one of the finest law-related movies of our generation and arguably the finest ever made in English with a judge as protagonist.

> *The Penalty Phase*. New World TV, 1986. Producer: Tamara Asseyev. Cinematographer: Steve Yaconelli. Film Editor: David Simmons. Music Score: Ralph Burns. Screenplay: Gale Patrick Hickman. Director: Tony

Richardson. Starring Peter Strauss (Judge Kenneth Hoffman) and Melissa Gilbert (Leah Furman). Featuring, in alphabetical order, Jonelle Allen (Susan Jansen), Karen Austin (Julie), Jane Badler (Katie Pinter), John Harkins (Mr. Hunter), Millie Perkins (Nancy Faulkner), Mitchell Ryan (Judge Donald Faulkner). With Richard Bright (Judge Von Karman), Richard Chaves (Nolan G. Esherman), Rossie Harris (Zach Hoffman), Art LaFleur (Pete Pavlovich). Also in the cast: Stuart Duckworth (Singleton), Ron Campbell (Chris), Michelle Guthrie (Miss Levine), Stacey Pickren (Clair Turnley), Mark Allen (Gil).

Understanding the film's significance requires a quick survey of law-related films from the early 1950s to the present. The years that roughly coincided with the Warren Court saw a resurgence in movies of this sort, which had been few and far between since the early 1930s. But the leitmotif of the Warren-era films tended to be idealistic, and most of what one remembers of the films from these years tends to cast law, lawyers and our legal system in a flattering light. One thinks of Don Siegel's *Count the Hours* (1953) where Macdonald Carey as the aptly named Douglas Madison is ostracized by both his fiancée and the community for defending a migrant farm couple falsely accused of a brutal murder; of Alfred Hitchcock's *The Wrong Man* (1956) where Anthony Quayle as a young attorney with little experience in criminal law defends the innocent Henry Fonda without thought of compensation; of *Trial* (1956) where Glenn Ford plays a law professor who goes to bat for a Chicano youth charged with the murder of a WASP girl; of the paean to the American jury in *12 Angry Men* (1957); of Spencer Tracy as Henry Drummond in *Inherit the Wind* (1961) fiercely defending the right of a teacher in the Tennessee Bible Belt to discuss evolution. Before any of these, of course, one conjures up Gregory Peck as Atticus Finch in *To Kill a Mockingbird* (1961) using all his forensic skills and oratorical power and moral authority to save an innocent black man (Brock Peters) falsely accused of rape. A few films of this era are somewhat less idealistic[4] but most share the dominant ethos.[5]

All that idealism quickly vanished as the Warren era in both legal and film history came to an end and was replaced in both legal and film history by a post-Warren Court anti-Warren Court era. The leitmotif of these films is an acid contempt for law, lawyers and the legal system. More precisely, the makers of most of these films radically denounce the legal system by employing more or less the same strategy: structuring them around defining events that are justified dramatically, psychologically, morally, indeed every way in the world except legally. Think of the crucial Kezar Stadium scene in *Dirty Harry* (1971) where director Don Siegel pulls back the camera into the night sky so that we see only two specks but hear the screams as Clint Eastwood tortures the wounded and helpless Scorpio (Andy Robinson) to make him reveal the place where he's buried a teen-age girl alive. Remember Al Pacino in . . . *And Justice for All* (1979) crying out to the jury that the sadistic judge (John Forsythe) he's been forced to defend on a brutal rape charge is guilty as hell. Set down in the same column Gary Oldman in *Criminal Law* (1989), trying to make amends for securing the acquittal of a psychopathic serial killer (Kevin Bacon) by befriending the man and betraying his confidential communications to the police. And Harrison Ford in *Presumed Innocent* (1990), who is in fact innocent of the murder he's been charged with but gets acquitted only because his attorney (Raul Julia) has blackmailed the corrupt judge (Paul Winfield) into making rulings favorable to the defense. And Tom Hanks in *The Bonfire of the Vanities* (1990) temporarily escaping the politically correct lynch mob in charge of the judicial system by committing perjury. And Nick Nolte in Martin Scorsese's version of *Cape Fear* (1991), who is hounded by his sociopathic former client (Robert DeNiro) because years before, while representing DeNiro, he had suppressed a report that the victim of his brutal rape was sexually active. And I haven't even mentioned any of the movies based on John Grisham novels! A few films from the past few decades are not quite so negative just as a few in the Warren era were not quite so idealistic as the pictures mentioned above.[6] But it's the films I've just evoked that sound the leitmotif for our generation.

Within this context the genius of Tony Richardson's *The Penalty Phase* becomes apparent. It's an artfully choreographed duel of juristic values between the spirit and ethos of the Warren films and those of the films of our own time. On first viewing it's easy to dismiss the film as unsubtle propaganda for the Warren court. But the more often one watches this amazingly rich and nuanced work, the more one becomes aware of what amounts to a second film, lying beneath the surface and perfectly consonant with it in terms of storyline, characterization and visual style but radically at odds with the surface film's moral and juristic valuations. The only way I can attempt to do justice to Richardson's vision is to construct a verbal model of the film, interspersed with readily identifiable subjective commentary in which I suggest how its Janus faces are related. If I succeed in drawing enough attention to this neglected gem, my detailed description will eventually have outlived its usefulness.

Under and immediately after the credits Richardson's images and Ralph Burns' music establish a mood of unease. Ominous looking courthouse facade. People waiting nervously in a corridor. Three women on a bench, joined by an obese bearded man. Lawyer drinking nervously in a nearby bar. A striking-looking black woman in her office studying a campaign poster for herself as a candidate in a judicial election. "The verdict is in." Judge Kenneth Hoffman (Peter Strauss) finishes lacing his sneakers, puts on his robe and takes the bench as the jury files in and their decision is handed to him and he begins to read. "People vs. Nolan G. Esherman. We the jury in the above entitled action find the defendant guilty of count one of the information, murder, victim Susan Cross, a violation of Penal Code Section 187." Cut. "People vs. defendant Nolan G. Esherman." Cut. "People vs. Nolan G. Esherman. We the jury in the above entitled action find the defendant guilty of count 53 of the information, rape, victim, Stacy Ann Foxmore, a violation of Penal

Code Section 261." Cut. "Count 54, People vs. Nolan G. Esherman, we the jury in the above entitled action find the defendant guilty of count 54 of the information, murder, victim Stacy Ann Foxmore, a violation of Penal Code Section 187." Interwoven with shots of Hoffman reading from the bench, becoming so hoarse that he has to pause every so often for a drink of water, we see the prosecutor Susan Jansen (Jonelle Allen), and a clean-shaven obese man among the spectators (John Harkins), and some of the families of the defendant's victims, and of course the murderer himself (Richard Chaves), bearded and dressed like an outlaw biker and glaring hate all around. Cut to the courthouse corridor with the media and prosecutor Jansen. "Would you care to speculate on the outcome of your race against Hoffman?" "I never feel safe with Judge Hoffman up there on the bench." TV reporter: "We are here with the mothers of three of the murder victims. [These are the three women we saw on the bench before a word of dialogue had been spoken.] Mrs. Foxmore, we noticed you were the first to cry during the reading of the verdicts. It must have been unnerving waiting four years for this terrible tragedy to end. . . . " Jansen: "Judge Hoffman's defense rulings are killing me. We have to get rid of Judge Hoffman." Obese man: ". . . We're all gonna be right back here on Monday morning and we're gonna stay here until that—that animal gets the death penalty." Reporter: "Thank you. That was Mr. Hunter, president of the Wasco County Citizens for Justice. . . . We will return next week when the penalty phase of the Nolan Esherman murder trial begins."

On the street outside the courthouse Judge Hoffman encounters Art Singleton (Stuart Duckworth), Esherman's assigned defense counsel. "Art, I want to see you when this trial is over. . . . I'm a little puzzled by some of the things you've been doing. Actually some things you haven't been doing. . . . Like why no insanity defense? . . . Why no search warrant challenge? You just come around and see me when the trial's over."

Next Hoffman joins the other judges of Wasco County who are running for re-election, including his former law partner Donald Faulkner (Mitchell Ryan), for a strategy session prior to a televised debate among all the candidates for judgeships. Most of Hoffman's colleagues are presented as time-serving buffoons who lack minimal integrity but are terrified that his refusal to mouth law-and-order slogans will cost all of them their cushy jobs. The most obnoxious and vocal of them even has a name that sounds like a Nazi. Judge Von Karman (Richard Bright): "Judge Hoffman, the voters aren't going to give a fat rat's butt about what a nice guy you might be." Katie Pinter, public relations person for the incumbents (Jane Badler): "People are afraid out there, Ken. There's no way that you can convey to them the subtleties of being a good judge."

Cut to high-school rowing practice on the Wasco River with Hoffman, his sneakers now explained, serving as coach. The comments he shouts to the team ("Jason, sit up taller! Pivot from your hips!") reveal him as a man with deep concern (obsession perhaps?) with proper technique. After practice comes a significant bit of dialogue when his son Zach (Rossie Harris), who is on the crew, mentions that one of his teammates seems to be suffering from serious back pain. "Do you think I should talk to him?" "It's your boat. You're the coxswain. Use your own judgment." This is followed by a brief exchange along the riverbank between Hoffman and Judge Faulkner's wife Nancy (Millie Perkins). "Such a beautiful river, Ken. . . . It'll be a year next week. I miss her so much." "Yeah, I know you do, Nancy. I miss her too." Previous casual remarks between Hoffman and Zach ("It's your turn to cook, you know") have made it clear that the judge is a single parent but not until much later will we understand his cryptic exchange with his former law partner's wife as opening the first of several trap doors, so to speak, between the surface of this film and its depths.

The next morning, obviously a Saturday, Hoffman and Katie Pinter and the judge's research attorney Leah Furman (Melissa Gilbert) are in the elevator heading for the debate when they encounter another young woman named Julie (Karen Austin). "She used to be Judge Faulkner's court clerk," he explains to Leah. Why she seems to have made him nervous he doesn't explain at all. Trap door number two.

The debate that follows, with the incumbent judges on one side of the stage and the challengers including prosecutor Susan Jansen on the other, vividly evokes the duel between the ethos of the Warren Court and that of this film's and our own time.

> Jansen: "The people are simply fed up with judges who put their interpretation of the law before the liberty and safety of the common citizen. Time and time again we see the criminal manipulating the system for his advantage. And judges such as these not only walk down the primrose path with them but they go out of their way to pave that path with newly created rights for which not even they can find constitutional precedent!"
>
> Hoffman: "I agree, but it's the appellate court that creates these laws. There's no one on this side of the room that wants to see criminals go free. . . . [To the moderator] I think the folks over there have a very low opinion of the average voter. They think they can press the fear buttons and all the sheep out there will vote them an emotional victory. . . ."

The rhetoric gets so heated that Judge Von Karman slips a note to Hoffman telling him to shut up.

That evening, with Zach having just left to go to a movie, Hoffman is alone at home and taking a shower when Leah walks in with some research he asked for and his day's mail from the courthouse. "Your son said to come in." Their dialogue, separated by the shower door, tells us more about Hoffman's earlier life. "Judge Faulkner seemed so— cautious. How long were you two partners?" "About seven years. Yeah, he's always been the conservative one." Then, as she studies a picture of Zach and a woman we haven't seen before: "Your son sure looks like his mother." "Yeah. They were very close." "And now you don't have a woman in your life?" "Are you practicing your cross-examination?" "I can be a little pushy sometimes." How pushy Hoffman discovers when he comes out of the shower wrapped in a towel and finds Leah naked in his bed. What would arouse the protagonists of most movies seems to embarrass this one. "Um, Leah, I'm, uh, uh—I'm sorry—it's, uh, it's just not the right time. . . ." Then, after she has hastily dressed and is about to leave: "Leah, I've, I've made terrible decisions when it comes to women." Trap door number three. As the front door closes behind her Richardson cuts to a table and one of the letters she's just delivered.

Now comes Monday morning and one of the most harrowing scenes in the film as prosecutor Jansen addresses the jury.

> "This is the part of the trial where you will decide to give Nolan G. Esherman life in prison without the possibility of parole, or death. During this hearing you will learn more about Mr. Esherman. His past victims will come here and show you what he did to them. At the end of this hearing I will ask you to order the death of Nolan G. Esherman, this murderer of seventeen innocent children. Ladies and gentlemen, if I could think of a worse penalty I would ask you to give him that. For indeed death is too kind. Slides, please. [During the rest of her address we see images of torment worthy of the Holocaust reflected on her face and body.] Remember the faces of these beautiful girls during your deliberations. I want these images seared into your memories. These are the same soft eyes Mr. Esherman saw, filled with innocent playfulness. Then fear. Then terror. Then the most unbelievable pain. Then death. Then death."

Cut to a recess with Hoffman opening a letter that came in the mail and, from the way Richardson presents it, clearly a duplicate of the one

Leah delivered to his house Saturday. "Get me the court file. . . . Get Jansen and Singleton and get 'em in here right away," he orders.

The ensuing scene between judge, prosecutor and defense attorney not only reveals what was in that letter and how those photographs of Esherman's butchered victims came into the prosecution's hands but brings to center stage the legal issue at this film's heart.

> Hoffman: "Art, am I blind or what? The court file tells me you didn't attack the search warrant in the preliminary hearing, you didn't attack it in the motion court. . . . Art, we've got a case here that rests entirely upon the photographs found in Esherman's apartment. The police dump the photographs in front of Esherman and he confesses. So the confession is linked to the photographs, right? . . . So all the probable cause is created by an anonymous informant. Now we've got a pen pal who says the police invented this anonymous informant and created their own probable cause to get into Esherman's apartment. . . . [Y]ou should have made a motion to suppress the photographs and the confession six months ago. You've got seventeen murder counts resting on the word of an anonymous informant!"
>
> Jansen (furiously): "May I inquire just who is the defense attorney here?"
>
> Hoffman: "The warrant should have been tested even without these letters. I've got to tell you, with them I don't see how we are going to avoid holding a hearing on it."
>
> Jansen: "We're in the penalty phase of this case. Are you telling me you want to stop this case and go back and hear a motion to suppress? . . . There's no precedent for that! You can't do that!"

The scene ends with Hoffman all but ordering Singleton to make a motion to suppress the next morning.

After hours comes another meeting of the judges up for re-election at which over Hoffman's indignant protest they agree to debate their challengers under the auspices of the Citizens for Justice organization. Katie: "It's not important that we win. It's sufficient that we appear to be concerned, willing to listen, willing to make a commitment." Hoffman: "A commitment to what?" Judge Von Karman: "How about a commitment to reality, Hoffman? If you . . . are so hot to get back out on the streets to hustle hypes and whores, then you can do the rest of us a favor and buzz off." Hoffman: "The public already thinks we're a bunch of political prostitutes. Why should we degrade ourselves further by doing one night stands?" Outside the meeting room Hoffman confronts the obese head of the organization: "I think you like to scare people, Mr. Hunter. I think you found a way to have a little power in your life and like most novices you don't know how to use it." Hunter: "Well, judges must be responsive to the people they serve. . . ." Hoffman: " . . . By and large, judges are hard working, unexceptional people. We don't perform very well with the smell of tar and torches in our courtrooms. . . ." Hunter: "We're watching you very closely, Judge Hoffman, I hope you appreciate that."

After these workday pressures Hoffman needs a few drinks, and the next scene takes place in an intime bar where the judge happens once again to encounter Julie, at the previous meeting with whom he seemed so ill at ease. Hoffman: "You look terrific." Julie: "I feel wonderful. Um, I really like the new job and, uh, I'm seeing someone now, um, a nice man, he's, um, an attorney. (Nervous laugh.) I know, I'm trying not to hold that against him." Hoffman: "I've thought about calling you." Julie: "No, you shouldn't do that. . . . I hope things work out for you too. It was nice seeing you." Hoffman moves to a table where a few minutes later Leah joins him and tries to apologize for the previous night. "I want a friend to sleep with. . . . What I would like to find is a man who's not a child. We've been working together for the last six months. I thought you might be him." Hoffman: "Leah, women and I always end up crying. I'm sorry."

Returning home that night, Hoffman listens to his voice mail and hears a message from yet another woman. "I'm the one who wrote you those letters. I just wanted to remind you that I expect you to look into that now. Those cops lied through their teeth about the search warrant. I'll be watching the newspapers to see what you do. . . ."

The next morning at another conference in chambers, Hoffman plays the tape for Jansen and Singleton and orders the defense lawyer to have an investigator question the cops who procured the warrant.

> Singleton: "And what do you think the cops are gonna say? 'Yeah, you caught us. We lied under oath. But you go ahead, let this mass killer out it took us years to put away.' Have you forgotten that we're dealing with real people out there? I'm going to make a motion to send this to Judge Faulkner. Now he issued the warrant. He's the one who should rule on it."
>
> Hoffman: ". . . The case stays here."
>
> Jansen: ". . . You may not like this suggestion, but I think you should transfer this to someone who's not up for election this time around."
>
> Hoffman: "The election does not exist inside that courtroom. The case stays here. [Then, to Singleton] Are you going to move on it or not?"
>
> Singleton: "And what if I don't?"
>
> Hoffman: "I will. I'll appoint an investigator and I'll open a hearing."
>
> Singleton: "Then, Your Honor, you try your case and I'll try mine."

When the fuming defense lawyer has gone, there is an exchange between the prosecutor and Hoffman which shows us that, even though she despises his ideology and wants his job, she also cares for him deeply. Jansen: "Ken, in all candor you're committing suicide."

Hoffman: "In all candor, Sue, if you're planning on wearing this robe you'd better be prepared to do the same thing."

The investigator Hoffman hires is Pete Pavlovich (Art LaFleur), a rumpled working stiff with a huge beer gut who among the several overweight men in the film is the only one presented as likable. Hoffman: ". . . What it boils down to is yes or no. Did they [Detectives Turnley and Dagenpatt] lie to Judge Faulkner on the search warrant? . . . Bad search? No case. Fruit of the poisonous tree. Mr. Esherman takes a walk." The next day, while Hoffman is coaching another practice session along the banks of the Wasco River ("Are you guys rowing or killing fish?"), Faulkner comes by to urge his former partner not to pursue the truth too vigorously and we learn that Pavlovich has gone to San Francisco where Detective Turnley is attending a police convention. "Ken, if this thing blows up, we're all back practicing law next year." (Sounds like a fate worse than death.) Hoffman replies: ". . . If I find out those cops lied to you on the search warrant I'm not going to have much choice, now am I?"

Richardson then returns us to the courtroom where the penalty phase is going forward. Without objection from Singleton, Susan Jansen presents medical testimony about the tortures Esherman inflicted on his victims. At the end of the day's session Pavlovich reports to Hoffman what he learned in San Francisco.

> "It's not easy keeping up with Detective Turnley when he's on one of his binges. . . . [He claims] he had nothing to do with getting the search warrant. It was Detective Dagenpatt's play all the way. . . . But he did say he was told they wouldn't have to testify about the warrant. . . . Dagenpatt and Mrs. Turnley have been taking recess together a little too often. . . . Turnley is drinking nonstop these days. He's near crackup. . . ."

That evening Hoffman goes to Faulkner's house for cocktails and poker with the other judges seeking re-election and the publisher of the local newspaper whose endorsement they want. "Okay, Don, just don't expect me to kiss his butt." "Come on, partner! You played politics to get a judgeship, you gotta play politics to keep it. Don't be so damn self-righteous!" Again Faulkner urges Hoffman not to push his investigation. "Damn it, Ken, why can't you wait till after the election? . . . Why don't you leave the whole thing alone?" Hoffman: "I can't do that. . . . It was your warrant, Don. I should think you'd be interested if the cops lied." An enraged Faulkner tells Hoffman to get out of his house.

The next day is Friday and we are back in court with Jansen questioning the only survivor among Esherman's victims, who testifies in sign language through an interpreter.

"He, he put me on a table. A workbench of some kind. He untied my ankles. He hurt me. I don't want to tell this. . . ."

"What did this man do to you after he raped you?"

"He cut my throat. He cut my vocal cords. Do I have to show them?"

After court Hoffman learns from Pavlovich that Detective Turnley killed himself earlier that day. "Stopped on the side of the freeway and put a hole in his head."

Between the end of the business day and the scheduled debate among judicial candidates that evening, Hoffman apparently has some free time. Richardson first shows him working out intensely on his rowing machine, then making a phone call, then enjoying another sort of workout in Leah's bed. Finally the new lovers go to the debate where Hoffman gives the news about Turnley's death to Faulkner. ". . . It's, uh, it's tragic, but at least you don't have to hold that hearing now." "Probably not. . . . I've got a couple of questions, though, I want to ask you. I looked at the Esherman file this morning. I noticed you appointed Singleton [as defense counsel]. I want to talk to you about that."

What Richardson shows us of the debate sponsored by Citizens for Justice makes most of the other incumbents and most of the challengers look like hypocritical hacks and Hoffman like the beleaguered lone champion of integrity. Under questioning by a judgeship-seeking prosecutor, Hoffman defends his dismissal of fifteen child molestation cases.

> ". . . [S]ome of those cases were so weak the DA waived jury and let the court take the heat. . . . You've got a weak case, you don't have the guts to dismiss it, so you let the judge do it. . . . In fact, Mr. Prosecutor, it appears to me that I've been getting a greater number of your losers since you guys decided to run against us. Now you, you haven't been playing politics with the trial calendar, have you?"

Then, after a torrent of lock-up-the-guilty-bastards rhetoric from Von Karman and other incumbents: "[W]e at this table shouldn't and I won't make you a promise I can't keep."

Saturday afternoon, while Hoffman is with Leah on the rowing machine in his boat shed, Katie drops by to tell him that he must run for re-election on his own: his colleagues have voted him out of their group and she can't serve as his PR person. "You're too honest to be a good client."

Later in Hoffman's chambers Pavlovich reports what he's discovered about the assignment of Esherman's defense counsel. "Singleton had a felony drunk driving charge. It was transferred to Faulkner's court. The charge was reduced to a misdemeanor, no jail, no fine. Even got to keep his bar card. . . ." Hoffman (studying the court file): "Faulkner appointed Singleton to the Esherman case on the same day. . . ." Hoffman then visits Faulkner's former clerk Julie at her house on the river in an effort to learn more about his former law partner's issuance of the Esherman search warrant but what we learn from her other comments is far more revealing. "Look, you're a year late coming through the door. . . .Were you really going to leave her for me?" "Yes," Hoffman replies. "Yes, I was."

Hoffman announces that he will hold a hearing on the legality of the search warrant and subpoenas not only the deputy DA who was present at its issuance but also Detective Dagenpatt and Judge Faulkner, who storms into Hoffman's house. Faulkner: ". . . Why did you subpoena me? What is it you want to know?" Hoffman: ". . . I'm going to have to ask you why you appointed Singleton. . . . And I'm going to find out why Singleton's been ducking the search warrant issue." Then Hoffman tells his ex-partner what he suspects.

> ". . . [T]hose cops had a problem with the Esherman case. They took the problem to [Deputy DA] Gene Waterman and . . . Waterman trotted down to Don Faulkner's chambers to get it solved. . . . Gene says: 'Don, . . . I need a judge willing to bend the law a little bit. All in the interests of justice, mind you.' . . . And then . . . you needed a defense attorney. One who would agree to look the other way on the search warrant. You thought of Singleton. . . . I think you bribed him, Don. . . ."
>
> Faulkner (in desperation): "Look, Ken, can't we find some middle ground? We're talking about fifteen years' friendship!"
>
> Hoffman: "I've got to call you. . . ."
>
> Faulkner (echoing prosecutor Jansen's previous statement): "You're committing political suicide. . . ."

The next scene takes us back to the courtroom and Hoffman's hearing on how the police obtained their search warrant. Under questioning by Hoffman is Detective Dagenpatt (actor uncredited). This new addition to Richardson's gallery of obese grotesques claims to have received a phone call from an anonymous informant to the effect that Esherman was keeping in his apartment photographs of the girls he'd mutilated. Then he testifies, he and his partner Turnley made out the search warrant affidavit which they took to deputy DA Waterman who in turn took it to Judge Faulkner. Subsequently they entered the apartment, found the photographs in a closet as the informant had claimed, and arrested Esherman when he arrived a few minutes later. "He's lying! He's lying, man!" screams Esherman. Dagenpatt goes on to testify that he and Turnley spent two and a half hours searching the apartment before they brought Esherman in for booking. Between segments of the fat sweaty detective's testimony comes a powerful exchange between Hoffman and the prosecutor.

> Jansen: "With all the respect due this court, it is infinitely clear to me that by this investigation the court has gone beyond its proper role. . . ."
> Hoffman: "Ms. Jansen. . . ."
> Jansen: "And has assumed the role of advocate."
> Hoffman: "Sit down, Counselor."
> Jansen: "I think you have already decided this case."
> Hoffman: "Sit down, Counselor. And if you finish that sentence I will have no choice but to hold you in contempt."
> Jansen: "With all respect. . . ."
> Hoffman: "If you accuse me of wilfully refusing to follow the law I'll have no choice, Ms. Jansen. NOW—SIT—DOWN!!"

That evening while the judge and his son Zach are preparing dinner comes another exchange.

> Zach: "Why don't you just have him castrated and let him bleed to death? (Pause) I don't get an answer? . . . Two of those girls went to my school. . . . I've got a right to think that way."
> Hoffman: ". . . I happen to have a job that doesn't

allow me to think those things. And if I do—and I'd be lying to you if I said I don't sometimes—then I'm not allowed to get emotional about it. . . ."

Zach: ". . . I can understand that. I just don't like it."

Hoffman (enraged): "Now where in the hell did you ever hear me say that I liked it?"

The next witness at Hoffman's hearing is Esherman himself. His version of events is that Turnley and Dagenpatt handcuffed him to his bed and searched his apartment without a warrant. After finding the photographs, Turnley left and only came back with a properly executed search warrant after the fact.

The following morning before court begins, Pavlovich shows up with the woman who sent Hoffman the anonymous letters: Clair Turnley (Stacey Pickren), widow of the detective who killed himself. She admits having been Detective Dagenpatt's lover but claims that he had told her the real story about the search warrant.

> "They knew he had done it, they just couldn't prove it. Anyway, he said he just decided to go inside and search the apartment and see what turned up. . . . [T]hey found all those photographs of those d-dead kids. And then all of a sudden Esherman came in and surprised them. And then [Dagenpatt] decided to try to get a search warrant to show that it was issued before they had gone into the apartment so that the search would be okay. . . . He said he took some of the photographs they had found and described what they showed. He wrote it into the . . . affidavit for the warrant and pretended an, an informant had told him all of that. . . . He said they'd never catch him unless they did it that way. He had to do it."

On cross-examination Jansen charges that as a detective's wife Clair had the knowledge to make up her story and that she had motive to do so because Dagenpatt had dumped her. She in turn claims that she had dumped him after he tried to molest her 14-year-old daughter but she admits that she had never made any such charge against the detective until now. Whether she's telling the truth about the molestation of her daughter we never learn and hardly matters since either way our moral judgment on her is equally devastating: by deciding to get even with Dagenpatt by sending those anonymous messages to Judge Hoffman, she has knowingly created a situation that may result in Esherman being set free to rape, mutilate and murder any number of girls her daughter's age.

Later in chambers, after court has adjourned for the day, Leah confesses to Hoffman that she believes both Esherman and Mrs. Turnley. "I don't think Dagenpatt had the warrant when they made that search." Everything hinges on the exact time Judge Faulkner issued the warrant but the numbers on the time stamp are smeared, which means that Hoffman will call Faulkner as a witness the next morning. As the judge is leaving court, his reporter (Mark Allen) takes him aside. "I, I just don't think you're doing the right thing, Ken."

Hoffman comes home to find Faulkner's wife waiting for him, and their dialogue at last begins to open the door wide to the underlying depths of his character and this film.

> Nancy: "If you're going to destroy my husband on the witness stand tomorrow, if you're willing to destroy my husband and my son and my life. . . . If you do that, I am going to do something so evil, so mean, so beyond my imagination of myself. . . ."
>
> Hoffman: "He has an obligation to tell the truth."
>
> Nancy: "Ken, isn't there a point where the legal games and the technicalities come to an end? Are we never allowed to say, no matter what, that man will not get a chance to kill again? Can't you find a way to do that, Ken?"

Hoffman: "Nancy, I don't have the right to do that."

Nancy: "How can you sit up there on the bench and forget the rights of those kids? What about their right to live? Their right not to be ripped apart by a monster? . . ."

Hoffman: ". . . Don has to tell the truth. I don't have the power to change that."

Nancy: "Then we shall all get a good strong dose of the truth, Judge Hoffman. We shall all live by the same rules. And tomorrow morning . . . I shall tell your son, Ken, that his mother did not just drown in that river out there last year. That she was weighted down by forty sleeping pills, the same day you told her that you were going to leave her for that cute little court clerk you were messing around with. . . . Diane had a desperate lovely little dream, Ken. She thought if you became a judge that you would settle down. . . . Do you know who she came to for that dream? My husband. . . . And then you broke her heart. I want to go home and tell my husband that he's not going to be crucified because he did the right thing."

Hoffman: "I'm sorry, I can't promise you that."

Nancy: "Then I will promise you this. If you don't call me by eight o'clock tomorrow morning, I'm telling Zach."

We have reached the crucial moment. Until now Hoffman has been presented as a man of great charisma and compassion and a man with a consuming passion for both personal and judicial integrity. Richardson and Hickman have wanted us to believe in this judge and to be for him. In order to push us in this direction, they have presented most of those who oppose Hoffman or who are threatened by his uncompromising integrity as crypto-Nazis, political hacks, unprincipled powerseekers, obese grotesques, alcoholic or child-molesting cops. There have been a few intimations of another side to the coin—the warnings from Sue Jansen (who has every selfish motive to see Hoffman destroy himself and therefore no selfish motive to warn him) and the court reporter (who has no stake in the matter) that he is on the road to making a horribly wrong decision, the hints about his relationships with women—but now we know the full truth about his womanizing and are torn as he is himself by the immediate decision he must make. If he forces Judge Faulkner to admit that he took part in a conspiracy to circumvent Esherman's rights, his son will know the truth about him. If he doesn't, all pretense of his sterling integrity is smashed.

The next moments display Richardson's seldom-seen flair for Hitchcockian suspense. Morning. Hoffman in his chambers, dangling a necklace with a heart-shaped pendant, gazing at a photo of his dead wife and their son. Zach and the crew innocently rowing on the river. The clock on the judge's desk approaching eight A.M. Faulkner pacing and smoking nervously in the corridor outside the courtroom. Finally Hoffman takes the bench. "The court will call," he says, and then pauses until we are on tenterhooks before he finishes the sentence, "no further witnesses."

Was his decision a selfish one? Has he fatally compromised his integrity in order to preserve his privileged status in the eyes of his son? Might the decision be seen as motivated at least in part by an unselfish desire to save from disgrace his former law partner and friend to whom he owes his own judicial appointment? The film gives us no clues either way but by this point no reasonable viewers see Hoffman in quite the same light as they saw him before. The die has been cast. The pedestal on which he stood has dissolved. From here on we listen to him not as believers taking in the priest's sermon but critically. Judging the judge. Prosecutor Jansen begins her closing argument.

> "Twelve citizens of Wasco County sat in this jury
> box for six horrible weeks and determined that Nolan
> G. Esherman tortured, molested, raped and murdered
> seventeen innocent children. . . . I don't think even this
> court is naive enough to believe [Esherman's and Mrs.
> Turnley's] testimony. If you do, if you dismiss this case

. . . then you are carving in stone a message . . . that our system of justice has failed."

Hoffman's response, which also constitutes his decision, is the longest speech in the film, and the most chilling, and the only sustained attempt by any character in a law-related film of the past few decades to defend the spirit and ethos of the Warren Court.

"Naive and reckless? No. Naive and reckless is when I refuse to follow the law because I don't like the taste it leaves in my mouth. . . . Once we start doing that, there is no law. A judge cannot pick and choose and fashion the law to reach an end he might personally desire. There are rules and they apply to everyone, even to Nolan Esherman. Our law is simple. If the police violate the law to obtain evidence, they don't get to use it. I can't imagine a tougher case for the application of that law. But I will not apologize for it and I will not accept the idea that our system fails when I follow it. And if you keep telling people our system fails when judges do their jobs, then pretty soon they're going to start believing the law doesn't matter anymore. And then there's just fear—and politics. Our law protects our freedoms. And it's my duty to apply that law even when it's painful. Even when it's tragic. There are times when we have to pay a price for our liberties. The testimony presented at this hearing leads the court to the clear conclusion that Detective Dagenpatt fabricated the anonymous informant. The search warrant was illegal and the photographs were illegally seized and the record in this case clearly shows that the defendant's confession was the fruit of the evidence illegally seized at the apartment. The court has no recourse but to order the photographs and the confession suppressed. The charges are dismissed. The defendant is discharged."

Since we are listening to this speech with critical ears, we may notice that most of what Hoffman says might just as well have been said by the Nazi judge played by Maximilian Schell in Stanley Kramer's *Judgment at Nuremberg* (except of course that Kramer doesn't believe in giving bad guys good lines). But the moment Hoffman has finished, critical thinking ends and hell erupts. Throughout the speech Richardson has cut between shots of Hoffman on the bench and the reactions of the three mothers and the bearded Foxmore and others in the courtroom: gasps of astonishment and rage, cries of "You bastard!", Esherman smiling gleefully. Amid screams from the other spectators Stacey Foxmore's father stands up with a gun in his hand. His face contorted by inarticulate fury, he kills Esherman where he sits and also wounds the court bailiff before being gunned down himself. At the end of this brief burst of violence we see Hoffman sitting alone and stunned in his chambers. Leah stands in the doorway, seems about to come in and console him but then, in a gesture that leaves us in no doubt who in her view did the right thing, shuts the door between them.

The final scene takes place in the now empty courtroom with Hoffman sitting alone and despairing in the vast chamber. Zach enters, sits next to him and says: "You had to let him go. You had to." Since we know that the boy is still ignorant of the truth about his father, we are compelled to look at his statement of support with the same critical eyes we fixed on Hoffman during his final speech. The film ends with a dark and quiet exchange between father and son.

> Zach: ". . . [W]hen I was a little kid I sat right here when you took the oath. You were up there. You seemed so high and far away. I was really proud of you then."
>
> Hoffman (on the brink of tears): ". . . It—was supposed to be an honor."

***

With a handful of new TV movies debuting on network or cable every week, few if any attract attention from the print media. In this respect *The Penalty Phase* fared better than most. John J. O'Connor in the New York *Times* described the film as "an unusually absorbing dramatic venture. . . ." which "generally sticks close to the bigger issues being confronted and, despite its portrayal of Judge Hoffman as a sensitive and dedicated hero, avoids simplistic answers. . . .Mr. Strauss's solidly intelligent performance, a fine supporting cast and Mr. Richardson's lean directorial style, wrapped in dramatic arrangements of shadows and light, add up to one of the more compelling movies of the season." [7] Judith Crist in *TV Guide* offered similar praise, saying that the film

> "offers a cogent consideration of judicial responsibility in the very face of vigilantism and public hysteria. Under Tony Richardson's direction, it is a taut, tense topical drama, as absorbing as it is stimulating . . .a thriller that is given complexity by the moral, legal and personal aspects of conflict between the letter and the spirit of the law. Strauss [is] at his best as the all-too-human jurist burdened by personal guilt and professional responsibility. . . ."[8]

Unfortunately the film, like almost every other movie first shown on television, quickly vanished into limbo and, except for a few off-the-cuff remarks of my own,[9] has never been the subject of any detailed discussion until this one.

As I have tried to show, a large part of this film's excellence and fascination stems from the in-depth characterization of Judge Hoffman. Indeed one might argue that at its deepest level the character harks back to perhaps the most profoundly tragic figure in all of Western literature, Sophocles' Oedipus Tyrannus.[10] After all, both Oedipus and Hoffman pursue their relentless quest for the truth despite being warned again and again that it will destroy them, as inevitably it does. At another level Hoffman seems a spiritual cousin to perhaps the most tormented judge in American literature: Captain Vere in Melville's *Billy Budd*. If we follow Richard Posner and other critics in seeing Vere as a good man who had no choice but to follow the law and commit the moral outrage of sentencing Billy to be hanged,[11] then perhaps Hoffman is a Vere for our own time, an equally good man who had no choice but to follow the law and commit the moral outrage of freeing the sociopath who murdered seventeen girls.

If like most present-day lawyers we are unversed in classical drama and high literature but know a bit more about contemporary popular fiction and film, the integrity and moral authority projected by Peter Strauss as Judge Hoffman will evoke Gregory Peck's unforgettable performance in *To Kill a Mockingbird*—so much so that we might well describe Hoffman as Atticus Finch in a black robe. But Atticus never faces a moral crisis and his situation, like that of most other protagonists in Warren-era law films, is presented in Manichaean terms of right against wrong. In several respects Judge Hoffman is closer to Barney Adams, the reluctant defender played by Robert Mitchum in *Man in the Middle*, who does indeed face a moral crisis: whether he should destroy his career in a foredoomed attempt to save the life not of a demonstrably innocent black man as in *To Kill a Mockingbird* but of a warped and violent white racist who just as demonstrably committed a cold-blooded and brutal murder.[12]

We might also view Hoffman alongside another cinematic jurist who predates him by only two years. The protagonist of *The Star Chamber* (1984) is Judge Stephen Hardin (Michael Douglas), whose passion for justice is so overpowering that, after being forced to release clearly guilty sociopaths because of police violations of their Warren Court-created rights, he joins a cabal of vigilante judges who conduct secret trials and impose sentences carried out by their private assassin. The first time the secret court makes a wrong decision and sends out the assassin to kill two sociopaths who in fact didn't commit the child-murder for which they were freed on a technicality, Hardin's passion for justice explodes once more. As he races into the night to stop the hit man, the film mutates into a conventional action thriller, at the end of which Hardin has turned informer and is setting up his Star Chamber colleagues for arrest. The plot of *The Penalty Phase* and the character of Judge Hoffman, whose passion is not for justice but for law, might well be understood as explicit condemnations of *The Star Chamber*—and also of *Dirty Harry* and . . . *And Justice for All* and all the other films of the past few decades which are built around an act that is justified in every way except under the law.

But if these reflections tempt one to see Peter Strauss' character as Atticus Finch in a black robe, we must remember that throughout *To Kill a Mockingbird* Atticus is seen through the uncritical eyes of his adoring young daughter. Judge Hoffman like Atticus is a widower and a single father but *The Penalty Phase* never adopts Zach's or any other idealizing viewpoint and one of the strengths of its last moments is our awareness that Zach does not know his father at all. However many similarities between Atticus and Judge Hoffman we may have ticked off, we are compelled by the last several minutes of *The Penalty Phase* to evaluate its protagonist with a stark objectivity we can never bring to Atticus Finch.

Time has been a friend to Richardson's film during the years of its obscurity. A man who combined a brilliant mind, great charm and charisma and attractiveness to women but who was later exposed as a compulsive womanizer and, far worse, as almost totally devoid of integrity came to prominence a few years after *The Penalty Phase* was made and left the national stage (but not for long) as the original version of this chapter was being written. For a viewer who has seen the film any time in the last several years or sees it for the first time today, the first person Judge Hoffman is likely to bring to mind is not Oedipus or Captain Vere or Atticus Finch or any other fictional character but Bill Clinton.

But anyone who makes this connection goes against the grain of the film, which compels us to reject the view that Judge Hoffman is unequivocally right but never invites us to see him as a hypocrite with a personal agenda. Alone among all the law-related films I have seen, *The Penalty Phase* seems to me best understood in terms of the theory of classical tragedy formulated in the early 19th century by the great philosopher G.W.F. Hegel, who "realized that at the center of the greatest tragedies of Aeschylus and Sophocles we find not a tragic hero but a tragic collision, and that the conflict is not between good and evil but between one-sided positions, each of which embodies some good. . . . One could not wish for more perfect illustrations of collisions in which neither side is simply wicked and some moral claims are present on both sides than we find in the *Oresteia* and *Prometheus* [by Aeschylus]. Indeed, the very words 'right collides with right' are encountered in *The Libation Bearers* [which is the second play in the Oresteia trilogy]."[13] And among all the films that take judges and justice and lawyers and law as their subjects one could not wish for a more perfect example of a Hegelian tragic collision than Tony Richardson and Gale Patrick Hickman gave us in *The Penalty Phase*.[14] While the seminal films of both the Warren and anti-Warren eras tend to present moral and juristic conflicts in terms of Manichaean simplicity, this one is artfully designed so that we the viewers are left divided as we see both sides of the coin simultaneously—an all but miraculous feat that guarantees *The Penalty Phase* an honored place in all serious discussions of the films whose province is judges and justice and lawyers and law.

NOTES

1. Precisely when the made-for-TV movie originated is not at all clear. The first films formally billed as such by networks were broadcast in the fall of 1964. But if a TV movie is defined as a film of feature length that tells a continuous story and was first seen in a single installment on the small screen, then the genre dates back to the thrillers and Westerns that

were aired roughly one week out of four, beginning in the fall of 1956, on the prestigious CBS anthology series *Playhouse 90*. And if one's definition does not require that the film be seen in a single sitting, then the TV movie dates back to the dawn of the medium and the first three episodes of *The Lone Ranger*, broadcast in September 1949 and discussed in Chapter 7 of this book.

2. Tony Richardson, *The Long Distance Runner: A Memoir* (Morrow, 1993).

3. *The Cinema of Tony Richardson: Essays and Interviews*, ed. James M. Welsh & John C. Tibbetts (State University of New York Press, 1999).

4. Otto Preminger's *Anatomy of a Murder* (1959) is often cited in the idealistic column, mainly perhaps because it's difficult to think of its star Jimmy Stewart in any other kind of role. But a strong case can be made that this story of how Stewart as shrewd country lawyer Paul Biegler manipulates the "irresistible impulse" doctrine so as to secure an acquittal for a man (Ben Gazzara) who seems to have coldbloodedly shot down his wife's lover is among the most cynical of the Warren era. Whether *Compulsion* should count as idealistic or its opposite depends, I suppose, on one's feelings about the death penalty.

5. One of the least known law-related films of the period, which is also one of the films most finely calibrated to the period's idealistic ethos, is discussed in Chapter 9 of this book.

6. Again, just which recent films should properly be classified as swimming against the tide is a matter on which reasonable minds can differ and which is beyond this chapter's scope. Most people would put *The Verdict* (1982) in the positive column; some would include *The Accused* (1988), *A Few Good Men* (1992) and *A Civil Action* (1998) or some combination of the three. But in most of the movies that are not clearly within the cynical mainstream, the film-makers hedge their bets, seeking like any savvy politician to be on both sides of a controversial issue at the same time. In *The Star Chamber* (1984) Michael Douglas plays a judge so outraged by having to let obviously guilty sociopaths loose on technicalities that he joins a cabal of jurists who render their

own verdicts and enforce them with a hit man. Sounds like it belongs squarely in the post-Warren Court anti-Warren Court column, but by the end of the film Douglas has informed on his fellow rogue judges and they are about to be arrested. In *A Time to Kill* (1996) Matthew McConnaughey plays a splendidly idealistic young lawyer representing a black client in the racist South. Sounds like a throwback to Atticus Finch idealism, but unlike Brock Peters in *To Kill a Mockingbird*, the client played by Samuel L. Jackson is guilty—and, by publicly blowing away the white scum who had raped and beaten his little daughter, he is all but indistinguishable from the other justified cinematic saboteurs of the legal system like Al Pacino in . . . *And Justice for All* and Nick Nolte in Scorsese's *Cape Fear*.

7. John J. O'Connor, *"Penalty Phase"* Looks at Problems of a Judge. New York *Times*, 18 November 1986, Section C, at 22 col. 1.

8. Judith Crist, film review, *TV Guide* (St. Louis edition), 15 November 1986, at A-5 and A-136.

9. See Francis M. Nevins, Book Review, 20 *Legal Studies Forum* 145, 146 (1996).

10. See Walter Kaufmann, *Tragedy and Philosophy* (Doubleday, 1968), especially Chapter IV, "The Riddle of Oedipus." The aspect of the play which connects it with *The Penalty Phase* is explored by Kaufmann in Section 25 where he discusses it as "the tragedy of the curse of honesty."

11. See Richard A. Posner, *Law and Literature* (2d ed. 1999). For a radically opposed view which sees Vere as an amoral hypocrite with a personal agenda, see Richard A. Weisberg, *The Failure of the Word* (1984), at 133-159, and *Poethics and Other Strategies of Law and Literature* (1992), at 104-116.

12. See Chapter 9 of this book.

13. See Walter Kaufmann, *Tragedy and Philosophy*, note 10 *supra*, at Section 42.

14. It is not surprising to learn that the director and the screenwriter of *The Penalty Phase* share roots in classical drama and the liberal arts. Among the literary and dramatic classics Richardson transformed into films are Faulkner's *Sanctuary* (1961), Fielding's *Tom Jones* (1963), Evelyn Waugh's *The Loved One* (1964), Shakespeare's *Hamlet* (1969), Vladimir Nabokov's *Laughter in the Dark* (1969), Edward Albee's *A Delicate Balance* (1973), and Fielding's *Joseph Andrews* (1977). See *The Cinema of Tony Richardson*, note 3 *supra*. Hickman took philosophy and English courses as a UCLA undergraduate and read fiction constantly while attending law school. See Allan Jalon, "Jurist's Script a Plea for Understanding," Los Angeles *Times* (Orange County ed.), 20 November 1986, Metro section, p. 1.

INDEX

Note: The titles of all novels, plays and nonfiction books are printed in italics, each title followed by the author's last name. The titles of all short stories and nonfiction works are in quotes, each title followed by the author's last name. The titles of movies are in italics, each title followed by the film's studio and copyright date.

INDEX

INDEX

413

INDEX

My Day in Court (Train), 62, 63, 68, 69, 73, 77, 80, 82, 85, 86, 95, 99
"My Friend at Bridge" (Post), 33
My Sin (Paramount, 1931), 200-201
"My Son, My Son" (*The Big Valley* TV series episode), 303
Mysterious Rider, The (Paramount, 1933), 229-230
"Mystery at Hillhouse, The" (Post), 46, 47
Mystery at the Blue Villa, The (Post), 45
"Mystery at the Mill, The" (Post), 52
"Mystery of Chance, The" (Post), 44

"Naboth's Vineyard" (Post), 43-44, 50
Nagel, Conrad, 198
Naish, J. Carrol, 192, 215, 216, 230
Nameless Thing, The (Post), 36
National Broadcasting Co. (NBC), 275, 276, 284, 287, 289, 299, 302, 306, 308
National Institute of Arts and Letters, 69, 70
National Legion of Decency, 231-232
Native Son (Wright), 6
Natteford, Jack, 228
Naughty Flirt, The (First National, 1930), 208
Nebel, Frederick, 215
Neill, Roy William, 175
Nero Wolfe (TV series), 300
Neville, John Thomas, 167
"New Evidence" (*The Cisco Kid* TV series episode), 268
New York *Times,* 395
New York Times Book Review, 320
New York University, 2, 149
New York Zoetrope (publishing house)
Newman, Paul, 368
Newmeyer, Fred, 207
Newspaper Days (Dreiser), 14
Nicholson, Jack, 96
Nietzsche, Friedrich, 44
Night Angel, The (Paramount, 1931), 199-200
Nijinski, Vaslav, 368
"Nine Points of the Law" (Train), 94-95
Niven, David, 321
Nixon, Marion, 205
Nixon, Richard M., 81
Nolte, Nick, 331, 332, 335, 336, 337, 341, 375

"Not Guilty" (*The Cisco Kid* TV series episode), 268
Nugent, Eddie, 203
Nugent, Elliott, 183
Nuisance, The (MGM, 1933), 190-191
Nuyen, France, 355, 364, 365, 366

Oates, Warren, 303, 304
Oakie, Jack, 208
Oakland, Simon, 288
O'Brian, Hugh, 275
O'Brien, George, 230, 252, 257
O'Connor, Carroll, 304
O'Connor, John J., 395
Office of Strategic Services (OSS), 312
O'Hanlon, James, 291
Oh, Promise Me (Robinson & Lindsay), 211
Oland, Warner, 217
Old Man Tutt (Train), 87
Oldman, Gary, 375
Oliver, Edna May, 219
Olney, George H., 66
Olson, James, 278
O'Malley, J. Pat, 278
On Trial (Warner Bros., 1928), 158, 165
"Once in Jeopardy" (Post), 26
One Man Law (Columbia, 1932), 223-228, 233, 243, 244
O'Neal, Zelma, 210
"1000 Feet Deep Brief, The" (*Dundee and the Culhane* TV series episode), 304
Oresteia (Aeschylus trilogy), 5, 398
Orth, Marion, 220
Osborn, John Jay, Jr., 61
Oswald, Gerd, 301
Outcasts, The (TV series), 289
Outlaws, The (TV series), 289
Ox-Bow Incident, The (20th Century-Fox, 1942), 41, 295
Oxford University, 63
"Ozark Gold" (*Cowboy G-Men* TV episode), 273

Pacino, Al, 375
Packer, Peter, 303
Padden, Sarah, 193

417

INDEX

INDEX

About the Author

Francis M. Nevins has won two Edgar awards from the Mystery Writers of America for his scholarly work on Cornell Woolrich and Ellery Queen. He is the author, most recently, of *Ellery Queen: The Art of Detection* (2013). By training a lawyer, he has written many essays on the nexus between fiction and the law. But to mystery fans, Mr. Nevins is at least equally known as the author of a number of novels and dozens of classic detective stories, many of them collected in *Night Forms* (2010).

CPSIA information can be obtained
at www.ICGtesting.com
Printed in the USA
LVOW03s1446230416

485016LV00004B/13/P